KV-648-877

Issues of Death

ISSUES OF DEATH

MORTALITY AND IDENTITY IN ENGLISH RENAISSANCE TRAGEDY

MICHAEL NEILL

CLARENDON PRESS · OXFORD
1997

Oxford University Press, Great Clarendon Street, Oxford OX2 6DP
Oxford New York
Athens Auckland Bangkok Bogota Bombay
Buenos Aires Calcutta Cape Town Dar es Salaam
Delhi Florence Hong Kong Istanbul Karachi
Kuala Lumpur Madras Madrid Melbourne
Mexico City Nairobi Paris Singapore
Taipei Tokyo Toronto
and associated companies in
Berlin Ibadan

Oxford is a trade mark of Oxford University Press

Published in the United States by
Oxford University Press, Inc., New York

British Library Cataloguing in Publication Data
Data available

Library of Congress Cataloging in Publication Data
Data available

ISBN 0-19-818386-0

1 3 5 7 9 10 8 6 4 2

Typeset by Graphicraft Typesetters Ltd., Hong Kong
Printed in Great Britain
on acid-free paper by
Biddles Ltd.,
Guildford and King's Lynn

For my Mother
and in Memory of my Father

First, then, we consider this *exitus mortis* to be *liberatio a morte*. . . . all our periods and transitions in this life, are so many passages from death to death. Our very birth and entrance into this life is *exitus a morte*, an issue from death, for in our mother's womb we are dead, so as we do not know we live, not so much as we do in our sleep. . . . But then this *exitus a morte*, is but *introitus in mortem*, this issue, this deliverance from that death, the death of the womb, is an entrance, a delivering over to another death, the manifold deaths of this world.

(John Donne, 'Death's Duel')

What is our life? a play of passion,
Our mirth the music of division,
Our mothers' wombs the tiring houses be,
Where we are dressed for this short comedy;
Heaven the judicious sharp spectator is,
That sits and marks still who doth amiss;
Our graves that hide us from the searching sun,
Are like drawn curtains when the play is done.
Thus march we playing to our latest rest,
Only we die in earnest, there's no jest.

(Sir Walter Raleigh, 'The Life of Man')

Acknowledgements

Completion of this book would have been impossible without the generosity of several institutions. I am indebted to the University of Auckland for provision of sabbatical leave, and to its research committee for helping to fund the project; to the Folger Shakespeare Library for their award of the Hanson Lee Dulin Fellowship, and to the Newberry Library for a short-term fellowship. Jason Freeman, Janet Moth, and their staff at Oxford University Press have been unfailingly helpful and efficient in shepherding this book through the various stages of publication. I should also like to record my gratitude to numerous friends and colleagues for their help and encouragement, especially Anne Barton, David Bevington, Sebastian Black, Albert Braunmuller, Jocelyn Harris, Mac Jackson, Jonathan Lamb, Mercedes Maroto Camino, Barbara Mowat, Roger Nicholson, Patricia Parker, Gail Paster, Mary Beth Rose, and Anna Wirz-Justice. To my immediate family, Makare, Anna, Tuataroa, and Te Ao Huri, I owe a debt which only they will understand.

Muriel Bradbrook and Harriett Hawkins, two scholars from whose kindness and intellectual generosity I have benefited enormously, both died while the book was in progress. The world seems thinner for their absence.

Earlier versions of some portions of this book have appeared in *Modern Language Review*, *Renaissance Drama*, *Themes in Drama*, and in Ian Donaldson (ed.), *Jonson and Shakespeare* (London and Canberra, 1983), and David Bergeron (ed.), *Pageantry in the Shakespearean Theatre* (Athens, Ga., 1985). I am grateful to the publishers for permission to reuse this material. Material from '"Hidden Malady": Death, Discovery, and Indistinction in The Changeling', *Renaissance Drama* XXII is reproduced in Chapter 4 by kind permission of the Northwestern University Press (© 1992 Northwestern University Press).

Contents

List of Illustrations

Note on Conventions Used in the Text

Punctuation and spelling have been discreetly modernized in all quotations from original texts and old-spelling editions, although Middle English texts are rendered in the original spelling. For bibliographic reasons, I have, however, chosen to leave titles in their unaltered form. In citations from the Riverside Shakespeare, I have silently modernized some old spellings preserved by the editor.

Introduction

> Death digs most deeply the jagged line of demarcation between physical nature and significance.
>
> (Walter Benjamin, *Trauerspiel*[1])

Inventing Death

> Nor dread nor hope attend
> A dying animal;
> A man awaits his end
> Dreading and hoping all . . .
> He knows death to the bone—
> Man has created death.
>
> (W. B. Yeats, 'Death')

Death, in Hamlet's haunting formula, is '[t]he undiscover'd country, from whose bourn, | No traveller returns' (*Hamlet*, III. i. 78–9); but there is something teasingly contradictory about this celebrated aphorism—not merely because the Ghost who haunts the Prince's consciousness professes to be just such a traveller, but because Hamlet's figure of speech locates death inside a contemporary geographic discourse according to which the 'undiscovered' is conceivable only as an explicit challenge to discovery. Such a paradox is perfectly appropriate, of course, to a play whose action is obsessively concerned with the exploration of mortality. It is often supposed that this morbid preoccupation reflects something peculiar to the psyche of Shakespeare's protagonist, but the frequency with which the play's unmasking of death is replayed in the charnel-house spectacles of the Jacobean stage suggests otherwise. Instead we should see episodes like Hamlet's interrogation of the Grave-digger as gestic demonstrations of what Renaissance tragic drama, at its core, is about—the discovery of death and the mapping of its meanings.

[1] In his *The Origin of German Tragic Drama* (London: Verso, 1985), 166.

This is less straightforward than it sounds; for discovery is never simply a matter of revealing what was always there—any more than mapping is a matter of representing a landscape already fixed and known. Both are part of a process that brings *terra incognita* into view by imposing a cultural template upon its shapeless 'emptiness'; and each involves a degree of invention. The idea that death might be invented in this way will seem paradoxical only if it is thought of as a natural given, rather than as the human fiction that thanatologists like Philippe Ariès have shown it to be—a fiction, moreover, of a particularly fluid kind. For 'death' is not something that can be imagined once and for all, but an idea that has to be constantly reimagined across cultures and through time; which is to say that, like most human experiences that we think of as 'natural', it is culturally defined.

A sense of the peculiar intimacy of culture and death is as old as Genesis, where the guilty knowledge of the Fall, the lapse into self-consciousness that renders humankind mortal, is figured as a discovery of dreadful undress. The First Parents' nakedness is a sign not merely of their newly socialized sense of shame, but also of their extreme vulnerability; it stands, in other words, for mortality, which is the true source of the body's shamefulness. Death comes into existence, this story tells us, only when a living being can imagine dying—until then the creature is immortal. All animals die, but only human beings suffer death—and their sense of what they suffer is, to a very large degree, imposed by the culture to which they belong.[2]

This was the truth irritably asserted by the writer Villiers de l'Isle-Adam when he found himself confronted by the florists, monumental masons, and other tradesmen of mortality who clustered about the entrance to the Père Lachaise cemetery in Paris: 'Those are the people who invented death'.[3] We have only to remember

[2] On the culturally constructed nature of death, see Philippe Ariès, *The Hour of our Death*, trans. Helen Weaver (London: Allen Lane, 1981). This magisterial history of changing Western attitudes towards death since classical times is usefully supplemented by a number of more local studies, including Clare Gittings, *Death, Burial and the Individual in Early Modern England* (London: Croom Helm, 1984); Ralph Houlbrooke (ed.), *Death, Ritual and Bereavement* (London: Routledge, 1989); Nigel Llewellyn, *The Art of Death: Visual Culture in the English Death Ritual* (London: Reaktion Books in association with the Victoria and Albert Museum, 1991); and Julian Litten, *The English Way of Death: The Common Funeral since 1450* (London: Robert Hale, 1991).

[3] D. J. Enright (ed.), *The Oxford Book of Death* (Oxford: Oxford University Press, 1983), 145.

the contrast between the sentimental cult of the dead enshrined in a great nineteenth-century cemetery and the *memento mori* didacticism so characteristic of fifteenth-century tombs to understand how different were the deaths 'invented' at Père Lachaise and at its late medieval predecessor in the cloister of Les Innocents.

It would be wrong, of course, to suppose that death was ever simply the invention of the professionals who supervised or contributed to its ritual practices. Of at least equal importance, as Ariès and others have shown, were the representations of death in literature and the visual arts—representations which, in the sixteenth and seventeenth centuries, developed an increasingly secular cast. It will be fundamental to the arguments of this book that the extraordinary burgeoning of tragic drama in late Elizabethan and Jacobean England was a crucial part of this secularizing process: tragedy, I will suggest, was among the principal instruments by which the culture of early modern England reinvented death.

Envisaging Death

> dost know
> Yon dreadful vizard? View it well.
>
> (*The Revenger's Tragedy*, III. i. 147–8[4])

The rereading of the Genesis myth in *Paradise Lost* gives a useful pointer to one of the most distinctive characteristics of the new death—its startling physical presence. The death of Genesis is without any substance; it can be evoked only through a metaphor of process: 'dust thou art and unto dust thou shalt return'. There is no such *thing* as death. In Milton's poem, by contrast, although those same words are spoken (x. 208), the Death brought into the world by the grand explorer Satan appears *in propria persona*: he is the third member of an infernal trinity, Satan's son by his own daughter, Sin, and builder of the prodigious bridge 'over the foaming deep' that fatally links 'this now fenceless world | Forfeit to Death' to the newly discovered regions of Hell (x. 301–4). This 'meagre shadow' is endowed with a terrifying personality, expressed

[4] Except where otherwise indicated, citations from non-Shakespearean plays are to Russell A. Fraser and Norman Rabkin (eds.), *Drama of the English Renaissance*, 2 vols. (New York: Macmillan, 1976).

in the emaciated frame, grotesque features, and monstrous appetite that identify him as one of humanity's grand antagonists:

> with delight he snuffed the smell
> Of mortal change on earth. As when a flock
> Of ravenous fowl, though many a league remote,
> Against the day of battle, to a field,
> Where armies lie encamped, come flying, lured
> With scent of living carcasses. . . .
> So scented the grim feature, and upturned
> His nostril wide into the murky air,
> Sagacious of his quarry from so far.
>
> (x. 272–81)

This construction of mortality in terms of an agonistic struggle with a cunning and remorseless foe had both biblical and classical antecedents, of course. Simply by nominalizing the process of dying language began to make a substantive thing of it; death could be imagined as if it were the opposite of life, as dark is thought of as the opposite of light, when it is simply the other's absence. The death which is apostrophized in Hosea 13: 14 ('O death, I will be thy plagues') and 1 Corinthians 15: 55 ('O death, where is thy sting?') is already halfway to acquiring an allegorical persona; and in the final book of scripture Death is fully incarnated as one of the Four Horsemen of the Apocalypse (Rev. 6: 8). But St John's allegory remains relatively thin and inert when compared with late medieval and Renaissance reworkings of the apocalyptic scene: only his sword and his pale horse distinguish him from his equally faceless companions. Similarly, in classical literature, while death may sometimes be allegorized as Thanatos or Mors, it is typically represented as mere cessation, extinction, or absence—a violent end whose symbols are the broken column and the inverted torch. Euripides, it is true, casts Death as Hercules' mightiest opponent in *Alcestis*, where the hero goes off to wrestle with the chthonic lord for the life of the stolen Queen. But even this contest is an off-stage one; for the actual *appearance* of Death in his theatre would be (in every sense) unimaginable. Moreover, such allegorizations are, as Ariès observes, 'infrequent, unobtrusive, marginal'.[5] It is not until the sudden flowering of macabre art towards the

[5] Ariès, *Hour of our Death*, 110.

end of the fourteenth century that Death begins to acquire an unmistakable personality.

In late medieval and Renaissance art Death is not merely imagined, but in the most literal sense *envisaged*, given a face: he becomes Milton's deformed monster, guarding the gates of Hell with his mother, Sin; or the grinning skeleton whose lineaments engravers loved to trace in the very branches of the Forbidden Tree (Fig. 1); or the sardonic jester who surprises his victims with unanswerable proof of their mortality (Fig. 4*b*). As King Death, the sibling of Time, and monarch of the earth, he acquires a realm and a power (Fig. 2), appearing, as in Samuel Rowlands's *A Terrible Battell betweene . . . Time, and Death*, in the form of

> God's great *Earl Marshal* over all the earth;
> Taking account of each man's dying hours,
> *Landlord of graves*, and tombs of marble stones,
> *Lord Treasurer* of rotten dead-men's bones. . . .
> God's speedy post, that ever runs and flies,
> Ender of all that ever was begun,
> That hast the map of life before thine eyes;
> And of all creatures since the world's creation,
> Hast seen the final dusty consummation.[6]

This transformation in ways of representing death corresponds, as historians have recognized, to an important transformation in social attitudes: death is represented differently because it is coming to be experienced differently; in particular, new images of destruction correspond to the new idea of 'the pathetic and personal death' whose emergence is signalled, for Ariès, in the late medieval elaboration of the *ars moriendi*.[7] Through a process that is only superficially paradoxical, Death comes to be credited with a personality precisely as dying comes to be felt, more acutely than ever before, as a cancellation of personal identity. In his rage to unfashion distinction, this Death takes a wicked pleasure in parodying, through the lively forms of Death the Antic, sardonic jester, grim summoner, and eldritch lover, the vivid self-exhibition of human identity. Personalized in this way, Death can be conceived as a threatening Other, or a morbid anti-self—the one we are each born

[6] Samuel Rowlands, *A Terrible Battell betweene the two consumers of the Whole world: Time, and Death* (London, [?1606]), sig. A3–A3^{v}.

[7] Ariès, *Hour of our Death*, 110, 112.

1. *The Fall of Man*, lithograph by Piloty after Frans Floris (1520–70), bound as extra-illustration in the Huntington Library 'Kitto' Bible (RB 49000 III. 375). By permission of the Huntington Library, San Marino, California.

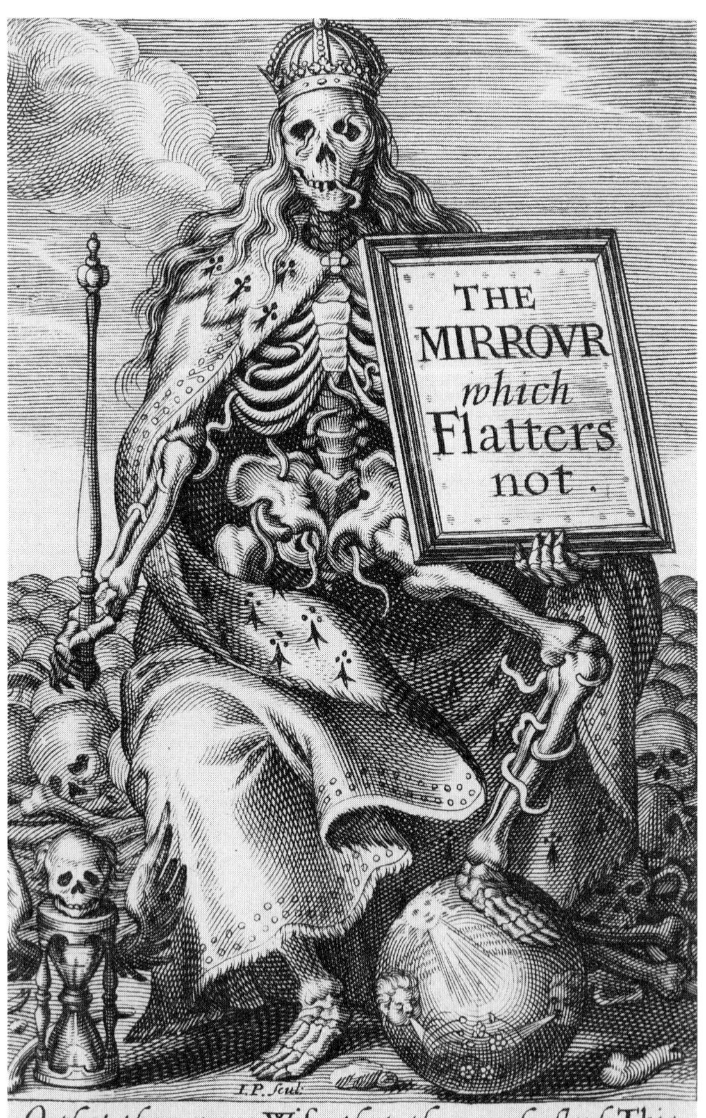

2. *King Death*, title-page engraving from T. Carey, *The Mirrour which Flatters not* (London, 1639) (British Library, 873F17). By permission of the British Library.

to meet, an uncanny companion we carry with us through life, a hidden double who will discover himself at the appointed hour.

Shameful Death

> I am not so much afraid of death, as ashamed thereof.
>
> (Sir Thomas Browne, *Religio Medici*[8])

The shamefulness of early modern death is its second striking characteristic. Shame, as we have seen, is already inscribed in the Genesis myth by the suddenly exposed nakedness of the fallen Adam and Eve; but it is given redoubled emphasis in Milton's version of the story, where Christ's deferral of the death sentence passed upon the fallen couple (x. 210–11) is implicitly equated with his pity for their disgracefully unclad condition:

> then pitying how they stood
> Before him naked to the air, that now
> Must suffer change . . .
> As father of his family he clad
> Their nakedness with skins of beasts . . .
> Nor he their outward only with the skins
> Of beasts, but inward nakedness, much more
> Opprobrious, with his robe of righteousness,
> Arraying covered from his Father's sight.
>
> (x. 211–23)

Here, as in the biblical version, nakedness stands most obviously for their sense of fearful exposure to the eye of God. But there is at least one other reason why nakedness came to be a sign of mortal shame in early modern culture, as an extraordinary story from late medieval Italy may help to show. In one of the *novelle* of Giovanni Sercambi, the central character, a furrier from the city of Lucca, makes an ill-fated visit to the public baths. No sooner has he removed his clothes than he is overwhelmed by the terrifying conviction that he is about to lose his identity amidst the crowd of naked, and therefore indistinguishable, bodies. As a desperate expedient, he attaches a straw cross to his right shoulder

[8] In his *Religio Medici and Other Writings*, intro. M. R. Ridley (London: Dent, 1965), 45; all citations from Browne are to this edition.

so that he may not lose himself; but his panic has been observed by a neighbour, who snatches the token and mockingly announces, 'Now I am you; begone, you are dead!' Out of his mind with fear, the furrier convinces himself that he has indeed died.[9] He is vulnerable to this panicky delusion only because he is naked.

For the furrier—whose very livelihood is, of course, dependent on a clothing market regulated by highly particularized notions of dress as the prime expression of social identity—the spectacle of mass nakedness at the baths releases a nightmare of indistinction so absolute as to be no different from death. It is as if for him the jostling rabble of bodies were suddenly transmogrified into something resembling the pile of undifferentiated corpses in a plague pit; and in a moment of uncanny fatality, he chooses for his badge of identity the very sign, a cross, conventionally used to mark a house that had been visited by the plague. The neighbour whose satiric humour strips the furrier of this last equivocal token of difference transforms himself into nothing less than the furrier's own morbid double—an avatar of Death, the mocking summoner. Sercambi's bizarre and disturbing parable appears to announce something like a crisis in the cultural accommodation of death: it is as if, in an increasingly competitive and status-conscious society, obsessed with the boundaries and badges of difference, the assaults of death have come to be experienced as something profoundly *un*natural, an unwarrantable annihilation of individual difference, imagined as a brutal stripping away of the outward persona. This obscene and shameful nakedness effectually unforms the self, producing that condition of absolute 'deformity' that appalled Sir Thomas Browne when he wrote that 'death is the disgrace and ignominy of our natures, that in a moment can so disfigure us that our nearest friends, Wife, and Children stand afraid and start at us'.[10]

The same sense of death as a condition of dreadful *disfigurement* is apparent in plague pamphlets such as William Bullein's *A Dialogue against the Fever Pestilence* (1578), where Civis, a wealthy citizen, laments to his wife: 'Now my body is past cure, no Physic

[9] Cited in Georges Duby and Philippe Braunstein, 'The Emergence of the Individual', in Philippe Ariès and Georges Duby (gen. eds.), *A History of Private Life*, trans. Arthur Goldhammer, 5 vols. (Cambridge, Mass.: Belknap Press, 1987–91), ii: Georges Duby (ed.), *Revelations of the Medieval World*, 507–630: 568–9.

[10] *Urn Burial*, 123, and *Religio Medici*, 45.

3. *The Stages of Life, with Death* by Hans Baldung Grien, 1476–1545 (Prado, Madrid, cat. no. 2220). By permission of the Museo del Prado, Madrid.

can prevail. . . . I shall be turned into a stinking carrion for worm's delight, dust, clay, rotten, most vile, forsaken of all men, poor without substance, *naked without clothing*, sown in dishonour, forgotten of my posterity, not known henceforth, vanish like a shadow, wither like a leaf, and fade as a flower.'[11] In Thomas Newton's verses on the death of Queen Elizabeth, the 'greedy worms' who feast upon the royal corpse are made to mock her nakedness:

For what's her body now, whereon such care
  Was still bestow'd in all humility?
Where are her robes? is not her body bare,
  Respectless in the earth's obscurity?[12]

For Bullein's Civis the degraded condition of nakedness is as distressing as the prospect of physical disintegration or of worldly oblivion. In fact—as in Hans Baldung Grien's *The Stages of Life, with Death*, where the process of mortal decay is accompanied by an increasingly obscene exposure of the flesh (Fig. 3)—it amounts to something like the same thing:[13] the dead body is 'vile' in the modern sense (filthy and repulsive), because it has been rendered 'vile' according to the root meaning ('base, common'), exposed to the 'vilification' that forms a theme of Donne's Grand Guignol sermonizing:

we must all pass this posthume death, this death after death, nay this death after burial, this dissolution after dissolution, this death of corruption and putrefaction, of vermiculation and incineration, of dissolution and dispersion in and from the grave, when those bodies that have been the children of royal parents, and the parents of royal children, must say with Job, *to corruption, thou art my father*, and *to the worm, thou art my mother and my sister*. Miserable riddle, when the same worm must be my mother, my sister, and my self! Miserable incest, when I must be married to my mother and my sister, and be both father and mother to

[11] Cited in Lucinda McCray Beier, *Sufferers and Healers: The Experience of Illness in Seventeenth-Century England* (London: Routledge & Kegan Paul, 1987), 155.

[12] Thomas Newton, *Atropoion Delion; or, The Death of Delia* (1603); in John Nichols, *The Progresses and Public Processions of Queen Elizabeth*, 3 vols. (London: John Nichols, 1823), iii. 639.

[13] According to Norbert Elias in *The Civilizing Process: The History of Manners*, trans. Edmund Jephcott (London: Basil Blackwell, 1978), the taboo on nakedness was virtually absent from medieval culture (pp. 163–5). If this is so, the emergence of the taboo may have as much to do with changing attitudes towards death as with a stricter policing of sexuality—though the two are inevitably intertwined.

my own mother and sister, beget and bear that worm which is all that miserable penury; when my mouth shall be filled with dust, and the worm shall feed, and feed sweetly, upon me; when the ambitious man shall have no satisfaction, if the poorest alive tread upon him, nor the poorest receive any contentment in being made equal to princes, for they shall be equal but in dust. . . . This is the most inglorious and contemptible vilification, the most deadly and peremptory nullification of man that we can consider.[14]

'Contemptible vilification', 'dissolution and dispersion', 'dilapidation', and 'peremptory nullification'—these are the characteristic terms of Donne's distress at a disgraceful transformation that threatens to abolish all the boundaries of humane definition and significance. In Newton's funeral ode, the grotesque physical proximity of the worms punningly enacts their levelling claim to kinship with the Queen: 'And we in life too filthy for her tooth, | Are now in death the *next* unto her mouth.'[15]

Vermiculation is an occasion less of physical disgust than of social outrage, because it is the process that renders the royal indistinguishable from the vile, the rich from the poor, the human from the inhuman, the animate from the inanimate. It is this that warrants Donne's grotesque incest conceit, since incest stands for the violation and confusion of the most fundamental of all natural boundaries. In this radical assault upon definition not even the most intimate distinctions of personal identity are immune from a universal bodily dispersion which reduces even the contemplative man 'that thought himself *his own* forever' to an indistinguishable dust that in turn must be '*mingled* with the dust of every highway, and dunghill, and *swallowed* in every puddle and pond'.[16]

What for Donne is so obscene about death is the sheer commonness figured in those public highways, dunghills, puddles, and ponds. As his fellow clergyman Samuel Purchas complained: 'In

[14] John Donne, 'Death's Duel', in *Devotions upon Emergent Occasions Together with Death's Duel* (Ann Arbor: University of Michigan Press, 1959), 176–7.

[15] Newton, *Atropoion Delion*, 639.

[16] For dirt as the sign of absolute undifferentiation, see Mary Douglas, *Purity and Danger: An Analysis of Concepts of Pollution and Taboo* (New York: Praeger, 1966): 'In [the] final stage of total disintegration, dirt is utterly undifferentiated. Thus a cycle has been completed. Dirt was created by the differentiating activity of mind, it was a by-product of the creation of order. So it started from a state of non-differentiation; all through the process of differentiating its role was to threaten the distinctions made; finally it returns to its true indeterminable character' (p. 161).

those houses of Death, *Diogenes* knows not King *Philip*'s ashes from a beggar's, or any other man's. . . . The beautiful and deformed, the strong and the weak, & whatsoever names of difference humanity acknowledgeth, are not distinguishable in the dark & silent grave. . . . If any difference be there found, it is that the fuller-fed paunch of the richer yields more worms, corruption, & stink.'[17] So too for Hamlet, brooding on the fate of Philip's son (and Diogenes' interlocutor) Alexander the Great, it is the outrage upon every last vestige of distinction embodied in a king's progress through the guts of a beggar that seems so bitterly offensive.[18]

Indifferent Death

> The other shape,
> If shape it might be called that shape had none
> Distinguishable in member, joint, or limb,
> Or substance might be called that shadow seemed . . .
> The likeness of a kingly crown had on.
>
> (Milton, *Paradise Lost*, II. 666–73)

For most modern readers, accustomed to interpreting what have become the clichés of 'Death the Leveller' in terms of a more or less egalitarian ethos, the social significance of the language used by our ancestors to figure the disgrace of death is liable to be obscured by a screen of deceptive familiarity—as though death's levelling involved nothing more than an ironic sanction of last

[17] Samuel Purchas, *Pvrchas his Pilgrim: Microcosmvs; or, The Historie of Man. Relating the Wonders of his Generation, Vanities of his Degeneration, Necessity of his Regeneration. Meditated on the words of David. Ps. 39.5. Verily, euery Man at his best state is altogether Vanitie* (London, 1619), 188–90.

[18] Douglas argues that 'So long as identity is absent rubbish is not dangerous. . . . Even the bones of buried kings rouse little awe and the thought that the air is full of the dust of bygone corpses has no power to move. Where there is no differentiation there is no defilement' (*Purity and Danger*, 160). This is so patently *not* true for Shakespeare and his contemporaries as to constitute evidence of the gulf that divides early modern from modern attitudes towards death. For readings of *Hamlet* that interpret its action in terms of the protagonist's triumphant 'resistance to the undifferentiation of death', see Richard D. Fly, 'Accommodating Death: the Ending of *Hamlet*', *Studies in English Literature*, 24 (1984), 257–74: 273, and Robert N. Watson, 'Giving up the Ghost in a World of Decay', *Renaissance Drama*, 21 (1990), 199–223—now incorporated in his *The Rest is Silence: Death as Annihilation in the English Renaissance* (Berkeley: University of California Press, 1994), 74–102.

resort against the hubris of the over-rich. But whilst such irony was by no means invisible to early modern moralists, its satisfactions were outweighed by the horror of death's power to degrade its victims—a degradation so absolute that (especially when compounded by the fearful confusions of epidemic disease) it seemed to threaten the very basis upon which the hierarchic order of society was founded. Death stands for all those natural forces that threaten to reduce the painstakingly constructed order of society to chaos, a mere tumbled heap: thus death itself is imagined in John Moore's *Mappe of Mans Mortalitie* as 'the *heap* whereupon the lives of all men shall be poured', while George Strode's *Anatomy of Mortalitie* imagines it as the ending of a chess game in which 'the men are *tumbled* together, and put into the bag'.[19]

When contemplating early modern representations of death it is easy to be seduced by their surface grotesquerie into diagnosing a morbid sensationalism indulged in for its own sake, when what the artists were struggling to express was the almost inconceivable horror of death's undifferentiating blankness. 'There is great difference in men,' wrote Strode, 'and greater respect had to some than to others . . . but when death cometh . . . then there will be no such difference in the grave, neither doth Death know any such difference for he spareth none.'[20]

In itself, as Robert N. Watson has observed, 'the anthropomorphising of death—even when it is disguised as a grim surrender . . . is in fact a consoling fiction. . . . The terror lies in its indifference, which steals away the differences by which and for which we live.'[21] It is in this sense that Death, as the Duke puts it in *Measure for Measure*, is 'a great disguiser' (IV. ii. 174).[22] Quibbling on the original meaning of 'disguise' as disfiguration or the stripping of usual guise, he reminds us that it is the very bareness of Death's masquerade that renders it impenetrable; for, as Sercambi's fable so poignantly insists, identity in the vestimentary system is always imagined as a kind of guise.

[19] John Moore, *A Mappe of Mans Mortalitie* (London, 1617), sig. D2 and George Strode, *Anatomy of Mortalitie*, 2nd edn. (London, 1632), sig. E3r, both cited in William E. Engel, *Mapping Mortality: The Persistence of Memory and Melancholy in Early Modern England* (Amherst: University of Massachusetts Press, 1995), 189 (emphases added).

[20] Strode, *Anatomy of Mortalitie*, loc cit.

[21] Watson, *The Rest is Silence*, 98.

[22] Except where otherwise indicated, citations from Shakespeare are to *The Riverside Shakespeare*, ed. G. Blakemore Evans (Boston, Mass.: Houghton Mifflin, 1974).

To turn from Sercambi and Donne to a masterpiece of macabre art, such as the great fifteenth-century Basel *Totentanz* (Fig. 4), whose frolicking cadavers trick out their nakedness in mocking fragments of their victims' costumes, is to be reminded how much this *memento mori* narrative is concerned with the same fear of uncovering, disfigurement, and the annihilation of identity. The bizarre liveliness of the figures of Death, on which viewers invariably comment, serves only to underline their impersonal sameness, stressing the paradox that to envisage death is to personify a radical defacement. Like the furrier's nightmare, the *Totentanz* expresses its anxiety about death partly as a morbid fear of absorption into an anonymous crowd, the hierarchical parade of estates contrasting as sharply as possible with the rout of bare, indistinguishable corpses into which they are drawn. The death most to be feared, these images announce, is mass death because of its extravagant multiplication of disfigured bodies. It is hardly surprising therefore that the growth of macabre art generally, and of the *danse macabre* in particular, should have been so strongly associated with the recurrent epidemics of plague that devastated European society for more than 350 years, beginning with the outbreak of the Black Death in 1347. No other single phenomenon had a more decisive effect than the plague in shaping the early modern crisis of death.

'[I]n an epidemic', writes Elias Canetti, vividly evoking the helpless terror of pestilence, 'people *see* the advance of death; it takes place under their very eyes. They are like participants in a battle which lasts longer than all known battles. But the enemy is hidden; he is nowhere to be seen and cannot be hit. One can only wait to be hit by him. In this battle only the enemy is active.'[23] Even more terrifying is the indiscriminate nature of the enemy's assault: 'As soon as an epidemic is acknowledged, it is felt that it can have only one end, and that is the death of everyone.'[24] By exposing populations to the trauma of mass death on an unprecedented scale, the plague repeatedly activated the fantasy of universal destruction. The threat of apocalyptic breakdown to a society preoccupied with the maintenance of hierarchical order was precisely to emphasize the role of death as the arbiter of indifference:

[23] Elias Canetti, *Crowds and Power*, trans. Carol Stewart (London: Penguin, 1981), 319.

[24] Ibid. 319.

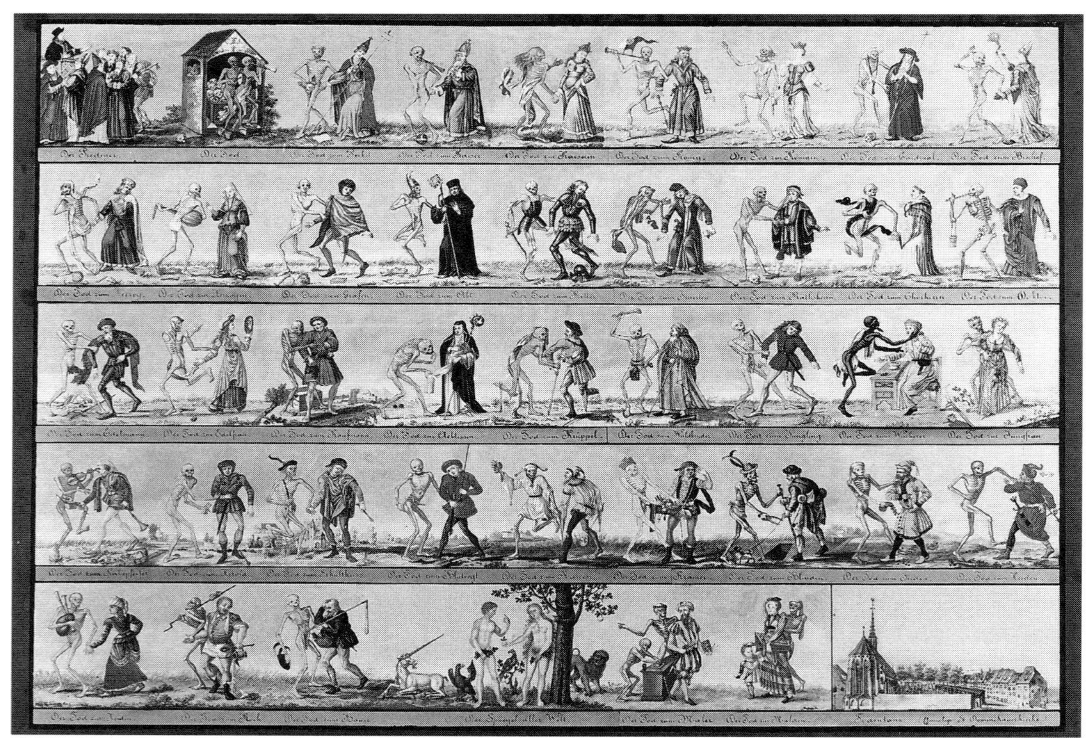

4(*a*). The Basel *Totentanz*, by Konrad Witz, *c*.1440?, Hans Hug Kluber, 1568, and others. Watercolour reproduction by J. Feyerabend, 1806). By permission of the Historisches Museum, Basel.

(*b*) Death and the Jester, detail from the Basel *Totentanz*.

'the distinctiveness of the plague', as René Girard puts it in a celebrated essay, 'is that it ultimately destroys all forms of distinctiveness. . . . All life, finally, is turned into death . . . the supreme undifferentiation.'[25] One of the words often used to describe the pestilence was 'wild'—as though its assault represented all those anarchic forces that lie beyond the bounds of civil order in what Thomas Dekker, the plague's most eloquent English chronicler, called 'the wild Irish country of worms'.[26] The plague was wild partly because of the suddenness with which it struck; cheating its victims of what Ariès has called 'the tame death', it brought the *mors repentina* or *improvisa* so repellent to the medieval imagination.[27] But, above all, the plague's wildness lay in its threat to wipe out the whole system of distinctions upon which civil order was founded. Thus it was more than just a fashionable taste for paradox that induced the author of *Newes from Graues-end*, writing in the aftermath of the terrible plague of 1603, to dedicate his verse tract to John Marston's mock-patron '*Sir* Nicholas Nemo, *alias* Nobody'.[28] With a fine witty flourish, the writer—almost certainly Dekker—subscribes himself 'Some-body', his sardonic hyphen serving as a reminder that the plague, with its gross demonstrations of bodily vulnerability, is what threatens to make nobody of everybody.[29]

Since the rites of funeral represent a traditional society's last line of defence against mortality, the horror of mass death is always most painfully felt in the breakdown of burial custom. Stripped

[25] René Girard, 'The Plague in Literature and Myth', in *To Double Business Bound: Essays on Literature, Mimesis, and Anthropology* (Baltimore: Johns Hopkins University Press, 1978), 136–53: 137.

[26] Dekker, *The Wonderfull yeare* (1603), in *The Plague Pamphlets of Thomas Dekker*, ed. F. P. Wilson (Oxford: Clarendon Press, 1925), 9. This perhaps is why the famous *Totentanz* at Basel, for example, seems to be danced out on a wild moorland outside the walls of the city.

[27] Ariès, *Hour of our Death*, 5–28. For the horror of plague as a bringer of sudden death, see e.g. Thomas Dekker, *A Rod for Run-awayes* (1625) and *London Looke Backe* (1625), in *Plague Pamphlets*, ed. Wilson, 159–62, 181.

[28] In 1602 Marston had dedicated *Antonio and Mellida* 'To the only rewarder and most just poiser of virtuous merits, the most honourably renowned Nobody, bounteous Maecenas of Poetry and Lord Protector of oppressed innocence' (cited from *The Selected Plays of John Marston*, ed. MacDonald P. Jackson and Michael Neill (Cambridge: Cambridge University Press, 1986), 7; except where otherwise indicated, citations from Marston are to this edition).

[29] *Newes from Graues-end: Sent to Nobody* (London, 1604), sigs. A3, C1^{v}. The pamphlet was published anonymously, but is generally attributed to Dekker.

of the decencies of interment, all are degraded to a condition of abject servitude by the common livery of death:

> No bells (the dead man's consort) playing,
> Nor any holy churchman saying
> A funeral dirge; but swift th'are gone,
> As from some noisome carrion. . . .
> There friend and foe, the young and old,
> The freezing coward and the bold,
> Servant and master, foul and fair
> One livery wear, and fellows are.[30]

Descriptions of pestilence from Thucydides to Defoe repeatedly focus on the abandonment of proper funeral rites as among the worst of its horrors. Such was the anarchy produced by the plague which devastated Athens in 427 BC that it seemed to Thucydides 'beyond description', resistant even to the retrospective ordering of narrative. The Athenians 'perished in wild disorder. The dead lay as they had died, one upon another. . . . The customs which had hitherto been observed at funerals were universally violated, and they buried their dead each one as best he could. . . . [and] made no scruple of using the burial-place of others.'[31] The plague-stricken cities of late medieval and Renaissance Europe were similarly forced to relinquish their elaborate rites of funeral in favour of the degrading practice of mass burial in common pits.[32] In many communities this would persist as the standard form of interment for the poorest members of society until well into the eighteenth century; but in times of pestilence the burial pit gaped for everyone, rich and poor, mighty and humble alike, reducing them all to the condition of the merest carrion. In the terrible autumn of 1418, according to the *Bourgeois de Paris*, 'so many people died in such a short space of time that it was necessary to dig huge pits, in each of which were placed thirty or forty persons with a few handfuls of dirt thrown on top'.[33] There were five great pits, such as the chronicler described, at Les Innocents alone, some holding up to 600 people; and the skulls and bones which filled

[30] Dekker, *Newes from Graues-end*, sig. E2–E3.

[31] Cited in Raymond Crawfurd, *Plague and Pestilence in Literature and Art* (Oxford: Clarendon Press, 1914), 30.

[32] Ariès, *Hour of our Death*, 56–7.

[33] *Journal d'un bourgeois de Paris au moyen âge*, ed. A. Tutey (Paris: Champion, 1881), Oct.–Nov. 1418, p. 116; cited in Ariès, *Hour of our Death*, 56–7 (emphasis added).

the adjacent charnels were mostly their end-products, heaped up as the ground was dug and redug to make room for new avalanches of the dead. Individual corpses lost all trace of identity in the shapelessness of 'heaps' and 'piles'.[34] In Boccaccio's Florence, at the height of the Black Death, as the sickness fell upon all classes without distinction, bodies were 'unreverently . . . thrown into the first open grave they found [so that] it plainly appeared, that the very like account was then made of Men or Women, as if they had been Dogs or Swine'.[35]

Thus the plague collapsed all differences between high and low, kinsfolk and strangers, humans and animals, and ultimately even between people and things:[36]

neither could the bodies have proper place of burial, according to our ancient custom: wherefore, after that the Churches and Churchyards were filled, they were constrained to make use of great deep ditches, wherein they were buried by hundreds at once, ranking dead bodies along in graves, *as Merchandises are laid along in ships*, covering each after the other with a small quantity of earth, and so they filled at last up the whole ditch to the brim.[37]

In an even more grotesque image the *Bourgeois* describes the dead as 'piled up like bacon' in the pits;[38] while for another eyewitness the thousands of bodies in the plague ditch at Vienna in 1679 resembled 'pickled game in a barrel'.[39] To Dekker the devastating

[34] The peculiar horror which attaches to the undifferentiating commonness of 'heaps' and 'piles' which strip corpses of their humanity is discussed by Canetti (*Crowds and Power*, 319).

[35] Boccaccio, *The Decameron*, First Day, cited from an anon. trans. of 1625 in Johannes Nohl, *The Black Death: A Chronicle of the Plague*, trans. C. H. Clarke (London: George Allen & Unwin, 1926), 26–7.

[36] The notion of becoming 'a loathsome *thing* which disgusts even those who love us most' is similarly imagined by Sir Thomas Browne as 'one of the principal horrors of death'; see Michael Stanford, 'The Terrible Thresholds: Sir Thomas Browne on Sex and Death', *English Literary Renaissance*, 18 (1988), 413–23: 415.

[37] Boccaccio in Nohl, *Black Death*, 28.

[38] *Bourgeois*, 116, in Ariès, *Hour of our Death*, 57. If the pig, as Peter Stallybrass and Allon White have shown, is a paradigm of lowness, emblematizing the challenge of the grotesque body to all the distinctions of the 'high', then in its dead form it represents undifferentiation redoubled, its preserved flesh a travesty of the embalmer's immortalizing art. See Peter Stallybrass and Allon White, *The Politics and Poetics of Transgression* (London: Methuen, 1986), ch. 2; see esp. pp. 44–59, 62–6.

[39] Cited in George Deaux, *The Black Death 1347* (London: Hamish Hamilton, 1969), 163.

London epidemic of 1625 revealed 'the Earth [as a] great warehouse, which is piled up with winding-sheets',[40] and his plague pamphlets are full of horrified reflections on the indignity of mass interment: corpses are heaped on corpses; people are tumbled 'into their everlasting lodgings (ten in one heap, and twenty in another) .... The gallant and the beggar ... together; the scholar and the carter in one bed';[41] men and women are 'buried like dogs' in the open fields.[42] Even more horribly, in some cases 'the mattock and shovel have ventured so far, the very common-shore [sewer] breaks into these ghastly and gloomy warehouses'[43] so that what began as food for the 'anthropophagized plague'[44] is reduced to the condition of mere excrement.

In *The Wonderfull yeare* Dekker imagines the suffering of a father, determined 'in despite of Death and his Plague, to maintain the memory of [his] child in the everlasting breast of Marble': 'thou must be forced with thine own hands [to] ... dig his grave, not in the church, or common place of burial ... but in thine orchard, or in the proud walks of thy garden, wringing thy palsy-shaken hands in stead of bells. ... [to] search him out a sepulchre'.[45] Again and again plague writing returns to this theme: in its wild assault upon difference the disease breaks all boundaries: human flesh becomes so much merchandise, or meat, or carrion; the grave becomes indistinguishable from the sewer, the orchard or the garden from the churchyard. No wonder that Dekker should figure the pestilence as an epitome of illegitimate mixture, its 'main army consisting ... of a mingle-mangle'. The plague for him is a creature whose protean and multiform nature seems to resist any ordering definition: 'all other infirmities and maladies of the body go simply in their own habit ... under their proper and known names',

[40] Thomas Dekker, *A Rod for Run-awayes*, in *Plague Pamphlets*, ed. Wilson, 139.

[41] *The Seven Deadly Sinnes* (1606), cited in F. P. Wilson, *The Plague in Shakespeare's London* (Oxford: Oxford University Press, 1963), 43–4.

[42] *The Wonderfull yeare*, in *Plague Pamphlets*, ed. Wilson, 36.

[43] Dekker, *A Rod for Run-awayes*, in *Plague Pamphlets*, ed. Wilson, 159.

[44] Dekker, *The Wonderfull yeare*, in *Plague Pamphlets*, ed. Wilson, 28. Metaphors of hunger and eating are especially abundant in Dekker as figures for the indiscriminateness of plague, in a way that helps to explain the intimacy of disease and appetite imagery in *Troilus and Cressida*, the archetypal plague-drama (see below, pp. 26–8). Ulysses' Appetite, the universal wolf, is nothing less than the undifferentiating principle of plague itself.

[45] *Plague Pamphlets*, ed. Wilson, 31.

but the plague, unmatched 'for violence, subtlety, catching, universality, and desolation', is simply 'THE SICKNESS', definable only by tautology, 'the *Sickness* of *Sicknesses*'.[46] Contained in that repetition is the threat of a self-consuming apocalypse whose 'universality' recalls the utter confounding of distinction produced by Ulysses' 'universal wolf' in *Troilus and Cressida* (I. iii. 121), or the self-cancellation emblematized in the impresa with which Holbein concluded his woodcut Dance of Death: *Death's Coat of Arms* (Fig. 5). In this blazon of Death heraldic difference punningly proclaims indifference: the skeletal arms which form part of the crest are clutching a rock with which they seem about to demolish the hourglass that sits where their skull should be, as though some ghoulish creature were about to dash out its own brains: Death's frenzy of annihilation, we are to see, will end by including even the very thing on which its being and power depend—Time.[47]

Theatre and Plague

The eminently bourgeois figures chosen by successive writers to suggest the monstrous undifferentiation of plague serve as reminders that the plague was essentially an urban phenomenon. Its inefficient bacillus could flourish only in the relatively large, overcrowded cities that developed in the late medieval and early modern period; but the grotesque comparisons of its heaped-up victims to 'merchandises', flitches of 'bacon', or 'pickled game in a barrel' suggest a parodic symmetry between its depredations and the activities of the urban world. The implication is that plague is the designated scourge of urban vice; and its endemic presence does much to explain the deep ambivalence with which the city came to be regarded. On the one hand, rapidly expanding metropolitan centres such as London, with their unprecedented wealth and growing pretensions to civic grandeur, were a source of legitimate pride to their inhabitants. Consciously invested with the trappings of the classical *urbs* or *polis*, the city stood for the very idea of civilization.

[46] Dekker, *The Wonderfull yeare* and *London Looke Backe*, in *Plague Pamphlets*, ed. Wilson, 31, 181.

[47] A simpler version of the same conceit is imaged in the Bridegroom of Holbein's *Dance*, where Death (as he does at the front of the Dance of Death Mural in Lübeck) is about to stamp on his own hourglass.

5. *Death's Coat of Arms*, woodcut by Hans Holbein from *Les Simulacres de la mort* (Lyons, 1538).

But, the city was also a place of dirt, corruption, and disease, and one whose sheer size and amorphousness was felt to undermine the traditional social order. Thus the same London whose civic pageantry gave it a serenely idealized form in the triumphal arches that identified it as a reborn Rome or New Troy could also be embodied in the rampaging mob of 2 *Henry VI*, or in the mutinous plebeians of *Coriolanus*, whose conviction that 'the people *are* the city' allegedly threatens 'To unbuild the city, and to lay all flat' (*Cor.* III. i. 197–9). To the imagination of a Coriolanus, the city crowd is not merely a source of disease, but in itself a kind of pustular 'plague' (I. iv. 31; I. vi. 43) whose taint of commonness will wipe out all 'distinction'.

In the vision of contemporary satirists, the city was a place whose swarming crowds and subjection to the universal solvent, money, rendered social identity dangerously fluid and uncertain —a place whose corruptions were uncannily mirrored in the undifferentiating depredations of the plague, as they are in Jonson's *Alchemist*, whose action implicitly equates the pestilence raging outside Lovewit's usurped house with the moral disease rampant within it. The Alchemist's den is not merely a microcosm of the city, of course; it is also presented as a type of fraudulent theatre— to the point where Face's epilogue actually identifies his ill-gotten pelf with the takings of the playhouse itself. The connection is hardly fortuitous, for the early modern ambivalence towards the city is nowhere more marked than in attitudes to the theatre. On the one hand, theatre is promoted by apologists like Heywood as the proper ornament of any metropolis that seeks to emulate the splendours of Greece and Rome;[48] on the other, it is identified by its enemies—and sometimes, surprisingly, even by its own practitioners—as a place of disorder, a bastion of the unruly mob, a leveller of proper distinctions, and a source of moral and physical disease.

Like the plague, the theatre was a phenomenon of the urban crowd; and their histories are entangled in a complex fashion. At the purely practical level the fortunes of the actors were materially dependent on the arbitrary violence of the plague, since the elementary precautions taken by the authorities in time of pestilence invariably included the closure of playhouses as places where the

[48] Thomas Heywood, *An Apology for Actors* (London, 1612), sig. C1–C2.

gathering of large crowds was likely to encourage the spread of infection.[49] Partly as a result, the theatre itself became tainted by its association with what Coriolanus calls 'the rank-scented meiny' (*Coriolanus*, III. i. 66). In the propaganda of their enemies, indeed, playhouses were often identified not merely as disseminators of pestilence, but as the original cause of such divine punishment. 'I.H.', the angry moralist of *This Worlds Folly*, for example, insisted that there could be no quelling of the plague until 'Bawdy Players' were banished from the commonwealth: 'neither can God's wrath be qualified, nor his pestilential arrows, which fly amongst us by day, & lethally wound us by night, be quivered up, till these *menstruous rags* be torn off (by the hand of *authority*) from the city's skirts, which so besoil and coinquinate her whole vesture'.[50] The plague here is traced to its corrupted source in the feminized body politic of the city, where a literal disease is produced by the taint of metaphoric uncleanness. The rhetorical shift is possible because playing, in the author's mind, violates the essential boundaries by which the distinctions of 'clean' and 'unclean' are preserved.[51] Behind his misogynist metaphor lie the elaborate prohibitions of Leviticus, which defines menstruation as a species of 'unclean issue' requiring 'separation', exactly as the defilement of 'plague' requires separation.[52] Marked with the sanguinary excrement of mortal corruption, players are at once the cause of pestilence's lethal 'wound', and part of its putrefying 'issue'.

Theatres became vulnerable to this kind of denunciation partly because of the rhetoric with which they successfully capitalized upon contemporary tropes of 'discovery': this was an important part of the symbolism of the Globe, after all, whose sign advertised the theatre's capacity to place the whole world on display before a curious public. The arts of the playwright vied with those of the geographer (whose atlases were themselves sometimes called 'theatres') in a project of universal discovery. In the judgement of its more hostile critics, however, the danger of theatre consisted in

[49] The best recent treatment of this subject is Leeds Barroll's *Politics, Plague, and Shakespeare's Theatre: The Stuart Years* (Ithaca, NY: Cornell University Press, 1991).

[50] I.H., *This Worlds Folly; or, A Warning-Peece discharged vpon the Wickedness thereof* (London, 1615), sig. B3.

[51] On 'the fear of impurity, of contamination, of "mixture", of the blurring of strict boundaries' aroused by theatre, see Jonas Barish, *The Anti-theatrical Prejudice* (Berkeley: University of California Press, 1981), 87.

[52] Lev. 13: 15.

its displaying precisely those things which—because they were too either too base or too lofty to touch—ought not to be spared such exposure. Thus for the preacher John Stockwood, the first of London's 'gorgeous playing place[s]' stood condemned by its very name, 'The Theatre', which, by virtue of its derivation from the Greek verb for 'view', identified it as 'a show place of all beastly and filthy matters';[53] while for the penitent playwright Stephen Gosson, the theatre was a place in which the humble were permitted to mimic the great in a fashion that subverted the good order of society, since by this means 'proportion is so broken, harmony confounded, that the whole body must be dismembered and the prince or the head cannot choose but sicken'. God's bow was bent, Gosson warned the players, ready to 'send you a plague, if you stay too long'.[54]

Accusing the players of 'barbarously diverting Nature, and defacing God's own image, by metamorphosing human shape into bestial form',[55] their detractors contrived to suggest that theatre's shameless confounding of difference was inseparable from its mimetic arts. In its blurring of moral distinctions, its counterfeitings, its violations of vestimentary order, its breaking of the accepted boundaries of hierarchy and gender—and even perhaps its promiscuous creation of a mass audience, heaped together in a pit—playing constituted, in fact, a kind of metaphoric plague for which actual disease was the proper and inevitable retributive substitute. Crewed by '*Fortune*-fatted fools, and Time's idiots, whose garb is the tooth-ache of wit, the plague-sore of judgement, [and] the common-sewer of obscenities',[56] theatres were imagined as a source of miasmic infection, every bit as dangerous as the plague pits themselves:

what voice is heard in our streets? Nought but the squeaking out of those . . . obscene and light jigs, stuffed with loathsome and unheard-of ribaldry, sucked from the poisonous dugs of sin-swelled theatres. . . . More have recourse to playing houses, than to praying houses, where they set open their ears & eyes to suck up variety of abominations, bewitching

[53] John Stockwood, *A Sermon Preached at Paules Crosse* (London, 1578), 134–5.

[54] Stephen Gosson, *Playes Confuted in fiue Actions* (1582), in E. K. Chambers, *The Elizabethan Stage*, 4 vols. (Oxford: Clarendon Press, 1951), iv. 218–19.

[55] *This Worlds Folly*, sig. B2. William Prynne's *Histriomastix* adumbrates such notions at great length.

[56] *This Worlds Folly*, sig. B2.

their minds with extravagant thoughts, & benumbing their souls with insensibility.[57]

The play which most conspicuously illustrates this sense of theatre as an agency of plague is *Troilus and Cressida*, whose nihilistic satire involves an exceptionally degraded view of theatrical imitation. Its nominal subjects are love and heroic warfare; but both are rendered as forms of epidemic disease, as plague is assimilated with syphilis, that other great scourge of early modern cities.[58] Just as Dekker's *Wonderfull yeare* represents the plague of 1603 as a siege of London by a great army of pestilence, so Shakespeare presents the epic siege of Troy as an outbreak of moral sickness—the true 'plague of Greece' denounced by Thersites (II. i. 12). The warriors of the play may fantasize their death in terms of the supreme heroic distinction conferred by single combat, but the degraded death of Hector, submerged in the rout of Achilles' Myrmidons (V. viii), makes brutally concrete Troilus' image of death in battle as a contemptuous stripping of 'distinction' among 'heaps' of anonymous bodies (III. ii. 26–9). Agamemnon envisages the war as one of those trials by which the gods seek 'To find persistive constancy in men', thereby revealing their essential selfhood in the distinct, 'unmingled' form proper to its true nature; in it

> *Distinction*, with a broad and powerful fan,
> Puffing at all, winnows the light away,
> And what hath mass or matter, by itself
> Lies rich in virtue and unmingled.
>
> (I. iii. 26–30; emphasis added)

But the actual progress of the war, as Ulysses suggests, has been one in which 'specialty of rule . . . degree, priority, and place, | Insisture, course, proportion, season, form, | Office, and custom' (I. iii. 78, 86–8), the whole system of distinctions by which society orders itself, has been undermined, to the point where 'Each thing meets | In mere oppugnancy' (lines 110–11). This collapsing of distinction and violent mingling of kinds threatens a terminal chaos of utter contradiction in which 'appetite, an universal wolf . . . Must

[57] *This Worlds Folly*, sig. B1^{v}.

[58] See Girard, 'The Plague in Literature and Myth', in *To Double Business Bound*, for some relevant discussion.

make perforce an universal prey, | And last eat up himself' (lines 121–4). All human qualities are reduced here to manifestations of this self-devouring principle: love becomes the 'lechery' which visibly 'eats itself' in the combat of Troilus and Diomed (v. iv. 35); heroic pride becomes the vanity that produces the self-destructive frenzy that Ulysses observes in Achilles:

> 'twixt his mental and his active parts
> Kingdom'd Achilles in commotion rages,
> And batters down himself.
>
> (II. iii. 175–7)

The quintessence of this same frenzy is to be found in the diseased genius of this deliberately botched play, the 'crusty botch of nature' Thersites. The seer of its levelling pestilential vision, he is significantly described as an 'indistinguishable cur' (v. i. 29). His satiric performances serve to confound all distinctions, 'matching [the Greek generals] in comparisons with dirt' (I. iii. 194); yet even as he lays open the 'botchy core' (II. i. 6), the plague-rotted heart of his society, his dissection exposes his own coruscating 'core of envy'.[59] He resembles, in fact, nothing so much as one of those self-anatomizing figures whose opened bowels obligingly illustrate the text of early modern anatomies.

In the degrading histrionics of Thersites theatre appears to operate exactly as the enemies of the stage complained, 'barbarously diverting Nature, and defacing Gods own image'; and his fury of indistinction replicates the satiric method of Shakespeare's own play, whose 'monumental mockery' undoes the very tale it pretends to memorialize. In its conspicuous refusal of tragic closure, *Troilus* flouts the convention of its nominal form; and as it ends

[59] The way in which the plague of 'war and lechery confound[s] all' in *Troilus* (II. iii. 75) is mirrored in *King John*, where the Bastard, with oxymoronic wit, describes how the 'undetermin'd differences' of kings reduce everything to 'havoc' and 'confusion' (II. i. 352–9), whilst Death comes to John himself as a besieging general, whose fantastic soldiery pour over the dying King in indiscriminate confusion:

> Death, having prey'd upon the outward parts,
> Leaves them invisible, and his siege is now
> Against the mind, the which he pricks and wounds
> With many legions of strange fantasies,
> Which *in the throng and press* to that last hold,
> *Confound themselves.*
>
> (v. vii. 15–20; emphasis added)

with Pandarus' venereal maledictions, its plague seems poised to engulf the audience themselves.

Mindful of such contamination, *This Worlds Folly* imagines the actors 'behung with chains of garlic, as an antidote against their own infectious breaths, lest it should kill their oyster-crying Audience'.[60] But the identification of the mass of playgoers with the city mob means that the audience too is felt as a source of contamination. In the case of Coriolanus, for example, the 'contagion' of the crowd is never more intensely felt than in the scene where, dressed in the borrowed robes of humility, he is forced to stage himself to the show for the approbation of a crowd whose gaze replicates that of the audience (II. iii); and his final rejection of the city is cast in language that mimics the standard tirades against the rabble of groundlings in the pit:

> You common cry of curs, whose breath I hate
> As reek a'th'rotten fens, whose loves I prize
> As the dead carcasses of unburied men
> That do corrupt my air—I banish you!
>
> (III. iii. 120–4)

It is as if for Coriolanus the contamination of 'the common file', with its danger of absorption into the crowd, threatens the very survival of his heroic selfhood; and one of the things that makes this play so uncomfortable to watch is that its tragic effect relies so much upon the hero's power to compel the audience into a self-contempt matching his own disdain for them. In this, however, *Coriolanus* merely carries to an extreme the tension that arguably underlies all tragic performance in a theatre where heroic transcendence of death is defined by the protagonist's ability to raise himself above the common herd who have come to witness his end.

Tragedy and Death

> All tragedies are finish'd by a death
> All comedies are ended by a marriage.
>
> (Byron, *Don Juan*, III. 9)

[60] *This Worlds Folly*, sig. B2. Cheryl Lynn Ross, 'The Plague of *The Alchemist*', *Renaissance Quarterly*, 41 (1988), 439–58 explores the kinship between plague, theatre, and masterless criminality as phenomena that appear to threaten the ordered definitions of society at its vulnerable margins.

Byron's reductive irony would have been quite invisible to Shakespeare's contemporaries. For them, as Theodore Spencer observed in his pioneering study, 'Death . . . *was* tragedy'[61] and its mere presence in the catastrophe of a play—even one as generically anomalous as Marlowe's *The Famous Tragedy of the Rich Jew of Malta*—was sufficient to identify it as belonging to the tragic kind, just as comedy was typically marked by its nuptial endings. The promiscuity of such a working definition reflects something more than the theoretical pragmatism and sensationalist bias of a popular art: for if, as Spencer claims, English Renaissance tragedy was 'more concerned with death than any drama that had previously existed'[62] (or any that followed it), this was because it catered for a culture that was in the throes of a peculiar crisis in the accommodation of death—one that reflected the strain of adjusting the psychic economy of an increasingly individualistic society to the stubborn facts of mortality.[63] We can see that strain most floridly displayed in the catastrophe of Marlowe's *Tamburlaine*:

> What daring god torments my body thus,
> And seeks to conquer mighty Tamburlaine?
> Shall sickness prove me now to be a man,
> That have been termed the terror of the world? . . .
> Come, let us march against the powers of heaven,
> And set black streamers in the firmament,
> To signify the slaughter of the Gods . . .
> See, where my slave, the ugly monster, Death,
> Shaking and quivering, pale and wan for fear,
> Stands aiming at me with his murdering dart,
> Who flies away at every glance I give,
> And, when I look away, comes stealing on.
>
> (2 *Tamb.* v. iii. 42–71)

[61] Theodore Spencer, *Death and Elizabethan Tragedy* (Cambridge, Mass.: Harvard University Press, 1936; repr. New York: Pageant Books, 1960), 232.

[62] Ibid. 232.

[63] See Ariès, *Hour of our Death*, part II; and Arnold Stein, *The House of Death: Messages from the English Renaissance* (Baltimore: Johns Hopkins University Press, 1986), 14–17. Ariès's emphasis on individualism as the primary motor in changing attitudes to death is, however, challenged by Houlbrooke (*Death Ritual and Bereavement*, 6–7); and it is possible to argue that individualist constructions of the self were themselves partly produced by the changing experience of death—just as it is precisely in Hamlet's prolonged and anxious meditation on death that we are made to experience the shaping of a distinctively modern subject. In a circular and mutually reinforcing fashion, new ways of responding to mortality probably helped to produce new forms of subjectivity, even as new subjectivities must have transformed the experience of dying.

The anxiety that inspires Tamburlaine's defiant rhetoric is registered plainly enough; and elsewhere it is only thinly concealed by the self-monumentalizing histrionics or theatrical stoicism with which such characters as Shakespeare's Cleopatra or Ford's Perkin Warbeck seek to clothe their endings:

Death? Pish, 'tis but a sound, a name of air,
A minute's storm, or not so much. To tumble
From bed to bed, be massacred alive
By some physicians for a month or two,
In hope of freedom from a fever's torments,
Might stagger manhood; here, the pain is passed
Ere sensibly 'tis felt. Be men of spirit;
Spurn coward passion! So illustrious mention
Shall blaze our names, and style us kings o'er death!

(*Perkin Warbeck*, v. iii. 200–8)

What is being resisted in such episodes is the notion of death as an arbitrary cancellation of meaning—the force of undifferentiation so overwhelmingly felt at the end of *King Lear* ('Why should a dog, a horse, a rat, have life, | And thou no breath at all?' v. iii. 307–8). That is why Perkin's imagination fixes on the narrative salve of 'illustrious mention', and why Cleopatra carefully stages her death in a royal tomb, masking it as a transcendent rite of coronation, and why the dying Tamburlaine surrounds himself with the emblematic badges of power and authority—chariot and scourge, map and crown.

The psychological value of tragedy's displays of agony, despair, and ferocious self-assertion, one might argue, was that they provided audiences with a way of vicariously confronting the implications of their own mortality, by compelling them to rehearse and re-rehearse the encounter with death. Thus tragedy served, in a fashion that was inseparable alike from its didactic pretensions and its entertaining practice, both as an instrument for probing the painful mystery of ending, and as a vehicle of resistance to the levelling authority of death. 'In constructing an illusion of death in the theater,' writes Kirby Farrell, 'people were collaborating, as they did in other areas of their lives, to convert the threat of pollution, instability, and nothingness into a source of fertility or productiveness: to make death yield heroic meaning that could sustain society.'[64] Thus tragedy, with its deliberate appropriation of the triumphalist motifs of funeral art, deserves be linked with a whole range of 'cultural artefacts' whose function, in the words of Nigel Llewellyn, was 'to teach the living how to die'.[65] Unlike them, however, tragedy (despite the claims of its sometimes disingenuous defenders) did not confine itself to the expression of pious orthodoxies. Its very secularity, combined with the dialectical tendency of all drama to incorporate contradictory and subversive voices, made possible the articulation of doubts and anxieties which orthodox forms of instruction were calculated to repress.

'To be knaved out of our graves,' wrote Sir Thomas Browne, 'to have our skulls made drinking-bowls, and our bones turned into pipes, to delight and sport our enemies, are *tragical abominations.*'[66] But at the same time as it paraded the emblems of undifferentiation, tragedy offered to contain the fear of death by staging fantasies of ending in which the moment of dying was transformed, by the arts of performance, to a supreme demonstration of distinction. Because tragedy rescues the dead from the uncertainty, obscurity, and confusion of 'the Land of Moles and Pismires', observes Browne, it offers a species of consolation: 'the *tragical ends* of noble persons [are] more favourably resented by compassionate readers, who find some relief in the election of such differences'.[67] Nowhere, perhaps, is the ambivalence of tragedy's relation to death more eloquently displayed than in Thomas Dekker's attempts, though a remarkable series of pamphlets, to come to terms with the experience of the plague. Seeking for a language adequate to horrors that seemed as indescribable to him as they had to Thucydides, Dekker draws repeatedly on his experience as a dramatist. In *Newes from Graues-end* he begins his description of the disease with an invocation of the Muse, not of history, but of tragic poetry—

> Thou Tragic Maid, whose fury's spent
> In dismal and most black ostent.
> In uproars, and in fall of kings,
> Thou of empire's change that sings,
> Of dearths, of wars, of plagues, and laughs
> At funerals, and epitaphs . . .

[64] Kirby Farrell, *Play, Death and Heroism in Shakespeare* (Chapel Hill: University of North Carolina Press, 1989), 10.

[65] Llewellyn, *Art of Death*, 7.

[66] *Urn Burial*, 120; emphasis added.

[67] Ibid. 116; emphasis added.

we will write
With pens pulled from that bird of night,
The shrieking owl; our ink we'll mix
With tears of widows, black as Styx;
The paper where our lines shall meet,
Shall be a folded winding-sheet,
And that the scene may show more full,
The standish is a dead man's skull.
Inspire us therefore how to tell
The *horror* of a *plague*, the *Hell*[68]

—and at the end of the same poem, Dekker reviews his narrative as a catalogue of tragic histories such as this Muse might approve:

These are the tragedies, whose sight
With tears blot all the lines we write;
The stage whereon the scenes are plaid,
Is a whole kingdom, who was made
By some, most provident and wise,
To hide from sad spectator's eyes
Acts full of ruth, a private room
To drown the horror of death's doom.
That building now no higher rear,
The *pest-house* standeth everywhere.[69]

It is difficult now, when the word 'tragedy' has become so worn from over-use, to sense the particularity of Dekker's theatrical metaphors; but they embody an attitude towards the genre which deserves some reflection. The grand tragic process, into which are absorbed all the small tragedies that the poet has described, is fully accomplished only at that moment of absolute undifferentiation, when 'The *pest-house* standeth everywhere', when all lines are blotted out, and the poem falls into silence. Tragedy here is specifically that kind of action in which human beings are shown in contest with the horror of indistinction, facing a world like Hamlet's, which threatens to collapse into 'a foul and pestilent congregation of vapours' (II. ii. 302–3), or like *The Duchess of Malfi*'s, where the 'huge pyramid' of aristocratic pride ends in 'a little point, a kind of nothing' (V. v. 79), or like Macbeth's, in which history is rendered down to an idiot's tale 'signifying nothing' (V. v. 28)—a world in which (as one English Dance of Death has it) 'death

[68] Dekker, *Newes from Graues-end*, sig. C3–C3^{v}. [69] Ibid., sig. E4.

hath brought all things to nought'.[70] Yet at the conclusion of what was to be the last of his plague pamphlets, Dekker returns to his theatrical metaphor, using it now as a figure for the human conquest of mortality. The trope is given a familiar pietistic twist, but nothing can conceal the defiant self-exhibition of the playwright as he breathes new life into one of the oldest metaphors for a good end—one in which performance snatches distinction from the very jaws of oblivion, and tames the wildness of death: 'On this stage are presented tragedies and comedies; the terriblest tragedy is that of the soul, fighting to get off (well) from the body. The best and most pleasing comedy is that of a white conscience, and peace of mind. . . . But in the conclusion, he that can get angels to sit in the galleries of Heaven, and clap his action with their immortal hands —he is the only Roscius of the time.'[71] Such a performer might stand, like the terrible Hero evoked by Elias Canetti, crowing upon the heaps of the dead.[72] By the fact of his art he joins those makers of tragic monuments whom his fellow dramatist Webster celebrated in the tag from Martial which he affixed to *The White Devil*: *Non norunt haec monumenta mori.*

In Webster's tragedy, as so often on this stage, death paradoxically becomes a powerfully individuating experience, the supreme occasion for exhibitions of individual distinction.[73] In that play the 'glorious strumpet' Vittoria can 'welcome death | As princes do some great ambassadors' (*White Devil*, v. vi. 208, 221–2), enacting the oxymoron of the title in a way that is matched by her black maid, Zanche ('I am proud | Death cannot alter my complexion, | For I shall ne'er look pale'; lines 231–3), by her brother Flamineo ('No, at myself I will begin and end. . . . Strike, thunder, and strike loud, to my farewell'; lines 259, 277), and even by their murderer, Lodovico ('I do glory yet | That I can call this act mine own'; lines 295–6). The death welcomed by these characters is quite explicitly the arbitrary *mors repentina* which the medieval imagination had found so terrifying: 'Of all deaths,' insists the swaggering Flamineo, 'the violent death is best' (v. vi. 115–17);

[70] [Richard Day], *A Booke of Christian Prayers* ['Queen Elizabeth's Prayerbook'] (London, 1569), sig. Oo1^{v}.

[71] Dekker, *The Blacke Rod and the White Rod* (1630), in *Plague Pamphlets*, ed. Wilson, 201.

[72] Canetti, *Crowds and Power*, 265–6, 322.

[73] For the Renaissance dramatization of dying as 'an episode of heightened [individual] awareness', see Stein, *The House of Death*, 14–16.

and his own murder, set against the hideous parody of the traditional 'good end' suffered by Brachiano (v. iii.), confirms his judgement. In this Webster follows the new philosophy of death advocated by Montaigne and others, according to which the 'happy' death is one 'which takes all leisure from the preparations of such an equipage'.[74] The ritualized drama of confession and absolution by which the 'good end' contained the chaos of death reduced the dying person to a passive sufferer whose only role was willingly to surrender the last frail trappings of selfhood; by contrast, to those who were ready to meet it, the once dreaded *mors improvisa* provided the occasion for an improvisational theatre of defiance in which the power of death was subordinated to self-display. '[N]o death is sudden to him that dies well,' Richard Brathwaite advises his *English Gentleman*;[75] for 'the readiness', as Hamlet puts it, 'is all' (v. ii. 222).

Deriving in part from classical moral philosophy, especially that of Seneca, this aesthetic depends upon the dying person's ability to make death the consummation of a life conducted according to immaculately theatrical precepts.[76] In Seneca's words, 'It fareth with our life as with a stage-play, it skilleth not how long, but how well it hath been acted. It importeth nothing in what place thou makest an end of life: die where thou wilt, think only to make a good conclusion.'[77] The metaphor became a favourite with

[74] Michel de Montaigne, *Montaigne's Essays*, trans. John Florio, ed. J. C. Harmer, 3 vols. (London: J. M. Dent, 1965), I. xix. 91. In a passage that might have supplied the programme for the staging of Brachiano's death 'mongst women howling', Montaigne argues that the truly dreadful death is that in which we are surrounded by 'the wailing of women and children . . . [in] a dark chamber: tapers burning round about; our couch beset round with physicians and preachers; and to conclude, nothing but horror and astonishment on every side of us' (ibid.).

[75] Richard Brathwaite, *The English Gentleman*, 3rd edn. (London, 1641), 206. The process by which the abhorred *mors repentina* gradually came to be regarded as the most desirable form of death is discussed by Ariès, *Hour of our Death*, 118–23.

[76] On the humanist transformation of the *ars moriendi*, in which 'every moment is seen as a form of death . . . [so that] the whole lifetime becomes a test . . . and the individual's disposition at the instant of death passes judgement on his whole life', see Phoebe S. Spinrad, *The Summons of Death on the Renaissance Stage* (Columbus: Ohio State University Press, 1987), 36–8. In this dispensation 'heroic dying becomes not only a spiritual victory but a temporal one as well; it can foil tyrants as well as devils when men die cheerfully' (p. 39).

[77] *The Workes of Lucius Annaeus Seneca both Morall and Naturall*, trans. Thomas Lodge (London, 1620), Epistle LXXVII, p. 323.

Seneca's Renaissance followers, including Montaigne, for whom death is 'the last act of [the] comedy, and without doubt the hardest',[78] and Pierre Charron, who expanded on Montaigne's aphorism to sketch a virtual poetics of human experience:

Our present life is but the entrance and end of a tragedy, a perpetual issue of errors, a web of unhappy adventures. . . . blindness and want of sense possesseth the beginning of our life, the middle is ever in pain and travail, the end in sorrow; and beginning, middle, and end in error. . . . He that judgeth of the life of a man, must look how he carrieth himself at his death; for the end crowneth the work, and a good death honoureth a man's whole life, as an evil defameth and dishonoureth it. A man cannot well judge of any, without wronging him, until he hath played the last act of his comedy, which is without all doubt the most difficult. . . . the reason is, because in all the rest a man may be masked, but in this last part, it is to no purpose to dissemble.[79]

To shape one's own end, these authors declare, is to render oneself immune to the unshaping hand of death.

Of course, as *Hamlet*'s pervasive nostalgia for the perfected decencies of ritual dying indicates,[80] the old idea of the 'good death' retained a good deal of cultural power; but the histrionic triumph over sudden death is what fascinates the dramatists in their innumerable variations on Charron's proverb 'the end crowneth the work' (*finis coronat opus*). This is equally apparent in the tight-lipped aesthetic satisfaction with which Lodovico surveys the scene of slaughter at the end of *The White Devil* ('I limned this night-piece, and it was my best'; line 299), and in the rhetorical self-display that consummates the heroic action of Chapman's *Bussy D'Ambois*.

In Chapman's play the fear of indistinction and dissolution is displaced onto human life itself by a Montaignean psychology that

[78] *Essays*, I. xviii. 72.

[79] Pierre Charron, *Of Wisdome Three Bookes*, trans. Samson Lennard, 2nd edn. (London, 1630), 121, 345–6. For further examples of this trope, see Stein, *House of Death*, 24–33, 83–94, 146–9, 174, and Michael Cameron Andrews, *The Action of our Death: The Performance of Death in English Drama* (Newark, NJ: University of Delaware Press, 1989), *passim*.

[80] For a full discussion of Christian *ars moriendi* and *memento mori* motifs in the play, see Ronald Mushat Frye, *The Renaissance Hamlet: Issues and Responses in 1600* (Princeton: Princeton University Press, 1984), ch. 6; and Harry Morris, *Last Things in Shakespeare* (Tallahassee: Florida State University Presses, 1985), ch. 1.

insists upon the fragile and unstable nature of identity ('None can be always one. Our griefs and joys | Hold several sceptres in us'; IV. i. 25–6), while death becomes the occasion of definitive self-fashioning, since its arrest, as Shakespeare's Cleopatra will discover, is what 'shackles accidents and bolts up change' (*A&C* V. ii. 6). In a world of radical instability whose 'ends' are governed as Monsieur insists, not by Providence but by a Nature who is 'stark blind' and 'works at random' (V. iii. 4–29), the hero can raise himself above arbitrary vicissitude only in the terminal confrontation with death. For Bussy, man is 'a torch borne in the wind', vulnerable to any sudden gust of passion or blast of fortune, a thing of no enduring substance—'a dream | But of a shadow' (I. i. 18–19); and the show of monumental constancy cultivated by 'great men' resembles the forgery of 'Unskillful statuaries [sculptors]' whose 'colossic statues . . . with heroic forms without o'er spread, | Within are nought but mortar, flint, and lead' (I. i. 6–17).

But in a triumphant reversal of this image, Bussy himself will be invested with the grandeur of true heroic sculpture at the very point when his flickering torch is about to be snuffed out. Rising above his own despair at death's peremptory nullification ('Nothing is made of nought'; V. iii. 133), he transforms it with a self-monumentalizing gesture that ushers in his virtual apotheosis: 'Here like a Roman statue I will stand | Till death hath made me marble' (lines 144–5). Unexpectedly rehabilitating the 'colossic statues' of his opening meditation, Bussy's marmoreal posture is now the form of a 'virtue' real and substantial enough to challenge the apparent futility of mortal extinction; and where the fiery imagery of that opening speech suggested only the self-consuming ephemerality of human life, Bussy's death is a tragic consummation that enables his brilliant spirit to mount above the sublunary world and 'Join flames with Hercules' (V. iii. 270).

This double metamorphosis into spiritualized fire and eternalizing marble anticipates the most celebrated of all such episodes, the 'Roman' suicide by means of which Cleopatra renders herself 'marble-constant' even as she rarefies to 'fire and air' (*A&C* V. ii. 240, 289). In the case of *Anthony and Cleopatra*, however, the meaning of the transformation is complicated by the fact that it is located inside a literal monument. Because this structure, with its freight of cultural meanings, is meant to be represented not by the usual stage property, but by the entire Globe stage, it makes an exceptionally powerful connection between the bravura of her performance and the monumentalizing power of the dramatist's own art. Placing theatre itself at the very centre of the confrontation with death, this move is repeated, as we shall see, in a number of the period's most powerful tragedies.

Memorializing Death

Tragedy's self-reflexive insistence upon its own ability to confer 'noble memory' on its heroes (*Coriolanus*, v. vi. 153) needs to be understood in terms of a wider preoccupation with the importance of remembrance in a culture forced to devise new ways of accommodating itself to the experience of mortality. Crucial in exacerbating the anxieties attendant upon death and dying for most post-Reformation English people were the changes in religious practice that resulted from the Protestant denial of purgatory. The abolition of the whole vast industry of intercession—indulgences, prayers of intercession, and masses for the repose of the soul—suddenly placed the dead beyond the reach of their survivors. What would have struck a visitor to any church in Catholic Europe from the twelfth to the eighteenth centuries, as Ariès remarks, would have been 'not so much the plowing of the ground by the gravediggers as the uninterrupted series of Masses [for the dead] said in the morning at all altars by priests for whom this was often the only source of income'.[81] In Protestant churches this liturgy of remembrance fell abruptly silent; and when it was no longer possible for the living to assist the dead by such pious interventions, then death became a more absolute annihilation than ever. Each individual's death was now (as *Doctor Faustus* vividly demonstrates) a painfully private apocalypse, whose awful judgement could never be reversed. In the process, as Natalie Zemon Davis puts it, 'All the forms of exchange and communication between souls in the other world and the living were to be swept away. God had not assigned to the saints the care of our salvation, Calvin said, but only to Christ. As for the dead, they were beyond our help, on their own: "There is nothing more that we can add or take away". . . .

[81] *Hour of our Death*, 173.

Thus the dead were to be done away with as an "age group" in Protestant society.'[82]

The deceased might still call upon the duty, love, and pity of the living,[83] but the new theology rendered all such emotion painfully ineffectual, as Sir Thomas Browne testified. Among those heresies by which he had been tempted in the course of his 'greener studies', the physician confessed, was

> a third . . . which I did never positively maintain or practise, but have often wished it had been consonant to truth, and not offensive to my religion, and that is the Prayer for the Dead; whereunto I was inclined from some charitable inducements, whereby I could scarce contain my prayers for a friend at the ringing of a bell, or behold his corpse without an orison for his soul: 'twas a good way, methought, to be remembered by posterity, and far more noble than an history.[84]

If even a good Protestant like Browne found the loss of such consolations hard to bear, to Catholic commentators of the time it seemed unconscionably cruel. To counteract such traumatic consequences, Protestants developed (in the words of Nigel Llewellyn) a 'theory of *memoria*, which stressed the didactic potential of the lives and deaths of the virtuous'.[85] Amongst the crucial instruments

[82] Natalie Zemon Davis, 'Ghosts, Kin, and Progeny: Some Features of Family Life in Early Modern France', *Daedalus*, special issue on The Family (1977), 87–114: 94–5.

[83] The force of the emotional claims exercised by the dead in *Hamlet* is only part of a large mass of literary evidence (including Ben Jonson's expressions of desolating grief at the death of his son) which renders Lawrence Stone's peculiarly bleak account of 16th- and 17th-century family life (*The Family, Sex, and Marriage in England 1500–1800* (London: Weidenfeld & Nicolson, 1977), ch. 6) peculiarly suspect. Like some other historians, Stone has never been willing to grant any historical status to literary evidence; but even the 'documentary' evidence is itself much more ambiguous than he would allow. Ariès's account of the burial instructions in 17th-century wills poignantly documents a wish to prolong the affection of family and friends beyond the grave; and more recent studies of the English evidence have significantly challenged Stone's account of it. One reason for the exceptional 19th-century popularity of *Hamlet* was surely its anticipation of attitudes towards death and bereavement which Ariès identifies specifically with Romanticism (*Hour of our Death*, 409 ff.). In their violent repudiation of those rituals of mourning which 'instead of allowing people to express what they felt . . . acted as a screen between man and death' (p. 327) both Hamlet and Laertes foreshadow the intense affectivity of a culture in which 'One person is dead and the whole world is empty' (p. 472). Ophelia's death (that favourite subject of Victorian painters) in Gertrude's idyllic description sounds uncannily like the idealized 'beautiful death' of the 19th century—she literally 'floats away'.

[84] *Religio Medici*, 9.

[85] Llewellyn, *Art of Death*, 28.

of *memoria* were the monumental trappings of funeral, all devoted to preserving 'the social body as an element in the collective memory'.[86] Both obsequies themselves, and the monuments which provided a permanent reminder of their costly pomp, were subject to extraordinary elaboration in this period; and while a tendency towards such secular display is apparent throughout sixteenth-century Europe, it was especially marked in Protestant England. Here, from the late fifteenth century, the organization of noble and princely funerals became the increasingly exclusive preserve of the College of Heralds, their extraordinary ostentation corresponding to their memorializing function as a testimony to both the greatness and lineage of the defunct and to the unassailable dignity of the social order in the face of death's assault.[87]

Funeral monuments, were, if anything, the object of even more extravagant attention, as Francis Bacon observed: 'There never was the like number of beautiful and costly tombs and monuments erected in sundry churches in honourable memory of the dead.'[88] The old chantry chapels, where priests had been retained to sing masses *in perpetuo* for the souls of the mighty, now became (where they survived at all) family mortuaries, in which the passive memorialization of inscriptions recording the virtue and piety of the deceased replaced the active rites of intercession. Unlike earlier tombs (as satirists like Webster did not fail to observe), the great memorials of this period were almost entirely retrospective in their appeal:[89] 'wholly bent upon the world' (*Duchess of Malfi*, IV. ii. 161), they were conspicuously secular substitutes for the liturgical *memento* of the Mass. The more splendid their marble

[86] Llewellyn, *Art of Death*, 46–9, 60–72, 81. The strong element of hierarchical propaganda in monumental art helps to account for the iconoclastic rage unleashed on church monuments in times of social upheaval.

[87] The fact that from the 16th century English funerals fell entirely under heraldic control (where in France their organization was shared with church functionaries) almost certainly suggests an intensification of the commemorative function of funeral in Protestant England.

[88] Bacon, *Observations on a Libel* (1592), cited in Gittings, *Death, Burial and the Individual*, 144. Ralph Houlbrooke's 'Death, Church, and Family in England between the Late Fifteenth and the Early Eighteenth Centuries', ibid. 25–42, similarly connects the burgeoning of elaborate funeral ceremonies and monuments with the abolition of intercession.

[89] *Duchess of Malfi*, IV. ii. 156–62; John Weever's complaint that contemporary monuments were becoming vain pattern-books for the latest fashions in dress is directed against the same worldly individualism; see John Weever, *Ancient Funerall Monuments* (London, 1631), 11. According to Ariès, it was 'the discovery of the

sculpture, the richer their gilding and painting, the more superb their heraldic ornamentation, the more eloquently these shrines of memory spoke of the longing for a species of immortality which, in spite of everything, it might remain in the power of the living to confer.[90] Frequently designed by the same heralds who organized the funeral itself,[91] and typically adorned with the figures of mourning wives and children, monuments functioned as the culminating episode of the heraldic obsequies, in which ephemeral pageantry was transformed to everlasting marble, freezing the triumphal symbolism of funeral rites for all time.

Whilst the iconography of tombs often incorporated elements of the macabre, in the form of skulls and *transi* sculptures, illustrating the grotesque reality of mortal decay, such details increasingly served only as a necessary counterpoint to the display of defiant secular pride criticized by contemporary moralists (Figs. 23–5). In much the same way, as we shall see, tragedy would stress the cruelty and shamefulness of death in order to point up its celebrations of human defiance; and it would do so typically in scenes that self-consciously stressed its own monumental function as a consolatory instrument of *memoria*. It is not for nothing that *Hamlet* sets the player's 'chronicles' against the musty oblivion of

individual . . . the desire to be oneself [that] forced tombstones to emerge from their anonymity to become commemorative monuments' (*Hour of our Death*, 293). Erwin Panofsky in *Tomb Sculpture: Its Changing Aspects from Ancient Egypt to Bernini*, ed. H. W. Janson (London: Thames & Hudson, 1964) follows the emergence of 'retrospective' monuments from their beginnings in the 13th century to the 'purely commemorative' programmes of 16th-century humanist design (pp. 56–74). Lawrence Stone, on the other hand, claims that in England realistic portrait sculpture 'was introduced from abroad by Nicholas Stone [in the 1620s]' (*The Family, Sex, and Marriage in England*, 225). Examples of realistic portraiture, however, can be traced at least as early as Torrigiani's Henry VII tomb in Westminster Abbey. The same individualizing tendency is apparent in the growing elaboration of biographical epitaphs (Ariès, *Hour of our Death*, 223). Eric Mercer, *English Art 1553–1625* (Oxford: Clarendon Press, 1962), 237–51, draws attention to both the increasing individualism and the enhanced emotional content of 16th- and 17th-century monuments.

[90] See Ariès, *Hour of our Death*, 202–3, 215: 'The survival of the dead man . . . was also dependent on a fame that was maintained on earth either by the tombs with their *signa* and inscriptions or by the eulogies of writers. . . . In common practice, in the sixteenth and seventeenth centuries . . . the commemoration of the living person was not separated from the salvation of the soul. Indeed, this is the fundamental meaning of the tomb.'

[91] Mercer stresses the importance of 'the universal display of heraldry, often of doubtful authority', on church monuments of this period (*English Art*, 218).

the grave-digger's 'houses': reflecting upon the universal appetite for remembrance, the seventeenth-century historian of funeral monuments John Weever would invoke the classical trope of poetry-as-monument to insist that literature itself constituted the most enduring memorial of all.[92]

Issues of Death

The essays which make up this book, while approaching the tragic encounter with death from a variety of perspectives, fall into three broad groupings. Those in Part I explore the representation of death as a trope of apocalypse. In Christian doctrine, apocalypse is of course a name for the End; and Chapter 1 looks at the apocalyptic images of mortality developed in the principal motifs of macabre art—the Dance and Triumph of Death[93]—and at the ways in which these were incorporated into the theatrical language of tragedy. But, as the terrible nakedness of death in the *danse macabre* reminds us, the literal meaning of apocalypse is unveiling or dis-covery. Apocalyptic thought imagines the End as a grand opening, a laying bare of all that has been hidden. The Gospels repeatedly look forward to such a moment—'For there is nothing covered, that shall not be revealed; neither hid, that shall not be known' (Luke 12: 2); and the New Testament's great book of the End (whose name is simply the latinized form of Apocalypse) takes the form of a visionary unveiling of the Discovery to come. Death in Revelation is both one of the Last Things that awaits the dreadful opening of the Angel's seven seals, and an instrument of judgemental discovery. The God of Revelation characteristically identifies himself as 'he that openeth [what] no man shutteth' (3: 7), and (even more graphically) as 'he which searcheth the reins and the hearts'—a ruthless anatomist of human secrets (2: 23). That last figure suggests a connection between the deeply ingrained idea of death-as-moral-discovery, and the secular revelations promised by the reborn science of anatomy, whose transformatory effect on attitudes to death and the human body is the

[92] Weever, *Ancient Funerall Monuments*, 3.

[93] The connection between plague and the origins of the Dance of Death, though widely accepted, remains contentious; see App.

subject of Chapter 2; and the connection is a fitting one, for anatomy took pains (as we shall see) to appropriate the moral authority of the apocalyptic tradition both through its habitually moralized iconography and through its highly theatricalized practice.

The Triumph and the Dance of Death shared close connections with the funeral arts which are the subject of Part III—the Dance as a motif which originated on the cloister walls of late medieval cemeteries, and the Triumph as a pageant-form that consciously travestied the hierarchical formalities of heraldic obsequies; and each, though deriving from contexts of religious moralization, was capable of more secular and subversive constructions which made it a potent source of literary and theatrical imagery. Of the two, it was the Dance, with its more episodic form and inherently dramatic contest between the living and the dead, that lent itself most easily to appropriation by playwrights. The ostensible moral of this motif was expressed by its ritualized undoing of order and degree, in which a procession of victims, representing all estates from the highest to the lowest, was drawn into the nullity of death. But this structural emphasis on death's levelling was undercut by a summoning narrative that insisted upon the paradoxical distinctness of each victim's fall into indistinction—especially in later versions of the Dance whose concentration upon the pathos and irony of the individual encounter with Death provided a perfect paradigm for tragedy. The Triumph of Death, by contrast, in which King Death's remorseless pageant car simply rolls over piles of corpses in which mighty and humble are heaped indiscriminately together, allowed no space for emotional complication or dramatic tension. Yet this motif, for all its appearance of grinding moral orthodoxy, was to form a primary model for one of the most heterodox tragic dramas of the period, Christopher Marlowe's *Tamburlaine*.

If the early modern experience of death was significantly shaped by the devastating impact of epidemic disease figured in macabre art, it was also conditioned in important ways by new understandings of the body and its relation to the 'inner' self. The distance between the powerful 'Nobody' of Dekker's superscription to *Newes from Graues-end* and the fragile 'Some-body' of his ironic subscription was effectively measured by the new science which grew up in the sixteenth century, quite literally in the shadow of the Dance of Death: anatomy, a discipline which offered to lay bare the hidden truths of the human microcosm in very much the way that navigators and geographers had uncovered the secrets of the macrocosm (Fig. 22).

In Chapter 2 I examine ways in which the literal 'opening up' of the human body by the new science of anatomy contributed to an emerging discourse of interiority by representing the human body as multi-layered container of 'secrets'. Since sixteenth-century physiology, with its heavy Galenic bias, had developed an elaborate system of physiological explanation for psychological phenomena, accounting for the 'inward motions' of the psyche in terms of physical motions in the humoral body itself,[94] it was inevitable that the anatomical 'discovery' of the body's interior should invite psychological applications. These might be either literal or metaphorical, or both. Investigation of the body's inner secrets, proclaimed the apologists of the new anatomy, was the perfect fulfilment of the ancient philosophic prescription *nosce teipsum*—know thyself. Not surprisingly, however, the wisdom revealed by dissection often amounted to nothing more than a new gloss upon old truisms: for what it uncovered at the very core of the human fabric was nothing other than the figure of Death itself. Recognizing the Vesalian body as a continent of enigmas, a structure that could be peeled back, layer by layer, to reveal the final secret of mortality, the Elizabethan preacher John More offered to introduce his congregation to 'some anatomy, in which you may see (as in a glass) the original of Death'.[95] Thus it was arguably the science of anatomy, tied as it still was to remnants of the *memento mori* and *vanitas* traditions, which did more than anything to produce that characteristically early modern conception of death described by Ariès, in which it is imagined as something always present 'in the inmost recesses of life . . . [or an eruption] out of the bodily envelope of the rottenness within'.[96]

From its inception under the innovatory genius of Andreas Vesalius (1514–64) the new anatomy had a strongly performative

[94] The best recent treatment of the early modern body is Gail Kern Paster, *The Body Embarrassed* (Ithaca, NY: Cornell University Press, 1992).

[95] John More ['preacher of the Gospel'], *A Lively Anatomie of Death . . . Tending to teach men to lyue, and die well to the Lord* (London, 1596), B3^{v}. For More the operation of Divine Law resembles the probing of an anatomist's instruments: 'The law then . . . revealed our nakedness . . . it opened the inward man with all his concupiscence. . . . [and showed] how all things, both within us and without us, were corrupted' (sig. C8–C8^{v}).

[96] Ariès, *Hour of our Death*, 121.

aspect, one that was underlined by the erection of purpose-built anatomy theatres—show-places of bodily discovery in which dissections were staged as elaborate entertainments before substantial, fee-paying audiences. Elizabethan and Stuart dramatists frequently exploited the physical resemblances between the two kinds of theatre to striking effect—not merely in episodes of spectacular violence, involving the literal cutting and dismemberment of the human body, but in scenes of psychological 'opening'. Chapters 3 and 4 go on to offer detailed readings of two tragedies—Shakespeare's *Othello*, and Middleton and Rowley's *The Changeling*—whose tragic catastrophes are presented as moments of apocalyptic discovery. In each play the villain's ruthless excavation of the protagonist's secret self can be seen as a kind of prolonged anatomical demonstration. For characters such as Iago and De Flores, as for the practitioners of anatomy described by William Heckscher, 'the chief objective of their enquiries is life and its secrets'; and like his anatomists they will discover that the price of such secrets is death.[97]

If the ideas of death and apocalypse discussed in Part I point towards tragedy as a profoundly teleological form whose full meaning will be uncovered in the revelation of its end, the essays in Part II explore the psychological and affective consequences of such fiercely end-driven narrative design. Literary endings are conventionally organized to gratify the human desire for a sense of aesthetic completeness, but in the process, as Frank Kermode has taught us,[98] they are always liable to become unsettling figures for our own end. Chapter 5 looks at a number of tragedies, including Kyd's *The Spanish Tragedy* and Marlowe's *Doctor Faustus*, in which the desire for narrative closure is pitched against a particularly intense dread of ending, and in which the imposition of an end is often figured as an act of writerly violence, committed by the author or his dramatic surrogate. Chapter 6 then offers an extensive treatment of *Hamlet* as an extreme example of the structural consequences of such anxiety. Its dramatic narrative is punctuated by a remarkable series of inset narratives whose conspicuously abrupted or incomplete form draws attention to the play's own difficulties in completing itself. These difficulties in turn are shown as directly related

[97] William S. Heckscher, *Rembrandt's Anatomy of Dr Nicolaas Tulp* (New York: New York University Press, 1958), 108.

[98] Frank Kermode, *The Sense of an Ending: Studies in the Theory of Fiction* (New York: Oxford University Press, 1979).

to the hero's problematic relationship with the conventional plot in which he finds himself trapped. Paradoxically, the nominal completion of Hamlet's revenge does little to resolve the play's anxieties about narrative closure, for the ending takes the form of a violent structural aposiopesis, in which the sudden 'arrest' of death seems to leave Hamlet's 'story' frustratingly suspended (as Kermode might say) 'in the middest'. It is, in more senses than one, a story without issue.

The given plot whose all-too-familiar end Hamlet vainly resists belongs, of course, to the popular subgenre of revenge tragedy; and in the final chapter of this section I go on to analyse revenge narratives as a response to particularly painful aspect of the early modern reimagining of death—the wholesale displacement of the dead from their familiar place in the order of things by the Protestant abolition of purgatory and ritual intercession. Revenge tragedy exhibits a world in which the dead, precisely because they are now beyond the help of their survivors, have become practically insatiable in their demands upon the living. Haunted by ghosts and other mementoes of the past, this genre speaks to the same anxieties that produced the cult of *memoria*, with its extraordinary elaboration of funeral rites and pompous monuments. It is therefore no accident that scanted or interrupted funerals, unburied corpses and disinterred skeletons, violated sepulchres and neglected tombs, should feature so prominently in the dramaturgy of plays like *The Spanish Tragedy*, *The Revenger's Tragedy*, *The Atheist's Tragedy*, *The Duchess of Malfi*, and, above all, *Hamlet*. In this most famous of all revenge dramas, the boundaries of the play world are marked by a ghost and a graveyard. Obsessed with the symbolic oblivion of shameful burial, *Hamlet* is dominated by a revenant 'from the grave' whose most intense emotion is the dread of being forgotten. Yet the very pathos of the Ghost's appeals will prove to be the corrosive poison that infects not only Hamlet but the whole body of Denmark. For revenge is revealed here to be merely the expression of remembrance at its savage extreme.

Hamlet's preoccupation with strategies of remembrance and intense concern for the proper performance of funereal rites leads naturally into the last section of the book. Part III focuses on the way tragedy articulates its challenge to the undifferentiating power of death through conventions and motifs borrowed from the funereal arts—from monuments, tomb sculpture, and the pageantry of heraldic funerals. In Chapter 8 I discuss how tragedy, which habitually dressed itself in the blacks of funeral custom, incorporated episodes of funeral pageantry into its action as a means of imposing an emblematic order upon the profoundly threatening havoc of its endings—to the point where more-or-less-stylized funeral processions became the recognized sign of tragic closure. Yet funerals embodied an equivocal message of which dramatists were quick to take advantage: speaking of the common necessity of ending, even as they proclaimed the human fantasy of triumph over death, they also bore a disconcerting resemblance to the very Triumphs of Death whose mocking lessons of mortality they sought to counter. Moreover, the control over the wildness of death asserted by these rites of passage was necessarily unstable, since any violation or disruption of due forms could seriously threaten their symbolism of transcendence. Funeral pageantry was thus perfectly adapted, by its instability and ambiguity, to the ironic ambivalence of tragedy's engagement with the issues of death.

In so far as heraldic funeral, like tragedy, was a teleological form, its ideal end lay not in the common earth to which the body of the deceased was committed, but in the splendidly ornamented tomb where its social symbolism was to be preserved for all time. Capitalizing on the iconic power of such monuments, sixteenth- and seventeenth-century dramatists frequently incorporated tomb properties into the action of their plays, making them the characteristic emblem of drama's memorializing power.[99] The remaining chapters of Part III are devoted to analyses of three plays—Shakespeare's *Anthony and Cleopatra*, Webster's *The Duchess of Malfi*, and Ford's *The Broken Heart*—in which actual tomb properties, as well as the trope of poetry-as-monument, are turned to particularly impressive effect. In each, through a kind of metatheatrical *trompe l'œil*, the memorializing art of the dramatist collaborates with the characters' art of dying to produce a brilliant troping of the tag with which the tragedy of the period so often signals the human transcendence of death: *finis coronat opus* ('the end crowns all'). Funeral is rewritten as wedding or coronation triumph, and death becomes the chosen instrument by which the protagonists fashion themselves

[99] Given this emblematic prominence, it is interesting to discover no fewer than three tombs among the relatively short list of stage properties in Henslowe's famous inventory; see Andrew Gurr, *The Shakespearean Stage 1574–1642* (Cambridge: Cambridge University Press, 1970), 123.

into a display of marmoreal perfection. In such moments tragedy realizes itself as a genre devoted to fantasies of mortal transcendence. The power of these plays, however, is dependent upon such fantasy's being tacitly recognized for what it is—a fragile artefact designed to dress the arbitrary abruption of mortal ending in a powerful aesthetic of closure.

Despite the fact that my title is culled from one of Donne's most famous sermons,[100] it will be apparent by now that my approach to the early modern representations of death has a heavily secular bias. This should not be taken to imply that I consider its religious dimension unimportant—it goes without saying that it remained crucial to the whole experience of mortality in early modern society. But, as Robert Watson has comprehensively shown, the increasingly strident assertions of Christian confidence that mark the orthodox teaching of the *ars moriendi* in this period can themselves be regarded as evidence of the erosion of ancient certainties and a gathering anxiety about the possibility of 'death as eternal annihilation'.[101] Eloquent testimony to the progressive secularization of death can be found in the complaints levelled by contemporary commentators at the increasing worldliness of funeral rites and mortuary art, in which they themselves diagnosed a culpable weakening of confidence in Christian prescriptions for the taming of death. Tragedy itself is among the most important cultural expressions of this secularizing process: to understand the nature of the crisis which it addressed, and to appreciate the power of the representations through which it helped to reinvent the experience of death, we need to look not at the mechanisms that were designed to keep death in its place, but at those which attempted to assign it a new one.

[100] Donne, *Devotions*, 165. The text for 'Death's Duel' is taken from Ps. 68: 20: 'Unto God the Lord belong the issues of death.'

[101] Watson, *The Rest is Silence*, 3 and *passim*.

PART I

'Within all rottenness': Tragedy, Death, and Apocalypse

I

'Peremptory nullification': Tragedy and Macabre Art

This is the most inglorious and contemptible vilification, the most deadly and peremptory nullification of man that we can consider.

(John Donne, *Devotions upon Emergent Occasions*)

It is wasted time to think of it, to count its grains,
Where all are alike and there is no difference in them.

(Sacheverell Sitwell, 'Agamemnon's Tomb')

The Dance of Death

I've always loved epidemics. They combine the greatest tragedies with wild revelry in cemeteries.

(Gabriel Garcia Marquez[1])

Ere sicknesses attack, young death is best,
Who pays before his death doth scape arrest.

(John Donne, '*H.W. in Hiber. belligeranti*'[2])

In the rich iconography that grew out of the early modern crisis of death, no motif enjoyed greater popularity, in northern Europe at least, than the Dance of Death. The earliest documented example of the Dance was the fresco from which the cycle derived its generic name, the celebrated Paris *Danse macabre*, painted on the cloister wall of the cemetery of Les Innocents in 1424–5. Accompanied by a series of moralizing verses—reputedly the work of

[1] Interview by Jean-Francois Fogel in *The Guardian Weekly* (*Le Monde* section), 12 Feb. 1995, 16.

[2] *The Poems of John Donne*, ed. H. J. C. Grierson (Oxford: Oxford University Press, 1912), 188.

Jean Gerson, Chancellor of the Sorbonne,[3] who may have devised the programme for the entire cycle—the mural depicted a hierarchically ordered chain of some thirty male figures, representing all ranks of society, each accompanied by a prancing figure of Death who summons him to join the grim dance to the grave. From this widely admired painting—destroyed in 1669, but surviving in the form of a late fifteenth-century woodcut copy—all other representations of the Dance are thought, whether directly or indirectly, to derive.[4] Imitations of it were soon amongst the most widely visited attractions of major northern cities, including London, Basel, Berne, Lucerne, Berlin, and Lubeck; whilst other large-scale representations, in both mural and tapestry, adorned the walls of palaces, castles, and parish churches. The popularity of the motif was further enhanced by the circulation of a wide variety of printed and manuscript versions, including Guyot Marchant's woodcut of the Paris *Danse* in 1485.[5]

Although none of the great English murals has been preserved intact, there is no doubt that the Dance enjoyed an extensive currency in England, its most spectacular example being one of the oldest in Europe. Dating from the early 1430s, the so-called *Dance of Paul's* was executed in the cloister of St Paul's Cathedral only a few years after the completion of the original *Danse macabre*. The *Dance of Paul's* was closely modelled on the French painting, whose accompanying verses, in a translation by John Lydgate, supplied its programme; and it achieved a comparable fame. It was to its images of 'bare bones hanging by the sinews' and to the accompanying display of 'dead heads in the charnel house' that Sir Thomas More, instructing his readers in the necessary 'Remembrance of Death', turned to evoke the 'loathly' ugliness of their

[3] On Gerson's involvement, see *The Danse Macabre of Women*, ed. Anne Tukey Harrison (Kent, Ohio: Kent State University Press, 1994), 7–8.

[4] See Hans Holbein, *The Dance of Death*, ed. James M. Clark (London: Phaidon, 1947); Clark gives a fairly comprehensive account of the surviving and recorded versions from Britain and continental Europe, tracing them all to their origin in the Paris *Danse macabre*.

[5] Guyot's full series, together with a parallel *Danse macabre des femmes* (added to his 3rd edition in 1486 and attributed in various texts to Martial D'Auvergne, Denis Catin, and Guyot himself) has been reproduced in facsimile as *La Grande Danse macabre des hommes et des femmes* (Paris: Baillieu, n.d.), and as *La Danse macabre de Guy Marchant*, ed. Pierre Champion (Paris: Éditions des Quatre Chemins, 1925).

mortal condition, and to prepare them to face the even more disturbing 'deep conceived fantasy of death in his nature, graven in [their] own heart[s]'.[6] Although this mural did not survive into the Elizabethan era, the wall on which it was painted being demolished in 1559, its memory remained fresh enough for Stow to record it in his *Survey of London* (1598). Describing a cloister full of monuments and tombs, which 'in number and curious workmanship, passed all other that were in that church', he recalled that 'About this cloister, was artificially and richly painted the Dance of Machabray, or dance of death, commonly called the Dance of Paul's, the like whereof was painted about S. Innocent's cloister at Paris in France; the metres or poesy of this dance were translated out of French into English by John Lydgate, the Monk of Bury, & with the picture of Death, leading all estates painted about the cloister.'[7] *Paul's* in turn probably supplied a model for several less prominent Dances of Death including the tapestry *Dance of Maccabre* kept in the Tower, the wall-painting which Stow records in the parish church of Stratford-upon-Avon,[8] and perhaps the mural in the Palace of Whitehall, reputedly the work of Holbein.[9] Holbein was, of course, the author of two woodcut Dances of Death, including the so-called *Great Death*, which remains the best known of all printed renditions of the motif. Holbein's versions circulated in numerous editions throughout Europe and probably helped, along with recollections of the *Dance of Paul's*, to inspire a popular broadside version of the Dance published in 1569,[10] as well as the most widely available English version—the elaborate ornamental border, with its seventy-six hierarchically arranged Dance of Death figures, that framed the entire second half of the much reprinted

[6] Sir Thomas More, *The Four Last Things*, in *The English Works of Sir Thomas More*, ed. W. E. Campbell, 7 vols. (London: Eyre & Spottiswoode, 1931), i. 467–8.

[7] Quoted in Beatrice White's intro. to John Lydgate, *The Dance of Death*, ed. Florence Warren (London: Early English Text Society, 1931), p. xxiii.

[8] See James M. Clark, *The Dance of Death in the Middle Ages and the Renaissance* (Glasgow: Jackson, 1950), 15; the painting is referred to in Stow's MS note on the relevant section of Leland's *Itinerary*.

[9] Clark, *Dance of Death*, 16; Francis Douce, *Holbein's Dance of Death* (London: G. Bell, 1902), 124–8; Aldred Scott Warthin, *The Physician of the Dance of Death: A Historical Study of the Evolution of the Dance of Death Mythus in Art* (New York: Paul B. Hoeber, 1931), 43.

[10] British Museum, Huth 50 (32), repr. in Willard Farnham, *The Medieval Heritage of Elizabethan Tragedy* (Oxford: Basil Blackwell, 1956), 292.

'Queen Elizabeth's Prayerbook', which originally appeared in the same year (see Fig. 6).[11]

Thus in England, as elsewhere in northern Europe, the Dance of Death acquired a significant place amongst those images that shaped people's sense of what it was to die, becoming part of the *Gestalt* of Death itself. Images from the Dance surface repeatedly in the literature of the period, not least in the drama, where its shaping influence on such plays as *The Revenger's Tragedy* has long been recognized.[12] The grotesque sexualization of Death in that play's Bony Lady scene (III. v) mirrors the perverse raptures of the Dance, sardonically inverting the popular episode of Death and the Bride, even as it recalls Death's warning to the Prostitute: 'Feel terror in your heart, | For you will be held tight.'[13] The motif is reworked again, with a similarly misogynistic twist, in another anonymous play, *The Second Maiden's Tragedy*,[14] where the hero, Govianus, hired as a painter to restore a semblance of life to the corpse of his own wife, daubs her lips with a poisoned cosmetic, betraying the necrophiliac Tyrant to a grotesque *mors osculi*:[15]

TYRANT. Wake, sweet mistress!
'Tis I that call thee at the door of life.
[*Kisses the body*.] Ha!
I talk so long to death, I'm sick myself.
(V. ii. 119–21[16])

[11] [Day], *A Booke of Christian Prayers*, 78–138 (I include the scenes of Apocalypse and Judgement bracketing the sequence proper, whose separate processions of male and female dancers are each repeated three times). This anonymous compilation, published by John Day and reissued by Richard Day in 1578, 1581, 1590, and 1608, became known as 'Queen Elizabeth's Prayerbook' from its frontispiece portrait of the Queen. Elizabeth's own copy is held at Lambeth Palace.

[12] See e.g. Samuel Schoenbaum, '*The Revenger's Tragedy*: Jacobean Dance of Death', *Modern Language Quarterly*, 15 (1954), 201–7; intro. to Cyril Tourneur [Thomas Middleton], *The Revenger's Tragedy*, ed. Brian Gibbons, 2nd edn. (London: A. C. Black, 1990); and Spinrad's more wide-ranging discussion of dramatized Dance of Death motifs in *Summons of Death*, ch. 5.

[13] *Danse Macabre of Women*, 102.

[14] Both plays are, perhaps significantly, often attributed to Thomas Middleton.

[15] On this motif, see Edgar Wind, 'Amor as a God of Death', in his *Pagan Mysteries in the Renaissance* (Harmondsworth: Penguin, 1967), 152–70. Ironically the Tyrant's grave robbery has been played out as a kind of rape upon death. Convinced that the '[grey-eyed] monument woos me: I must run and kiss it' (IV. iii. 9, 23), the Tyrant struggles to 'Pierce the jaws | Of this cold, ponderous creature', forcing it to 'yield' to his importunate 'mastery' (lines 25–6, 43, 49).

[16] All citations from this play are to *The Second Maiden's Tragedy*, ed. Anne Lancashire, The Revels Plays (Manchester: Manchester University Press, 1978).

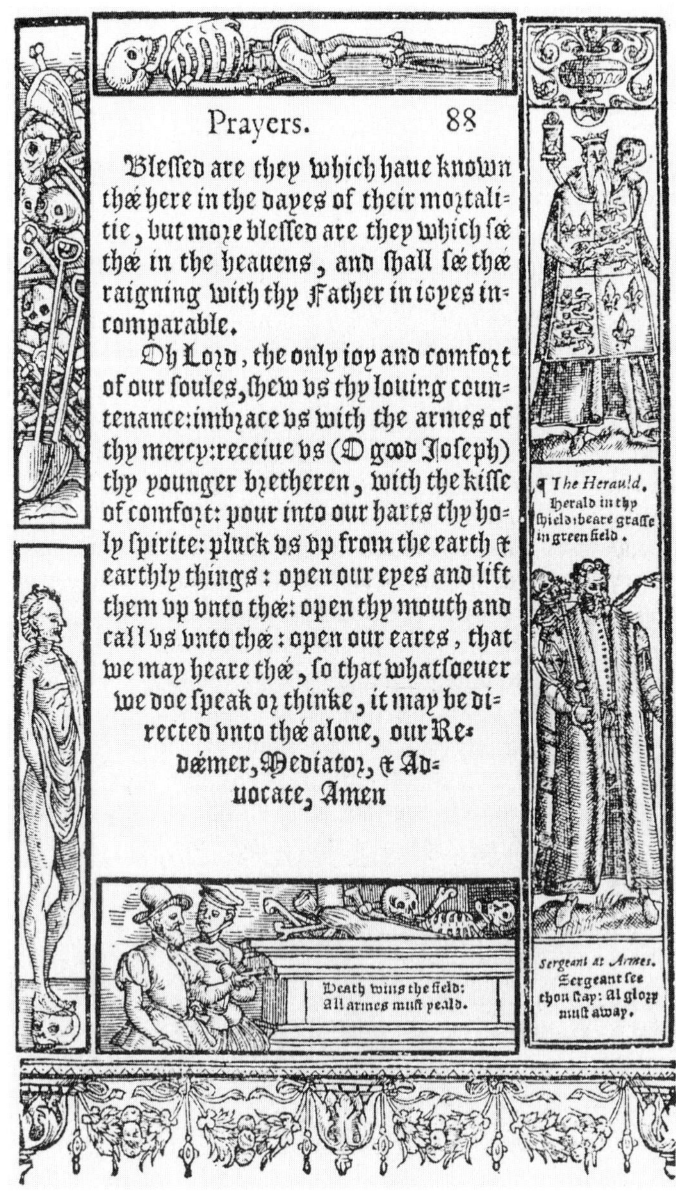
Prayers. 88

Bleſſed are they which haue known thée here in the dayes of their moꝛtali-tie, but moꝛe bleſſed are they which ſée thée in the heauens, and ſhall ſée thée raigning with thy Father in ioyes incomparable.

Oh Loꝛd, the only ioy and comfoꝛt of our ſoules, ſhew vs thy louing countenance: imbꝛace vs with the armes of thy mercy: receiue vs (O good Ioſeph) thy younger bꝛetheren, with the kiſſe of comfoꝛt: pour into our harts thy holy ſpirite: pluck vs vp from the earth & earthly things: open our eyes and lift them vp vnto thée: open thy mouth and call vs vnto thée: open our eares, that we may heare thée, ſo that whatſoeuer we doe ſpeak oꝛ thinke, it may be directed vnto thée alone, our Redéemer, Mediatoꝛ, & Aduocate, Amen

6. Dance of Death episodes from *A Booke of Christian Prayers* ('Queen Elizabeth's Prayerbook') (London, 1569).

(*a*) Death with a Herald and a Sergeant.

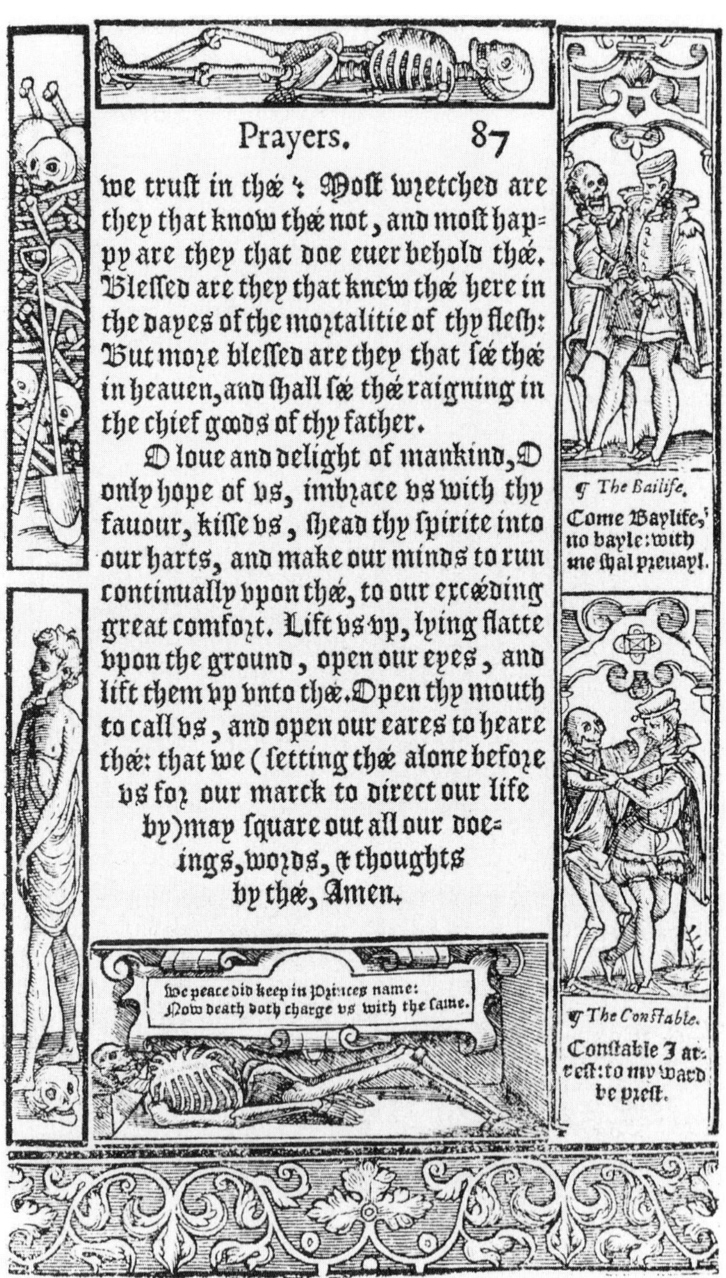

Prayers. 87

we trust in thee: Most wretched are they that know thee not, and most happy are they that doe euer behold thee. Blessed are they that knew thee here in the dayes of the mortalitie of thy flesh: But more blessed are they that see thee in heauen, and shall see thee raigning in the chief goods of thy father.

O loue and delight of mankind, O only hope of vs, imbrace vs with thy fauour, kisse vs, shead thy spirite into our harts, and make our minds to run continually vpon thee, to our exceeding great comfort. Lift vs vp, lying flatte vpon the ground, open our eyes, and lift them vp vnto thee. Open thy mouth to call vs, and open our eares to heare thee: that we (setting thee alone before vs for our marck to direct our life by) may square out all our doings, words, & thoughts by thee, Amen.

(*b*) Death with a Bailiff, and a Constable.

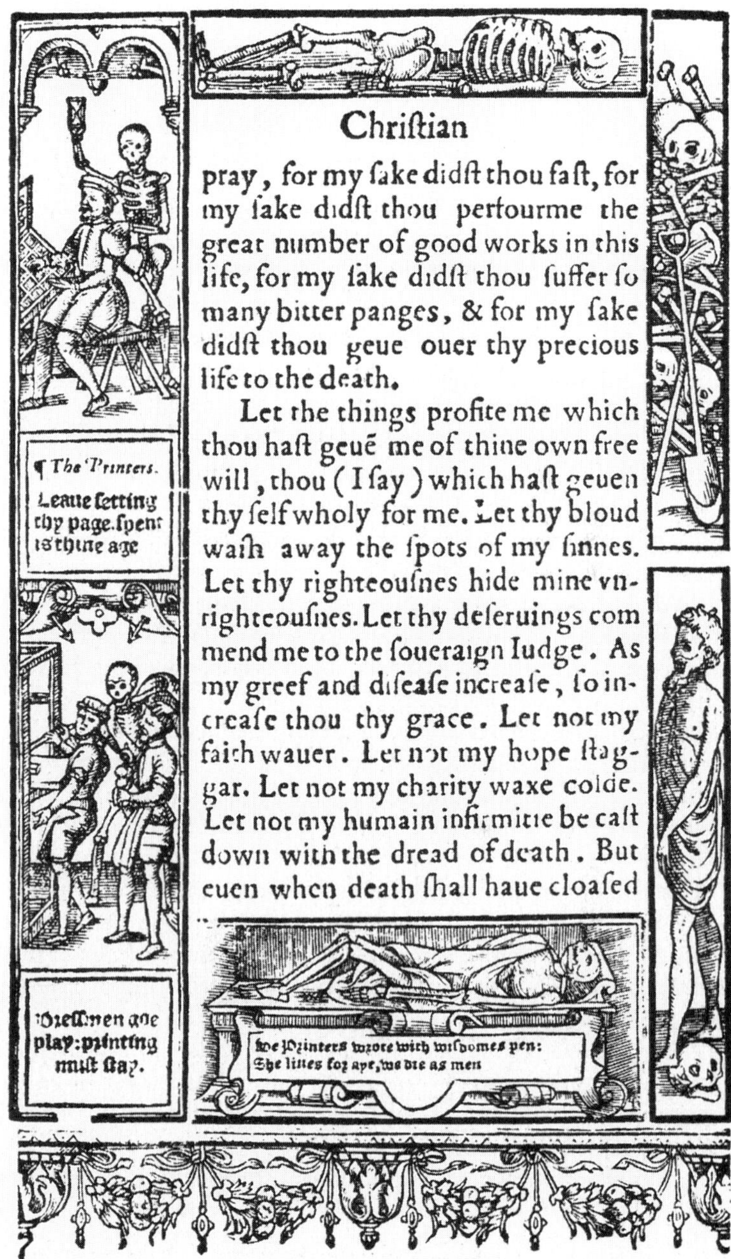

Chriſtian

pray, for my ſake didſt thou faſt, for my ſake didſt thou perfourme the great number of good works in this life, for my ſake didſt thou ſuffer ſo many bitter panges, & for my ſake didſt thou geue ouer thy precious life to the death.

Let the things profite me which thou haſt geuẽ me of thine own free will, thou (I ſay) which haſt geuen thy ſelf wholy for me. Let thy bloud waſh away the ſpots of my ſinnes. Let thy righteouſnes hide mine vnrighteouſnes. Let thy deſeruings commend me to the ſoueraign Iudge. As my greef and diſeaſe increaſe, ſo increaſe thou thy grace. Let not my faith wauer. Let not my hope ſtaggar. Let not my charity waxe colde. Let not my humain infirmitie be caſt down with the dread of death. But euen when death ſhall haue cloaſed

(*c*) Death Visits the Printer.

In a rather different key, the conceit of Death as usurping Bridegroom orchestrates the climactic action of *Romeo and Juliet*, where the elaborate play on sexual 'dying' echoes the complaints of Newlywed and Bride in the Danse of Women as they are led away by Death:

> Why die so soon?
> It is not sweetness I feel, but fury . . .
> Death, why do you lust
> For me, why take me so quickly?[17]

The summons with which Bosola ends his moralizing dirge in *The Duchess of Malfi* ('End your groan, and come away'; IV. ii. 195), following the hellish Dance of Madmen, deliberately recalls the fatal summons of the Dance, just as Delio's concluding *sententia* (V. ii. 120–1) seems to paraphrase the figure of Guyot's *Acteur*, gesturing to another Duchess in the *Grande Danse*: 'All one takes away is the deed well done.'[18]

For audiences in this culture even relatively insignificant details whose connection with the Dance are now obscured may have set up powerful resonances. When, for example, the dying Falstaff is said to have 'babbl'd of green fields' (*Henry V*, II. iii. 16–17) he was perhaps less filled with pastoral nostalgia for Shallow's Gloucestershire than haunted by an episode in the Dance where Death accosts a Herald with the verse, 'Herald in thy shield: beare grass in greene field', above the motto 'Death winnes the field | All armes must yield' (Fig. 6*a*).[19] When Tamburlaine's physician informs him that the condition of his urine 'imports . . . death' (2 *Tamb*. V. iii. 90), he echoes the summons of Death the Physician: 'By thy water, I do see: thou must away with me';[20] while Macbeth's despairing 'Tomorrow, and tomorrow, and tomorrow' (V. v. 19) oddly recalls the Latin verses that precede Death's encounter with the Bath-house Attendant: 'Noli per cras cras tibi longas ponere metas | Per cras cras cras cras omnis consumitur etas.'[21] Even more significantly, to miss the recollections of the Dance in a play like *Hamlet*, with its extended meditation on death, is to blur an important dimension of its meaning. Among the rich assortment

[17] *Danse Macabre of Women*, 80, 112.
[18] Ibid. 54.
[19] *A Booke of Christian Prayers*, 88.
[20] Ibid. 87^{v}.
[21] *Danse Macabre of Women*, 104.

of *memento mori* images that inform the brooding wit of the graveyard scene, for example, we might discover the figure of the Acteur at the end of the *Grande Danse*, gesturing at the worm-eaten body of a king, above verses which declare that 'The body has rotted in the soil, the name is stripped of fame' ('Corpus humo putruit, nomine fama caret') (Fig. 7*b*);[22] while behind the 'soldier's music' ordered by Fortinbras for the dead Hamlet, we should probably hear the apocalyptic drumming of the Dance in 'Queen Elizabeth's Prayerbook': 'We drum that doomsday now at hand: | Doth call all soldiers to death's hand.'[23] When the mortally wounded Prince recognizes the grip of a 'fell sergeant' whose 'strict . . . arrest' no man can refuse, he consciously frames his end as an episode from the Dance of Death, in which Death usurps the role of Sergeant, Bailiff, or Constable (Figs. 6*a,b*)—just as the poet himself had done in Sonnet 74, anticipating the moment 'when that fell arrest | Without all bail shall carry me away'. In Hamlet's case, however, the trope has an additional glint of irony, since Death's summons replicates his own arrest of Claudius, giving a further unexpected turn to the circle of vicious mimesis so characteristic of revenge tragedy.

The figure of Death as Sergeant summoning his mortal counterpart to final judgement is, of course a recurrent one in the literature of the period: he is, for example, the fearful 'Sergeant with the Black Rod' who stalks the pages of one of Thomas Dekker's plague pamphlets, his sudden arrest representing the arbitrary power of epidemic disease.[24] But he made his first appearance in the Dance of Death, appearing in the earliest sequences of all, including the original *Danse macabre* at Les Innocents and the *Dance of Paul's*. Here the grim Sergeant's mortal counterpart vainly protested his immunity in words that Hamlet seems to remember:

> Howe darst thou deth set on me arrest
> Which am the kyngis chosen officeer
> And yistirday walkyng est & west
> Myn office did with ful dispitous cheere
> But now this day I am arrest[ed] heere
> And may nat flee thouh I hadde it sworn

22 Ibid. 130. 23 *A Booke of Christian Prayers*, 89.

24 Dekker, *The Blacke Rod and the White Rod* (1630), in *Plague Pamphlets*, ed. Wilson, 202.

7. Figures from Guyot Marchant's *Mirroir tressalutaire* (1492), a woodcut version of the Paris *Danse macabre* (British Library, 11483. i. 44). By permission of the British Library.

(*a*) Monk and Usurer.

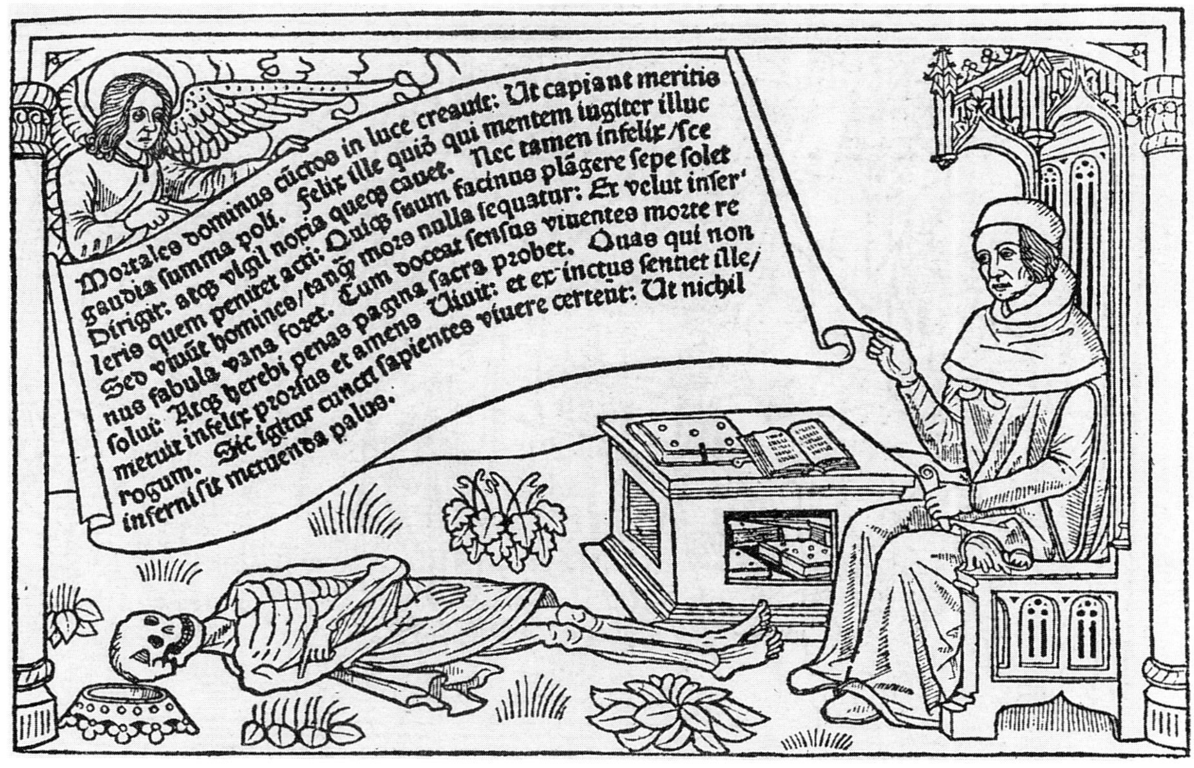

(*b*) The Dead King, showing the *Acteur*, or presenter-figure.

Eche man is loth to deie ferr or neer
That hath nat lernyd [for] to deie afforn.[25]

The ostensible lesson here is fundamentally the same as that enforced by every episode of the Dance. It is threefold: Death is an impartial leveller who spares no condition or estate; the moment of his arrest is sudden, arbitrary, and unpredictable; and the shock of his summons will be unbearable to those who have not spent their lives preparing for it. But the meanings of so rich a set of images could not in the end be confined to illustrations, however vivid, of *memento mori* truisms; and beneath the apparently unimpeded flow of the Dance it is possible to trace the emergence of a powerfully resistant undertow, whose pull the viewers of *Hamlet* were likely to feel with exceptional force.

Envisaging Death: From the Danse Macabre *to the* Totentanz *of Basel*

The precise origins of the *Danse macabre* (and even the significance of its name) remain obscure, but the painter of Les Innocents was clearly able to draw on a number of existing traditions. His design had affinities with the older motif of *Les Trois Vifs et les trois morts,* in which three men in the prime of life stumble upon three dead who rise from their coffins to warn them of mortality and admonish them to lead a godly life.[26] The *Danse* extended and transformed the *memento mori* moral of this scene by combining it with the idea of the hierarchic procession to death from *Vadomori* poetry.[27] Subsequent versions of the Dance, like the Basel *Tod*, would further develop this connection by capitalizing

[25] The translation is Lydgate's, in the Lansdowne MS version (cited from Warren's edition, stanza lii, pp. 49–51).

[26] This motif, deriving from the 13th-century French poem *The Legend of the Three Living and the Three Dead*, is widely represented in visual arts from the 13th to the early 16th centuries. For discussion of its possible connections with the Dance of Death, see Clark, *Dance of Death*, 95–6; Douce, *Holbein's Dance of Death*, 24–9; Warthin, *Physician of the Dance of Death*, 5.

[27] Clark, *Dance of Death*, 101–2; Clark discusses a late 13th- to early 14th-century Latin *Vadomori* from France in which a succession of eleven characters (later expanded to twenty-three) from Pope to Fool make their complaints as they pace on towards their death. Death himself does not appear in the poem, however.

on the suggestion, apparent in later versions of the *Trois Vifs,* that the dead are in some sense the doubles of the living, phantoms of the personal death which lies in wait for each of them.[28] But perhaps the most important transformation effected by the Paris artist lay in turning the old encounter with the dead into an encounter with Death itself. The human participants in the Dance are displayed in the very moment of arrest—as if caught in the liminal instant before the distinct social identities announced by their costumes dissolve into the anonymity of the grave.

Connected with this emphasis on the levelling insolence of Death was the painter's most striking visual innovation: the presentation of Death as the orchestrator of a black carnival—musician, capering dancer, and jester—from which the whole rich tradition of Death the Antic appears to derive (Fig. 7*a*). The sinister merriment and abandoned postures of the dancing cadavers may suggest additional influences. James Clark recalls the popular superstition that at certain times the graveyard dead would rise and dance—a belief which may be related to the widespread custom of churchyard dances and revelry amongst the living.[29] Alternatively, Johannes Nohl and others have suggested a connection between the Dance of Death and *choreomania*, the peculiar form of frenzied dancing—

[28] Guyot Marchant seems to acknowledge the relation between the two motifs by including a version of 'les dis des trois mors, et trois vifz' in his *Grande Danse macabre*. In his chapter 'Death and Experience', in *The Moment of Self-Portraiture in German Renaissance Art* (Chicago: University of Chicago Press, 1993), Joseph Leo Koerner notes how often 16th-century Deaths are made to parody the attributes of their victims, and suggests that the origins of this notion can be traced to the *Trois Vifs* tradition (pp. 280–4), in which (as Phoebe Spinrad has shown) the Dead gradually acquire the distinguishing marks of their living counterparts—so that, as in later versions of the *danse macabre*, la Mort is transformed into le Mort, 'an image of the self after selfhood . . . the individual facing his own end' (*Summons of Death*, 4–5, 11–12). Clark (*Dance of Death*, 108–11) discusses the possibility of such an interpretation, only to dismiss it, maintaining that 'the dance is the symbol of death and nothing more'; Werner Gundersheimer, on the other hand, inclines to the view that 'the subject is really a dance of the dead, rather than a dance of death'; see *'The Dance of Death' by Hans Holbein the Younger: A Complete Facsimile of the Original 1538 Edition of 'Les simulachres et historiees faces de la Mort'*, intro. Werner L. Gundersheimer (New York: Dover, 1971), p. xi. As we shall see, in many versions of the Dance we are required to read the cadavers *both* as abstract symbols of the general death, *and* as the morbid doubles of those they seize. A Dance of Death misericord in St George's Chapel, Windsor, for example, described by Clark himself, shows 'three skeletons . . . made to resemble the living characters; *they are in fact their doubles*' (*Dance of Death*, 15; emphasis added). See also John Kerrigan, '*Henry IV* and the Death of Old Double', *Essays in Criticism*, 40 (1990), 25–53: 30.

[29] Clark, *Dance of Death*, 106.

later known as St Vitus's Dance—that seems to have accompanied outbreaks of the plague;[30] and these phenomena may in turn be remembered in folk-games like the middle European Dance of Death which, according to Nohl, became popular after the great pestilence.[31] But the grim humour of Death's summonses gives the revelry of the true *danse macabre* a sardonic colouring absent from these analogues.

From the beginning the Dance seems to have histrionic connections: the presentation of Death as a Summoner is closely paralleled in late medieval dramas, like *Everyman* and *Pride of Life*;[32] and it is likely that his characterization as a satiric reveller was shaped by other theatrical performances of which only the sketchiest record remains, such as the *Chorea Machabaeorum* recorded at a church in Besançon in 1453, or the 'play, history, and morality relating to the fact of the *Danse Macabre*' offered to the Duke of Burgundy by the painter Niçaise de Cambray and others in

[30] Nohl, *Black Death*, ch. 12, esp. 250–2. For an interpretation of the *Totentanz* as a reaction to the plague's violent assault on emergent individualism, see Gittings, *Death, Burial and the Individual*, 35.

[31] Ibid. 264. Nohl's description of the dance is worth quoting for its vivid evocation of the carnival grotesequerie of these performances:

> In the Dance of Death the guests paired off, and young and old began to dance merrily with joyous chattering and laughter, but suddenly the music stops with a shrill note and deep silence falls on the assembly; shortly after a low, melancholy tune is heard, which ultimately develops into a dead march, as played at funerals. A young man of the company now has to throw himself on the ground and play the dead man, the women and girls dance around him with graceful motions, endeavouring to caricature mourning for the dead in as comical a manner as possible; at the same time they sing a dirge, but sing it so merrily that it produces general laughter. On completion of the dirge the women and girls, one after another, go up to the dead man and kiss him till a round dance of the whole company terminates the first part of the dance. The second part resembles the first, only that now the men and youths dance round a dead woman or girl. When now the kissing part came the fun was great, for the dancers endeavoured to inflict the kiss as tenderly and comically as possible.

In the eldritch laughter of this game, however, it is the living whose defiant dancing appears to mock the power of Death in a wild travesty of funeral rites. In the true Dance of Death, by contrast, all the mocking energy of the revel belongs to the ministers of mortality—the living are reluctant partners in the dance, frozen in gestures of horrified refusal, so that (in the paradox observed by many commentators) it is the figures of Death which seem most startlingly alive.

[32] Spinrad examines connections between this theatrical tradition and the Dance of Death, arguing that Last Judgement plays in particular 'appear to have their roots in the Dances of Death, which expand the moment of death into a recapitulation of life and an adjustment to the act of dying' (*Summons of Death*, 69).

1449.[33] It must be significant, too, that from the beginning the painted *danses* were closely associated with orders of mendicant Friars, especially the Dominicans. Working from such small hints, Clark has suggested that the origins of the Dance may have lain in a kind of sermon-drama—a suggestion given colour by the convention of including a Preacher, acting as a kind of presenter-figure, at the beginning or end of the series (Figs. 4, 7*b*).[34] A description of one Frère Richard at Les Innocents in 1429 offers a glimpse of a preacher evidently using the Paris *Danse macabre* itself as an illustrative prop, just as the Prediger is doing in the Basel *Tod* (Fig. 4), and very much as other preachers might have used a sermon-drama. Every day for a week, from five until ten or eleven in the morning, the friar harangued an audience of five or six thousand people in the small cemetery, the great crowd of the living facing the heaped remains of their dead: 'He preached from the top of a platform almost a fathom and a half high, his back to the charnels, his face towards the cartwright's workshop, *right by the danse macabre*.'[35] According to the sixteenth-century curators of the Basel *Predigerkirche*, Dance of Death images were expressly designed to encourage 'serious philosophizing' of the sort on which Frère Richard no doubt sought to capitalize.[36]

The usefulness of such images as a prop to sermonizing upon

[33] Clark, *Dance of Death*, 91–2. See also Beatrice White's intro. to Lydgate, *Dance of Death*, pp. x–xi, and Warthin, *Physician of the Dance of Death*, 3, 10–11. Clark notes that the poet Jean Lefèvre in his *Le Respit de mort* (1376) wrote of himself as one who had made or performed a Dance of Death ('Je fis de Macabre la danse'); whether Lefèvre intended this literally, or whether (as is usually supposed) it was a metaphoric description of the pestilential sickness he had recently survived, he was clearly alluding, some fifty years before the completion of the Innocents painting, to a well-understood form.

[34] Clark, *Dance of Death*, 94–5, 102–6. Émile Mâle, *L'Art réligieux de la fin du moyen âge en France* (Paris: A. Colin, 1908), 401 cites the performance of a *danse macabre* as an adjunct to a penitential sermon preached at Caudebec in Normandy, 1393. Clark finds further evidence for connection with mendicant preaching in the *Totentanz*'s pervasive hostility towards the rich and powerful. However, the Preacher is also a figure for the Preacher of Ecclesiastes: 'all is vanity. All go unto one place; all are of dust, and all turn to dust again' (Eccles. 3: 19–20).

[35] Cited in Ariès, *Hour of our Death*, 65 (emphasis added). These charnels, most of them placed in the covered gallery above the arcaded cloister, provided an essential frame for the Paris *Danse macabre*, as they also did for the Basel *Tod* and *Dance of Paul's*—one which, as Thomas More's recollection of the skulls at St Paul's reminds us (see above, p. 52), we need to remember when attempting to imagine the full impact of the original paintings.

[36] Maurer, *Kunstdenkmäler des Kantons Basel-Stadt*, 2.

the unimpeachable lessons of *memento mori* and *vanitas vanitatum* is apparent enough; and it seems revealing that the sites favoured for Dance of Death paintings should have been of a liminal character, as if emphasizing the fragility of the boundary separating the world of the living from the attendant world of the dead. The cloister walls at Les Innocents, St Paul's, and the Predigerkirche marked the border between polis and necropolis, boneyard and street; and if the spectacle of the Dance offered, as the Poet of the Basel *Tod* reminded the viewer, a panorama of 'beginning, middle and end', its narrative concentration upon the instant of arrest—a moment strictly *between* life and death—projected a sense of fearful intermediacy, of human life as a state in the midst of which its denizens were already in death.

Yet for all its didactic usefulness, the morbid grotesquerie of the Dance of Death may still seem excessive, suggesting that it has more to reveal about early modern attitudes to death than its official function would allow. In the obsession with physical corruption that it shares with other forms of macabre art, some historians have detected a pathological loathing of the flesh and its frailties—the reaction they suppose of a profoundly outraged hedonism.[37] To concentrate upon the mere Grand Guignol surface of the imagery can be misleading, however; and if we wish to understand more about the cultural construction of death in this period, we need to think about what this elaborate parade of horrors might stand for.

To begin with, it may be useful to focus on the most obvious (and consequently least discussed) feature of the way Death is pictured: its shocking nakedness. Until the mid-sixteenth century at least, Death, though it might sometimes be symbolized as a skull, was almost never represented as a skeleton; instead it took the form of a cadaver, and one conspicuously stripped of the decencies of winding-sheet or shroud.[38] In the Dance of Death the most

[37] The latter is the view of Theodore Spencer, for example, for whom the late medieval preoccupation with death is an expression of increased worldliness: 'The more joyous the voice of life grew, the louder became the hollow tones of death'; *Death and Elizabethan Tragedy*, 36.

[38] Holbein's is the first Dance to show most of its deaths as skeletons. The skeleton who dances with the physician in the Basel *Tod* is generally recognized as a mid-16th-century alteration, its detail being dependent on the anatomic representations of Vesalius. While the skeletal form reduces the scandal of the uncovered corpse, the stripping away of 'costly three-piled flesh' from 'bare bone' may be thought of as the extreme of nakedness, as it clearly is in *The Revenger's Tragedy*.

immediate and startling contrast between the figures of Death and their reluctant partners lies not in the morbidity of one and liveliness of the other, since the dead bodies often seem more vigorous and animated than the living, but in the shameful and indiscriminate nakedness of the gambolling corpses set against the elaborately hierarchized costumes of their chosen victims. In a similar fashion much of the emotional power of fifteenth- and sixteenth-century *transi* tombs depends on the extremity of the contrast between the opulent robes of the portrait figures which crown them and the scandalous undress of the rotting corpses sculpted beneath—a sense of scandal only enhanced by the ostentatious care taken to cover the privy parts of the exposed cadaver. Such nakedness, as we have already seen, interprets the shamefulness of death in a culturally specific fashion: death is shameful because it is an extreme form of defacement, a stripping away of the constituent forms of social identity that amounts to nothing less than an absolute undoing of the self.

In the Les Innocents *Danse,* and the other great paintings deriving from it, this sense of Death's cruel cancellation of distinction, its dismal uniformity, was further enforced by the uninterrupted sweep of the design.[39] 'O cruel deth that sparist non estat', exclaims Lydgate's Gentlewoman, fixing this peculiar sense of death as an outrage upon social order, 'To old and yong thou art indifferent.'[40] And despite the hierarchical sequence of victims, from Pope to Fool, the chainlike arrangement of the interlocking figures, where each of the living is in the grasp of two leering cadavers, powerfully conveys the undiscriminating nature of the mortal process in which all are caught up, underlining the fearful sameness of all these naked figures of death, who are differentiated only by skittish variations in their dancing postures (Fig. 7*a*). Their irremediably *common* fate is represented, as the women of the *Danse des femmes* are reminded, by the grotesque confusion of the plague pit and the charnel-house:

> Women, imagine yourselves in a heap [*ung tas*],
> Of bones from people who have died,

[39] The book form of Guyot's version necessarily reduces this effect, especially because of the disproportionate structural prominence it gives to the arcading that frames nearly every group of four dancers; but it is still possible—allowing for both the relative crudity of his technique and the updating of the costumes—to get from it some sense of the original.

[40] Lydgate, *Dance of Death*, stanza xlvi (Lansdowne MS], ed. Warren, 57.

Who have filled many worldly roles
In their time past
And [who] now are piled [*sont entassez*]
One on other, fat and thin . . .
Rotted flesh, bones all bare [*tous nudz*].[41]

Like the elaborately ordered processions of late medieval and Renaissance funerals,[42] the Dance of Death simultaneously displays the hierarchic order of earthly distinction and announces its inevitable cancellation, for ironically (as the Queen observes in the *Danse des femmes*), 'The grandest are the first ones seized.'[43] But where in funeral obsequies the formal precession enacts a rite of remembrance designed to proclaim ultimate mastery over mortal oblivion, in the *danse macabre* the balance shifts decisively in favour of death's annihilation of difference. The embodied moral is that voiced most clearly in the first and last dialogues of the Paris sequence: in the first, Death reminds the Pope that (as Lydgate phrases it) 'deth ne sparith high nor Low degre'; in the last, the Fool is made to recognize that enemies and friends, wise men and fools, high and low, all ranks and conditions are indistinguishable in death: 'quand Dieu l'accord | Tous mors sont d'un estat commun.' The Fool's moral is restated in the ensuing picture, not properly part of the Dance, but a kind of visual motto to it, in which a king lies stretched on the earth, his crown having tumbled onto the ground beside him (Fig. 7*b*). Like an incarnation of Sidney's idea of tragedy, he lies there to make 'kings fear to be tyrants' and to show 'upon how weak foundations gilden roofs are builded'.[44] This 'kynge liggyng dede & eten with wormes' addresses the reader, rather as the Trois Morts had addressed the Trois Vifs, offering a mirror of their common fate:

Ye folke that loken vpon this purtrature
Beholdyng here alle the estates daunce
Seeth what ye ben & what is yowre nature
Mete unto wormes not elles yn substaunce
And have this myrroure euer yn remembraunce
[H]ow I lye here som-tyme crowned kynge

[41] *Danse Macabre of Women*, 48.

[42] See below, Ch. 8, pp. 267–81.

[43] *Danse Macabre of Women*, 52.

[44] Sir Philip Sidney, 'An Apology for Poetry', in Edmund D. Jones (ed.), *English Critical Essays (Sixteenth, Seventeenth and Eighteenth Centuries)*, 2nd edn. (London: Oxford University Press, 1947), 26.

To al estates a trewe resemblaunce
That wormes fode is fyne of owre lyuynge.[45]

'Is this the fine of his fines,' asks the Prince of Denmark, as if the indistinguishable skulls of the graveyard have put him in mind of Lydgate once again, 'to have his fine pate full of fine dirt' (v. i. 107–8). In the Paris *Danse* the King's body has indeed become 'a thing . . . of nothing' (*Hamlet*, IV. ii. 27–30), an emblem of death's power of 'contemptible vilification . . . [and] nullification', as Donne imagined it: 'That monarch, who spread over many nations alive, must in his dust lie in a corner of that sheet of lead, and there but so long as that lead will last. . . . and (such are the revolutions of the grave) be mingled with the dust of every highway.'[46] However much the imagination may be made to dwell on the physical horrors of mortification, it is required to do so only as a way of making vivid the true horror of death, the blank indifference of its 'dissolution and dispersion'—the absolute loss of distinction that an Anthony finds mockingly pictured in the dissolving clouds at Alexandria (*Anthony and Cleopatra*, IV. iv. 2–14).

As Anthony's attempt to assume the active role of 'bridegroom in my death' (line 100) might remind us, however, the living do not always abandon themselves passively to the clutch of indistinction; and among the many imitations inspired by the original *Danse macabre* at Les Innocents, one in particular has interesting things to reveal about the gradual articulation of such resistance, making it a highly suggestive document of evolving attitudes to death in the century and a half that followed the painting of its Parisian model.

The so-called Gross Basel *Tod*, the great mural in the graveyard cloister of the Predigerkirche in Basel, was commissioned (perhaps from the prominent local artist Konrad Witz) in about 1440,[47] and

[45] Stanza lxxx (Ellesmere MS), ed. Warren, 74.

[46] John Donne, 'Death's Duel', in *Devotions*, 177.

[47] Both the dating (which we owe to the first engraver of the series, Merian) and the attribution are contentious. For a long time it was supposed, partly on the authority of Büchel, that the *Predigerkirche*, or Gross Basel *Tod*, was a copy, made in about 1480, of the less well-known Klein Basel *Tod* in the Klingental convent across the river; and this view is argued by Warthin, *Physician of the Dance of Death*, 16, and by Clark, *Dance of Death*, 60–4. Clark supposes that it was actually the Klingental *Tod* that was painted as a response to the Basel plague, but that, since this painting was not open to public view, its history became displaced onto the Prediger painting. However, more recent opinion has reverted to the original precedence, and has become more sympathetic to the claims of Witz: see François Maurer, *Die Kunstdenkmäler des Kantons Basel-Stadt* (Basel: Birkhäuser

several times repainted and modified in the sixteenth and seventeenth centuries. The painting itself was destroyed, except for a few fragments, in 1805; but a good sense of how it looked at various stages in its history can be gathered from engravings published by Matthäus Merian in 1621, and from the water-colours made by Emanuel Büchel in 1773 and by Johann Feyerabend in 1806 (Fig. 4).[48] From these we can see that the Basel *Totentanz*, the earliest of two which once adorned Dominican buildings in the city,[49] was among the more splendid realizations of this motif; and it remains in some respects the most interesting of all because of the striking clarity with which its painter—or painters, since later restorers made significant alterations to the detail of the design—illuminated and modified certain crucial meanings of the Dance of Death. Moreover, through its influence on Henry VIII's court painter, Hans Holbein, a former resident of Basel, the *Tod* made a contribution to the English Dance of Death tradition second only to that of the Paris *Danse* itself.[50]

Although the Basel *Tod* offers an altogether richer and more complex set of images than its predecessor, at first glance one is likely to be struck by its generic resemblances to the Paris *Danse*. At one end stands a charnel-house out of which issue the two Deaths with trumpet and tabor, musicians of the Apocalypse, who seem to orchestrate the Dance, leading the dancers towards their common end amid the heap of indistinguishable skulls. The dance proper consists, in its surviving copies, of thirty-seven pairs of figures, arranged in a hierarchic line, from Pope to peasant; attached

Verlag, 1966), v. 2–13. Elisabeth Landolt, *The Basel Dance of Death*, Basel Historical Museum pamphlet (Basel, n.d.).

[48] Merian's engravings also preserve the verses attached to each image in the series. Feyerabend clearly knew both Merian's engravings and Büchel's paintings, but was by no means wholly dependent on them.

[49] Büchel also executed a copy of the so-called Klein Basel painting, which, because of its less extensive history of restorations, was probably closer in many of its details to the original Groß Basel version.

[50] See Maurer, *Kunstdenkmäler des Kantons Basel-Stadt*, 8–10. Once thought to have been the painter of the Prediger mural itself, Holbein returned to its ferocious imagery in a number of works both grand and miniature—in the design for a dagger-sheath, in now lost murals of his own (including one at Whitehall), and above all in his famous woodcut series. Transmitted throughout Europe in a huge number of editions from 1530, his *Great Death* soon became so much the best-known of the *danses macabres* that it apparently influenced the 1568 restoration of the Basel *Tod* itself.

to each pair are sets of verses enforcing the familiar levelling moral of Les Innocents. Death addresses the Lawyer in the accents of the fell Sergeant, warning him that men and women, spiritual and worldly alike, are subject to his absolute law. Death gleefully informs the Physician that he must now become the cadaverous simulacrum of those that his physic has hurried on their mortal way ('Dann du hast manchen auch hing'richt, | Der eben gleich wie ich jetzt sicht'). The threat is of a likeness so absolute that it makes redundant the very terminology of likeness and difference—a horror which the Basel *Tod* makes especially vivid in the Bishop's reply to Death:

> Ich bin gar hoch geachtet worden
> Dieweil ich lebt in Bischoffs-Orden:
> Nun ziehen mich die Ungeschaffnen
> An ihren Tantz, als einen Affen.[51]

[While I was alive and invested in Bishop's orders, I became the object of the greatest esteem: now the shapeless ones drag me off, as if I were an ape.]

In their nakedness these figures of death stand for an undifferentiation even more absolute than that represented by the mere interchangeability of human corpses: they are *die Ungeschaffnen*, 'the shapeless or uncreated ones', incarnations of formlessness itself, of the kind of death for which the imagination of a Claudio struggles to find metaphors:

> Ay, but to die, and go we not where;
> To lie in cold obstruction, and to rot;
> This sensible warm motion to become
> A kneaded clod; and the delighted spirit . . .
> To be imprisoned in the viewless winds
> And blown with restless violence round about
> The pendant world.
>
> (*Measure for Measure*, III. i. 117–25)

A more considered examination of the Basel *Tod*, however, shows that its heightened emphasis on the fear of indistinction is matched by an intensified sense of the resistant individuality of the

[51] Cited from *Totentanz der Stadt Basel* (Basel: G. S. Beck, n.d.), a 19th-century reprint of Merian's engravings.

living, a number of whom were reputedly portrait-figures.[52] The chainlike arrangement in which the identity of the Paris dancers is subsumed is replaced by a succession of distinct encounters, as if to emphasize the particularity of each experience of arrest.[53] The effect is to highlight the gestures of shock and refusal apparent in most of the figures, many of whom (in anticipation of Holbein) have clearly been surprised in the midst of their daily occupations: the Lawyer clutches a sealed brief; the startled Physician drops his diagnostic urine flask; the Noblewoman, looking in the mirror to approve her fashionable attire, finds her own Death gazing back at her; the Usurer is called to an uncanny account; the Bride is accosted by an unexpected bridegroom; the Pedlar finds himself doing business with an unusually demanding customer; the Blindman is tricked into his grave by a Death with shears who severs the lead of his guide-dog; the Farmer with his flail and basket of poultry is grabbed on his way home from the fields.

At the same time, in another striking departure from the Paris *Danse*—for which a sixteenth-century restoration may have been partially responsible—several of the Deaths are shown in ways that seem to identify them particularly closely with their victims.[54] The Empress and the Queen, for example, are partnered with cadavers

[52] In this the Basel painter may have been anticipated by his recent predecessor at St Paul's, who seems to have given a more individual cast to his series, by including at least one portrait from life, since Lydgate's Tregetour (Juggler) is named as 'Mr John Rikill', Henry VI's jester; see Clark, *Dance of Death*, 12. Lydgate also omitted the Queen from the Paris sequence, presumably because Henry VI was still unmarried. The practice appears to have been carried furthest by the painter of the Lucerne Dance in 1635, who allegedly modelled most of his faces after local worthies (ibid. 76). On the heightened individuality of the human figures in the Basel version, see Maurer, *Die Kunstdenkmäler des Kantons Basel-Stadt*, 10–11.

[53] The fragmentation of the classic chainlike arrangement of Les Innocents is equally striking in the illuminated manuscript version, which makes no attempt to preserve Marchant's linked pairs, but devotes a separate illustration to each moment of summoning. At another level the fragmentation of the dance-procession may mimic the frantic drive to individual separation which Canetti discerns as a classic symptom of plague with its terror of contagion: 'It is strange to see how the hope of survival isolates them, each becoming a single individual confronting the crowd of victims' (*Crowds and Power*, 320).

[54] If Maurer and others are right in supposing that the Klingental painting is closer to the original of the Gross Basel *Tod* than the surviving copies, then the *doppelgänger* effect is probably largely the contribution of the 1568 restorer, Hans Hug Kluber. For doubling as an expression of the undifferentiation associated with the plague, see Girard, 'The Plague in Literature and Myth', in *To Double Business Bound*, 142–3.

whose flowing locks and full breasts mark them, in a disconcerting violation of the conventional asexuality of such figures, as female.[55] Other Deaths usurp properties or costume from their victims: the Cardinal's Death wears a cardinal's hat and the Abbot's a mitre; the Knight's Death boasts half-armour and flourishes the Knight's own sword; the Cripple's Death has, like him, been treated to primitive prosthesis, and seems to wrestle for the use of his crutch; the moral depravity of the most hated figure in the sequence, the Usurer, is mirrored in the grisly black cadaver which climbs over a counting desk to seize him ('Ein schwarzer Todt is dein Gefehrt');[56] the Maiden's Death is crowned, like her, with a chaplet of flowers; the Mayor's sports a jaunty feathered hat that seems to parody his victim's stylish bonnet; the Cook's carries a spit with a roasting fowl on it. Most strikingly of all, the Jester is swept into the dance by a mocking partner whose costume almost exactly mimics his belted jerkin, cap, and bells, except that it is shroud-white, drained of distinctive coloration. Underlying this transformation of the anonymous *Morts* of Les Innocents is a notion of death as not merely imminent (as in the *memento mori* tradition) but *immanent*, as an ending implicit in every beginning, and constantly present in every middle.

This was the Death to whose immanence Dekker traced the origins of the plague itself: 'For every man within him feeds | A worm which this contagion breeds';[57] the Death envisaged by John Moore, when he wrote that 'Death and Life are as two twins, united and knit together, until the separation of the soul and body, which separation is called death';[58] or the Death which John Donne imagined as already inscribed upon the foetus whose progress metaphorically prescribes the dismal circle of our lives:

[55] The hair which crowns the cadaverous heads of Death in the *Danse macabre des femmes* may perhaps be meant as a marker of gender, but their bodies are conspicuously unsexualized.

[56] The 'schwarzer Tod' has sometimes been associated with the figure of a negro trumpeter of death at Les Innocents, as an emblem of the 'Black Death' itself; but since that name for what was called the 'Great Pestilence' did not become common before the later 17th century, and seems altogether unknown before the middle of the 16th century, these details are presumably coincidental. Perhaps, like early uses of 'black death', the Basel figure is merely a literal rendering of the Latin *atra mors*; —see Philip Ziegler, *The Black Death* (London: Collins, 1969), 17–18.

[57] Dekker, *Newes from Graues-end*, sig. D1^{v}.

[58] John Moore, *A Mappe of Mans Mortalitie* (London, 1617), sig. S2^{v}, cited in Engel, *Mapping Mortality*, 141.

We have a winding-sheet in our mother's womb, which grows with us from our conception, and we come into the world wound up in that winding-sheet, for we come to seek a grave. . . . We celebrate our own funerals with cries even at our birth, as though our threescore and ten years' of life were spent in our mother's labour, and our circle made up in the first point thereof. We beg one baptism with another sacrament, a sacrament of tears.[59]

The immanent death figured in the Basel *Tod*'s prancing cadavers is the Death that each mortal carries about with him, his *Gefehrt*, or travelling-companion, the stealthy *comes* (companion) of the *Danse des femmes*, an uncanny double who watches our every footstep ('Passibus invigilat nostris mors').[60] This is the morbid double with which Webster's Ferdinand wrestles when he attempts to throttle his own shadow, or which the Cardinal glimpses in his fish-pond when he catches sight of 'a thing, armed with a rake | That seems to strike at me' (*Duchess of Malfi*, v. ii. 38, v. v. 6–7);[61] and it is subtly refigured in that half-recognized *alter ego*, the 'malignant . . . Turk' who returns to claim Othello at the moment of his death (*Othello*, v. ii. 353).

The irony of Othello's suicide lies in the fact that the very action that is designed to reassert his heroic difference from the barbarian world of the Turkish Other effectually collapses that difference—just as in the Dance of Death the ragged trappings of the *Gefehrt* amount only to a sardonic travesty of difference. Beneath them there is, in the end, always the same Death waiting to be discovered.

In the Basel *Tod* this collapse into sameness is grotesquely imagined as a kind of sexual undoing—playing on the familiar idea of erotic consummation as a 'little death'. Each victim is drawn into the dance by a Death who assumes the conventionally masculine role, forcing his partner to adopt the feminine posture of

[59] Donne, 'Death's Duel', in *Devotions*, 169–70.

[60] *Danse Macabre of Women*, 54. On Death as a double who both 'accompanies or is within each individual at all times and yet is characterised as the alien, the other', see Engel, *Mapping Mortality*, 74–5, 81–3, 169–88.

[61] Here the rake functions as a travesty of his crozier; but compare Time's description of Death in Rowlands, *A Terrible Battell betweene . . . Time, and Death*, sig. E4^{v}: 'From ear to ear thou hast a mouth unshut, | With arms and hands like to a Gardeners rake.' Spinrad notes several instances in which Deaths are armed with a rake, including the Fourth Horseman in Dürer's Apocalypse woodcuts (*Summons of Death*, 210).

bashful resistance.[62] Moreover, these Deaths are so conspicuously eroticized in their nakedness that not even their identification as the victims' morbid *doppelgängers* can disguise the suggestion that each pairing announces a grim coupling of sorts—one that parodies the union of the first couple, 'the Mirror of the whole World' ('Der Spiegel aller Welt') as the caption calls them, whose mortal sin initiates the dance itself.[63] To make love, in the popular idiom of Tourneur's *Atheist's Tragedy*, is 'to dance the beginning of the world';[64] but to join that giddy round is, the painting suggests, to begin the dance of the world's end—the painter's conceit paralleling that in an English ballad, Thomas Hill's *The Doleful Dance, and Song of Death*, in which Death begins begins his summons with a grotesque quibble on a popular euphemism for copulation, 'Can you dance the shaking of the sheets?'[65] This erotic aspect of

[62] On the 'subversive, trans-sexual' character of the Deaths in the *danse macabre*, see Llewellyn, *Art of Death*, 22.

[63] It is not clear at what point in the evolution of the Basel *Tod* this framing episode was included: since there is no record of it before Merian's 1621 engravings, it may have been added as late as Emmanuel Bock's 1614–16 restoration. Perhaps the Fall took the place of the Turk, who is given as the last dancer in the first detailed description of the mural by Hans Frölich in 1588. On the other hand Frölich may simply have regarded the scene as extraneous to the Dance proper. A representation of the Fall seems to appear first in the Dance of Death at La Chaise-Dieu in the Auvergne (*c.*1460), while Holbein's *Dance* similarly begins with a Genesis sequence, featuring the Creation of Adam and Eve, the Fall, the Expulsion, and the condemnation of humankind to labour. The motif is repeated in an elaborate engraving from Augsburg by the brothers Ridinger which once again describes death as a grotesque coupling: the border is decorated with twelve pairs of dancers from the *Totentanz*, while the central illustration shows a graveyard in which a ring of nine women and their skeletal partners dance around a coffin in which two skeletons lie in a fast embrace; the four corners display images of the Crucifixion and the Fall on one side, and of the Judgement of the Blessed and the Damned on the other. This engraving dates from the mid-18th century, but its figures are in 16th-century costume, indicating that the makers were consciously imitating work of that period.

[64] II. v. 66. All citations from this play are to *The Atheist's Tragedy*, ed. Irving Ribner, The Revels Plays (London: Methuen, 1964).

[65] The erotic tone of Death's invitation is apparent in several stanzas:

> Can you dance *The shaking of the sheets?*—
> A dance that everyone must do—
> Can you trim it up with dainty sweets,
> And every thing as 'longs thereto?
> Make ready then your winding sheet,
> And see how you can bestir your feet,
> For Death is the man that all must meet.
>
> * * * *

the *Tod* is predictably apparent in Death's embrace of the Maiden—a motif which developed a life of its own outside the *danse macabre*;[66] but it is more disturbingly expressed in the painter's fascination with the cadavers' absent genitalia. Some conceal their genital regions with chastely angled limbs, or convenient flutters of drapery; but others brazenly expose themselves, revealing how the embalmer's knife or the worms of corruption have stripped them of their secret parts; while still others parade obscene simulacra of them. The Pope is led by a Death whose loins are adorned with a shin-bone and skull resembling an erect penis and swollen testicles, a motif echoed in the bone and lantern of the Hermit's companion; the Minstrel's prancing fiddler has a box strapped suggestively to his groin; the Cardinal's dancing-partner sports a phallic worm protruding from his open belly—a visual pun mirrored in the vermiculating bowels of the Youth's cadaver, and again in the entwined serpent about the waist of the Executioner's Death, who clutches indecently at his anus. Worms and serpents

And you that lean on your ladies' laps,
And lay your heads upon their knees,
And think to play with beauteous paps,
And not to come and dance with me?
No! fair lords and ladies all,
I will make you come when I do call,
And find you a pipe to dance withal.

* * * *

For I can quickly cool you all,
How hot or stout so e'er you be . . .

(lines 1–7, 43–9, 64–5)

(Quoted from *The Roxburghe Ballads*, 9 vols. (Hertford: printed for the Ballad Society by S. Austin, 1871–99), iii. 184–6). The earliest printed version of this ballad (Roxburghe Collection, I. 499) is tentatively dated 1625, but it must be older, since a ballad with the same title was licensed to John Awdelay in 1568–9, and its opening clearly lies behind Dekker's grim euphemism for plague-death—to 'daunce . . . the shaking of one sheet', *The Meeting of Gallants at an Ordinarie* (1604), in *Plague Pamphlets*, ed. Wilson, 125. The eroticization of Death's arrest is given a bizarre late twist in the wrestling-match of William Hogarth's sketch *Death Giving George Taylor a Cross-buttock* (*c.*1758–9).

[66] For a suggestive account of this tradition and the eroticization of Death's 'bite', especially in the work of Hans Baldung Grien, see Koerner, *Moment of Self-Portraiture*, ch. 14; Baldung's iconography systematically associates Death and the Maiden with his own peculiarly eroticized representations of the Fall, to the point where in *Eve, the Serpent, and Death* (*c.*1530), Adam himself becomes the figure of Death.

alike are to be seen as the spawn of the primal Serpent twined about the forbidden Tree where the fig-leaved First Parents stand, enacting the fall into sexual knowledge and death.[67] These obscenities at once sign the vicious place of begetting as the fountainhead of death, and identify the dance itself as a revel of monstrous uncreation. The moment of arrest, when Death performs the 'rape' of which Tourneur's Atheist complains (*Atheist's Tragedy*, v. ii. 267), is the moment at which the living are inducted into the world of *die Ungeschaffnen*, crossing the boundary into formlessness and indistinction.

Of course the Basel *Tod* is not simply a series of discrete encounters: it also presents a narrative of sorts. As in the Paris *Danse*, this takes the simple form of a processional movement from life to death. But in this case the sequence can be read from either end; and one may elect to see the narrative either as including the figures who frame it—the Preacher at one end and the Painter at the other —or as being composed of an entirely discrete inner action, upon which these characters comment.[68] It is important that, while the Preacher and his audience seem to have been part of the original design, the second framing group, featuring the painter himself, with his wife and son, seems to have been added in the course of Hans Hug Kluber's extensive refurbishment of 1568. Apparently borrowing a conceit from Nicolas Manuel's Berne *Totentanz*,[69] this addition substantially altered the meaning of the original.

From one point of view, the painting begins with the Preacher, who appears to call the narrative into existence, acting as a kind

[67] Stanford, 'The Terrible Thresholds', notes that the same grotesque image, 'the surreal and terrifying picture of a snake arising from the spine of a cadaver', is used in Browne to associate vermiculation with sexuality and with the Serpent of Genesis; for Browne too the serpent's association with death and reproduction symbolizes the terrible circularity of life (pp. 416–17).

[68] The preacher appears to have been part of the original design, though the face was altered by the 16th-century restorer, Kluber, to resemble his contemporary the Basel reformer Oekolampad—perhaps to protect the work from the defacement of iconoclasts.

[69] In the final scene of the Berne series, as Clark describes it, 'complete with brush, maulstick and palette, dressed in the mode of the day, stands the artist himself, with the features of Nicolas Manuel. He is seen putting the finishing touches to his great work. Death creeps along with the hour-glass on his back and grasps the maul-stick, interrupting the painter in his studio' (*Dance of Death*, 74). A later version of the conceit appears in panel 8 of the Totentanz on the Spreuer Bridge in Lucerne, 'Death and the Painter' (1626–35).

of presenter for the sequence, like the moralizing Acteur (Author–Authority) of Guyot Marchant's *Danse*, or, more exactly, like Frère Richard incorporating the original *Danse macabre* into his sermon at Les Innocents. The Prediger is surrounded by a crowd of listeners whom he instructs, following his model, the Preacher of Ecclesiastes, on the levelling morality of the charnel at whose heap of skulls he seems to gesture ('O Mensch betracht | Und nicht Veracht | Hie die Figur, | All Creatur | Die nimmt der Tod | Früh und spot, | Gleichwie die Blum | Im Feld zergoht': 'Behold, O people, and don't despise, the image of all human creatures whom Death seizes, sooner or later, like flowers in the meadow'). His audience, though, are hardly as one would imagine a crowd in the cemetery of the Predigerkirche—in fact, in a second remarkable doubling, they seem to represent the victims of the Dance itself. Among them one can distinguish Pope, Emperor, King, Queen, and Cardinal, as well as (less certainly) Abbot, Abbess, Doctor, and Farmer. In this context the Preacher's gesture may be interpreted as directed less at the monitory signs of mortality than at the Last Judgement painted on the tympanum of the charnel-house above; and indeed his verses begin with a passage dealing with resurrection and judgement, based on the apocalyptic conclusion of the book of Daniel 12: 'What shall be the end of these things?'[70] This image proposes a transcendental consummation for the Dance—an ending which reasserts the principle of distinction in spiritual terms, as the damned upon the left are cast into the pit, and the blessed upon the right are summoned to bliss.

Once the viewer's attention has been drawn to the Judgement scene, the Dance begins to assume the aspect of a symbolic history of the world, a reading powerfully reinforced by the inclusion of the Genesis scene. In this image the First Parents are shown beneath

[70] Daniel 12: 8; the entire chapter is cited at the head of the Prediger's verses. The chapter, which offers a vision of judgement and resurrection, is marked by a powerful rhetorical stress on the idea of ending: 'But thou, O Daniel, *shut up* the words, and *seal* the book, even to the time of the *end*. . . . And one said to the man clothed in white linen . . . How long shall it be to the *end* of these wonders. . . . And I hear the man clothed in linen [say] that . . . when he shall have accomplished to scatter the power of the holy people, all these things shall be *finished*. . . . then said I, O my Lord, what shall be the *end* of these things? And he said, Go thy way, Daniel: for the words are *closed up* and *sealed* till the time of the *end*. . . . But go thy way till the *end* be: for thou shalt rest, and stand in thy lot at the *end* of the days' (12: 4–13; emphases added).

the Tree of Knowledge, about to taste its mortal fruit; and the attached verses invite us to read it as an encapsulation of the universal history which the Dance plays out: 'Behold this mirror of the world, placed before us so that we may quickly and thoroughly understand the beginning, middle and end of things.'[71] Adam and Eve appear both as the progenitors of humankind and as the authors of that fatal choice which brought death into the world and all our woe. The peasant who hurries away from them, loaded with the instruments of toil and mopping his sweating brow, might almost stand for Adam himself, expelled from the Garden;[72] but the ineluctable movement towards death which he initiates (and which is further emphasized by the advancing age of the living figures) is qualified by the promise of the Judgement, which offers to restore the offspring of Adam to a transfigured version of the immortality lost to them in the Garden. Each of the individual lives in the sequence reenacts in little the process of this grand history.

That at least is the comfortably orthodox reading which the *Tod* will readily accommodate. The sceptical eye might observe, however, that the Judgement scene seems disproportionately small in relation to the whole scheme, and that it exists only as a kind of fiction-within-a-fiction (or perhaps within several fictions). Kluber's addition of his own self-portrait complicates matters further, asserting an individualism which was perhaps only possible in a specifically Protestant reworking of the Dance. The Painter is both of the Dance and not of it. Like the victims of the *Tod*, he and his family are each attended by a personal Death: a Death in female headdress mockingly removes the dress-cap from Barbara's head; an infant Death, who has put down his hourglass in order to play with the artist's equipment, waits for little Hans behind the coffin-like bench; a third Death, crowned with deathless bays, slaps his hand on the artist's shoulder:

> Now Hans Hug Kluber, cease to paint
> On other matters now we're bent

[71] In a similar fashion the Lübeck narrative proceeds from a beginning, symbolized by the cradled infant to an end represented by Death's foot poised over the hourglass.

[72] Holbein's *Dance* also begins with a Genesis sequence, featuring the Creation of Adam and Eve, the Fall, the Expulsion, and the condemnation of humankind to labour.

Your art, pains, labour all are vain
When you are called like other men.

As he speaks, Death gestures at the line of dancers, inviting the painter to join it.[73] But of course the Dance, as Kluber is careful to remind the viewer, is his own creation: he has painted himself with palette and brushes still in hand, as if walking away from the great painting he has just finished restoring. It is like that disturbing moment at the conclusion of the printed *Doctor Faustus* when the hero's midnight ending threatens to lap over the boundaries of its fiction to engulf the author himself: *Terminat hora diem; terminat author opus*. Yet, as in the case of Marlowe's motto, the gesture is ambiguous: that last *terminat*, after all, is a reminder of the artist's power, and an assertion of his presence in face of the absence signified by the blank paper below; Kluber's eyes roll in alarm at the sensation of death's arrest, his face is a mask of consternation, yet his stance is marked by a relaxed confidence that distinguishes him from every other figure in the series—as well it might, since, with all its ironies, this last grouping represents the signature of immortality. The artist acknowledges his subjection to death, it is true, but he has also placed himself—like his opposite and double, the Preacher of the Word—outside time:

O, God, I pray thee stand by me,
Since I too from this world must flee:
To thy hand I my soul commend,
When comes the hour my soul must end
And Death my soul from body drive;
I hope my memory may survive
So long this work its tale shall tell.
God bless you all! I'm off, farewell.

The defiant paradox celebrated here in Kluber's self-portrait, none the less moving for the impudence which imposes the (borrowed) stamp of his own personality upon on a dead painter's work, is exactly that articulated in a set of Latin verses by Holbein's friend Borbonius proclaiming that his pictures of Death have rendered

[73] In Feyerabend's version, where the Genesis scene is placed between Kluber and the Dance proper, Death gestures at an apple still hanging from the mortal tree, as though mockingly inviting Kluber to re-enact the First Parents' sin.

the artist immortal;[74] and it is repeated in the Printer's scene of the 'Queen Elizabeth's Prayerbook' Dance, whose reflexive motto, defying Death's interruption of Compositor and Pressman, proclaims: 'We printers wrote with wisdom's pen: | She lives for aye, we die as men' (Fig *6c*).[75] By such conceits the Dance of Death is transformed from a memento of death's commonness and indifference into a monument of personal fame.[76]

Theatre and the Macabre

If the strange mixture of irony, pathos, and triumphant defiance that infuses Kluber's revision of the *Totentanz* seems powerfully reminiscent of the mood of Jacobean tragic endings, that is perhaps no more than we should expect, given the extent to which the early modern *Gestalt* of Death was shaped by macabre art. But, as we have seen, it also reflects the way in which tragedy absorbed motifs from the Dance of Death. The effects of such cross-fertilization are most apparent in plays such as *Hamlet*, *The Atheist's Tragedy*, *The Revenger's Tragedy*, and *Hoffman* which make extensive use of macabre spectacle, though they are by no means confined to them. The very didactic seriousness with which tragedy in general professed to confute the enemies of drama by exposing the weak foundations of authority's gilden roofs pushed it towards an ironic levelling that repeatedly recalls the Dance of Death. The notoriously ambivalent deposition scene in Shakespeare's *Richard II*, for example, presents a ritual unfashioning of royal identity, in which 'the pompous body of a king' is publicly stripped of every mark of royal distinction ('I have no name, no title, | No, not that name was given me at the font'; IV. i. 255–6), transforming his body to a mere 'nothing', an undifferentiated emblem of common mortality that belongs exactly to the graveyard

[74] Cited in H. Noel Humphreys, 'A Concise History of the Origin and Subsequent Development of the Subject', in *Hans Holbein's Celebrated Dance of Death* ([? London], 1868), 28. Holbein's own, rather more ambiguous version of the conceit is contained in the *Death's Coat of Arms*, where the artist and his wife appear as heraldic supporters.

[75] [Day], *A Booke of Christian Prayers*, 90^{v}.

[76] Ann Harrison discerns a similarly contradictory tendency in the manuscript women's *Danse*, where the sequence of 'elegantly dressed women' tends to encourage 'a wholly positive reading . . . that is not altogether consistent with the [heavily moralized] text' (*Danse Macabre of Women*, 24).

kingdom of Antic Death evoked in Richard's earlier 'talk of graves, of worms, and epitaphs' (III. ii. 145):

But what e'er I be,
Nor I, nor any man that but man is,
With nothing shall be pleas'd, till he be eas'd
With being nothing. (V. v. 38–41)

In Marlowe's companion-tragedy, *Edward II*, a similar cancellation of royal identity is enacted with brutal literalness as the King's anointed person is washed in 'channel water', preparatory to his induction into the symbolic darkness of Killingworth (V. iii. 27–36), where his tragedy will be disclosed as an illustration of the sinister pageant-mottoes chosen by Lancaster and the deadly Mortimer, *Undique mors est* and *Aeque tandem* ('Death is everywhere' and 'Equal at last'; II. ii. 20, 28). The presiding figure of the play's catastrophe is the Mower, who betrays the King to his murderers, an avatar of levelling Death whose 'remember me' (IV. vi. 115) points up his resemblance to the summoners of the Dance.

Even in the ostensibly more optimistic world of a play such as *1 Henry IV*, which resists the habitual accommodation of historical drama to the norms of tragedy, Hal's triumphant reclamation of his royal identity is balanced by Sir Walter Blunt's pageant of 'grinning honour', his dead body 'Semblably furnish'd like the king himself' (V. iii. 21); and this transformation of the royal double into a sign of Death's authority anticipates an ending in which the Prince's own *alter ego*, Hotspur, having yielded to 'the earthy and cold hand of death', is transformed to 'dust | And food for . . . worms' (V. iv. 84–6). Like Guyot's King, the high priest of heroic distinction is consigned to 'two paces of the vilest earth' in the degrading mock-funeral that reduces him to a mere piece of shapeless 'luggage' hauled on Falstaff's back (lines 91, 156). He too has become nothing, the mere 'counterfeit' of himself, like one of the Deaths of Les Innocents, an image of his own undifferentiated absence. In such a context all Hal's graceful talk of memorializing epitaph is finally no more effectual than the funeral distinctions which Belarius magnanimously urges for Cloten in the tragical false ending of *Cymbeline*:

Though mean and mighty, rotting
Together, have one dust, yet reverence
(That angel of the world) doth make distinction

Of place 'tween high and low. Our foe was princely,
And though you took his life, as being our foe,
Yet bury him as a prince.

(*Cymbeline*, IV. ii. 246–51)

For all these gestures of 'reverence' and 'distinction', nothing will now serve to distinguish the headless Cloten even from his opposite, Posthumus—all of whose distinguishing marks he posthumously seems, in Imogen's demented gaze, to bear. If Death is the great disguiser, it is because his vizard renders all masquers alike, stripping them of what Sir Thomas Browne called 'these scenical and accidental differences between us',[77] and obliterating every sign of distinction.

In Tourneur's *The Atheist's Tragedy* the whole action turns upon the horror of such indifference, for what drives the villain, D'Amville, is the despair induced by the prospect of a mortal 'revolution' which renders 'man and beast . . . *The same*, for birth, growth, state, decay and death' (I. i. 6–7; emphasis added). In a play which projects a vision of human activity reminiscent of Donne's 'universal churchyard'—a world animated by a peculiar *danse macabre* in which 'the life and motion that the greatest persons have . . . is but as the shaking of buried bodies in their graves by an earthquake'[78]—it is entirely appropriate that the fourth act should be played out in a graveyard and its adjacent charnel. But, if the grave's collapsing of difference is the real source of its horror for the individualist D'Amville, for his pious adversary Charlemont it is a fund of consolation. With its impartial cancellation of misery and happiness, death promises him the ultimate equality of 'humble earth': this is 'The world's condition at the best . . . since to be lower than | A worm is to be higher than a king' (IV. iii. 3–22). To Charlemont, like the Basel Preacher, the charnel-house is a storehouse of improving emblems: the skull on which he leans and falls is a sign of the untrustworthiness of his the mortal condition; the death's heads on which he and Castabella compose themselves for rest are the emblematic 'pillows whereon men sleep best' (line 204); and Death himself is a companion he is happy to embrace ('Now, sweet death, | I'll bid thee welcome'; lines 180–1). For D'Amville, and the corrupt Puritan Snuffe, by contrast, the graveyard is a place of nightmare where their lecherous

[77] *Religio Medici*, 87. [78] Donne, 'Death's Duel', in *Devotions*, 171.

designs are transmuted to terrifying episodes from the *danse macabre*. Reaching to clasp the whore Soquette, Snuffe finds himself obscenely coupled with a corpse 'of the masculine gender'—as it were with his own morbid double (line 211); pursuing his attempted rape of Castabella (which makes her dream of being 'bound to the carcass of a man | For ever'; lines 170–2), D'Amville is fittingly arrested by the sight of a death's head, whose stare reminds him, in a macabre metaphor, of his affair 'with that same strumpet, Murder' (line 220).

The bizarre sexual coloration that such scenes, like the *danse macabre*, give to the encounter with death is even more pronounced in *The Revenger's Tragedy*. If Tourneur's recollections of the Dance of Death belong to a scheme that often resembles a formal dramatic lesson on the art of dying well, *The Revenger's Tragedy* makes use of macabre devices to produce something much closer to the wild spirit of the original. Vindice stages his revenge on the old Duke as if it were an episode from the Dance: in his opening soliloquy, where he stands like the Basel Preacher, moralizing on the procession of corrupt courtiers, he looks quite through the 'silk and silver' of court display and the bodily covering of 'costly three-piled flesh' to the 'hollow bones' of the Duke's immanent Death; and through his grisly puppeteering with the skull, that 'terror to fat folks' (I. i. 52, 46, 6, 45), Vindice introduces himself as 'a bone setter'—both a kind of Grim Physician, and one who 'sets bones together' (I. iii. 43–4), the bawd of Death who will subsequently contrive the adulterous coupling of the Duke with his last partner.

For the Duke this encounter proves to be nothing less than the discovery of his own Death: the 'Bony Lady' with whom he grapples in the chthonic darkness of the 'unsunned lodge | Wherein 'tis night at noon' (III. v. 120, 18–19) is the old man's mortal Other, the Death inside him animated by the unnatural, self-consuming lust of 'marrowless age [that] stuff[s] the hollow bones with damned desires' (I. i. 6); to kiss this painted skull, its lips daubed with his own corrosive poison, is to surrender to the deadly embrace of his own *Gefehrt*. Ironically enough the Duke's corpse will play an uncannily similar role for Vindice in the murderous burlesque of Act IV, scene iv. As he gazes down on the body he has dressed up in the clothes of his *alter ego* Piato, it is as if Vindice too were facing the image of his Death ('I must stand ready here to make away myself yonder'; v. i. 6); and, in the mime of self-murder that ensues, he perfectly anticipates the wickedly reflexive ironies of his arrest in the closing minutes of the play ''Tis time to die when we are ourselves our foes' (v. iii. 110).

A similarly uncanny moment announces the imminent destruction of Hector in *Troilus and Cressida* where the Trojan hero, like the horrified knight of the *Totentanz*, comes face to face with his own *Gefehrt* in the form of a 'putrefied core' (*T&C*, v. viii. 1) tricked out in sumptuous trappings like Titian's *Death in Armour* (Fig. 8). But it is in *Hamlet*, a play whose notorious doublings contribute so much to its sense of uncanny fatality, that the most suggestive of such encounters occurs.[79] Just as Laertes is assigned his *Gefehrt* in the form of the French gallant Lamord–La Mort, who tested his mettle at the fence, so Hamlet encounters his in the scene of verbal fencing with the equivocating Clown of the graveyard. The Clown is ostensibly a sexton preparing for the burial of Ophelia, but his unnerving claim to have begun his grave-digging vocation 'that very day that young Hamlet was born' (v. i. 147) identifies him as a figure of the Prince's immanent death—an immanence that is also implicit in his identification of digging as 'Adam's profession' (v. i. 31). Like the antic figures of the *danse macabre*, the Clown stands for a death that is at once personal and common. Leaning on his spade in a fashion that recalls the Sexton Death of the *danse* as well as the digging skeleton of Vesalius (Fig. 12),[80] he sings of the universal levelling of mortality. His song sardonically ventriloquizes the skulls in his cure, giving them a voice even as it strips them of identity:

But age with his stealing steps,
Hath clawed me in his clutch,
And hath shipped me into the land,
As if I had never been such.

(v. i. 71–4; emphasis added)[81]

[79] On repetition and the uncanny in *Hamlet*, see Marjorie Garber, *Shakespeare's Ghost Writers* (New York: Methuen, 1987), 124–76.

[80] In Rowlands's *A Terrible Battell* Death's weapons include 'A Spade, and pickaxe, Hourglass, and Dart', sig. E4. For Vesalius' digging skeleton, see below, Ch. 2, p. 106 and Fig. 12.

[81] According to E. R. Chamberlin, *The Black Death* (London: Jonathan Cape, n.d.), grave-diggers, hated and feared for their association with mortality, were sometimes known as 'Death' (p. iv).

8. *Death in Armour*, engraving after Titian, early sixteenth century.

Significantly the Clown's graveyard kingdom is the only space beyond the claustrophobic walls of Elsinore to which the stage gives a concrete reality, establishing it as the undifferentiating Other of the hierarchic palace world—a region where the blank remains of politician, courtier, lawyer, peasant, prince, and fool lie confused together in a 'pit of clay', a place where Alexander and Caesar become literally indistinguishable from the dirt used to stop a beer-barrel.[82]

The graveyard with its anonymous pit of clay is the play's most brutal sign of mortal ending; but it is not of course where the play itself ends. Against its skeletal images of *die Ungeschaffnen*, the last scene sets the nostalgic providentialism of Hamlet's 'divinity that *shapes* our ends'—a longing for coherent form which language and spectacle reinvigorate as aesthetic defiance. To Fortinbras the final spectacle of slaughter may resemble a triumphal banquet of death, where undifferentiating 'havoc' levels 'so many princes at a shot' (v. ii. 364–7). But, as I shall argue in later chapters, the carefully orchestrated rites of funeral closure, together with the gathering rhetorical emphasis on the memorializing power of narrative, serve to reassert the human claim to put a shape upon the confusion of death. Death is both what silences Hamlet's story, and what compels him to have it told. 'Tous mors sont d'un estat commun,' proclaimed the Fool's Death at Les Innocents, anticipating both Gertrude's complacent 'thou knowst 'tis common' and the lessons of Yorick's skull; but it is precisely this blank commonness that Hamlet's story, like Hans Hug Kluber's painting, refuses. In the Prince's repudiation of the 'common' at the very moment of his surrender to Death's arrest the play takes us as close as we ever get to the stubborn heart of his mystery. It is a gesture that he shares with other very different tragic heroes, and one that Marvell well remembered when, in the 'Horatian Ode', he wrote the epitaph not merely for a particular 'Royal Actor' but for the whole style of aristocratic dying that had characterized the 'Tragick Scaffold':

> He nothing common did or mean
> Upon that memorable scene:
> But with his keener eye

[82] Frye sees the graveyard as 'Hamlet's Imaginary Dance of Death' (*The Renaissance Hamlet*, 237–430).

The axe's edge did try;
Nor called the Gods with vulgar spite,
To vindicate his helpless right,
But bowed his comely head,
Down as upon a bed.[83]

The Triumph of Death

O proud death,
What feast is toward in thine eternal cell,
That thou so many princes at a shot
So bloodily hath strook.

(*Hamlet*, v. ii. 364–7)

The second great motif of macabre art, the Triumph of Death, proved rather more resistant than the *danse macabre* to the revisionist inscriptions of the Renaissance. It had emerged like the Dance, in the shadow of the plague with its apocalyptic threat of mass annihilation. But where the Dance of Death was from its very inception a north European motif, the Triumph seems to have originated in Italy, spreading north to become the perhaps the most widespread of all macabre motifs. In the Triumph King Death is once again presented as a remorseless leveller who spares neither young nor old, neither high nor low degree; but its admonitory celebrations of Death's assault are without the Dance's ambivalent play with hierarchy; and where the organization of the Dance as a series of individual encounters with Death concentrates upon the pathos and irony of each moment of surrender, the Triumph displays its dead as so much spoil in a wholesale assault upon the social order. What is represented here, as Philippe Ariès observes, is not 'the personal confrontation between man and death, but the collective power of death'.[84] In this, the motif reflects its origins in the apocalyptic tradition—a connection which is particularly apparent in those earlier versions where Death is explicitly the figure on a pale horse from Revelation, who, with his companions, War, Famine, and Pestilence, brings down judgement upon 'the kings

[83] Andrew Marvell, 'An Horatian Ode upon Cromwell's Return from Ireland', lines 57–64; cited from, *The Poems and Letters*, ed. H. M. Margoliouth (Oxford: Clarendon Press, 1927), 88–9.

[84] Ariès, *Hour of our Death*, 119.

of the earth, and the great men, and the rich men, and the chief captains, and the mighty men, and every bondman, and every free-man' (Rev. 6: 15). However, in the classic fifteenth- and sixteenth-century versions of the motif, shaped by the imagery of Petrarch's extremely popular *Trionfi*, the apocalyptic suggestiveness of the heaps of indiscriminate dead was modified by the transformation of Death's careering steed into a stately pageant-car. The dark monarch's progress had now become a formal triumph *all'antica* (Fig. 9): mounted in splendour, like the monarch of some Renaissance royal entry, King Death rides through the world on a magnificent parade chariot, hauled by a team of jet-black oxen over the heaps of his victims, grinding their corpses into the final anonymity of earth. In place of the original emphasis on the wildness of Death's assault, the stress is now upon the solemn, almost mechanical irresistibility of his progress.

Just as the Dance of Death murals seem both to have been derived from and to have provided a model for actual performances, so the Triumph paintings, as well as imitating the style of street pageantry, appear to have been transformed in their turn to actual pageants—as, for example, in Piero di Cosimo's Florentine Triumph of 1433:

> A huge wagon drawn by oxen rumbled along, quite black and painted over with skulls and crossbones and white crosses; upon it stood Death with his scythe, surrounded by covered graves. From time to time the procession halted, there was a dull blast of a trumpet, the graves opened, the dead arose; they were men in black clothes on which the outline of a skeleton was painted, and sat down on the edges of the graves and sang. The song began 'Dolor, pianto, e penitenzia' ('pain, lamentation, and penitence'), and further on the following verses occurred:
>
> Morti siam: come vedete:
> cosi morti vederem voi.
> fummo gia come voi sete,
> voi sarete come noi.
> (We are dead, as you see,
> Thus dead you will also be,
> We were formerly as you are,
> And you will be as we are.)
>
> Before and behind the wagon there rode men on meagre horses each with four servants in a similar mask, who bore black torches and a large black

9. *Triumph of Death*, Florentine School, late fifteenth century. Courtesy of the Pinacoteca, Siena.

flag with a skull and cross. Ten similar flags closed the procession, and thus it moved along while with tremulous voices they intoned 'Miserere'.[85]

What was imaged in shows of this kind was a species of monstrous anti-funeral—a suggestion underlined in numerous illustrations by the way in which the triumphal car is surmounted by a coffin, pall, or funerary urn. Thus Death appropriates and burlesques the very ceremonies of distinction by which society reckons to keep his levelling wildness in check.[86] This subversion of funeral decorum is made unusually explicit in a Florentine painting (Fig. 9), where Death's triumphal ride is juxtaposed with an actual funeral procession.[87]

In such images, as Philippe Ariès has stressed, the emphasis is less upon 'the equality of conditions and the necessity of death [than upon] its absurdity and perversity. The Death of the Triumphs goes straight ahead, like a blind man.'[88] This absurdity is most apparent in the mordant contradiction between the ceremonial formality of triumphal pageantry and the grotesque disorder represented by the indiscriminate piles of carrion beneath Death's wheels. It reflects the same monstrous contradiction that is figured in Thomas Dekker's description of the plague's triumphant siege of London in *The Wonderfull yeare* (1603). Here the levelling confusion of Death's assault is created by an enemy force that is itself a 'mingle-mangle', its 'main army' consisting of a rout of 'dumpish mourners, merry sextons, hungry coffin-sellers, scrubbing bearers, and nasty grave-makers . . . that are employed only (like moles) in casting up of earth and digging of trenches'.[89] The transformation of the very agents of funeral practice into the disorderly soldiery of King Death makes a powerful point about death's undoing of the social fabric. As they dig the plague pits designed to receive the cascades of nameless dead, these 'pioneers of the camp' seem to undermine the very order they are supposed to serve.

[85] Nohl, *Black Death*, 256.

[86] Ariès notes how in a number of versions Death's triumph car explicitly resembles 'the chariot from a royal funeral procession' (*Hour of our Death*, 118).

[87] The presence of the funeral, together with the prominent coat of arms on Death's chariot, may suggest that (like the Unton portrait) this painting was commissioned as a memorial; it is tempting to speculate that the deceased is among those who ride in front of Death's car.

[88] Ariès, *Hour of our Death*, 119.

[89] Dekker, *The Wonderfull yeare* (1603), in *Plague Pamphlets*, ed. Wilson, 31–2.

'This my fatal chair': Marlowe's Tamburlaine *and the Triumph of Death*

The Triumph of Death was actually staged for English theatre-goers as part of the abbreviated sequence of Petrarchan Triumphs around which Fletcher and Field built their strangely masquelike *Four Plays; or, Moral Representations in One* (*c.*1612–15), in which the didactic application of each brief allegory or fable is fixed by the pageant that follows it and from which it derives its title. Thus the third play is Fletcher's 'The Triumph of Death', and it concludes in a 'black and dismal Triumph' (Prologue, line 8) in which all those who have died in the course of its action parade across the stage, accompanied by '*four Furies with bannerets inscribed* Revenge, Murder, Lust, *and* Drunkenness, *singing*. . . . [and followed by] *a Chariot with* Death, *drawn by the Destinies*' (scene vi, 3rd interlude). This show forms no part of the abbreviated tragedy to which it is attached, however, serving only as a kind visual motto that freezes the meaning of the fable; and in general the Triumph of Death, by virtue both of its conspicuously linear design and of its apparently inflexible didacticism, lent itself less easily than the *danse macabre* to the purposes of tragedy. Whereas each episode of the *danse* constituted the agonistic climax of an implied narrative—the catastrophe, as it were, of a tragic individual struggle with death—the Triumph remained a fundamentally undramatic form, admitting no space for resistance to the undifferentiating advance of death. There was, however, one splendid exception; and it was no accident that when Dekker sought a figure to express the overwhelming and indiscriminate violence of Death in the fearful epidemic that marked the end of Elizabeth's reign, his mind should have turned to the London theatre's first authentic masterpiece, Christopher Marlowe's *Tamburlaine the Great* (1587): 'Death (. . . like a stalking *Tamberlaine*) hath pitched his tents (being nothing but a heap of winding-sheets tacked together) in the sinfully polluted suburbs; the Plague is muster-master and marshal of the field; burning Fevers, Boils, Blains, and Carbuncles, the leaders, lieutenants, sergeants, and corporals. . . . Fear and Trembling (the two catch-polls of death) arrest every one.'[90] The singular

[90] *Plague Pamphlets*, ed. Wilson, 31–2. For Tamburlaine as Death, see David Hard Zucker, *Stage and Image in the Plays of Christopher Marlowe*, Salzburg Studies in

appropriateness of Dekker's comparison lay in its witty reversal of the very figure that underlies the structure of Marlowe's two-part tragedy, whose hero systematically usurps the attitudes, heraldry, and prerogatives of King Death. In a career which exhibits all the blind, mechanical urgency that Ariès associates with the Triumph of Death, this self-proclaimed 'Scourge of God' sweeps through the world, meting out destruction like some catastrophic pestilence, his chariot-wheels rolling, like those of Death's car, over 'heaps of carcasses' (*2 Tamb.* v. i. 72), while 'Emperors and kings lie breathless at [his] feet' (*1 Tamb.* v. i. 471). 'Tread[ing] on emperors' (*1 Tamb.* IV. ii. 32), and leaving the streets of conquered cities 'strow'd with dissever'd joints of men | And wounded bodies gasping yet for life' (*1 Tamb.* v. i. 324–5), this 'general of the world', consciously clothes himself in the usurped panoply of 'imperious Death' (*1 Tamb.* v. i. 111), whom he claims to have reduced (like his other royal victims) to abject servitude ('my servant Death | Sitting in scarlet on [my horsemen's] spears' (*1 Tamb.* v. i. 116–17). Just as his 'triumphant host' is preceded by Death and the Fates as his sweating forerunners, so the symbolic colours of his tents, trappings, and banners (*1 Tamb.* v. i. 49–61) arrogantly mimic the infernal sequence of white, red, and black horses in the Apocalypse (6: 2–5),[91] suggesting (as Zabina's 'Hell, Death, Tamburlaine, Hell!' implies) that the 'fell and stout Tartarian steed[s]' of his horsemen (*1 Tamb.* v. i. 318, 332) are creatures of Tartarus and much as Tartary, following their commander as Hell follows Death in Revelation (6: 8).

With its remorselessly linear design, declamatory rhetoric, and driving verse rhythms, Marlowe's play constantly draws attention to the pageant-like nature of its action—above all through the fascinated repetition of the word 'triumph', which rises to a climax in the hero's celebrated incantation of 'ride in triumph through Persepolis' (*1 Tamb.* II. v. 50–4). The Tamburlaine who promises to 'triumph over all the world', claiming to 'hold the Fates fast

English Literature (Salzburg: University of Salzburg Press, 1972), 48. Zucker (p. 48) notes that Tamburlaine's symbolic colours are given to the darts of Death in a 16th-century plague pamphlet, where they symbolize the apocalyptic afflictions of pestilence, war, and famine. Cf. also Spinrad, *Summons of Death*, Ch. 6 *passim*.

[91] It is worth noting that the same symbolic colours also dominate the colour schemes of the Unton portrait and the Siena Triumph (Figs. 9, 25), suggesting that each is to be read as an apocalypse in little.

Le Char de Renommée.

SIx hommes bien en point & armes des principales pieces, d'vng harnoys, feruoyent de conduyre les cheuaulx, Sur le train de derriere d'icelluy char estoit posée vne Chaire subtillement vmbragée de fin or, par dessus vng Trophée ou montioye de despeuilles de guerre. Dedens ceste Chaire seoit d'ung graue geste, moderé de bonne grace, vne Dame d'incomparable beaulté, qui representoit Renommée, Elle estoit vestue d'vng surcot de drap d'or frizé sur champ d'Azur semé de perles à gros bouillons, Sa coste ou basquine de drap d'argent à grans fleurons d'or esleuez de broderie, les brasures de mesmes à grosses ronsles sur la ioincture des espaulles & à l'endroict du coulde la toille d'arget rayé bouffat parmy. Pour affut de teste elle auoit vng Rayz ou cussion

10. Pageants from the Entry of Henri II into Rouen, 1550. Both by permission of the Bibliotheque Municipale, Rouen.

(*a*) Triumph of Fame (Bibliotheque Municipale, Rouen, Norm. 112 Res. Impr., fo. 15).

(*b*) Triumph of Fortune (Bibliotheque Municipale, Rouen, MS Y 28 Gde res., 5e miniature, *Le Roi Couronne par la Fortune*).

bound in iron chains' and to turn Fortune's wheel with his own hand (*1 Tamb.* I. ii. 174–5), effortlessly appropriates the triumphal attributes of Fame and Fortune (Fig. 10); but it is the pageantry of Death above all that is suggested by the unfolding of the 'bloody spectacle' that reduces the corpses of his butchered enemies to so many 'sights of power to grace my victory' (*1 Tamb.* V. i. 341, 475).

In Part I Tamburlaine's self-identification with the universal power of King Death goes virtually unchallenged—the only serious monitory note being struck by Zenocrate's lament for Bajazeth and Zabina. Her litany mocks the most extravagant of her husband's 'sights of power' by transforming it into a familiar *memento mori*:

> Those that are proud of fickle empery
> And place their chiefest good in earthly pomp,
> Behold the Turk and his great empress!
>
> (*1 Tamb.* V. i. 354–6)

In Part II, where Marlowe capitalizes upon the powerful iconic suggestions of Tamburlaine's chariot to enhance the pageant-like effect of the action, the resemblance of his progress to a Triumph of Death becomes, if anything, even more explicit. For Theridamas, admittedly, his emperor, whose pageantry incorporates, even more elaborately than before, the iconography of Fortune, Fame, and Death, remains the supreme *triumphator*

> That treadeth Fortune underneath his feet,
> And makes the mighty god of arms his slave;
> On whom Death and the Fatal Sisters wait
> With naked swords and scarlet liveries;
> Before whom, mounted on a lion's back,
> Rhamnusia bears a helmet full of blood,
> And strows the way with brains of slaughtered men;
> By whose proud side the ugly Furies run,
> Hearkening when he shall bid them plague the world;
> Over whose zenith, clothed in windy air,
> And eagle's wings joined to her feathered breast,
> Fame hovereth, sounding of her golden trump.
>
> (*2 Tamb.* III. iv. 52–63)

And Tamburlaine's own language repeatedly evokes the scene of Death's pageant-car rumbling over the anonymous piles of the dead:

For in a field, whose superficies
Is covered with a liquid purple veil
And sprinkled with the brains of slaughtered men,
My royal chair[92] of state shall be advanced;
And he that means to place himself therein,
Must armed wade up to the chin in blood.

(2 *Tamb.* I. iii. 79–84)

Where Belus, Ninus, and great Alexander
Have rode in triumph, triumphs Tamburlaine,
Whose chariot wheels have burst th'Assyrians' bones,
Drawn with these Kings *on heaps of carcasses.*

(2 *Tamb.* V. i. 69–72; emphasis added)

All this rhetorical explicitness, however, cannot mask the frenzy with which the Scythian tyrant responds to the gathering evidence of his common mortality; nor can it disguise the increasingly ironic gap that opens between himself and Death, who now appears as Tamburlaine's rival in a one-sided contest for supremacy: 'Death, with armies of Cimmerian spirits | Gives battle 'gainst the heart of Tamburlaine!' (2 *Tamb.* V. iii. 8–9). The effect, whether or not this second play formed part of Marlowe's original scheme, is to quite alter the meaning of Part I, subordinating it to a diptych pattern in which Tamburlaine's usurpation of the panoply of Death proves to be only the prelude to his ultimate humiliation as the last and mightiest of Death's victims.[93]

This disconcerting reorientation is foreshadowed from the very beginning of the second part: its title-page highlights both the hero's 'Impassionate fury, for the death of his lady and love, fair Zenocrate' and 'the manner of his own death', while the Prologue presents the entire action as a brutal reversal of Part I, in which 'Death cuts off the progress of his pomp, | And murderous fates throws all his triumphs down' (2 *Tamb.*, Prol. 4–5). Indeed the Prologue suggests that in so far as Tamburlaine's progress maintains its triumphal aspect, it is only through its translation into an

[92] 'Chair' punningly identifies Tamburlaine's throne (*OED* 'chair' sb. *1*. 1) with his chariot (*OED* sb. 2).

[93] For a reading of Part II which also stresses the importance of Death as the concealed Antagonist, see Susan Richards, 'Marlowe's *Tamburlaine II* as a Drama of Death', *Modern Language Quarterly*, 26 (1965), 375–87. According to Richards, at the end of the play 'Death is revealed ... as a kind of Mephostophilis to Tamburlaine's Faustus—the servant who gives unlimited power only to become the master' (p. 377).

elaborate funeral rite for Zenocrate, in which his victories become pageants to rival the 'masks and stately shows' with which 'Infernal Dis' greets his conquest of Olympia (2 *Tamb.* IV. ii. 93–4):[94]

> And with how many cities' sacrifice
> He celebrated her sad funeral,
> Himself in presence shall unfold at large.
>
> (2 *Tamb.*, Prol. 7–9)

The death and funeral of Zenocrate provide the spectacular focus of Acts II and III, the first recapitulating her *memento mori* over the corpses of Bajazeth and Zabina ('I fare, my lord, as other empresses'; 2 *Tamb.* II. iv. 42 ff.), the second articulating Tamburlaine's defiance of the chthonic powers through the formal preservatives of remembrance. The funeral rites conclude in the expected fashion with the consecration of a monument to the dead Queen:[95]

> CALYPHAS. This pillar, placed in memory of her,
> Where in Arabian, Hebrew, Greek, is writ,
> *This town, being burnt by Tamburlaine the Great,*
> *Forbids the world to build it up again.*
> AMYRAS. And here this mournful streamer shall be placed
> Wrought with the Persian and Egyptian arms,
> To signify she was a princess born,
> And wife unto the Monarch of the East.
> CELEBINUS. And here this table as a register
> Of all her virtues and perfections.

[94] The death of Olympia in Act IV, which repeats Zenocrate's death and Tamburlaine's outrage in a minor key, reinforces the sense of unfolding pageant:

> THERIDAMAS. Infernal Dis is courting of my love,
> Inventing masks and stately shows for her,
> Opening the doors of his rich treasury
> To entertain this queen of chastity;
> Whose body shall be tombed with all the pomp
> The treasure of my kingdom may afford.
>
> (2 *Tamb.* IV. ii. 93–8)

Chastity, in the scheme of Petrarch's *Trionfi*, triumphed over Love, but Death triumphed over Chastity: those 'masques and stately shows' are the pageants of Death's Triumph, for which Theridamas' promised 'pomp' only provides an earthly shadow.

[95] Whilst portable tomb properties were often used in funeral scenes of this kind, the implicit stage directions here show that the twin columns and tiered façade of the *frons scenae* could be used to evoke the grander forms of triumphal monument. Cf. also my discussion of *Anthony and Cleopatra* below, Ch. 9.

TAMBURLAINE. And here the picture of Zenocrate,
To show her beauty which the world admired.

(2 *Tamb.* III. ii. 15–26)

For all its heraldic orthodoxy, however, this is a funeral without an interment; and its deferral of the promised end creates a sense of unease that is exacerbated by other details of the scene. In particular, the spectacle of the burning town recalls the promises of the Prologue and invites us to see the whole of Tamburlaine's subsequent military career as a continuation of Zenocrate's obsequies—a reading which his principal gesture of defiance, the stubborn refusal to yield up Zenocrate's corpse, ironically makes even more inescapable:

Where'er her soul be, thou shalt stay with me,
Embalmed with cassia, amber greece, and myrrh,
Not lapped in lead, but in a sheet of gold,
And till I die thou shalt not be interred.

(2 *Tamb.* II. iv. 129–32)

The installation of a hearse, containing the embalmed body of Zenocrate, as its centre-piece transforms the iconic significance of Tamburlaine's triumphal progress, making it seem more a ritual of mourning than a celebration of *virtu*.[96] In the process the colour which in Part I signalled the extreme of Tamburlaine's identification with the power of Death—

Black are his colours, black pavilion;
His spear, his shield, his horse, his armour, plumes,
And jetty feathers menace death and hell

(1 *Tamb.* IV. i. 59–61)

—becomes the sign of his helplessness in the face of Zenocrate's mortal frailty: 'Black is the beauty of the brightest day' (2 *Tamb.* II. iv. 1). Moreover, the mournful ostentation of II. iv and III. ii is tellingly juxtaposed with the brilliance of Callapine's coronation pomp in III. i, so as to emphasize the complex ironic relationship between the rites of coronation and funeral:

[96] Tamburlaine's morbid attachment to Zenocrate's hearse is less extravagant than at first appears: the melancholic Earl of Essex, commanding a Parliamentary army during the Civil War, chose 'to encumber the baggage train of his already sufficiently discouraged army with his own coffin' (Mercer, *English Art*, 245).

Enter the Kings of TREBIZON and SORIA, one bringing a sword and the other a sceptre; next NATOLIA and JERUSALEM with the imperial crown; after CALLAPINE; and, after him, other Lords [and ALMEDA]. ORCANES and JERUSALEM crown him and the others give him the sceptre.

[Enter] TAMBURLAINE with USUMCASANE, and his three sons; four bearing the hearse of ZENOCRATE, and the drums sounding a doleful march; the town burning. (2 *Tamb.* III. i, III. ii)

Zenocrate's hearse will remain to point the silent moral of Tamburlaine's increasingly frantic hubris until the last scene of the play. There it is formally incorporated in the obsequies which the dying hero orders for himself in a fashion that subtly modifies all that has gone before:

Now fetch the hearse of fair Zenocrate;
Let it be placed by this my fatal chair,
And serve as parcel of my funeral.
(2 *Tamb.* V. iii. 211–13)

Placed beside the pageant-car that is the most distinctive symbol of Tamburlaine's royal authority, the hearse reveals that 'fatal chair' for what it has always been, itself a 'parcel' of a funeral pageant that began on the very day that he was born; and with redoubled irony it simultaneously identifies the newly crowned Amyras, even as he enthrones himself upon his father's 'royal chariot of estate', as another of the helpless 'sights of power' that grace the triumph of King Death. Fittingly, it is at precisely this point that Tamburlaine yields to his grinning adversary the title he himself stole from Bajazeth, 'monarch of the earth' (*1 Tamb.* III. i. 41; 2 *Tamb.* V. iii. 217), exposing in the process the grisly pun which it always mockingly concealed.

If the ironic complexities of Marlowe's dramaturgy sometimes disguise the extent of his dependence on the hieratic simplicity of pageant-forms, this was certainly apparent to his sixteenth-century imitators, such as the author of *Soliman and Perseda* (*c.*1589–92). Another tragedy of oriental tyranny written in emulation of *Tamburlaine*, *Soliman* turns Marlowe's metaphoric play with the Triumphs of Fortune, Fame, and Death to didactic explicitness: at the end of the play, after the corpse of Soliman has been carried silently from the stage in doleful procession, there ensues a formal debate between Love, Fortune, and Death in which the latter demonstrates that 'powerfull *Death* best fitteth tragedies'. Death's orgulous litany invites the audience to respond to the entire action of the play as a concealed Triumph of Death—perhaps suggesting that the dramatist intended to round off this dramatized epilogue with an appropriate pageant procession:

> And now, to end our difference at last,
> In this last act note but the deeds of Death.
> Where is Erastus now, but in my triumph?
> Where are the murderers, but in my triumph?
> Where judge and witnesses, but in my triumph?
> Where's false Lucina, but in my triumph?
> Where's fair Perseda, but in my triumph?
>
> * * * * * *
>
> And where's great Soliman, but in my triumph?
> Their loves and fortunes ended with their lives,
> And they must wait upon the car of Death.
>
> * * * * * *
>
> Aye, now will Death, in his most haughty pride,
> Fetch his imperial car from deepest hell,
> And ride in triumph through the wicked world.
>
> (*Soliman and Perseda*, v. v. 15–26[97])

Death's pageant effectually annihilates the implicit claims of Soliman's funeral procession to bring his tragedy to a triumphal close; and the ironic pun in the first line identifies Death's Triumph not merely as writing *finis* to his debate with Love and Fame, but as signalling the end of all difference.

Tamburlaine, in which the significance of funeral pageantry is repeatedly turned awry by the iconoclastic thrust of Marlowe's imagination, might be easily be read as pushing towards a similar conclusion. Predictably, however, Marlowe's intentions prove a little harder to scrutinize. The second part draws to a close with apocalyptic rant from Amyras ('Meet heaven and earth, and here let all things end'; v. iii. 250), which is infused with a fierce sense of nature's self-consuming destructiveness: 'Earth hath spent the

[97] Quoted from *The Works of Thomas Kyd*, ed. F. S. Boas (Oxford: Oxford University Press, 1941). This tragedy has been attributed to Kyd mainly on the grounds of his inclusion of a dramatic paraphrase of *Soliman and Perseda* in his best-known play, *The Spanish Tragedy*—though the stylistic resemblances to Kyd's known work are less than decisive.

pride of all her fruit, | And heaven consumed his choicest living fire' (lines 251–2). But the pessimism of this conclusion is modified by something of the same defiance that infuses the motto on the playwright's supposed portrait: *Quod me nutrit me detruit*;[98] and *Tamburlaine* is finally no easier to accommodate to the formulaic utterances that frame its ending than *Doctor Faustus* will prove to be.

In strict theatrical terms, for example, it might be noticed that all things *do not* end with Amyras's invocation of apocalypse. For, although the original Quarto supplies no stage direction, the preceding action and dialogue make it plain that Marlowe intended to end Part II as he had ended Part I with a grand funeral procession. Just as Part I caps the coronation of Zenocrate with the 'solemn exequies' which Tamburlaine decrees for Arabia, Bajatheth, and Zabina (*1 Tamb.* v. ii. 535), so Part II sets the coronation of Amyras against the funeral which Tamburlaine has ordered for himself. The effect in each case is to create a striking histrionic oxymoron, tensely yoking together shows of celebration and mourning. The obvious difference between the two is that in Part I Tamburlaine's triumphalist rhetoric invites us to subsume the exequies of his victims among the sights of power he devises for his forthcoming 'rites of marriage' (line 536); while in Part II Amyras's lament for his father seems to purge all suggestions of 'mirth in funeral', making of his own coronation a mere prologue to the final show of mourning. But, while there is a clear contrast in the emotional balance of the two episodes, in each case the silent eloquence of the funeral procession allows a considerable margin of ironic ambivalence. Even Amyras's frenzied invocation of apocalypse, then, is significantly qualified by a display of funeral order which, as we shall see in Chapter 8, conventionally asserts both individual transcendence, and the power of the social order to resist the levelling anarchy of Death.

[98] The motto is inscribed on the supposed portrait of Marlowe in Corpus Christi College, Cambridge.

2

The Stage of Death: Tragedy and Anatomy

> Erect, valiant Republic, funerary Theaters. . . . This House we found for Death, this hall is rigid with skins forcibly removed. Here, keenly intent, we behold whatever we are inside, and that which is hidden in our bodies' *fabrica* is brought to light. This structure is the seat of the soul, this is the venerable tabernacle of the mind, this insignificant receptacle contains divinity concealed. Whatever we were we are no longer. Behold, a life's span has withered. And once the light has been extinguished, man disintegrates in putrefaction. Behold this, O citizens, and tell your Magistrates that here you can learn the ways of death and a desire to shun death.
>
> (Caspar Barlaeus, 'On the Anatomical House which can be Visited in Amsterdam', *c.*1638; Fig. 11[1])

Anatomy and Death

Through examining the evolutionary history of the *danse macabre*, I have argued, it is possible to trace the gradual adjustment of early modern society to the ravages of plague and to its attendant terror of undifferentiation—an adjustment that issued in a defiant reimagining of the human encounter with mortality. But the trauma of epidemic disease was by no means the only factor contributing to the early modern reinvention of death. Of particular importance, in educated circles at least, was the reinvigorated science of anatomy which, from the mid-sixteenth century, helped to produce an entirely new understanding of the human body and its processes of morbidity.

The bible of this revolutionary science was the magnificent *De*

[1] Quoted in Heckscher, *Rembrandt's Anatomy of Dr Nicolaas Tulp*, 114.

11(*a*). Anatomy of Dr Paaw at Leiden, engraving by Bartolomeo Dolendo after J. C. Woudanus, early seventeenth century. By permission of the Rijksmuseum, Amsterdam.

(*b*) Anatomical theatre, Leiden, engraving by Willem van Swanenburgh after J. C. Woudanus, 1610. By permission of the Academisch Historisch Museum, Leiden.

Humani Corporis Fabrica, written by the Flemish physician Andreas Vesalius (1514–64). Within half a century of the publication of Vesalius' masterpiece in 1543, the classically derived pieties that had ruled scholastic anatomy for several hundred years had been utterly displaced. Medieval practice had been so dominated by its inherited texts that anatomy lessons took the form of readings from some received authority, to which the actual dissection served only as an illustrative accompaniment performed by uninstructed menials. Vesalius, by contrast, insisted on restoring the investigative, exploratory role of dissection, which the anatomist must now perform in person. Like the macrocosm with which it was habitually analogized, the microcosmic body was to be treated as a site of discovery, with important consequences for the understanding of human biology and pathology. The central mystery exposed by the anatomist's probing knife, as the illustrations to Vesalius' text repeatedly remind us, was that of death itself.

The *Fabrica* is acknowledged as one of the founding masterpieces of modern Western medicine; but, as critics have increasingly begun to recognize, it is also a key document in the larger cultural history of its period.[2] Vesalius' own sense of the work's importance was indicated by the care he took in supervising its production. He chose Basel to publish his treatise because of the pre-eminent reputation of its printers, just as he commissioned the prestigious studio of Titian to produce the outstanding illustrations. But—like the Basel painter Hans Hug Kluber, whose restoration of the *Totentanz* included a homage to the great anatomist in the representation of the Physician's Death as an unmistakably Vesalian skeleton (Fig. 4)—Vesalius might have acknowledged a special appropriateness in the place of publication. For his career in anatomical experiment had begun, whilst he was still at student at the University of Paris, at the site of the original *Danse macabre*, the great ossuary of Les Innocents, where (with his fittingly named partner, Matteus Terminus) he had first attempted a

[2] Most notably, perhaps, Devon Hodges in her *Renaissance Fictions of Anatomy* (Amherst: University of Massachusetts Press, 1985) has shown how anatomy provided a discursive model for a wide range of Renaissance texts. For other relevant commentary see Francis Barker, *The Tremulous Private Body: Essays on Subjection* (London: Methuen, 1984); and Luke Wilson, 'William Harvey's *Prelectiones*: The Performance of the Body in the Renaissance Theatre of Anatomy', *Representations*, 17 (1987), 62–95.

complete articulation of the human skeleton;[3] and while Vesalius was often at pains to emphasize the scientific detachment of his practice, it seems inescapable that the vividly moralized context of these early studies played a significant part in shaping both the iconography and the ideological stance of the new anatomy.

In the strange epic poem with which he introduced the Vesalian body to an English literary audience, Phineas Fletcher included a figure of Death culled directly from the *danse macabre* tradition:

> No state, no age, no sex may hope to move him;
> Down falls the young, the old, the boy, and maid:
> Nor beggar can intreat, nor King reprove him;
> All are his slaves in cloth of flesh arrayed:
> The bride he snatches from the bridegroom's arms,
> And horror brings, in midst of love's alarms. . . .
> A dead man's skull supplied his helmet's place,
> A bone his club, his armour sheets of lead.[4]

It was no mere freak of a provincial imagination that led to the appearance of this piece of traditional grotesquerie in what Fletcher probably regarded as a serious contribution to the dissemination of scientific knowledge, for the *Fabrica* itself provided an impeccable precedent. Although Vesalius' text generally maintains an air of strict objectivity, the woodcut plates, whose production he closely controlled, are organized according to a clear didactic programme. The ingenious conceits of these illustrations, whose execution is generally attributed to Titian's pupil Jan Calkar, have interested literary scholars,[5] though most historians of anatomy have dismissed

[3] Years later Vesalius was to recall the 'long hours in the Cemetery of the Innocents in Paris turning over bones. . . . [when] I was gravely imperilled by the many savage dogs' (letter of 1546, cited in C. D. O'Malley, *Andreas Vesalius of Brussels, 1514–1564* (Berkeley: University of California Press, 1964), 59). According to O'Malley, Vesalius and Terminus amused themselves at Les Innocents with blindfold identification tests (p. 60), but were ultimately frustrated by the decayed condition of much of their material—as Vesalius complained in his chapter on the maceration of bones in the *De Humani Corporis Fabrica* (Basel, 1543): 'you will never find all the bones of any one body, as is the case . . . in the cemetery of the Innocents at Paris, even though you were to dig up as many piles of bones as those that afforded us such abundant supply when I first studied bones with Mattheus Terminus' (p. 333).

[4] P[hineas] F[letcher], *The Purple Island; or, The Isle of Man* (Cambridge, 1633), canto XII, stanzas xxxvii–viii.

[5] See e.g. Frye, *Renaissance Hamlet*, 220–1.

them as ornamental curiosities.[6] In plate after plate skeletons and cadavers adopt the attitudes of figures from the *memento mori* tradition—above all from the *Totentanz*. These figures (followed by their innumerable sixteenth-, seventeenth-, and eighteenth-century imitations) play the part of Death the Sexton, leaning on a spade (Fig. 12); parodying the familiar *topos* of a Young Man with a Skull, they contemplate their own mortality with wittily redundant melancholy (Fig. 13); they kneel at tombs (Fig. 14), and stare, as if appalled, at emblems of *vanitas*—blown lilies and blasted tree-stumps (Fig. 15); or, peeling back their own flesh in a postures of aristocratic narcissism, they seem to anticipate the satiric stripping of 'costly three-piled flesh' in the macabre court of *The Revenger's Tragedy* (Fig. 16). Arranged in proper sequence, moreover, they can be seen to compose a fantastic procession whose arrangement across a panoramic wilderness[7] vividly recalls the famous *Totentanz* of Basel.

The power of Vesalius' didactic programme is nowhere more impressive than in Calkar's masterpiece, the great woodcut title-page (Fig. 17*a*), whose scene of dissection corresponds to the Judgement, which forms the (implicit or explicit) climax of every *danse macabre*. Iconographically the woodcut is designed as a bold announcement of Vesalius' departure from the traditional

[6] J. B. deC. Saunders and C. D. O'Malley, for example, in their edition of *The Illustrations from the Works of Andreas Vesalius of Brussels* (Cleveland: World Publishing, 1950), despite noticing the derivation of the skeleton with a spade from the Dance of Death, regard this as a purely ornamental adaptation of the supports required to keep standing skeletons intact (p. 84); and they treat the scythe in the second version of the *Fabrica* title-page as merely 'a decorative *motif* which Vesalius himself recommends while describing the method of articulating the specimen' (p. 44). Of the standard treatments of Vesalius, only K. B. Roberts and J. D. W. Tomlinson's *The Fabric of the Body: European Traditions of Anatomical Illustration* (Oxford: Clarendon Press, 1992), makes any effort to place his illustrations in the larger context of the late medieval and Renaissance preoccupation with death. By contrast André Chastel, in *La Crise de la Renaissance* (Geneva: Skira, 1968), 146–7, emphasizes how anatomical texts were inevitably framed by a larger moral discourse that encouraged reading them as part of 'a gigantic *memento mori*'; cited in Frank Lestringant, *Mapping the Renaissance World*, trans. David Fausett (Berkeley: University of California Press, 1994), 78. The fullest treatment of the didactic iconography of such 'sacred anatomy' is in Jonathan Sawday's interesting *The Body Emblazoned: Dissection and the Human Body in Renaissance Culture* (London: Routledge, 1995).

[7] Apparently that of the Euganean Hills, just outside Padua, where Vesalius held the chair of anatomy; see T. V. N. Persaud, *Early History of Human Anatomy* (Springfield, Ill.; C. C. Thomas, 1984), 168.

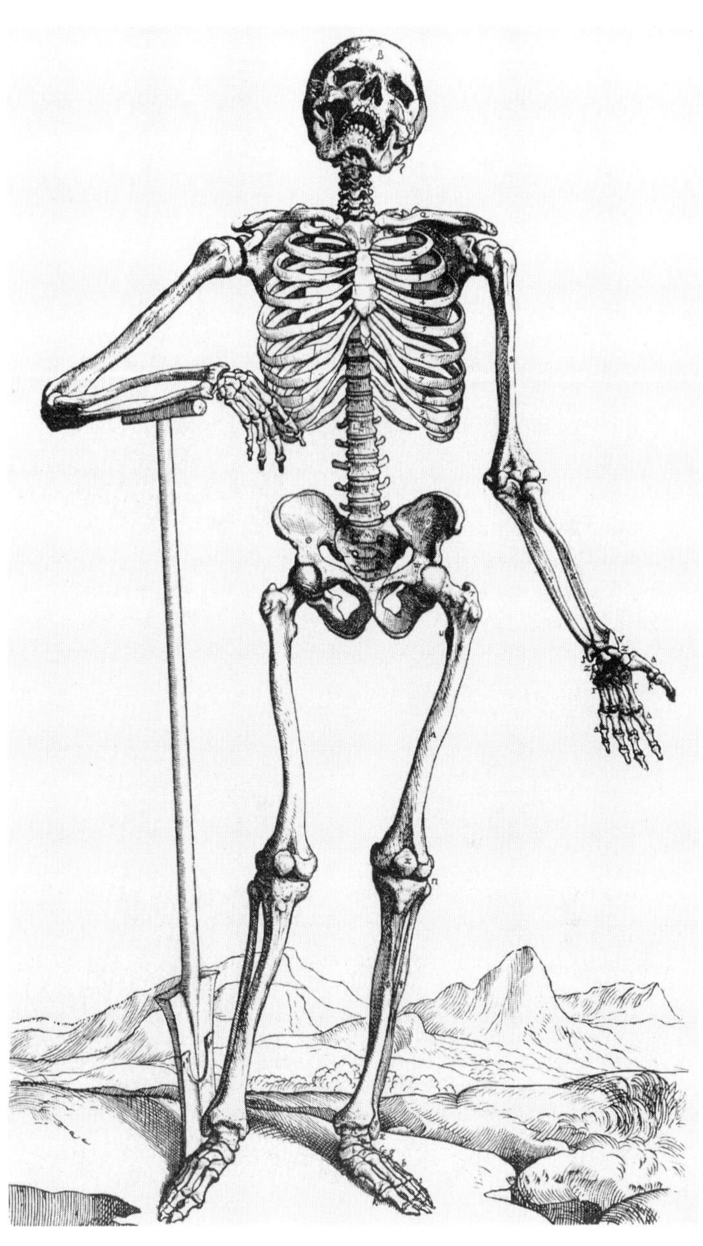

12. Skeleton with a spade, from Andreas Vesalius, *De Humani Corporis Fabrica* (Basel, 1543).

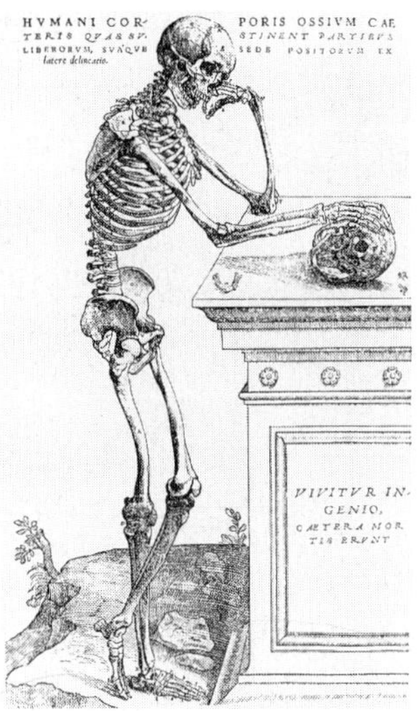

13. Skeleton contemplating a skull, from Andreas Vesalius, *De Humani Corporis Fabrica* (Basel, 1543).

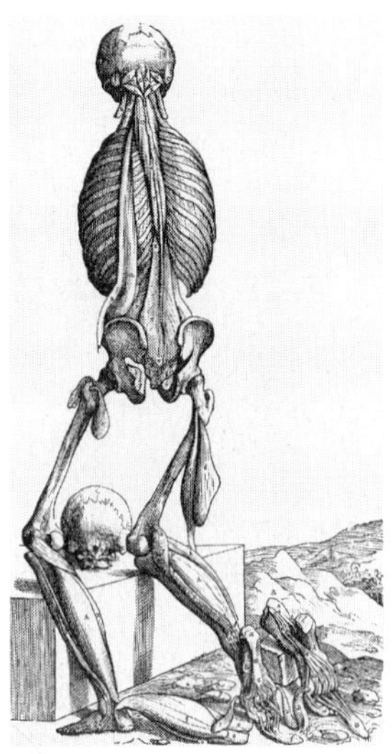

14. Cadaver kneeling at a tomb, from Andreas Vesalius, *De Humani Corporis Fabrica* (Basel, 1543).

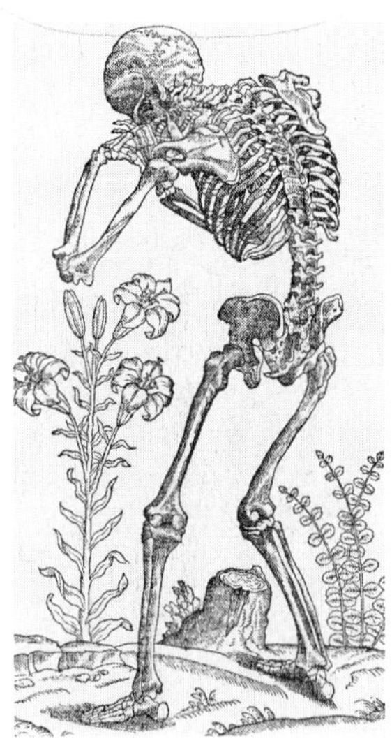

15. Skeleton contemplating a lily and a blasted tree-stump, after Vesalius, from John Banister, *The Historie of Man* (London, 1578).

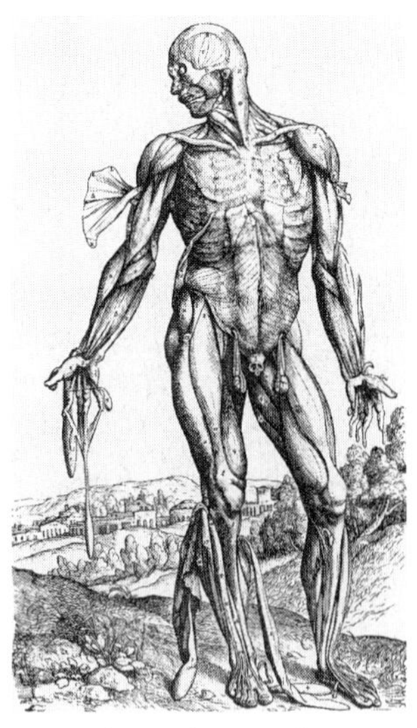

16. Cadaver, from Andreas Vesalius, *De Humani Corporis Fabrica* (Basel, 1543).

ANDREAE VESALII
BRVXELLENSIS, SCHOLAE
medicorum Patauinæ professoris, de
Humani corporis fabrica
Libri septem.

CVM CAESAREAE
Maiest. Galliarum Regis, ac Senatus Veneti gra-
tia & priuilegio, ut in diplomatis eorundem continetur.

17. Title-pages of Vesalius, *De Humani Corporis Fabrica*.

(*a*) First edition (Basel, 1543).

(*b*) Second edition (Basel, 1555).

practice of medieval anatomy lecturers, the *praelectores*, who sat enthroned above the dissection reading from their textbooks ('like jackdaws aloft in their high chair, with egregious arrogance croaking things they have never investigated', as Vesalius satirically described them),[8] whilst the routine task of opening the corpse was performed by the menials below. On the *Fabrica* title-page, by contrast, the anatomist, whose revolutionary practice required that he wield the knife himself, stands confidently in the foreground, one hand reaching into the very bowels of the corpse. But although the anatomist projects himself as the active hero of this drama, he has lost the central, controlling position occupied by his predecessors as they intoned the ancient texts *ex cathedra*. This place has been usurped by the figure at which the lecturer, in a gesture repeated by the subjects of numerous later Anatomy Lessons (Fig. 18), points with his left index finger. This rhetorical stress upon the prominence of the skeleton—added, interestingly enough, after the artist had submitted his original sketch[9]—has been glossed by anatomy historians simply as a reference to Vesalius' doctrine that 'the study of anatomy begins with the bones, to which constant reference must be made during the process of dissection'.[10] But certain details resist this reductive reading—the skeleton's unaccountably heroic scale,[11] and its seated posture, which seems to contradict Vesalius' instruction in the *Fabrica* that it should be displayed in a standing position 'supported by an iron rod'.[12]

Of course these things would scarcely have seemed anomalous to anyone schooled in the iconographic tradition by which Vesalius' own imagination was shaped. The title-page is much more than

[8] Preface to the *Fabrica*, cited in Roberts and Tomlinson, *Fabric of the Body*, 133.

[9] The sketch, together with the different versions of the woodcut, is reproduced in *Illustrations from the Works of Vesalius*.

[10] *Illustrations from the Works of Vesalius*, 42. Cf. also Harvey Cushing, *A Bio-bibliography of Andreas Vesalius* (Hamden, Conn.; Archon Books, 1962), 83. Similarly, for Thomas Laqueur 'the lordly skeleton' serves primarily to enforce Vesalius' conviction that 'the opened body is the unquestioned source of all authority' (*Making Sex: Body and Gender from the Greeks to Freud* (Cambridge, Mass.: Harvard University Press, 1992), 72). Sawday, though his reading of the details of Calkar's woodcut is often strained, is one of the few commentators to recognize its powerful *memento mori* drama (*The Body Emblazoned*, 71–2).

[11] 'The skeleton,' complains O'Malley, 'seems rather large, but whether it was that of an unusually large person, or whether the size is the fault of the artist, or a means of drawing attention to the importance of osteology is not known' (*Andreas Vesalius*, 143).

[12] Ibid. 143.

18. *The Visceral Lecture Delivered by Barber-Surgeon Master John Banister*, anon., 1581 (Glasgow University Library MS Hunter 364, v. 1. 1). By permission of Glasgow University Library, Department of Special Collections.

Thomas Laqueur's 'picture about the majestic power of science to confront, master, and represent the truths of the body'.[13] Its skeleton is enthroned in the familiar fashion of King Death, monarchizing over a crowd of mortals: on one level its presence probably serves to distance the anatomist from the theatre of degradation in which he is now actively involved, reminding the viewer that he is merely the instrument of an ineluctable judgement;[14] on another, it functions as a reminder of Death's inevitable triumph over the triumphant anatomist himself, exposing his exercise of power over the prostrate corpse as nothing other than the discovery of his own mortality. Vesalius (whose own features were later to adorn a printed 'flap anatomy'),[15] thus finds his expository gesture sardonically reinterpreted as part of a familiar *memento mori* spectacle, showing his position to be fundamentally no different from that of the figures of death who brood so absurdly on mortality in the succeeding plates—like the flayed cadaver which kneels at a skull-crowned tomb, bearing the motto, 'All splendour is dissolved by death . . .'.[16] The didactic thrust of Calkar's title-page was to become even more apparent when Vesalius had a new version prepared for the second edition of the *Fabrica* (1555). Historians have been puzzled as to why the finest of all the original woodcuts should have been displaced by this technically inferior revision; but the substitution makes perfect sense as an attempt to highlight the didactic programme of the illustrations. For here the skeleton is not only slightly more prominent than before, but his beribboned staff has been replaced by the menacing scythe of Death the Mower—an icon borrowed directly from the *memento mori* tradition (Fig. 17*b*).[17]

To anyone approaching the *Fabrica* with hindsight via the great

[13] Laqueur, *Making Sex*, 72.

[14] Jonathan Sawday ('The Fate of Marsyas: Dissecting the Renaissance Body', in Lucy Gent and Nigel Llewellyn (eds.), *Renaissance Bodies: The Human Figure in English Culture c.1550–1660* (London: Reaktion Books, 1990), 111–35) rightly stresses the need for the new anatomy to protect itself from the odium that might be invited by the dissector's collaboration in the 're-assertion . . . of sovereign power over the body of the condemned criminal' (p. 116).

[15] Roberts and Tomlinson, *Fabric of the Body*, 52. For 'flap anatomy' illustrations, see below, p. 123.

[16] The motto appears only in the version printed in the *Epitome* of the *Fabrica*; see *Illustrations from the Works of Vesalius*, p. 79.

[17] Commentators generally remark on the technical inferiority of the second version, whose minor alterations to the original include a number of apparently misunderstood details; but it is difficult to believe that the changes to the central figure (for which no explanations are usually offered) were not among Vesalius'

tradition of anatomical illustration, extending into the early nineteenth century, which it initiated, this linking of spectacles of human dissection with traditional *memento mori* and *vanitas* motifs may seem to be almost a generic given. Yet oddly enough it turns out to have been a Renaissance innovation, and one for which Vesalius himself was principally responsible. Although successive artists of the Anatomy Lesson genre, from Rembrandt and Hogarth, would reach back to fifteenth-century models such as the Justice Painting for some of their didactic detail, and although fifteenth-century representations of scholastic dissections often exhibit a strong morphological resemblance to Judgement scenes, medieval anatomy illustrations themselves bear surprisingly little trace of the moralizing treatment of the body which became routine in the sixteenth and seventeenth century.[18] There are hints of what was to come in Berengario da Carpi's *Isagoge Breves* (1523), where a skeleton, newly risen from its grave, balances a skull in either hand, and especially in Dryander's *Anatomiae . . . Corporis Humani* (1537), whose illustration of the skull shows it balanced on an hourglass, above the motto 'Inevitabile fatum'. But it was the *Fabrica* that institutionalized this way of reading the spectacle of dissection.

Vesalius and the Scene of Dissection

This didactic programme was by no means confined to the tradition of textbook illustration initiated by the *Fabrica*, however; as

reasons for producing a new version of the woodcut—especially since he specifies the scythe as a particularly suitable prop for anatomical skeletons. The evolution of the title-page through a series of sketches and drawings makes it plain that its didactic aspect became an increasingly important element in successive stages of the design; and this didacticism would become even more explicit in the designs for later anatomy texts, such as the frontispiece engraving by Cornelis Visscher in 1652 in which 'Anatomia' is represented by a winged hourglass mounted on a skull over the legend 'Memento Mori'; see A. Pfister, *Tod und Totentanze* (Basel: Henning Opperman, 1927), pl. 4 and cat. no. 1303.

The widespread incorporation of skeletons with scythes and hourglasses in anatomy theatres is a reminder of the frequent interchangeability of Death and Time, and is interestingly echoed in a mid-17th-century engraving, where Time with an hourglass and scythe presides over a scene of geographers dissecting the globe (Fig. 22). Time, after all, as Death puts it in one Jacobean poem, is only a Death awaiting anatomy—'Remove the veil of flesh and blood away, | 'Tis *Death's* true picture all the world will say'; Rowlands, *A Terrible Battell betweene . . . Time, and Death*, sig. F1.

[18] For the moralization of anatomy pictures as a 16th-century innovation, see Roberts and Tomlinson, *Fabric of the Body*, 33.

Vesalius' frontispiece suggests, it was also incorporated into the practice of anatomy itself. For the new science was at pains to exhibit its cultural prestige through the institution of elaborately mounted public lectures at which not merely medical students, but crowds of interested amateurs, could participate in the excitements of exploring the human body. The *mise-en-scène* of these events was carefully calculated to emphasize their moral sigificance. Renaissance anatomy lectures were highly self-conscious performances, whose strikingly histrionic nature has been extensively documented by William Heckscher.[19] From their inception in the late fifteenth century, public dissections were organized as festive and triumphal occasions, accompanied by processions, music, and feasting, and timed to coincide with midwinter celebration—or even occasionally with Carnival. From the mid-sixteenth century, their quasi-commercial character was emphasized by the growing practice of selling tickets to the large audiences attracted through public advertisement; and their consciously theatrical effect was enhanced by the erection, in many parts of Europe, of increasingly lavish, purpose-built amphitheatres, where two or three hundred spectators could watch the brilliantly illuminated spectacle, which typically lasted for up to five days (Figs. 11, 17, 19).[20] By the early seventeenth century a number of centres, including Padua, Bologna, Leiden, and Amsterdam, had established permanent structures of this sort, which, like London's Barber-Surgeons' Hall, became regular places of resort;[21] and in 1636 London acquired a purposebuilt theatre, designed for the Barber-Surgeons by the doyen of theatre

[19] See Heckscher, *Rembrandt's Anatomy of Dr Nicolaas Tulp*, 5–14, 24–33, 43–6. For further comment on the theatricality of anatomical demonstrations see, A. M. Lassek, *Human Dissection: Its Drama and Struggle* (Springfield, Ill.: C. C. Thomas, 1958), 71; Giovanna Ferrari, 'Public Anatomy Lessons and the Carnival in Bologna', *Past and Present*, 117 (1987), 50–107; Wilson, 'William Harvey's *Prelectiones*', 68–74; Sawday, *Body Emblazoned*, 42–3, 62, 190, 212, and 'Fate of Marsyas', 114, 131.

[20] Some, however, were even more extensive: Vesalius, when Professor of Anatomy at Padua, 'dissected the entire day for a period of three weeks' in a marathon performance 'attended not only by medical students, but by many members of the university, government officials, clergy, artists, and prominent citizens of the city'; see Persaud, *Early History of Human Anatomy*, 157.

[21] From the reign of Henry VIII the Company of Barber-Surgeons was licensed by Parliament to conduct four anatomies of criminal bodies every year, while a further annual anatomy was instituted at St Bartholomew's in 1569, where the first Reader was the subsequently notorious Queen's physician Dr Lopez (Heckscher, *Rembrandt's Anatomy of Dr Nicolaas Tulp*, 101). Regular dissections were also performed in Edinburgh, Oxford, and Cambridge; while the College of Physicians

19. Anatomy theatre designed by Inigo Jones and Isaac Ware for the Company of Barber-Surgeons, London, 1636. By permission of Worcester College, Oxford.

architecture Inigo Jones, and modelled on the famous *teatro anatomico* in Padua (Fig. 19).

Renaissance anatomy theatres had a double function. Contemporary engravings show the Leiden theatre employed by Dr Paaw as a kind of *Kunst-und-Wunderkabinett*, perhaps 'the nearest thing to a public art musueum' that its visitors would have encountered (Fig. 11*b*).[22] For most of the year such buildings served as 'devotional and moralizing museums' in which were displayed 'skeletons of man and beast, human skins, and an occasional corpse, displayed in an atmosphere calculated to remind the visitors of St Paul's ominous words that "Death is the Wages of Sin."'[23] But on the occasion of the grand public lectures, they became, in the full sense, 'theatres', show-places of the body and stages of improving spectacle, where the anatomist acted a drama of the human encounter with death. Since the primary purpose of anatomical shows was demonstrative rather than investigatory, bodies were carefully prepared beforehand to ensure the smooth unfolding of the anatomist's design, and the entire event took the form, as Heckscher demonstrates, of 'a dramatic play that in all its particulars was carefully rehearsed with a view to its public *mise-en-scène*'.[24] In the words of the Dutch poet Caspar Barlaeus, urging the city fathers of Amsterdam to erect an anatomy theatre, as a proper adjunct to pulpit and playhouse, these were 'funerary Theaters. . . . House[s] . . . ound[ed] for Death', and dedicated not to the patroness of venery, but to 'cruel *Venus Libitina*', the goddess of funerals.[25] Pre-dating the commercial playhouses of northern Europe, whose designs they resembled (Figs. 11, 19), anatomy theatres offered entertainment as well as instruction, and deserve to be recognized (as Heckscher has argued) not merely for their scientific significance but as 'important chapters in the historical development of the stage'.[26]

in London had the right to anatomize four criminal bodies a year (Sawday, *Body Emblazoned*, 56). In addition, study at the great European centres of anatomy had become commonplace for English practitioners by the late 16th century; and many other Englishmen (including players) on their travels in Europe must have become acquainted with the spectacular attractions of their anatomy theatres.

[22] Heckscher, *Rembrandt's Anatomy of Dr Nicolaas Tulp*, 98. Sawday similarly describes it as 'an architectural lesson in human mortality—a cabinet of death' (p. 73).

[23] Ibid. 98.

[24] Ibid. 5.

[25] Cited ibid. 112.

[26] Ibid. 28. He goes on to point out that '[t]he success of an anatomy, just like that of any other theatrical performance, depended largely on the size and sympathetic response of its audience. The anatomies of this type were expressly designed

A later set of verses by Barlaeus, inscribed on the gallery of the new Amsterdam anatomy theatre in 1639, reminded the audience that dissection and admonition were to be recognized as part and parcel of a single drama of death and judgement: 'Skins teach without voices. Mortal remains though in shreds warn us not to die for crimes.'[27] In the theatre of anatomy the shameful nakedness of death was violently dramatized in the progressive stripping of the corpse to expose the signs of death within. It was an important feature of this ritual that the bodies so disgracefully exposed to the prying gaze of the crowd should have been those of condemned criminals. For it was precisely the public display of all that should remain hidden which rendered this final punishment so degrading.[28] The drama of dissection extended the humiliation of the malefactor beyond execution, with an exemplary cruelty that not even prolonged exposure upon a gibbet could match, and at the same time enhanced the moral lessons of the whole theatre of punishment. 'Dead bodies', as Webster's Cardinal Monticelso reminds Vittoria in her trial scene, with thinly veiled menace

are begged at gallows,
And wrought upon by surgeons, to teach man
Wherein he is imperfect.

(*White Devil*, III. ii. 96–8)

No wonder, therefore, that Thomas Geminus in the *Anatomy* which he dedicated to Henry VIII in 1545 should have wittily joined two

to attract and to hold large numbers of onlookers. They needed financial success, also, and had therefore to depend on the support and approval of the masses no less than Shakespeare's plays in London or Vondel's in Amsterdam' (p. 28). For analogies with other forms of theatrical entertainment, including miracle plays, *intermezzi*, tableaux, royal entries, *trionfi*, academic debates, and other forms of public entertainment, see pp. 45–6, 117–21.

27 Cited ibid. 112.

28 On the punitive aspect of dissection, see Sawday, *Body Emblazoned*, ch. 4. It was this aspect of anatomy as revenge ritual that allowed Dekker to present *The Wonderfull yeare* as an anatomy of the plague (as it were, of the disgraceful corpse of Death itself): 'arm my trembling hand, that it may boldly rip up and anatomize the ulcerous body of this anthropophagized plague' (in *The Plague Pamphlets*, ed. Wilson, 28).

Significantly no particular stigma seems to have attached to private dissections, respected families being willing to surrender their dead for the anatomical investigations of Leonardo, for example (Heckscher, *Rembrandt's Anatomy of Dr Nicolaas Tulp*, 44–5).

figures from Vesalius' *Epitome* (1543) to present them as Adam and Eve, the authors of our mortal imperfection and initiators of the Dance of Death—a conceit repeated in the macabre decoration of the Leiden anatomy theatres, and perhaps echoed in the paired skeletons of Inigo Jones's London design (Figs. 11*b*, 19).[29]

A Renaissance public dissection, then, was at least as much a piece of drama, a species of didactic tragedy, as it was a scientific event;[30] and as with other kinds of tragedy, its dramatization of the human encounter with death was not confined to the simple moralization of imperfection. In the midwinter staging of these spectacles of death with their systematic degradation of the bodies of criminals, Heckscher detects an echo of the same ancient scapegoat rituals, designed to banish the threat of sin and death from an anxious community, which shaped the development of tragedy. In this reading the anatomist's performance becomes a 'triumph . . . of communal science over the egotistical ignorance of sin. The inevitable and deserved eradication of the criminal, which repeats itself year after year, makes it possible for the chief anatomist to rise vicariously, like a phoenix, from another man's ashes, as it were, to lasting fame.'[31] Even as it emphasized the abject rottenness of human flesh, the anatomy lesson, by offering to expose 'the ways of death', constituted a paradoxical demonstration of human transcendence and power that justified the anatomist's self-representation as defiant 'Triumphator'.[32] On the title-page of the *Fabrica* Vesalius' coat of arms is conspicuously imposed on the scene, above the imperious figure of Death, in a fashion that realizes the motto from another of the woodcuts, where a Hamlet-like skeleton ponders

[29] In Leiden the First Parents were represented by two skeletons, in London (according to a description published in 1708) by 'Two humane skins on the wood frames, of a man and a woman, in imitation of Adam and Eve' (cited in Sawday, *Body Emblazoned*, 76).

[30] On the public anatomy as 'theatre of cruelty' involving a 'fusion of punishment and science', see Barker, *Tremulous Private Body*, 73–4, 90.

[31] Heckscher, *Rembrandt's Anatomy of Dr Nicolaas Tulp*, 120. Revd James Townley's verses inscribed beneath Hogarth's great anatomy engraving (Fig. 20), the final plate from the Progress of Cruelty series, neatly invert this monumental moral, reducing the scene (appropriately in a version where the dominating figure of a black-capped justice stresses the iconography of final Judgement) to an unambiguous Triumph of Death: 'Behold the villain's dire disgrace! | . . . His heart expos'd to prying eyes, | To pity has no claim: | But, dreadful! from his bones shall rise, | His monument of shame.'

[32] Heckscher, *Rembrandt's Anatomy of Dr Nicolaas Tulp*, 90, 120.

over a skull, placed on a tomb inscribed with the words 'Vivitur ingenio, caetera mortis erunt'—'Genius lives on, all else is mortal' (Fig. 13).[33]

Heckscher is by no means the only commentator to have remarked upon the theatrical appearance of such events. Observing the extraordinary 'theatricality' of Vesalius' plates, the two most recent historians of anatomical illustration are reminded of the self-mutilations of Oedipus, or the tragedies of Shakespeare.[34] But it seems significant that the connection between anatomy and tragedy was first, and most provocatively, argued by a poet and dramatist, Thomas Lovell Beddoes, whose primary avocation was as an anatomist. Beddoes explored the relation between his two crafts in a remarkable letter written to his friend Thomas Forbes Kelsall in 1825. The poet was then studying as an anatomy student in Göttingen, but was already at work on his masterpiece, an overblown but oddly compelling pastiche of Jacobean tragedy entitled *Death's Jest-Book* (1829, rev. 1844). In the letter he reflects upon the relation between his medical studies and the poetic that informed his tragic experiments: 'even as a dramatist, I cannot help thinking that the study of anatomy . . . is that which is most likely to assist one in producing masterly and correct delineations of the passions: great light would be thrown on Shakespeare by the commentaries of a person so educated. The studies . . . of the dramatist and the physician are closely, almost inseparably allied; the application alone is different.'[35] Beddoes's insistence upon the essential relatedness of tragedy and 'Anatomy the grim',[36] which was to shape both his anatomical and dramatic practice over the next quarter-century, and even to condition the bizarre staging of

[33] Devon Hodges finds even in the postures of Vesalius' anatomical figures 'a sign that the heroic human subject has not been completely conquered. By the end of the 'muscle-men' series a skeleton is all that remains—yet the bones are posed to retain signs of human suffering. They function as *memento mori* rather than as medical illustrations' (*Renaissance Fictions of Anatomy*, 5).

[34] Roberts and Tomlinson, *Fabric of the Body*, 139.

[35] *The Works of Thomas Lovell Beddoes*, ed. H. W. Donner (Oxford: Clarendon Press, 1935), 609. Beddoes was clearly laying out the programme for his own masterpiece; he went on: 'it still remains for someone to exhibit the sum of his experience in mental pathology & therapeutics, not in a cold technical dead description, but a living semiotical display, a series of anthropological experiments developed for the purpose of ascertaining some important psychical principle—i.e. a tragedy'.

[36] Verse letter to Bryan Waller Procter, 7 Mar. 1826, in *Works*, 614.

his own suicide in 1849,[37] grew out of an eccentric conjunction of scientific, philosophic, and literary interests. His immersion in the arcana of Renaissance philosophy and medical lore was matched by a characteristically Romantic fascination with the 'Gothic' extravagance of Jacobean tragedy. In the work of Tourneur, Marston, Webster, Shakespeare, and their contemporaries, he discerned a peculiarly intense version of the same quest to lay bare the relation of body and soul which he himself had derived from the speculative metaphysics of Paracelsus and, above all, from the anatomical discoveries of Vesalius. For Beddoes, tragedy was the exact literary counterpart of anatomy, whose ultimate object was the triumphant uncovering, and thus (he believed) the mastery, of death itself. His own tragic practice was designed

> To rob [death], to uncypress him i'the light
> To unmask all his secrets. . . .
> To conquer him and kill. . . . you see
> Contempt grows quick from familiarity.
> I owe this wisdom to Anatomy—[38]

Beddoes might, of course, have justified his opinions by appealing to Sir Philip Sidney, for whom tragedy did indeed work like a species of moral surgery or anatomy: '[it] openeth the greatest wounds and showeth forth the ulcers that are covered with tissue'.[39] Sidney's celebrated formula was not simply a striking figurative variation on the Aristotelian idea of catharsis, for it was grounded in a perception that tragedy and anatomy, through their common preoccupation with unveiling, opening, and discovery, were not merely analytic but (in the most literal sense) apocalyptic arts; and the original force of his metaphor depended upon a potent resemblance between the staging of anatomical and dramatic performances. Consciously or not, Sidney was paraphrasing a passage from one of the most popular medical handbooks of the time, *The English Mans Treasure* (1548), by the Henrician barber-surgeon, Thomas Vicary. For Vicary, whose book includes illustrations copied from the *Fabrica*, the 'deepness of the [surgeon's]

[37] Beddoes, who opened an artery with his anatomist's knife, killed himself in Basel, near the site of the great *Totentanz* that had been demolished some forty years earlier, as if deliberately acting out his own epigraph to *Death's Jest Book*: 'Down from the Alps Paracelsus came | To dance with Death at Basel'.

[38] Ibid. 615.

[39] Sir Philip Sidney, 'An Apology for Poetry', 26.

art' was demonstrated by its capacity to probe 'grievous wounds, ulcers, and fistules, as other hid and secret diseases upon the body of man'.[40] Thus if Beddoes found his interest in Jacobean dramatic poetry resonating so profoundly with his anatomical studies, that was entirely conistent with his fascinated interest in Vesalian practice and with the mode of thinking that made the early modern anatomy lesson resemble a protracted tragic drama in a number of quite specific ways—in its suggestive mimicry of scapegoating rituals and the scene of judgement; in its fascination with the stripping away of surfaces to discover their enfolded secrets; and in its ironic exploitation of the tension between these didactic impulses and a powerful drive towards humanist triumphalism. Nor were these resemblances merely inert or one-sided; for, as we shall see, dramatists in their turn would capitalize upon them to extraordinary theatrical effect.

Anatomy and Discovery

The primary function of the practitioner's *technē* in early modern surgery, as texts like Vicary's reveal, was not curative but demonstrative. Unsurprisingly in an age when medicine was justifiably suspected of killing far more than it saved, the true power of surgery was expressed not in its uncertain interventions upon living bodies, but in its magisterial operations upon the corpses of the dead—in the progressive stripping away of layers of skin and tissue that took place in the anatomy lesson or the post-mortem inquest. The idea of the human body as a cabinet of physical secrets awaiting discovery by the surgeon's probe—spectacularly

[40] Thomas Vicary, *A Profitable Treatise of the Anatomie of mans body* (London, 1577), Epistle Dedicatory [p. vii]. Vicary's textbook was first published under this title, which was also used in the 1577 reprint issued by the Surgeons of Bart's, but it became better known as *The English Mans Treasure*—the title adopted in numerous late 16th- and 17th-century reprints, which appended a catalogue of popular remedies for various wounds and diseases to Vicary's anatomical treatise. Vicary's sense of the body as a closet of secret corruptions is paralleled in Francis Bacon's probing of 'the secrecies of [its] passages' to lay bare its myriad 'imposthumations, exulcerations, discontinuations, putrefactions, consumptions, contractions, extensions, convulsions, dislocations, obstructions, repletions, together with all the preternatural substances, as stones, carnosties, excrescences, worms, and the like' (*The Advancement of Learning*, ed. G. W. Kitchin (London: Dent, 1973), 113–4, cited in Sawday, *Body Emblazoned*, 94–5).

embodied in Vesalian 'flap anatomy'[41] illustrations which invited the viewer to peel back successive layers of a cadaver until the skeleton lay revealed in all its bareness—easily lent itself to moralizing inflexion. It became a recurrent trope of the period, and one that is crucial to understanding the peculiar relationship between tragic and anatomical performance. In his *Historie of Man* (1578), the Elizabethan surgeon and anatomist John Banister announced that 'I haue earnestly, though rudely, endeavoured to set wide open the closet door of nature's secrets, whereinto every godly artist may safely enter, to see clearly all the parts, and notable devices of nature in the body of man.'[42] Varying the trope a little, Phineas Fletcher's anatomical poem *The Purple Island; or, The Isle of Man* imagines the surface of the body as a 'veil' behind which the 'rougher frame' may 'lurk unseen'.[43] It is almost as if the body, like the discovery space which gave the Elizabethan stage its structural focus, existed to challenge the curious gaze, as if it were there *to be opened.* The mysteries it contained were not merely physiological, but moral-ontological, and psychological. In a fashion ambiguously poised between the metaphoric and the literal, the interior of the body was imagined as inscribed with the occult truths of the inner self. Thus, in the exemplary openings of the body that crowned the execution of traitors, the victim's heart would be displayed as the sign and proof of his hidden wickedness—as it is at the climax of Fletcher's 'The Triumph of Death', when the villain's 'false heart' is thrown down to the assembled court by the vindictive heroine (scene vi, lines 188–9). In much the same way a coroner's excavations could be expected to uncover autoptic evidence of repressed emotion—as they did in the celebrated case

[41] For a description of these teaching devices, in which paste-on sections of the body could be lifted to disclose successive layers of muscle-tissue, internal organs, and bones, see Roberts and Tomlinson, *Fabric of the Body*, 52.

[42] John Banister, *The Historie of Man, sucked from the sappe of the most approued Anathomistes* (London, 1578), sig. B1^{v}. Writing of Hippocrates and Galen, Banister asks: 'what secret so dainty, that they have not uncovered? yea, what mystery so covert, the door whereof they have not opened?' (sig. Bii). Banister is perhaps best known as the first English subject of a painted anatomy lesson—a genre whose popularity, extending to the 19th century, originates in the title-page woodcut that adorned Vesalius' *De Humani Corporis Fabrica.* Banister's book, despite its conservative reverence for Galen, whom Vesalius despised, begins by citing 'the words of *Vesalius*', almost as though they were holy writ (sig. C1); and Banister was unscrupulous in raiding the *Fabrica* for its own illustrations (Fig. 15).

[43] F[letcher], *The Purple Island*, canto II, stanzas vii–viii.

of Elizabeth's maid of honour Margaret Ratcliffe, whose corpse was opened before the Queen to reveal the unmistakable proofs of her broken heart.[44]

This way of imagining the body as a container of secrets was so deeply ingrained that it inflected the thinking even of so confirmed a rationalist as Vesalius. In a telling passage in the *Fabrica* Vesalius discusses the curious belief ('WELL KNOWN TO MAGICIANS AND DEVOTEES OF OCCULT PHILOSOPHY') that the human body contained a bone (the so-called *luz*, or 'Albadaran') 'similar in shape to the chickpea, which [resisting] all decay, [would remain] hidden in the ground like a seed after death, and which [would] reproduce the person at the last day of judgment'. Vesalius wrily suggests that the mysterious bone might be identified with one of the sesamoid ossicles in the foot 'which is very similar to a dried chickpea' and is indeed 'surprisingly resistant to decay'—although experiment shows that it 'can in fact be broken and burnt just like other bones'. Then, as if aware that his scorn for followers of the occult is in danger of leading him into treacherous regions of doctrine, the anatomist mockingly renounces any interest in the physics of resurrection or problematic metaphysics of body and soul:

> We shall leave the theologians to argue over the dogma which maintains that a whole person, whose wondrous fabric we are at present describing, will be propagated from such a bone; after all, it is they who lay exclusive claim to freedom of opinion and argument on the subject of resurrection and the immortality of the soul. So because of them we shall add nothing further about the miraculous occult powers of the inner ossicle of the right big toe. But we may make the point that in taking our supply of these bones from the public dissection of a thief or a paramour who has been hung we are at least doing better than the three depraved Venetian harlots who, in order to secure this bone and the heart of a young virgin boy, killed an infant, *ripped out his heart before he died* and, as they richly deserved, suffered the ultimate penalty for their crimes.[45]

[44] For a fuller version of this argument, containing detailed accounts of the execution of Sir Everard Digby and the post-mortem dissection of Margaret Ratcliffe, see my ' "What Strange Riddle's This?" Deciphering *'Tis Pity She's a Whore*', in Michael Neill (ed.) *John Ford: Critical Re-visions* (Cambridge: Cambridge University Press, 1989), 153–79.

[45] Vesalius, *De Humani Corporis Fabrica*, book 1, ch. 28. I am grateful to Dr Will Richardson of the Department of Classics at the University of Auckland, and to his collaborator, Professor John Carman of the Department of Anatomy, for

The savage irony of this anecdote registers Vesalius' disdain for superstitious anatomies which, treating the body as the physical container of metaphysical properties and powers, sought to locate these in particular organs—whether hearts or big toes. Vesalius' own dissections fill him with reverence for the complex mechanical operations of the 'wonderful fabric' that his knife patiently unpicks; but the notion that to cut out a person's heart is somehow to possess oneself of the properties traditionally invested in that organ strikes him as absurd. Yet for all his resolute materialism, Vesalius could not altogether divorce himself from the habit of mind which saw the body as a container, a site of naturally inscribed, but often occluded, meanings.[46] Indeed both the iconography of his own work and the propaganda of those who were influenced by his new anatomy make it plain that anatomy involved moral as well as biological discovery, and that this science was to be esteemed partly for its ability to lay bare truths about human beings that were to be found deep within the fabric of the body (Figs. 20, 21).

The idea of discovery is inscribed in the theatrical form of Vesalian anatomy. Where medieval dissections had been essentially static and iconic, Vesalius' is presented as dynamic and dramatic;[47] and carefully staged though it may be, what is being mimed here is not the familiar ritual of confirming authority, but a scene of revelation and discovery. In its project of opening up the hidden truths of the human fabric, anatomy self-consciously associated

providing me with the MS translation from which all my quotations are taken. Emphases are my own. Vesalius' scepticism about this 'hidden and philosophical myster[y]' is repeated in rather more pious tones by Banister: were it true, he remarks, 'the goodly martyrs, whose bodies, for the profession of Christ, have been burnt to death, shall never rise again . . . which doctrine . . . is to be shunned and detested of all true believers of Christ' (sig. M1ᵛ).

[46] Compare Sir Thomas Browne's evident anxiety about anatomy's inability to locate the seat of the soul: 'In our study of anatomy there is a mass of mysterious philosophy. . . . yet, amongst all those rare discoveries, and curious pieces I find in the fabric of man, I do not so much cóntent myself, as in that I find not, there is no organ or instrument for the rational soul; for in the brain, which we term the seat of reason, there is not any thing of moment more than I can discover in the cranny of a beast. . . . Thus we are men, and we know not how, there is something in us that can be without us, and will be after us, though it is strange that it hath no history what it was before us, nor cannot tell how it entered in us' (*Religio Medici*, 41–2).

[47] On the dynamic aspect of Vesalian anatomy, see Wilson, 'William Harvey's *Prelectiones*', 69–70.

20. *The Reward of Cruelty*, engraving by William Hogarth (third state, 1750).

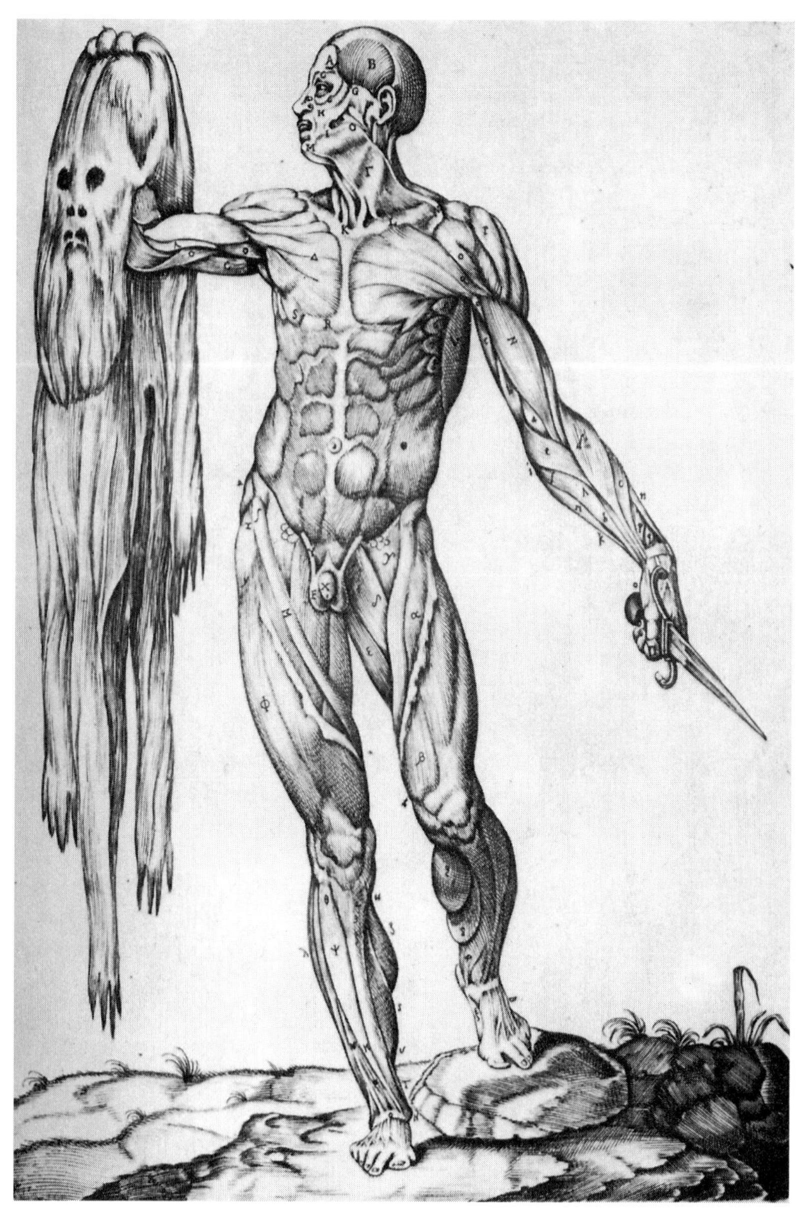

21. Muscle-man holding his own skin, copperplate engraving by Nicolas Beatrizet from Juan Valverde, *Anatomia del corpe humano* (Rome, 1560).

22. Geographers dissecting the globe, with the assistance of Time, frontispiece engraving for Olaus Rudbeck, *Atlantica* (Uppsala, 1689). By permission of the British Library.

itself with the larger discourse of discovery that found its most characteristic expression in the geographic and cartographic literature of the age. 'The frenzy of knowing', Michel de Certeau has written, in a passage that suggestively associates anatomical and geographical exploration, 'and the pleasure of looking reach into the darkest regions and unfold the interiority of bodies as surfaces laid out before our eyes.'[48] Not for nothing does Vesalius' title-page feature so prominently another of the great anatomist's aptly named associates, Columbus, who stands on the right, gesturing towards the opened body. Indeed one of Vesalius' most prominent English followers, Helkiah Crooke, using the same macrocosmic analogy that inspired Donne's 'Anatomy of the World', as well as an extraordinary seventeenth-century print, *Geographers Dissecting a Globe* (Fig. 22), would self-consciously compares his anatomical investigations to a voyage of discovery:

> In my journey, if I have not made many new discoveries; yet certainly I have sounded the depths more truly, entered farther into the continents, coasted the shores, plied up the firths, discovered the inhabitants, their qualities, tempers, regiment of life, their diet, their apparel, their employments; and in a word, I have made it easy for thee to reap the profit of men's labours, and of mine own. Yet thou must understand this but as a letter of advertisement from the coast.[49]

Asserting that 'We carry with us the wonders we seek without us; there is all Africa and her prodigies in us,' the physician Sir Thomas Browne placed medicine among the arts that enabled him to 'travel . . . in the cosmography of myself';[50] and the title of Phineas Fletcher's *The Purple Island* announces its elaboration of the same conceit in which the exotic marvels of discovery literature will be outmatched by the wonders of that 'strange, though native coast' the human body.[51] Just as the macrocosmic achievements of cosmography served to 'unlock the locks which the Ocean had closed since the flood', enabling the discoverers to pry into 'the marrow of these great and innumerable secrets, which remain to

[48] 'Ethno-graphy', in de Certeau, *The Writing of History*, trans. Tom Conley (New York: Columbia University Press, 1988), 232.

[49] Helkiah Crooke, *Mikrocosmographia: A Description of the Body of Man* (London, 1618), preface to book 13, p. 925.

[50] Browne, *Religio Medici*, 17.

[51] F[letcher], *The Purple Island*, canto 1, stanza xxxiv.

be discovered',[52] so the microcosmic science of anatomy, in John Banister's words, 'endeavoured to set wide open the closet door of nature's secrets'. Such projects for expanding the domain of human understanding were, however, always open to the charge of Faustian hubris; and just as geographers and cartographers often chose to adorn their work with deprecatory emblems of *vanitas*, admitting death as the final end of wordly discovery,[53] so the iconography favoured by anatomists presented death as the last of the body's closeted secrets: 'to peer into the body', as Jonathan Sawday puts it, 'was to undertake a journey into a corrupt world of mortality and decay . . . a voyage into the very heart of the principle of spiritual dissolution'.[54]

The work of Thomas Laqueur has shown how, on one level, the purpose of the new style of 'extravagantly public theatrical dissection' was to 'advertise . . . the conviction that the opened body was the font and touchstone of anatomical knowledge'.[55] The lessons involved, however, could never be of a purely scientific character. As with the tragic drama, in the instructional programme of such events, the informative nature of the display was almost invariably elided into the didactic. Thus for Browne, the art of dissection was as much a form of spiritual exercise as of physiological investigation: far from rendering him 'insensible of [death's] dread and horror', this 'raking into the bowels of the deceased, [together with] continual sight of Anatomies, Skeletons, or Cadaverous reliques', had materially assisted him in coming to terms with death by 'marshalling all the horrors, and contemplating the extremities thereof'.[56] In this way, as its advocates repeatedly proclaimed, it offered a path to fulfilment of the ancient Apollonian prescription, *nosce teipsum*.

No one illustrates better than Helkiah Crooke how the anatomy theatre's project of discovery overlapped with its didactic purposes; for he devotes the first book of his significantly named

[52] Las Casas, *Historia de las Indias*, and Oviedo, *Historia general y natural de las Indias*, cited in Anthony Pagden, *European Encounters with the New World* (New Haven: Yale University Press, 1993), 101, 58.

[53] See e.g. the elaborate frontispiece to Purchas, *Haklvytvs Posthumus: Purchas his Pilgrimes*.

[54] Sawday, *Body Emblazoned*, 21. Sawday stresses the recurrent analogies made between dissection and terrestrial exploration in the early modern period; see pp. 23–8, 87–9, 95, 180.

[55] Laqueur, *Making Sex*, 70.

[56] *Religio Medici*, 43.

treatise *Mikrocosmographia* (1618) to a justification of the art of dissection as a route to divine and philosophical enlightenment: citing a series of *loci classici* for the idea of self-knowledge as the ground of all wisdom, he declares that 'by the dissection of the body, and by anatomy, we shall easily attain unto this knowledge. . . . [and since the soul can only operate through the body] whosoever will attain unto the knowledge of the soul, it is necessary that he know the frame and composition of the body'.[57] But even more typical than Crooke's humanist enthusiasm, perhaps, is the moralizing tone adopted by writers like Martinus Bogdanus and Caspar Barlaeus. In his advertisement for a public dissection at Basel in 1660, Bogdanus promises to

> reveal to the sight of any of you who are curious . . . what Nature has enshrined in all of us [quae Natura in nobis omnibus occlusit]. Not out of a desire to vent malice upon the work of God but so that you may come to know yourself when you examine with eyes and ears the two palaces of the inferior sex [in sequiori sexu]. To wit the one in which you first received your soul, and the other in which the soul resides as long as you live.[58]

Similarly, for Barlaeus the anatomy theatre, never a temple of pure science, became a place where an elaborate display of traditional *memento mori* was consummated in an anatomical performance whose revelatory spectacles of 'whatever is hidden in our bodies', produced a forcible demonstration of both outward corruptibility and inward corruption: 'Whatever we were we are no longer. Behold, a life's span has withered. And once the light has been extinguished, man disintegrates in putrefaction. Behold this, O citizens, and tell your Magistrates that here you can learn the ways of death and a desire to shun death.'[59] In the laying open of the corpse they would witness a perfect emblematic display of fallen man's mortal condition:

> Here lies spread out Man and offers to all the World spectacles of his piteous state. To miserable mortals he exposes his naked limbs, and since this happens on account of the Fall of Sin, he lacks shame. Here stands

[57] Crooke, *Mikrocosmographia*, 12. The prevalence of the *nosce teipsum* trope in anatomical discourse is also observed by Sawday (*Body Emblazoned*, 110 ff.).

[58] Cited in Heckscher, *Rembrandt's Anatomy of Dr Nicolaas Tulp*, 14.

[59] Caspar Barlaeus, 'On the Anatomical House which can be Visited in Amsterdam', cited ibid. 114.

the Table, bloody like that of Thyestes. . . . Brow, finger, kidney, tongue, heart, lung, brain, bones, hand, afford a lesson to you. . . . While . . . you contemplate [this medical knowledge] in the remains of the defunct, learn it is through God that you live hale, teach this to yourself.[60]

For Barlaeus anatomy is above all an instrument of moral revelation: 'Here, keenly intent, we behold whatever we are inside, and that which is hidden in our bodies' *fabrica* is brought to light [quae latet in media fabrica luce patet].'[61]

Thus the same habits of thought which made Sidney's hidden ulcers a natural metaphor for (and sign of) the occulted moral corruption exposed by tragedy encouraged anatomists and their audiences to regard the opening of the body as a species of apocalyptic dis-covery, a baring of mortal corruption. It is no coincidence that Fletcher's *The Purple Island,* which begins with a vision of creation, should end with a literal apocalypse (in which King James figures as an angelic anatomist who 'open lays the Beast's and Dragon's shame'; canto XII, stanza lv); for the poem's structure is a symbolic reminder that the supreme type of all anatomical openings, on which their staging deliberately drew, was the terminal 'opening' of the great Judgement itself.[62] By the end of the sixteenth century, indeed, the preacher John More could invoke anatomy as a natural figure for the necessary contemplation of Last Things:

To the end therefore that the remembrance of Death drive us not to despair, but may rather comfort us in our conflicts, it will not be amiss if (according to my skill) I show you some anatomy, in which you may see (as in a glass) the original of Death, and from whence it came, what it is by nature, with the power, strength, and sting thereof; and what through Christ to the faithful.[63]

[60] Caspar Barlaeus, 'On the Anatomical Table' (1646), cited in Heckscher, *Rembrandt's Anatomy of Dr Nicolaas Tulp*, 113.

[61] 'On the Anatomical House which can be Visited in Amsterdam', cited ibid. 114.

[62] Compare John Cotta, *The Triall of Witchcraft, shewing The Trew and Right Methode of the Discovery* (London, 1616), 15, cited as an epigraph to Ch. 4 below. In Leiden, where the anatomy theatre was built in a converted chapel, the staging of the dissection as a Judgement narrative was emphasized by placing the dissection table in the position formerly occupied by the high altar (Heckscher, *Rembrandt's Anatomy of Dr Nicolaas Tulp*, 31), as well as by the prominent display of two skeletons re-enacting the Fall.

[63] John More, *A Lively Anatomie of Death*, B3^{v}.

For More, divine law is itself imagined as operating like an anatomist's knife:

> The law then convinced us of sin, and revealed our nakedness, which our fig leaves had hidden; it opened the inward man with all his concupiscence; it showed us our shame and confusion, our uglesome shape, most monstrous to behold, how we were transformed from the image of God, to the similitude of the devil. . . . how all things, both within us and without us, were corrupted. (C8–C8^{v})

More's emphasis on the 'uglesome shape' disclosed by the dissector's knife helps to explain why the sixteenth century should have made 'anatomy' a synonym for 'skeleton'—and hence for the bony figure of Death himself, the 'fell anatomy' hailed by Constance in *King John* (III. iv. 40); for what the science of dissection ultimately seemed to disclose was nothing less than the 'original of Death'—the death that is always already inside us, its presence marked by the very structure that, in Banister's words, comprises 'the body's framework' or 'foundation'.[64]

Through its impressive public displays, then, surgery, which remained so helpless in the face of the actual processes of morbidity, took care to exhibit its symbolic control over life and death. Thus the 'Godly Artist' celebrated by Banister was also *godlike* in his capacity to 'set wide open the closet door of nature's secrets'.[65] Yet, as the majestically enthroned figure of Death on the Vesalius frontispiece insists, this unlocking of the privy cabinet of human flesh produced an ambiguous apocalypse, for in its disclosure of the hidden lineaments of death, it invited the audience to witness an ironic restaging of one of the most popular episodes from the Dance of Death—the Physician's encounter with his own mortal double (Fig. 4*a*). The effect was to set up a tension between the triumphant and abject in the anatomist's performance that gave it

[64] Banister, *Historie of Man*, sigs. M1^{v}, C1; F[letcher], *Purple Island*, canto II, stanza v. Banister's section on the 'frame' is accompanied by his rough copy of Vesalius' digging skeleton (Fig. 12).

[65] The claim to godlike knowledge is even more explicitly advanced in Crooke's *Mikrocosmographia*, which argues that since man is made in the image of God, to study the human body is to study the divine (preface to book 1, pp. 1–2), and that since '*The invisible things of God* (saith the Apostle) *are knowne by those things that are visible*' (book 1, ch. 6, P. 18), dissection is a sure path to the discovery of divine wisdom.

a distinctly tragic cast, pointing up the resemblances between the two stages of death and their spectacles of discovery.

Anatomy in the Theatre

If the power of Vesalian theatres to instruct their audiences depended in large part upon their ability to exploit the histrionic potential of the anatomist's performance, London playhouses were equally able to make capital out of their physical resemblance to the scene of dissection. In *Volpone*, for example, a satire built around numerous variations on the theme of hidden mortification and discovery, the acting space is successively transformed into a mountebank-doctor's booth-stage and an arena of dissection. When Corvino proposes to strip Celia to the last nakedness that will reveal her secret whorishness, he casts himself as a new Vesalius, poring in her corpse for the signs of corruptibility, and visiting upon her the extreme desecration of a public dissection:

> I will make thee an anatomy,
> Dissect thee mine own self, and read a lecture
> Upon thee to the city, and in public.
>
> (*Volpone*, II. iii. 70–2)

Corvino's deranged fantasy, by collapsing the idea of moral uncasing into that of anatomical discovery, briefly threatens to tip this unstable comedy into a tragic register. It is the satiric counterpart of the imaginary opening of Regan's body with which, in the Quarto version of *King Lear,* Lear concludes his first judgement scene: 'Then let them anatomize Regan; see what breeds about her heart? Is there any cause in nature that make these hard hearts?' (*King Lear*, III. vi. 76–8) Devon Hodges has recognized the metonymic significance of these lines for a play which she reads as a tragic Anatomy of the World.[66] But, as the stage business traditionally associated with the scene suggests (and as Edward Bond's reworking of the play insisted),[67] it is to the literal violence

[66] Hodges, *Renaissance Fictions of Anatomy*, ch. 5, pp. 68–88.

[67] For the way in which actors habitually act out the dissection and display of Regan's heart, see Marvin Rosenberg, *The Masks of King Lear* (Berkeley: University of California Press, 1972), 72. Bond's post-holocaust *Lear* (London: Methuen, 1972) makes dissection and dismemberment one of its controlling image patterns.

of the imaginary spectacle that we are required to attend first. Not for nothing is Lear's anatomy immediately followed by the mutilation of Gloucester; not for nothing is it ushered in by the barking of 'The little dogs and all, | Blanch, Tray, and *Sweetheart*', recalling the snapping curs who waited for choice pickings from the dissection table, before themselves being offered to the scalpel (Figs. 17, 20).

In Tourneur's *Atheist's Tragedy*, the bony relics of whose graveyard scenes emblematize the true secret that awaits the anatomist's probing knife, the folly of Lear's anatomical fantasy is echoed in the maddened curiosity of D'Amville, who begs his nephew's body from the scaffold in order that he may uncover the occult source of Charlemont's outward resolution:

I would find out by his anatomy
What thing there is in Nature more exact
Than in the constitution of myself.
Methinks my parts and my dimensions are
As many, as large, as well compos'd as his,
And yet in me the resolution wants
To die with that assurance as he does.
The cause of that in his anatomy
I would find out.

(*The Atheist's Tragedy*, v. ii. 142–53)

What such moments do is to activate a pervasive anxiety about the maddening opacity of the human body, which in certain tragedies erupts in shockingly literal displays of anatomical violence. If Lear's baffled grief over the unspeaking body of the daughter whose very name, *Cor*delia, associates her with the heart—'Do you *see* this? *Look*, her lips. | *Look* there, *look* there' (v. iii. 311–12)—resonates with his imaginary excavation of Goneril's stony heart ('*see* what breeds about her heart'), it does so partly because the tragic stage plays so insistently upon its resemblance to the theatre of anatomy. Thus when, at the end of Ford's *'Tis Pity She's a Whore* Giovanni enters like some deranged anatomist to display his sister-lover's impaled heart, the extraordinary discharge of tension (so admired by Artaud[68]) is produced not merely by his literalization of one of the play's most obsessive image patterns,

[68] See Antonin Artaud, *The Theatre and its Double* (London: Calder & Boyars, 1970), 18–31.

but by the abrupt making visible of a whole set of submerged associations between tragic and anatomical performance. Addressing the assembled banqueters, Giovanni forces their horrified gaze upon Annabella's eviscerated heart:

> I came to feast, too, but I digged for food
> In a much richer mine than gold or stone
> Of any value balanced; 'tis a heart,
> A heart, my lords, in which is mine entombed.
> Look well upon't; d'ee know't?
>
> * * * * * *
>
> 'Tis Annabella's heart; 'tis; why d'ee startle?
> I vow 'tis hers; this dagger's point plowed up
> Her fruitful womb, and left to me the fame
> Of a most glorious executioner.
>
> ('*Tis Pity She's a Whore*, v. vi. 26–35)

His triumphant display makes literal the play's recurrent figuration of the body as a container of emotional secrets waiting to be 'ripped open'.[69]

In Henry Chettle's *Tragedy of Hoffman*, where the revenger's apocalypse is emblematized in the recurrent 'discovery' of an anatomically displayed skeleton, the transformation of playhouse into anatomy theatre is made even more explicit. The play opens with an extraordinary unveiling in which the hero '*strikes ope a curtain where appears a body*'.[70] These remains are quickly identified as 'his father's anatomy' stolen (as the anatomist's specimens commonly were) 'from the gallows' (I. i. 104).[71] The brows of this 'dead remembrance of my living father' (line 8) are encircled (in a deliberate echo of the iconography of King Death) with the crown that killed him. The father's 'bare bones' will hang there, now hidden, now uncovered, throughout the play, their 'nerves and arteries | In dead resoundings summon[ing] up revenge' (I. i. 3–4). The presence of the skeleton gives a strange hallucinatory life to Chettle's insistent anatomical imagery—as when Otho's death becomes a living maceration:

[69] For a more detailed analysis of this scene, see my 'What Strange Riddle's This?'.

[70] Henry Chettle, *The Tragedy of Hoffman* (Oxford: Malone Society, 1950–1), I. i. 8–10 All citations from *Hoffman* are to this edition.

[71] Vesalius' first successfully articulated skeleton, after his difficulties at Les Innocents, was secured in just this way.

OTHO[.] Death like a tyrant seizeth me unawares;
My sinews shrink like leaves parched with the sun,
My blood dissolves, nerves and tendons fail,
Each part's disjointed, and my breath expires.
(*The Tragedy of Hoffman*, I. i. 230–3)

Hoffman casts himself as a 'surgeon' seeking revenge upon the 'filthy mountebanks' whose 'incision knives' have opened his father's body, allowing them to 'thrust their dastard fingers in his flesh': 'I'll play Mercury,' he snarls, 'And like fond Marsyas flay the quacksalver' (I. iii. 390–5), duly stripping Otho's bones and hanging a second viciously crowned 'anatomy' beside his father's. But even as he dresses the stage to resemble the Barber-Surgeons' moralized theatre of dissection, the vindictive anatomist unconsciously prepares the way for a wickedly apt catastrophe in which he too will be 'outstript | In his own fashion' (V. I. 2205–6). At the end of the play Hoffman is forced to gaze 'with . . . blood-shed eyes on . . . bare bones' which have now become 'justices to punish [his own] bare bones' (V. ii. 2570–1) in a last fearful maceration:

oh wretched eyes
That have betray'd my heart; be you accurst;
And as the melting drops run from my brows,
So fall they on the strings that guide your heart
Whereby their oily heat may crack them first.
Aye so, boil on, thou foolish idle brain . . .
(V. ii. 2592–7)

In Chettle's play the carefully orchestrated sequence of unveiled 'anatomies' mimics, with increasing insistence, the grand discovery towards which the revenge action is ineluctably leading. Shakespeare allegorizes a similar discovery in the last act of *Troilus and Cressida*, where Hector tears away the 'hide' of sumptuous armour that covers his latest adversary to reveal the 'putrefied core' that is the sign of his own immanent death (*T&C* V. vi. 31; V. viii. 1);[72] and Webster's *The Duchess of Malfi* is haunted by images of grotesque anatomical disclosure. Bosola's meditation on the '[ulcerous] deformity' concealed beneath the 'outward form of man',

[72] In so far as his 'putrefied core' recalls Thersites' satire of Agamemnon as a 'botchy core' (II. i. 6), the dead Greek is clearly also a sign for the corrupted heart of the play's whole society (Trojan and Greek). The figure suggests a literalization of the pun which Samuel Purchas detected in the Latin word for body itself (see below, p. 140).

the 'rotten and dead body, [that] we delight | To hide in rich tissue' (*Malfi*, II. i. 51–67), is echoed in the mad longing to expose his own secret animality, which Ferdinand acts out in the graveyard where he 'dig[s] dead bodies up':

> One met the Duke, 'bout midnight in a lane
> Behind St Mark's church, with the leg of a man
> Upon his shoulder; and he howled fearfully,
> Said he was a wolf; only the difference
> Was, a wolf's skin was hairy on the outside,
> His on the inside; bade them take their swords,
> Rip up his flesh, and try.
>
> (*Malfi*, V. ii. 13–19)

Just as he attempts to throttle his own shadow (V. ii. 38), so it is really his own body that Ferdinand has in mind when he attacks the doctor, threatening to 'flay off his skin, to cover one of the anatomies this rogue hath set i'th'cold yonder, in Barber-Chirurgeons' Hall' (lines 76–8).

But perhaps the nearest analogue for Chettle's scene of anatomical discovery is to be found in *The Revenger's Tragedy*, a play whose whole action is constructed as an elaboration of its opening tableau, where the dramatist carefully pairs Vindice's metaphoric anatomy of the corrupt court world with his rhetorical dissection of Gloriana. The hero's imagination progressively strips his dead mistress of her 'costly three-piled flesh' to expose that 'terror to fat folks', the skull which he then advances for the contemplation of his audience. Of course the bitter music that sounds from the 'fret' of Vindice's 'abused heart-strings' is a reminder that *The Revenger's Tragedy* will be as much concerned with laying open the hero's own hidden corruption as with exposing the rottenness at the heart of the court; and what the extraordinary staging of this monologue forces us to see is a moral anatomist becoming his own Marsyas, peeling back the layers of his outward person to expose the deathly corruption within. Soliloquy here visibly constitutes a kind of self-dissection, recalling those self-demonstrating figures in anatomy textbooks who open their own bodies to display their inward operations and framework (Fig. 21).[73]

[73] In a similar vein, Sawday explores images of self-dissection as 'a literal interpretation of the searching, inward gaze recommended by philosphical self-perception' (*Body Emblazoned*, 117) and uses them as a key to Donne's poetry of self-examination.

The idea that the discourse of psychological discovery, the exploration of inwardness, constitutes a species of anatomical practice is enshrined in the title of Robert Burton's treatise *The Anatomy of Melancholy*; and it is made perfectly explicit by the greatest self-anatomizer of the age, Michel de Montaigne, in the prolonged soliloquy which he called the *Essays*: 'I wholly set forth and expose my self: it is a *skeletos*, where at first sight appear all the veins, muscles, gristles, sinews, and tendons, each several part in his due place. . . . I write not my gests, but my self and my essence.'[74] Montaigne's conceit can help to explain the subliminal connection between anatomical imagery and the obsessive soliloquizing that characterizes the Shakespearean tragedy in which, as it happens, the influence of the *Essays* is most intensely felt—*Hamlet, Prince of Denmark*. This play's remorseless interrogation of 'that within which passes show', its satiric urge to expose Denmark's 'vicious mole of nature', its searching of hidden 'imposthumes', and its obsession with 'pluck[ing] out the heart of [the] mystery' reach a climax in the closet scene where the 'daggers' that Hamlet speaks to his mother work like a surgeon's knife, piercing the 'penetrable stuff' of her heart (*Hamlet*, III. iv. 37), and peeling back the 'skin and film' to expose Gertrude's 'inmost part' as 'an ulcerous place', the source of a 'rank corruption [which], mining all within, | Infects unseen' (lines 20, 147–9). Like the spectators of an anatomy lesson, or the audience of Sidneian tragedy, the Queen is subjected to a moral spectacle that turns her eyes into her 'very soul' to reveal the taint of her own wickedness: 'And there I see such black and grained spots | As will not leave their tinct' (lines 90–1). But this whole process of moral dissection is brought to a *reductio ad absurdum* in Hamlet's anatomy lesson over Yorick's bones ('Here hung those lips that I have kiss'd I know not how oft'; V. i. 188–9). It is no coincidence that this should also be the scene which finally appears to silence the Prince's compulsion to soliloquize; for there is an exact and exacting congruence between the progressive laying open of his own *skeletos* enacted in the hero's self-flaying meditations, and the larger movement from the opening 'Who's there?' on the battlements to the mute eloquence of the skull's supremely reductive answer at the graveside.

To philosophize, the neo-Stoic orthodoxy of the Renaissance

[74] *Essays*, II. vi. 60. Cf. Meditation 9 of Donne's *Devotions*: 'I have cut up mine own *Anatomy*, dissected myself . . .'.

never tired of insisting, was to learn how to die. If Hamlet's inward delving leads quite logically to the excavations of the boneyard, that is because, in ways that Montaigne's practice illustrates, the exploration of self-consciousness was linked at a fundamental level to the early modern reinvention of death. Anatomy, I have been suggesting, provided the essential discursive link between the two. Conceived as a discipline that offered a resolutely material solution to the ancient philosophic precept *nosce teipsum*, it provided an age without a well-developed language of interiority with indispensable metaphors for thinking about the mysterious spaces of the inner self; but because early modern anatomy could never entirely detach itself from the traditional Christian obsession with the hidden corruptions of the flesh, these metaphors were inevitably coloured by the didactic bias of the discipline itself. Thus when Samuel Purchas comes to inspect the human microcosm, he does so through a moralized 'anatomy' that reveals the body, though designed as 'the house or tabernacle of the diviner spirit'[75] to be no better than, '[as] the Greeks call it . . . a sepulchre', its true nature punningly disclosed in its Latin name *cor-pus*: 'is not COR the first syllable, as the heart, life, excellency of our first estate, fallen away in man's Fall, and now as before was said, we are . . . only PUS, the last syllable . . . nothing but *vulnus & livor, & plaga tumens: no soundness in it, wounds and bruises, and putrefying sores*' (pp. 141–2). To search within, to scrutinize one's 'essence', was inevitably to encounter the admonitory signs of corruption and death, or the mocking presence of Montaigne's *skeletos*.

In the next two chapters I shall be examining a pair of tragedies whose preoccupation with opening up the mysterious spaces of the inner self, though less expressly coloured by the images of the anatomy theatre, would be almost unimaginable without the discursive shift that this new science had produced. In each case the process of self-discovery leads ineluctably to the discovery of death.

[75] *Mikrocosmus*, 18.

3
Opening the Moor: Death and Discovery in *Othello*

Anatomy is that branch of learning which teaches . . . through ocular inspection and dissection.

(William Harvey, *Prelectiones*[1])

For now is nothing hid,
Of what fear did restrain.
No secret closely done,
But now is uttered.
The text is made most plain
That flattery gloz'd upon,
The bed of sin reveal'd.
And all the luxury that shame would have conceal'd.
The scene is broken down,
And all uncov'red lies,
The purple actors known
Scarce men, whom men despise.

(Samuel Daniel, *The Tragedy of Cleopatra*, Chorus 1)

Truly to know [a man] we must look into his inward part, his privy chamber. . . . If we will know man we must . . . [take] him in all senses, beholding him with all visages, feeling his pulse, sounding him to the quick, entering into him with a candle and a snuffer, searching and creeping into every hole, corner, turning, closet, and secret place, and not without cause. For this is the most subtle and hypocritical, covert and counterfeit of all the rest, and almost not to be known.

(Pierre Charron, *Of Wisedome*[2])

[1] In *The Anatomical Lectures of William Harvey*, trans. Gweneth Whitteridge (Edinburgh: E. and S. Livingston for the Royal College of Physicians, 1964), 1.
[2] pp. 6–7.

'Show me thy thought'

Near the beginning of the great temptation scene which determines the course of his tragedy Othello makes an extraordinary, impossible demand of Iago: 'If thou dost love me, | Show me thy thought' (III. iii. 115–16). Not 'tell' or 'confess', but 'show'—as if thought were (like the handkerchief, which comes to stand for all that is hidden from Othello's frantic gaze) a substantial thing, something that might be displayed and offered for inspection.[3] In the subdued pun which Iago's own habitual language makes unavoidable, it is like some precious commodity, hidden in the 'purse' of Iago's contracted brow (line 113), or like a living creature with an obscene life of its own, 'some monster . . . too hideous to be shown' (lines 107–8). Through nearly fifty lines of teasing evasion from Iago, the Moor will keep rephrasing his demand: 'I prithee speak to me as to thy thinkings . . . give thy worst of thoughts | The worst words. . . . Thou dost conspire against thy friend . . . and mak'st his ear | A stranger to thy thoughts . . . By heaven, I'll know thy thoughts' (lines 131–62). The language here, reflecting the effort of rationality, is more conventional; but Iago's flat denial, when it finally comes, quite deliberately reinstates the desperate materialism of the original demand: 'You cannot, *if my heart were in your hand*' (line 163; emphasis added).

In Iago's imaginary scene of evisceration, Othello is cast in the role of baffled anatomist, delving in the ensign's body for the core of secrets which he supposes to be contained there. The jibe is cruelly effective because this is exactly how Othello, under Iago's tutelage, has begun to think: the 'monster' of Iago's 'horrible conceit' is terrifyingly substantial to him. Shortly he will begin to imagine his own inner world in similarly hideous terms, as Iago discloses to him the seeming presence of the monster's anthropophagous double lurking in the recesses of his own mind:

> O, beware, my lord, of jealousy
> It is the green-eyed monster which doth mock
> The meat it feeds on. (lines 164–6)

[3] Emilia will employ the same idiom in IV. ii: '*Remove your thought*; it doth abuse your bosom. | If any wretch hath *put this in your head*, | Let heaven requite it' (lines 14–16; emphases added).

The whole dynamic of the temptation scene depends on this carefully engineered reversal, which turns back upon Othello the scopic longing aroused in him by Iago's self-presentation as a man with something to hide. The effect is to foster in the Moor the horrifying sense that it is his own secret self that is being opened to the scandal of public view. The 'palace whereinto foul things | Sometimes intrude' (lines 137–8) is ostensibly Iago's own bosom; but, as the ensign's teasing enquiry ('Who has that breast so pure . . . ?' lines 138–41) already insinuates, it will presently be exposed as the polluted castle of Othello's inner self—whose fabric includes the dank 'dungeon' and foul 'cistern' of his corrupted sexual imaginings (III. iii. 271; IV. ii. 61).[4]

The preoccupation of the temptation scene with interpreting what Othello, in a telling oxymoron, calls '*close dilations* working from the heart' (III. iii. 123)—enigmatic physiological signs through which occulted interior motives are exposed to view[5]—is exceptionally intense, but by no means exceptional; for no play in the canon is more obsessively concerned than *Othello* with the idea of laying open. Indeed, as I have argued elsewhere, the peculiarly uncomfortable effect of this tragedy depends upon its power to arouse in the audience a diseased fascination with a hidden scene of 'unnatural' coupling—a fascination that is ultimately rewarded in the most shocking fashion by the theatrical 'discoveries' of the murder scene with its overwhelming focus on Desdemona's violated bed.[6]

[4] Anatomical texts habitually make use of the familiar medieval figuration of the body as a palace or castle of the soul: thus, for example, Helkiah Crooke urges 'princes and peasants' alike to learn from the organization and government of the body, noting in particular how the 'the milt and the reins do purge and cleanse the princely palace, & thrust, as it were, out of the kitchen, down the sink, all the filth and garbage' (*Mikrocosmographia*, 13); and see below, Ch. 4.

[5] For some brilliantly suggestive discussion of the motif of hiddenness and opening–unfolding in the play, see the series of essays by Patricia Parker, '"Dilation" and "Delation" in *Othello*', in Patricia Parker and Geoffrey Hartmann (eds.), *Shakespeare and the Question of Theory* (New York: Methuen, 1985), 54–74; 'Fantasies of "Race" and "Gender": Africa, Othello, and Bringing to Light', in Margo Hendricks and Patricia Parker (eds.), *Women, 'Race', and Writing in the Early Modern Period* (London: Routledge, 1994), 84–100; and '*Othello* and *Hamlet*: Spying, Discovery, Secret Faults', ch. 7 of her *Shakespeare from the Margins: Language, Culture, Context* (Chicago: University of Chicago Press, 1996). Parker's approach to the discourses of anatomy and discovery in Othello, though strongly inflected by her interest in gender, has a number of parallels with my own.

[6] See Michael Neill, '"Unproper Beds": Race, Adultery and the Hideous in *Othello*', *Shakespeare Quarterly*, 40 (1989), 383–412.

Closely associated with this gathering pressure for physical disclosure, and prefiguring its inevitable catastrophe, is the pressure for psychological unveiling created by Iago, and progressively gratified by his ruthless opening out of Othello's inner world. These two processes are not merely paralleled, but entangled in such a way as to force Othello to experience the one as the objective form of the other, so that to recognize the handkerchief's occult demonstration of adultery is to witness the 'ocular proof' of his own secret monstrosity. Like Banister's 'closet door of nature's secrets', Iago's promised 'door of truth' (III. iii. 407) will be as much a door into the dark of Othello's inner world as a port of discovery for the occluded scene of adultery.

Through his patient excavation of the 'encaved' Othello, Iago presents himself as the true anatomist of the play, offering to the shame of public exhibition precisely those regions of Othello's person that (like Hamlet) he delights in insisting are inaccessible in himself:

For when my outward action doth demonstrate
The native act and figure of my heart
In complement extern, 'tis not long after
But I will wear my heart upon my sleeve
For daws to peck at. (I. i. 61–5)

Iago's mocking response to the demand that he 'show' his thought makes plain how Othello's desire repeats the anatomical folly of a D'Amville, baring the Moor himself to a curiosity about others that nothing can ever allay. In the process it also exposes him to an alienated self-inquisition that will prove even more tormenting. The monstrous array of 'bloody thoughts' that Othello discovers, or imagines he discovers, inside himself may be nothing more than what Iago's anatomy lesson has taught him to recognize, but it will take the radical surgery of the final scene (the very incision that he cannot bear to make upon Desdemona's immaculate body, for fear of what he might find) to excise it.[7] Ironically, however,

[7] For a reading of *Othello* which treats the play's anatomical tropes as part of a gendered discourse specifically aimed at opening up the secret space of female interiority, see Howard Marchitello, 'Vesalius's *Fabrica* and Shakespeare's *Othello*: Anatomy, Gender, and the Narrative Production of Meaning', *Criticism*, 34 (1993), 529–58.

it is this very cut which leaves Othello's corpse (for all his rhetorical attempts to dress himself again in the glamour of deeds and gestures) mercilessly open to the gaze of Venetian onlookers, who recoil from it as they might from the spectacle of 'disgrace' upon an anatomist's table: 'the object poisons sight, | Let it be hid' (v. ii. 364–5). They have seen too much.

Othello's Darkness

As Iago presents his systematic opening of Othello—and as it is often read—he does no more than expose the barbarous Moor concealed beneath the 'civil' forms and manners of Venetian general, ensuring that this 'erring stranger' cannot (in the significant phrase of one sixteenth-century traveller) 'conceal [his] Moorish nature'.[8] Professing to lay open the exotic person of Othello to a 'discovery' or 'view' like those announced in the tract-literature of early empire—as though the Moor were alien territory to be subjected to the colonizer's all-mastering optic—Iago seeks to persuade not merely the audience, but Othello himself, of the accuracy of his revelations: like any colonizing project, that is to say, his will involve inducting the colonized into the colonizer's discourse.

The question what precisely constituted the 'nature' of foreign peoples was, of course, a fiercely contested one at a time when the modern ideology of 'race' was only beginning to be hammered out on the anvil of European empire.[9] But in a play so concerned with the problematic relation of exterior signs to inward realities, it is inevitable that the markers of racial difference should come under particularly fierce scrutiny. Capitalizing on the ancient prejudices associating blackness with evil and death, Iago sets out to demonstrate that the tokens of malign otherness inscribed on the Moor's 'visage' correspond to the inward truths exposed by his anatomical method.

[8] *John Huighen Van Linschoten his Discours of Voyages into yᵉ Easte and West Indies* (London, 1598), 156. The phrase occurs in the course of an anecdote that constitutes an odd mirror-image of *Othello*—in it an adulterous Goanese mestizo and her Moorish mother contrive to murder the mestizo's innocent husband in his bed.

[9] For discussion of the extensive literature on race in *Othello* see my 'Unproper Beds', 391–5 , and Emily Bartels, 'Making More of the Moor: Aaron, Othello, and Renaissance Refashionings of Race', *Shakespeare Quarterly*, 41 (1990), 432–54.

'Can the black Moor change his skin? or the leopard his spots?' demands the prophet Jeremiah, '*Then* may ye also do good, that are accustomed to do evil.'[10] In the biblical text colour has a complex analogical function: in the first instance it simply stands for that which cannot be changed: the indelibility of the Moor's skin matches the indelibility of Judah's sin. But, by implication at least, his colour—like the spots that blemish the leopard's coat[11]—also resembles the sin itself, since it is not merely an aspect of his physical constitution, but a manifestation of the curse placed on the adulterate offspring of Ham. It is the proper sign, that is to say, of his essential nature, the visible expression of an inward depravity, something that naturally corresponds to the darkness of the inner self.[12] This helps to explain the paradox whereby hidden vice is analogized to a highly conspicuous outward attribute—as the context makes plain, it is a way of expressing the fearful visibility of secret wickedness to the jealous eye of God: 'For the greatness of thine iniquity are thy skirts discovered, and thy heels made bare. . . . because thou hast forgotten me, and trusted in falsehood. Therefore will I discover thy skirts upon thy face, that thy shame may appear. I have seen thy adulteries, thy neighings, the lewdness of thy whoredom, and thine abominations . . . Woe unto thee, O Jerusalem! wilt thou not be made clean? when shall it once be?' (Jer. 13: 22, 25–7). The whole passage is a reminder

[10] Jer. 13: 23 (Geneva Bible). Interestingly, this same passage is paraphrased by Gertrude at the climax of Hamlet's moral anatomy lesson in the closet scene: 'Thou turn'st my eyes into my very soul, | And there I see such black and grained spots | As will not leave their tinct' (*Hamlet*, III. iv. 90–2).

[11] In the bestiary tradition a leopard's spots were the mark of its adulterate nature as the offspring of 'the adultery of a lioness with a pard'; see *The Book of Beasts*, trans. and ed. T. H. White (London: Jonathan Cape, 1954), 13–14.

[12] According to a widely circulated explanation for the existence of black peoples (available in both Leo Africanus and Hakluyt), blackness was originally visited upon the offspring of Noah's son Ham, or 'Cham', as a punishment for the adulterate disobedience of his father. Flouting his father's taboo upon copulation in the Ark, Cham, in the hope of producing an heir to all the dominions of the earth, 'used company with his wife. . . . for the which wicked and detestable fact, as an example for contempt of Almighty God and disobedience of parents, God would a son should be born whose name was Chus, who, not only itself but all his posterity after him, should be so black and loathsome, that it might remain a spectacle of disobedience to all the world. And of this black and cursed Chus came all these black Moors which are in Africa' (George Best, in Richard Hakluyt, *The Principal Navigations, Voyages, Traffiques and Discoveries of the English Nation*, ed. Walter Raleigh (Glasgow: J. MacLehose, 1903–5), vii. 264.

of how discovery (as both founding myth of Genesis and the closing vision of Revelation insist) is inseparable from judgement, punishment, and death. In Jeremiah the black Moor's skin is shown as a mark of disclosure: making apparent his hereditary sin and the punitive sentence to which he is subject, it speaks of death and apocalypse. It is perhaps for this reason that in the iconography of early modern maps, as John Gillies has observed, 'Africans seem to be interchangeable with skulls'—a tradition apparently echoed in the 'carrion Death' discovered by the tawny Prince of Morocco in Portia's courtship trial (*Merchant of Venice*, II. vii. 63).[13] The medieval identification of Death as 'der schwarze Mann' seems to have been reinforced, as William Engel has pointed out, by a sixteenth-century habit of punning on Moors–Mors.[14]

But blackness is not only the apparent sign of sin and death—'the badge of hell, | The hue of dungeons, and the [?shroud] of night', as Navarre has it (*Love's Labour's Lost*, IV. iii. 250–1); by virtue of its seeming opacity, it can also, as Jeremiah suggests, stand for a vicious hiddenness—as, for example, when Aaron the Moor in *Titus Andronicus* mockingly proclaims its superiority to the 'treacherous hue' of white skin 'that will betray with blushing | The close enacts and counsels of thy heart' (IV. ii. 117–18). Thus blackness proves to be oddly like death, a disfiguring exposure so absolute that it becomes a 'great disguiser'.

The heart of Iago's project is to teach Othello and the audience with him to 'read' his blackness in just this fashion. Othello must learn to recognize it not merely as the badge of his own damnable savagery, but as the analogical proof of Desdemona's hidden (but now, to *his* jealous eye, shockingly visible) adultery:

> Her name, that was as fresh
> As Dian's visage, is now begrim'd and black
> As mine own face. (III. iii. 386–8)

The audience, too, must be tempted into identifying it as the sign of Othello's inherent corruption, the secret viciousness beneath his noble Venetian persona—so that the path from the oxymoronic 'noble Moor' and 'Moor of Venice' to the vicious tautology of

[13] John Gillies, *Shakespeare and the Geography of Difference* (Cambridge: Cambridge University Press, 1994), 161. For further discussion and a useful selection of maps illustrating this practice, see Engel, *Mapping Mortality*, 151–8.

[14] Engel, *Mapping Mortality*, 72.

'blacker devil' and 'dull Moor'[15] seems natural and inevitable. The long and unpleasant history of interpretations which see *Othello* as the study of a man reverting to innate barbarity is a proof of how well Iago succeeds.[16]

Yet (as the history of its critical reception also shows) the play itself will not rest content with such gross explanations; for it keeps suggesting—not least by the way in which Othello progressively begins to speak Iago's language—that the entire revelation may amount no more than a horrible conjuring-trick; that what Iago (along with his collaborators in the audience) discovers 'inside' Othello is only what he himself has put there, a tautologous demonstration of what his audience, like the Venetians, have always expected to find ('what you know, you know', v. ii. 303)—that it amounts, indeed, to nothing more than what Othello (with unwitting perspicuity) calls a 'horrible *conceit*'. The word 'conceit', with its subtle play on two sense of 'conceive', sends us back to Iago's speech the end of Act I, reminding us that the 'monster' shut up in his thought is in effect the same creature whose 'monstrous birth' is envisaged in that first soliloquy, where Iago represents the invention of his plot against the Moor as an obscene engendering (I. iii. 403–4). At the same time, the lurid chiaroscuro of that speech, resonating as it does with the play's racial imagery, is part of a linguistic pattern that actually prepares us to accept the horrible substitution by which Iago's 'conception' will appear to be brought 'to the world's light' from out of Othello's dark interior.[17]

In this fashion the play keeps forcing the audience to ask questions about the 'real' Othello hidden 'beneath' the unruffled magniloquence of the first two acts. The questions remain, of course, fundamentally undecidable—not so much because they imply a

[15] The quibble on two familiar senses of 'dull' ('stupid', and 'not bright, obscure, gloomy'—i.e. 'dark') is complicated by a secondary quibble on Latin *mōrus* (= stupid—from Greek *moros*) and the unrelated medieval Latin *mōrus* (= Moor—from Greek *mairos* = Moor, via Latin *mauros;* cf. also Gk. *mauros* = black). It seems probable that this constellation of words made its own subterranean contribution to European racial prejudice.

[16] For a useful historiography of *Othello* criticism, see Julie Hankey's intro. to *Plays in Performance: Othello* (Bristol: Bristol Classical Press, 1987), 1–121.

[17] For further discussion of how the figures of pregnancy and birth operate in the play's unsettling displacements of gender roles, see my 'Changing Places in *Othello*', *Shakespeare Survey*, 37 (1984), 115–31.

psychological essentialism that Shakespeare and his contemporaries were well capable of questioning,[18] but because the play itself refuses any good grounds for an answer. In the process it may even exploit the audience's suppressed awareness that 'behind' a character's words, 'within' the actor's personation, there is, after all, nothing at all. Yet that, of course, is not sufficient to cancel the naggingly intrusive power of such questions. To the contrary, it only increases the audience's frustration, cranking up their desire to 'know' until the very last moments of the play, when the entire enigma can seem to be concentrated in a single, intensely perplexed verb:

> Then must you speak . . .
> Of one not easily jealous, but being *wrought*,
> Perplexed in the extreme.
>
> (v. ii. 343–6; emphasis added)

The fierce stressing of 'wrought' here draws attention to its alternative meanings: either 'worked upon', 'worked up', or 'fashioned'. What does it mean to be 'wrought' as Othello has been? Does the play mean to suggest that Iago has done no more than work upon the Moor's *inherent* savagery? Or is the 'dull Moor' of the final scene to be understood as a creature of Iago's perverted fashioning?

Such uncertainty is possible partly because, of all Shakespeare's tragic heroes, none is more absolutely and confidently externalized than Othello for the first two and a half acts. We are never allowed the illusion of seeing into him; and this impression of opacity, through its contrast with the brooding interiority of Iago, comes to seem part of his strangeness, even of his exotic magnificence. Othello appears to know himself—and we are allowed to apprehend him—entirely as a 'person' in the seventeenth-century sense of that word, as one defined by his actions, his outward attributes, and his office. Indeed it is as if he *had* no inner self to disturb the impeccably performed surface. It is almost impossible

[18] For accounts of early modern notions of subjectivity which perhaps overstress the anti-essentialist tendency apparent in the sceptical writings of Montaigne, Burton, and others, see Jonathan Dollimore, *Radical Tragedy* (Brighton: Harvester, 1983), and Catherine Belsey, *The Subject of Tragedy: Identity and Difference in Renaissance Drama* (London: Methuen, 1985).

to imagine such a man in soliloquy: what would he have to say? Desdemona may boast of seeing 'Othello's visage in his mind' (I. iii. 252); but, narrowly inspected, her phrase has a kind of paradoxical obscurity that is oddly reminiscent of Iago's notorious obliquities—as though *even* in Othello's mind 'visage' were all there were to be seen.

'Visage', of course, is precisely the kind of surface that Iago teaches us to mistrust. In a first scene that is almost paranoically obsessed with questions of 'face' (in several senses), Iago has spoken contemptuously of 'visages of duty' (I. i. 50); and his entire proceeding is concerned with opening up the gap between the face of 'outward action' and the 'native act' behind it. What maddens him about Othello is the apparent seamlessness of the surface he presents: the sense that in him there is nothing hidden and nothing to hide: 'The Moor is of a free and open nature' (I. iii. 399). To be 'open' in this way is not only to be beyond opening; it is also to be incapable of imagining the closedness of others, and so to '[think] men honest that but seem so' (line 400). Such ingenuous openness is insufferable to Iago because, by the envious dialectic that governs his construction of the world, it at once defines and insults his own closed-off secrecy. The whole point of Iago's anatomical 'opening' of Othello will be to unpick the seamless fabric of his person and thereby to 'show' the 'erring barbarian' hidden in the 'civil' Moor.

But to open Othello to the world, Iago will first have to open the Moor to himself—forcing him to discover what John Cotta called the 'seminar[y] . . . of corruption and putrefaction . . . hidden in the body'.[19] To do this he must hollow him out and make him empty. Desdemona is the instrument he unerringly chooses. By persuading Othello that 'She's gone' (III. iii. 267) Iago exposes him to a sudden sense of desolating lack at the very centre of his being, deep inside himself 'where I have garner'd up my heart' (IV. ii. 57). Around this unfamiliar absence, the 'hollow hell [or "cell"]' in which vengeance lurks (III. iii. 447),[20] Othello will strive to close himself.

[19] Cotta, *The Triall of Witchcraft*, 15.

[20] The differences between the Quarto and Folio texts of *Othello* appear to represent a process of significant authorial revision; and here, as often elsewhere, there are grounds for regarding there the Quarto and Folio readings ('cell' and 'hell') as independent alternatives.

Opening Iago

If it is Iago who introduces his victim to the realm of the hidden, acting (in the phrase that Othello ironically applies to Emilia) as the 'closet lock and key of villainous secrets' (IV. ii. 21),[21] he can do it partly because from the beginning he is distinguished from those around him by a ferocious and possessive inwardness. While in the first half of the play Iago's complex interior life is repeatedly opened out to the audience in soliloquy, he jealously guards it from the scrutiny of the Venetian world with the misleading semaphore of his 'flag and sign of love' (I. i. 156). In contrast to the 'free and open nature' he contemptuously acknowledges in Othello, Iago's mind, as Patricia Parker has noticed, is like the closed purse with which his rhetorical imagination repeatedly plays.[22] Indeed he teases his gull, Roderigo, by boasting of the disjunction between public persona and private self—'I am not what I am' (I. i. 65)—relishing the hiddenness of his pursed-up motives like a miser's pelf.

Iago's hoard is at once a treasure and a torture to him—a treasure because it is uniquely and unassailably his own ('the *native* act and figure of my heart'), but a torture because it so easily metamorphoses into the 'poisonous mineral' whose corrosive action 'Doth . . . gnaw my inwards' (II. i. 297). At the core of his being, that is to say, Iago recognizes the principle of his own destruction; and the point of his seduction is to bring Othello to the same discovery. If Iago's consciousness *is* the hidden poison that devours him, then his psychological penetration of Othello is properly figured as an aural poisoning or infection: 'I'll pour this pestilence into his ear' (II. iii. 356). But it is also figured as an obscene impregnation: 'gnaw', after all, seems to attribute a sinister life to Iago's tormenting thoughts, as if the psychological purse were a kind of womb whose unnatural offspring (like 'the green-eyed monster' of jealousy)

[21] For a brief but extremely suggestive account of the temptation scene as Othello's induction into 'internality' or 'withinness', see Kenneth Burke, '*Othello*: An Essay to Illustrate a Method', in Susan Snyder (ed.), *Othello: Critical Essays* (New York: Garland, 1988), 127–68 (esp. pp. 138–9). On the closet as a trope for secrecy and inwardness, see Alan Stewart, 'The Early Modern Closet Discovered', *Representations*, 50 (1995), 76–100.

[22] Patricia Parker, *Literary Fat Ladies: Rhetoric, Gender, Property* (London: Methuen, 1987), 95. Compare also the 'pursed' brow that reveals to Othello the concealed monster 'shut up' in Iago's brain (III. iii. 113).

were consuming it from within; and, of course, it was precisely as such a monstrously quickened womb that Iago figured his secret self in the soliloquy that closed Act I. The function of the temptation scene is to reproduce this obscene pregnancy in the hero himself.

The language of this scene traces the progressive emergence of the 'foul thing' coiled at the heart of the tempter's psychic darkness (line 166): as this creature comes to light, the confession of Iago's supposedly hidden thoughts gradually slides into the revelation of Desdemona's supposedly hidden deeds. Iago, the audience knows, has a real secret, but it is only that his *apparent* secret is wholly fictive, a fabrication of his malice. In seeming to 'unfold' it, however, he discovers to his victim the existence of a whole unsuspected realm of hiddenness. By a characteristic slide, the occulted nature of 'honest' Iago's thoughts seems to demonstrate the concealed viciousness of 'honest' Desdemona's response to what Iago presents as the 'hidden loose affection' of Cassio (II. i. 241): 'In Venice they do let God see the pranks | They dare not show their husbands' (III. iii. 202–3); just as the acknowledged 'foulness' of Iago's monstrous imagination helps to make probable the 'Foul disproportions, thoughts unnatural' of Desdemona's covert deformity (line 233). With an even more cruel circularity, the very opening up of Othello's magnanimous persona to disclose the unsuspected jealousy 'within' gives a further colour of probability to Desdemona's secret lust. Perversely it is just the fact that her adultery *cannot* be seen that seems to prove its existence; or (as Iago puts it, in a characteristically teasing formulation) 'Her honour is an essence that's not seen; | They have it very oft that have it not' (IV. i. 16–17).

From his hints of invisible vice, the tempter edges, with his technique of elaborate *occupatio*, rhetorically exhibiting what he repeatedly insists can never be shown, into the scopophile excitements of erotic encounters evoked in increasingly lubricious visual detail, opening the supposed 'door of truth' upon his gallery of promiscuously copulating beasts:[23]

> Would you, the supervisor, grossly gape on?
> Behold her topp'd. . . .

[23] 'Topped' here is simply a variant of 'tupped', a verbal form deriving from the dialectal 'tup' = ram (*OED*).

> It were a tedious difficulty, I think,
> To bring them to that prospect; damn them then
> If ever mortal eyes do see them bolster
> More than their own. . . .
> It is impossible you should see this,
> Were they as prime as goats, as hot as monkeys,
> As salt as wolves in pride, and fools as gross
> As ignorance made drunk.
>
> (III. iii. 395–405)

The still merely verbal, but powerfully suggestive, metonym 'bolster' gives way to a ruthlessly detailed night-piece in which Iago claims to have been himself the unwilling partner in Cassio's dream of fornication. Once again nothing is directly shown—the love act is merely a sleeping fantasy, 'Desdemona' is only 'Iago'. Yet this doubly fictive scene of adultery is made to seem doubly adulterate by the homoerotic displacement of the kisses that grow upon Iago's lips—kisses which themselves disturbingly mirror the one real adultery of the play, the seduction of Othello in which Iago is at this very moment engaged.[24] Iago's revelation is given an extra stamp of authenticity, moreover, by being presented as Cassio's unwitting self-betrayal in a moment of compulsive secrecy: 'Sweet Desdemona, | Let us be wary, let us *hide* our loves' (lines 419–20; emphasis added). The ensign's invention seems to part the curtains to expose not merely the hidden scene on the bed, but hidden thoughts themselves; and his final triumph of prestidigitation is to use his own concocted fantasies as a vehicle for revealing an apparently essential truth about Othello himself: 'There's many a beast then in a populous city, | And many a civil monster' (IV. i. 63–4).

At the beginning of the temptation scene Iago's 'echoing' of Othello is what appears to disclose the secret monster of his own thought (III. iii. 105–8); by the time we reach Act IV, scene iii it is the general who has become his ancient's echo, acting out the way in which his 'inmost' thoughts are the product of Iago's ventriloquy:

[24] See my 'Changing Places in *Othello*', 130. The element of homoerotic displacement in Iago's fantasy is further examined in Arthur L. Little, Jr., '"An essence that's not seen": The Primal Scene of Racism in *Othello*', *Shakespeare Quarterly*, 44 (1993), 304–24: 317–19.

IAGO. Will you *think* so?
OTHELLO. *Think* so, Iago?
IAGO. What!
To kiss in private?
OTHELLO. An unauthorized *kiss*!
IAGO. Or to be *naked* with her friend *in bed*
An hour or more, *not meaning any harm*?
OTHELLO. *Naked in bed*, Iago, and *not mean harm*?
(IV. i. 1–5; emphasis added)

In this exchange the violated marriage-bed is brought into full imaginative view for the first time, in a rhetorical unveiling that is a counterpart to the physical 'discovery' of the final scene. Through it the tainted palace of Iago's imagination is finally confirmed as a mirror for the polluted interior domain which his whispering has opened in the Moor himself, the place where the 'poison' of 'dangerous conceits' burns 'like the mines of sulphur' (III. iii. 325–9). It is his newly wakened interiority that will keep Othello for ever from 'that sweet sleep | Which thou owd'st yesterday' (lines 332–3), imprisoning him in the dank dungeon of introspection glimpsed in his first soliloquy (lines 270–3). And in accordance with the play's tangled logic of vicious substitution, that same dank prison will become a figure for Desdemona's hiddenness, identified as the corrupted 'place', both psychic and sexual, in which Othello's entire sense of self-possession has been locked away. Her body is the profoundly secret (but all too public) enclosure in which Othello's imagination locates the deep but morbidly tainted source of his own being:

there, where I have garner'd up my heart,
Where either I must live, or bear no life;
The fountain from the which my current runs,
Or else dries up: to be discarded thence!
Or keep it as a cistern for foul toads
To knot and gender in! (IV. ii. 57–62)

The final irony of this process, of course, is that at the end of the play, just when the spectacle of butchery on Desdemona's marriage-bed lays the 'truth' of Othello's hidden savagery so naked to the public gaze that even the censorious Venetian onlookers cannot bear what they see, Iago withdraws into a secrecy so gloatingly absolute that even the audience may begin to doubt whether he has ever really opened himself at all: 'Demand me nothing; what you know, you know: | From this time forth I never will speak word' (v. ii. 303–4) 'Torments will ope your lips,' snarls the frustrated Gratiano. But Iago stands there 'encaved' (to use his own word) in a triumphant privacy that no instrument of torture will ever penetrate.

The Encaved Self: Othello *and Inwardness*

It was, of course, the jealous Othello whom Iago advised to 'encave' himself, the better to eavesdrop on Cassio; and no term better expresses the transformation wrought in Othello—the Iago-like encrypting of his formerly 'open' self—than this marvellous coinage:

Do but encave yourself,
And mark the fleers, the gibes, and notable scorns
That dwell in every region of his face,
For I will make him tell the tale anew:
Where, how, how oft, how long ago, and when
He hath, and is again to cope your wife.

(IV. i. 81–6)

The scene which Iago constructs, we should notice, is like a perverted version of Othello's account of his own wooing (I. iii. 127–70), with its 'travel's history' of twice-told tales. The earlier Othello's openness was exemplified by the innocence of that narrative whose teller merely 'pass'd' the fearful sights of Barbary like some wide-eyed Mandeville, as if untouched even by those 'distressful stroke[s]' that reduced his listener to tears. In this strangely fractured replay, where the place of Barbary's wild inhabitants has been taken by the marks of savage scorn 'that dwell in every region of [Cassio's] face', the nonchalant observation of the traveller is replaced by the obsessive gaze of the spy, and Othello must 'encave' himself, as though he had become a lurking denizen of one of those 'antres vast' whose looming presence he had once so carelessly remarked. Of course the stage business merely acts out what has already begun to happen at the psychological level, where Othello's monster-self is by now profoundly encaved, shut up within the hollow cell of his newly discovered lack, gazing out with the green eyes of jealousy.

In the gathering frenzy of the second half of the play the protagonist's need for encavement grows in exact proportion with his longing to tear open and discover. We can see these contradictory drives acted out in the brothel scene, where Othello's determination to prise open the 'closet lock and key of villainous secrets' is matched by his repeated insistence that Emilia 'shut the door . . . turn the key, and keep our counsel' (lines 28, 94); and once again in the murder scene, where his locking and unlocking of the door, like his repeated opening and closing of the bed-curtains, mimics the terrible double compulsion both to discover and to conceal.

Iago's imposture can work upon Othello as immaculately as it does not just because the Moor is a man who straddles two worlds, but because he is caught at the junction of two historically conditioned modes of subjectivity. The work of recent cultural historians and critics has made us familiar with the argument that the experience of subjectivity which we regard as 'natural', with its characteristically 'inward' notion of the self, is as much a cultural construction as the 'outward' persona to which it is habitually opposed.[25] Impossible as it may be to think oneself into the forms of subjectivity characteristic of another time, Anne Ferry constructs a plausible case for supposing that in the Renaissance 'inward experience was not conceived as necessarily antithetical to outward, or radically different in kind, or widely distanced from it'.[26]

[25] See e.g. Elias, *The Civilizing Process*; Dollimore, *Radical Tragedy*; and Belsey, *The Subject of Tragedy*. For a trenchant critique of this position, see Katharine Eisaman Maus, 'Proof and Consequences: Inwardness and its Exposure in the English Renaissance', *Representations*, 34 (1991), 29–52. Maus shows how the prosecution of such crimes as treason and witchcraft was conceived in English legal process as a ritualized 'discovery' of hidden inner 'monstrosity'; and she provides a suggestive analysis of *Othello*, showing how its obsession with the interpretation of outward signs mirrors judicial models of enquiry 'that define . . . inwardness as guilty secrecy' (p. 43). Maus's arguments about the nature of early modern interiority are further developed in her *Inwardness and Theatre in the English Renaissance* (Chicago: University of Chicago Press, 1995).

[26] Anne Ferry, *The 'Inward' Language: Sonnets of Wyatt, Sidney, Donne and Shakespeare* (Chicago: University of Chicago Press, 1983), 65. To say that selfhood was not primarily an inward phenomenon is not, obviously, to say that there was no such thing as inward experience, but only that, rather than being the continuous ground of one's being, it was imagined as intermittent *activity*—something to be consciously undertaken. For their moral and spiritual well-being, individuals were required, in the revealing phrase, to 'discourse with themselves'—an activity that should properly take place in some withdrawn private room, as if in conscious enactment of withdrawal into the privacy of inner space. In a detail of great significance, Ferry observes that the language used to describe such discourse makes

In such a culture selfhood, rather than being located specifically *within* the body of an individual, may be thought of as dispersed through the whole person—very much as Othello's seems to be before Iago opens the 'door of truth' and forces him into the dungeon of inwardness. Yet Ferry's own evidence suggests that this way of experiencing the self was already under considerable pressure; for she draws attention to the rapid development of literary forms concerned in various ways with the exploration or expression of inwardness—the sonnet, the Montaignean essay, autobiographical memoirs, and especially the dramatic soliloquy.[27] All of these point towards a psychological formation in the process of rapid redefinition; and the work of Norbert Elias, in particular, suggests that our own deeply ingrained way of thinking about the self as something contained *within* the body was very much an artefact of the early modern period in Europe.[28]

no clear distinction between spoken and silent thought: private prayers are habitually accompanied by groans and gestures of the sort that normally accompanied outward expression, while 'thinking is identified with utterance in all but sound, and . . . a person alone thinks, or talks aloud to himself in a formal pattern that differs significantly from speech to an outside listener only in the respect that it is not overheard' (pp. 53–5). For a culture whose encounter with inwardness was of such a studied and performative character, there need have been nothing particularly artificial about the device of soliloquy as a way of representing the processes of thought. It is conceivable, indeed, the powerful inhibitions that deter people from speaking their thoughts aloud are to some extent (like silent reading) a modern phenomenon. This might account for the complex metatheatrical joke by which Congreve, having mocked in his dedicatory epistle to *The Double Dealer*, the ridiculous and outdated convention that allowed soliloquy to be overheard by other characters, nevertheless allows Maskwell to gull the elderly Lord Touchwood with a pretended soliloquy: 'He shall know my thoughts, or think he does' (v. i. 15–16); cited from *The Comedies of William Congreve*, ed. Anthony G. Henderson (Cambridge: Cambridge University Press, 1982).

[27] For some fascinatingly detailed material on radical Protestant expressions of inner selfhood, see Nigel Smith, *Perfection Proclaimed: Language and Literature in English Radical Religion* (Oxford: Clarendon Press, 1989), ch. 1, pp. 23–72. Smith notices the Ranter Joseph Salmon's apparent attempt to distinguish typographically between the 'I' which refers to the outer 'fleshy' man, and that which refers to the inner, 'spiritually regenerate self' (pp. 59–60); and he records how the female prophet Anna Trapnel, when she installed herself at Whitehall in 1654, withdrew to her bed for twelve days: 'while in bed the closeness of her inner self to God was registered by her outer body ceasing to operate: she did not move and her faculties of sense did not function, especially during her speeches, vision and prayers' (p. 50).

[28] Elias, *The Civilizing Process*, 245–63. See also Karin S. Coddon, '"Suche Strange Desygns": Madness, Subjectivity, and Treason in *Hamlet* and Elizabethan Culture', *Renaissance Drama*, 20 (1989), 51–75.

Elias argues that, in the course of that gradual internalization of discipline and control which he calls 'the civilizing process', individuals developed the sense 'that their own "self", their "true identity," [was] something locked away inside them'—confined within a social carapace of manners that was intuitively identified with the body. By the same token the body itself came to be imagined simply as 'the vessel which holds the true self', whose skin constituted a 'frontier between "inside" and "outside"'. This was the experience of a new kind of human subject, whom Elias dubs '*homo clausus*', a creature 'severed from all other people and things outside' by the 'wall' of the body.[29]

Nothing is more eloquent of the relation between *homo clausus* and the outside world than the metaphor by which personal confession was expressed as 'opening' one's 'self', one's 'bosom', or one's 'heart'—as if intimacy somehow resembled the self-anatomizing gestures by which Vesalian cadavers laid open their inward fabric. There was, of course, a convenient symmetry between the emergent discourse of psychological interiority and the new anatomy pioneered by Vesalius. Indeed, because it spatialized the human body in a similar fashion, making use of the same kinds of architectural metaphor ('fabric', 'frame', 'palace', 'door'), anatomy came to provide an essential rhetorical underprop for new ideas of inwardness. Thus, in spite of Vesalius' sceptical materialism, the proof of 'that within which passes show' typically began to be expressed in anatomical terms—plucking out the heart of the mystery, holding the heart in one's hand—as if dissection could provide a physical route to the discovery of metaphysical truths. And such imaginings, which at certain points barely seemed metaphorical at all, were made brutally literal not merely in the action of plays like *'Tis Pity She's a Whore*, but in the language of public executions, where the climactic display of a traitor's heart constituted the public proof of his hidden treachery.[30]

[29] In fact, of course, as Elias emphasizes, 'there is nothing that resembles [a container or] a contained—nothing that could justify metaphors like that of the "inside" of a human being. The intuition of a wall, of something "inside" man separated from the "outside" world, however genuine it may be as an intuition, corresponds to nothing in man having the character of a real wall' (*The Civilizing Process*, 259).

[30] See my 'What Strange Riddle's This?', in *John Ford*, 157. Cf. Maus, 'Proof and Consequences', 39: 'The traitor comes to the scaffold quite literally to spill his guts, to have the heart plucked out of his mystery.' The ostentatiously opened body of Christ, displaying his sacred heart, which appears for the first time in baroque art, may be read as a sacralized counterpart of this anatomical trope.

One way of accounting for Othello's psychological crisis is to see it as produced by the stress of his violent induction into this new discourse of interiority. To begin with, his sense of other people seems as undisturbed by any intimations of depth as his sense of himself; and that is why Iago's carefully staged self-exhibition as a man with something to hide is so devastating in its effect—not just because it renders Iago (and Desdemona, and Cassio) suddenly impenetrable to the Moor, but because it uncovers the terrible, vertiginous possibility of hidden depths in himself ('By heaven, he echoes me').

Opening Masculinity

The peculiar cultural dynamics of a play that sets heroic Moor against 'super-subtle Venetian' make it inevitable that we should associate the shock of Othello's discovery with his racial otherness; and in so far as the noble simplicity of his 'free and open nature' is linked to his barbarian origins, the play may seen as drawing on (and contributing to) that cultural discourse whereby Europeans came to understand 'savage' peoples as constituting a living record of their own lost past.[31] As an African, Othello, for all his royal lineage and Venetian *savoir faire*, can be imagined as belonging to a pre-reflective world. Thus it might be argued that the play colludes with (or helps to invent) the familiar colonialist fantasy that denies true subjectivity to the colonial Other, seeing it as a gift (or, in primitivist versions, a curse) conferred by civilization—the gift which Prospero so ambiguously confers on Caliban when he teaches him to 'know [his] own meaning'.

Yet the very different case of the almost equally externalized hero who dominates the first half of *Anthony and Cleopatra* should give us pause; and it is important to observe that if the anxious interiority of Othello's encaved self is culturally marked, the dislocation (or loss of 'occupation') it produces is also (like Anthony's crisis of identity) presented in significantly gendered terms. 'Masculinity', Walter Ong has written, 'is difficult to interiorize, a kind of stranger to the human psyche. Since being human means living from interiority, masculinity is an especially acute problem for

[31] On this point, see Pagden, *European Encounters*, 13–14 and chs. 4–5.

human beings.'[32] This is particularly true of the extreme style of performative masculinity in which Othello's sense of self is invested —the heroic.

Having less to do with inner essence than with external performance, heroic identity, as Ulysses has occasion to remind Achilles in *Troilus and Cressida*, knows itself not by introspection but by reflection:

For speculation turns not to itself,
Till it hath travell'd and is mirror'd there
Where it may see itself.
(III. iii. 109–11)

If interiority of the kind classically explored in *Hamlet* is recognized as new, painful, and potentially dangerous,[33] it is also seen as inimical to this peculiarly masculine self-construction: so that for Hamlet, the hero *manqué*, to 'unpack [his] heart', in the private language of soliloquy, is to experience inner debate as a kind of unmanning that reduces him to a 'whore' or 'drab' (II. ii. 585–6). If soliloquy feminizes Hamlet by taking the place of heroic action, in *Anthony and Cleopatra* the process of psychological emasculation that 'robs' the hero of his 'sword' is inextricably linked with his drift into a mode of fatal introspection. To look within (as Montaigne had discovered) is to discover an identity that is never self-identical, a self that always seems to be slipping away from itself.[34] Thus Anthony feels himself becoming 'indistinct as water is in water', as though he were dissolving into the very element that defines the feminine other (*A&C* IV. xiv. 10–11).

In so far as the Othello we meet at the beginning of his play has

[32] Walter J. Ong, *Fighting for Life: Contest, Sexuality and Consciousness* (Ithaca, NY: Cornell University Press, 1981), 98.

[33] On this, see Ferry's 'Introduction: The *Inner Life*, the *Real Self*, and Hamlet', in *'Inward' Language*, 1–30. When Horatio warns Hamlet against the ghost's leading him to a giddy brink above the roaring sea, we may read it as a figure for the very abyss which the play opens within the Prince, and for the loss of distinction that must ensue from the failure to maintain the heroically constructed outward persona.

[34] See e.g. 'Of the Inconstancy of our Actions', *Essays*, II. i. 11, 14: 'He whom you saw yesterday so boldly venturous wonder not if you see him a dastardly meacock tomorrow next. . . . We are all framed of flaps and patches and of so shapeless and diverse a contexture, that every piece and every moment playeth his part. And there is as much difference found between us and our selves, as there is between our selves and [an]other.'

moulded himself to a similar ideal of masculine virtue, he is a character who must continually construct himself from without, centring his identity upon a carefully fashioned performance. Speaking of the love between himself and Desdemona, Othello typically accounts for it in terms of her admiring reaction to this publicly represented persona ('She loved me for the dangers I had passed'; I. iii. 167), and of his own grateful response to Desdemona's sympathetic inwardness ('I loved her that she did pity me'; line 168). The inward is implicitly identified as feminine; while masculine identity proclaims itself in outward magnificence. Desdemona's love, in exactly the specular fashion Ulysses describes, is what enables Othello to recognize himself in the strange world of Venice; beyond that externalized guarantee of identity, what remains is 'chaos', another name for annihilation (III. iii. 92). Thus to yield, as Othello does, to the inward gaze that Iago wakens in him will be to experience an unmanning, a real undoing of the self—in effect a kind of death ('Othello's occupation's gone'; III. iii. 357); and his struggle against this morbidly emasculating process is registered (like Hamlet's) in a rhetoric of distress that vainly seeks to transform the feminized interior 'place' into a locus of masculine action where 'bloody thoughts, with violent pace' can sweep towards revenge (line 457):

> Arise, black vengeance, from thy hollow cell!
> Yield up, O love, thy crown and hearted throne
> To tyrannous hate! Swell, bosom, with thy fraught,
> For 'tis of aspics' tongues! (III. iii. 447–50)

Ironically this last image, with its odd, unconscious evocation of Cleopatra's suicide, undercuts him—just as his 'bloody thoughts' end not as the agents, but as the victims, of a revenge that will 'swallow them up' (line 460); but all of Othello's rhetorical effort is nevertheless directed towards re-creating himself as the externalized incarnation of 'Black vengeance'. Inevitably, therefore, at the very end of the play (after a revenge that seems as much concerned with extinguishing the searing light of jealous introspection as with the murder of a living woman), Othello tries to defend himself from everything that is revealed in the fearful discovery on the bed by ceremoniously reconstituting his externalized masculine persona. He does it by means of the oddly self-dividing parable of the turbaned Turk, in a speech of recollection whose strikingly distanced perspective ('in your letters, | When you shall these unlucky deeds relate, | Speak of me . . . Then must you speak | Of one . . . Set you down this; | And say besides . . .'; v. ii. 340–52), returns to the narrative mode of his first romantic autobiography. Once again speculation finds itself by travelling, recognizes itself heroically mirrored in the gaze of others. But by now such a restoration is possible only at the cost of yielding to the self-cancelling embrace of his own uncanny Gefehrt—in the form of the barbarous other whom Iago has taught him to recognize within.

Drawing the Curtain: Apocalypse in the Bedchamber

The turbaned traducer of the Venetian state, of course, is also a 'circumcised dog' bearing marks of racial and cultural difference that reflect other aspects of the conflicted identity on which Othello means to exact retribution. Perhaps the most telling of the many self-betrayals in the Moor's original vow of revenge, indeed, may be found in the phrase 'Black vengeance' itself. For if vengeance's 'hollow hell/cell' is the space within Othello that Iago has excavated, then the demon-prisoner who dwells there (like a monstrous parody of those white manikins used by medieval artists to represent the soul) is an image of the Moor's own blackness; and this moment of intuitive (mis)recognition marks a critical point in the hero's surrender to Iago's notion of the hidden truth about him.

This transformation is completed in a murder scene whose imaginative chiaroscuro disturbingly exaggerates the play's symbolism of light and dark, black and white. Here Othello imagines his own catastrophe in a rhetoric of eschatological confusion:

> Methinks it should be now a huge eclipse
> Of sun and moon, and that th'affrighted globe
> Should yawn at alteration. (v. ii. 99–101)

In his longing for obliteration, the Moor envisages a kind of anti-apocalypse, a covering of himself against the horror of light; and, through his absolute internalization of the very values that define his alienation from the Venetian order, his language yields to the symbolism that identifies his colour as the badge of both indelible wickedness and secret vice. On one level this is simply part of the process by which the play produces a peculiarly European idea of racial difference;[35] but it also has to do with the psychological process through which a man learns to look inside himself and uncovers the tokens of his own damnability and death. The last scene of Othello is in more senses than one a 'discovery scene', but to understand the nature of its disclosure we need to think more about the way the play constructs its ideas of 'inside' and 'outside', and how it represents the invention of a particular kind of fatal inwardness.

There is, it might be noticed, a curious symmetry between Othello's first entry in Act I, scene ii 'with torches' and his final entrance in Act V, scene ii 'with a light'. In the first scene he has been summoned from his nuptial bedchamber, in the second it is to the bedchamber itself that he enters. Both episodes have to do with discovery: the first is ushered in by Roderigo's promise to 'discover' Othello to Brabantio; the second is a true 'discovery scene', a nightmare staging of that promised revelation. One way of measuring the distance between the two entries would be to notice that the first shows a public man returning to a public world, while the second shows the same man effectively stripped of his public 'place' and relegated to what he called 'the circumscription and confine' of the private domain (I. ii. 27). In the first he is conspicuously the general, followed by attendants, talking with his officer, and insisting on the primacy of public affairs ('My services which I have done the signiory | Shall out-tongue his complaints'; lines 18–19); in the second, standing over the sleeping Desdemona 'in her bed', he is alone with himself, in converse only with his own 'soul'. Othello's 'soul' had figured in the earlier scene, but only as an externalized aspect of the public self—'My parts, my title, and my perfect soul'—something that can '*manifest* [him] rightly' (I. ii. 31–2; emphasis added); in the last it stands for his innermost self, a region of obscure knowledge which recognizes a 'cause' too deep for the ostentation of words, too dark for the light of articulate consciousness. The transformation that has occurred might be registered in this way: the Othello of Act I, incapable of soliloquy, is projected as a speaking-voice whose only inwardness is that of audience to its own conscious magniloquence; the Othello of Act V, scene ii, by contrast, is a man whose being is registered *primarily* in the deep interiority of monologue—one

[35] See my 'Unproper Beds', 407–12.

who can withdraw into it even in the presence of others, as he does at line 272, when he turns to address Desdemona's corpse ('Now—how dost thou look now?'), and who can restore the semblance of his public self only by a feat of vicarious self-imagining. Thus it is entirely appropriate that the end-point of the hero's fatal retreat inside himself should be accomplished in a scene that conducts the audience into a space that has been defined throughout the play as 'within'—somewhere hidden and secret, an object of recurrent prying speculation. The effect—whether we imagine a parting of the arras that masks the 'discovery space' itself, or the drawing aside of the curtains around an on-stage tester bed is to register a moment of theatrical discovery as a picture of psychological disclosure.

As I have previously argued,[36] the extraordinary effect of this disclosure depends upon its being staged as a climactic repetition and realization of an obscene spectacle which, from the wild antics outside Brabantio's house in I. i ('an old black ram | Is tupping your white ewe'; lines 88–9) to the corrupt intimacy of the murder pact in IV. i ('Strangle her in her bed, even the bed she hath contaminated'; lines 208–9), has been repeatedly illuminated by the glare of Iago's garish imagination, whilst remaining physically shut away from the audience's prurient gaze. In the process the bedchamber becomes a metonymic figure not merely (as in *Cymbeline*) for the female body, but for the fiercely contested private spaces of the psyche itself. As a result, *Othello* can establish the tormenting equivalency between off-stage action (what happens 'within') and psychological event (what happens 'inside'), that allows it to flourish its final discovery as a psychic unveiling, an apocalyptic 'opening' in which audience as well as characters are caught up.

As Othello moves towards his murderous exposure of those 'villainous secrets' for which Emilia is 'a closet lock and key', the bed becomes more and more explicitly the 'place' upon which the action is centred. Punningly revealed by Jacobean pronunciation even in the innocent syllables of Lodovico's ill-judged praise of Desdemona ('Truly, an o*bed*ient lady'; IV. i. 248), it is the submerged theme of the demented outburst that exposes Othello's breakdown to the embarrassed Venetian delegates: 'And she's obedient, as you say, obedient, | Very obedient. . . . Cassio shall have

[36] Neill, 'Unproper Beds', 396–403.

my place' (lines 255–61). The bed is the emotional focus, too, of Desdemona's two scenes before the murder, where (as though in unconscious collusion with Othello's fantasies) she perfects the scene of murderous consummation:

> Prithee to-night
> Lay on my bed my wedding sheets, remember;
> And call my husband hither. (IV. ii. 104)

Desdemona shrouds herself here in a narrative of eroticized self-immolation as self-consciously as Othello in his final speech will dress himself in the narrative of heroic self-conquest. The programme of the tableau she devises is supplied by the fashion, increasingly popular amongst aristocratic women in the early seventeenth century, for having one's corpse wound in the sheets from the marriage night:[37] 'If I do die before thee, prithee shroud me | In one of those same sheets' (IV. iii. 24–5). The fetishistic significance of wedding-sheets derived, of course, from the bloodstains that witnessed the sexual consummation of a marriage, which, in the conventional metaphor of epithalamic poetry, accomplished the death of the virgin bride and her rebirth as wife. To be buried in one's wedding-sheets was thus to enact a peculiarly feminine defiance of mortality, one in which perfected identity could be resurrected, paradoxically enough, only through an extreme act of self-abnegation—as it is, for example, by Ford's Princess Calantha when she reconstitutes her death as a wedding-rite: 'Thus I new marry him whose wife I am' (*Broken Heart*, V. iii. 66). The significance of Desdemona's ritual is reinforced by the metonymic relationship (so brilliantly explored by Lynda Boose[38]) between the wedding-sheets and the strawberry-spotted handkerchief, 'dy'd in mummy . . . Conserv'd of maidens' hearts' (III. iv. 74–5), which was Othello's 'first token' of love. In Othello's imagination, the handkerchief is invested with the same magical significance as a wedding-ring: like Calantha's ring (or the Duchess of Malfi's), it is the symbolically charged bequest of a dying parent and embodies the

[37] See Gittings, *Death, Burial and the Individual*, 111–12. Gittings cites the case of Lady Frances Stuart, whose will projected her funeral as a ceremonious re-enactment of her wedding-night: 'Let them wind me up again in those sheets . . . wherein my Lord and I first slept that night we were married' (p. 193).

[38] See her now classic 'Othello's Handkerchief: "The Recognizance and Pledge of Love"', *English Literary Renaissance*, 5 (1975), 360–74.

very union out of which he himself was born. Though it ostensibly represents the power of the wife to 'subdue [the husband] | Entirely to her love' (III. iv. 59–60), that power is revealed as wholly contingent upon the husband's gift (V. ii. 215–17). It is in the context of such ritualized subordination to the husband's identity that Desdemona's self-inculpation ('Who hath done this deed?' | 'Nobody; I myself'; V. ii. 123–4) makes a painful kind of sense. When, within the patriarchal system, husband and wife become one flesh, the woman is, almost literally, no-body.

Yet, of course, as the metaphysical frustrations of a Donne[39] or the jealous frenzies of Webster's Ferdinand[40] confirm, this no-body is also all body, the originary site and source of mortal frailty; and in *Othello* the blood-stained sheets (through their metonymic substitute, the handkerchief) become the very sign of that corrupted bodiliness by which the hero's imagination is possessed. Activating the ancient taboos associated with female blood, Iago's lurid concentration upon 'the bed she hath contaminated' hangs out Desdemona's sheets to Othello's imagination like a flag not of love, but of defilement and death: 'Thy bed, lust stain'd, shall with lust's blood be spotted' (V. i. 36). Thus, by the time we reach the final scene with its long-postponed discovery of Desdemona's bedchamber, the bed (symbolically associated with the exposure of hidden truth via the complex metonymy of the handkerchief[41]) has itself been constructed as a continent of deadly secrets—a theatrical

[39] This aspect of Donne is exhaustively analysed by Watson in *The Rest is Silence*, ch. 4.

[40] See e.g. *Duchess of Malfi*, IV. i. 121–3: 'Damn her! that body of hers, | While that my blood ran pure in't, was worth more, | Than that which thou wouldst comfort, called a soul.'

[41] The handkerchief's effectiveness as 'ocular proof' of Desdemona's inner viciousness is symbolically associated with the claim that it was woven by a prophetess who dyed it with a decoction 'of maiden's hearts', and once owned by an Egyptian 'charmer' who could 'almost read | The thoughts of people' (III. iv. 57–8). Compare Burke, '*Othello:* An Essay': 'this handkerchief that bridges realms, being the public surrogate of secrecy . . . is an emblem's emblem. . . . Since it stands for Desdemona's privacy, and since this privacy in turn had stood magically for his entire sense of worldly and cosmological order, we can readily see why, for Othello, its loss becomes the ultimate obscenity' (in Snyder (ed.), *Othello*, 160). For useful historical detail on the significance of the handkerchief, see Karen Newman, '"And wash the Ethiop white": Femininity and the Monstrous in *Othello*', in Jean E. Howard and Marion O'Connor (eds.), *Shakespeare Reproduced: The Text in History and Ideology* (London: Methuen, 1987), 141–62. Newman notes how the strawberry spots draw on the allegorical symbolism of the strawberry plant as a sign of deceit (p. 156).

emblem of all that is (in Othello's resonant phrase) 'too hideous to be shown' (III. iii. 108). What is *hid*eous, the word-play here reminds us, is what should be kept *hidden*, off-stage, out of sight, occluded.[42] The bed is now the visible sign of all that has been improperly revealed and must now be hidden again from view—the unnameably 'horrible conceit' which Othello glimpsed in the dark cave of Iago's racial imagination (III. iii. 114–15); it is the token of everything that must not be seen and cannot be spoken ('Let me not name it to you, you chaste stars'; V. ii. 2), everything that the second nature of culture seeks to efface or disguise as 'unnatural'—all that should be banished to outer (or consigned to inner) darkness; a figure for the very unlicensed desires that Lodovico's 'let it be hid' means to erase.[43] But knowledge, as Iago's sardonic adieu gloatingly insists, cannot be *un*-known. Like the Vesalian anatomist, patiently cutting back the layers of tissue to expose the hidden signs of an all-too-familiar mortality, Iago has stripped away the fabric of Othello's civil self to expose precisely the secrets that he has taught the audience to expect. They are secrets, moreover, that, exploiting the tautology implicit in the Tragedy of a Moor—one whose colour suggests an affinity to the realm of death that even Hamlet's inky suit cannot claim, Iago insists were always blazoned on Othello's skin. Othello's uncannily replayed murder of the Turk may be read as an attempt at violent cancellation of that tautology; but from the chilling perspective of Shakespeare's catastrophe it merely confirms it in a final self-annihilating repetition. No prophecies are more compelling, or more difficult to unpick, than the self-fulfilling kind. *Othello* at once invents and naturalizes the horrors it reveals, declaring them unproper, even as it implies that they were always 'naturally' there.

[42] The word-play, which may well reflect a folk-etymology, occurs elsewhere in Shakespeare: see e.g. *Twelfth Night*, IV. ii. 31 ('hideous darkness'), and *King John*, V. iv. 22.

[43] The staging proposed by Richard Hosley, in which the bed is 'drawn in' to the discovery space, neatly exhibits its function as a willed un-discovery; see 'The Staging of Desdemona's Bed', *Shakespeare Quarterly*, 14 (1963), 57–65.

4
'Hidden malady': Death, Discovery, and Indistinction in *The Changeling*

[The Serpent's] creeping undoes me; for howsoever he begin at the heel, and do but bruise that, yet he, and *death in him, is come into our windows*; into our eyes and ears, the entrances and inlets of our soul. He works upon us in secret, and we do not discern him; and one great work of his upon us is to make us so like himself as to sin in secret that others may not see us; but his masterpiece is to make us sin in secret so as we may not see ourselves sin.

(John Donne, *Devotions upon Emergent Occasions*[1])

Are not divers secret and hidden apostemations, & other inward collections of vicious matter in the body, daily seminaries of unexpected and wondered shapes of corruption and putrefaction, which lying long hidden in the body, and by an insensible growth taking deep root, in the end suddenly break forth beyond all possible expectation, or thought of the most excellent, exquisite, and subtle circumspection and disquisition?

(John Cotta, *The Triall of Witchcraft, shewing The Trew and Right Methode of the Discovery*[2])

The Changeling *and* Othello

Othello's anatomizing gaze and its complementary fascination with both psychological interiors and the secrets of the social body are extended and taken in new directions by *The Changeling*. Middleton and Rowley's domestic tragedy was written eighteen years after *Othello*, but significantly in the very year that saw the publication

[1] *Devotions*, 65. Donne is paraphrasing St Jerome here: 'If you see a woman to lust after her, death shall come in through the window' (cited in Koerner, *Moment of Self-Portraiture*, 305).

[2] Cotta, *The Triall of Witchcraft*, 15.

of the first Quarto of Shakespeare's play (1622); and in both the details of its execution and its larger metaphoric structure it often appears to be a self-conscious rewriting of the earlier tragedy, adapting and recombining elements of its model to create a disturbing sense of familiarity-in-strangeness. The main plot of *The Changeling* shifts attention from the racial anxieties at the centre of the earlier tragedy to the bitterness about rank and status evident at its margin. Once again the action includes a murderous struggle to control the body of an aristocratic woman; once again the marriage-bed will become a place of murder, its linen turned to winding-sheets. But the dramatic focus has now shifted from the abused husband to the woman herself, and to the usurping subordinate who engineers her downfall. Superficially at least, it is as if Desdemona had been transformed to the embodiment of female changefulness that Iago made of her, and the Iago-figure, though as vicious as ever, promoted to become an object of sympathetic psychological attention. The husband, by contrast, has been stripped of the magnificence and the grandeur-in-suffering that constituted the Moor's claim to heroic singularity, and relegated, a bland and colourless figure, to the marginal position conventionally assigned to wives and servants. Like Webster's tragedies, *The Changeling* radically disturbs the accepted hierarchy of interest, but in so doing begins a quite un-Websterian assault on the principle of tragic distinction itself, which at the end carries everything—or nearly everything—before it.

Like *Othello*, *The Changeling* is structured around tropes of opening, discovery, and hidden secrets: like *Othello* it can be read as a species of psychological anatomy lesson designed to 'shew forth the ulcers that are covered with tissue' and expose the core of mortal corruption in the social body—the 'hidden malady | Within' of Alsemero's opening speech (I. i. 24–5). Working away in the bowels of Shakespeare's Venice is the emotional cancer that Iago feels as a 'poisonous mineral' gnawing at his inwards (II. i. 297); this poison is the source of the 'pestilence' he pours in Othello's ear (II. iii. 356), and from it wells the 'poison' that begins to 'Burn like the mines of sulphur' in the Moor's blood (III. iii. 325–9). At the end of the play Lodovico's horrified reaction to the spectacle on the bed makes it appear like a revelation of this hidden corruption: 'The object poisons sight' (V. ii. 364). It is as if this murderous tableau, tainting the sight as the deadly effluvia of plague were thought to infect the smell, threatened a fresh round of infection; and as if closing off the scene of discovery might somehow protect the Venetians from contagion. The ending of Shakespeare's tragedy shows us a society incapable of learning, desperate only to cover what it feels should never have been disclosed. Colluding in effect with the villain's defiant walling away of his inner self, Lodovico's gesture leaves the Venetian body politic encysted upon the moral poisons of its own secret corruption. In *The Changeling* the hidden plague which threatens to destroy society from within is once more embodied in a corrupt subordinate whose sight is 'poison' to the protagonist (I. i. 110–16); here again the same malignancy that devours the seducer will be discovered in his victim—who will come to recognize herself as polluted blood, a source of dangerous infection that must be removed from sight ('I am that of your blood was taken from you | For your better health; Look no more upon't'; v. iii. 150–1). Here too the outraged survivors of the catastrophe will collude in wilful self-deceit—even if their suppression of the truth is authorized in this case more by smug self-approval than by the panic and disgust that overwhelm the Venetian world.

The villain of *The Changeling* is a character whose energy, sardonic humour, and psychological acuity, combined with his sobriquet of 'honest De Flores', identify him as a deliberate reworking of Iago.[3] Like the ensign, De Flores is a man 'out of his place',[4] in Alsemero's phrase (I. i. 137)—a gentleman whom 'hard fate has thrust . . . out to servitude' (II. i. 48–9), naggingly conscious of disparity between his fortune and his imagined deserts. Even the servile office to which he is reduced remains vulnerable, since the mistress of his household, Beatrice-Joanna, treats him with undisguised scorn and is privately resolved to be rid of him: 'The next good mood I find my father in, | I'll get him quite discarded' (II. i. 92–3). De Flores' need to revenge himself for the wound of displacement involves him, like Iago, in a scheme of adulterous usurpation; but the object of his vindictive design—as if Iago were

[3] That contemporaries sensed the connection between the two is apparent from Ford's *Love's Sacrifice*, for example, where the character of D'Avolos ingeniously recombines elements of Iago and De Flores in a fashion that the audience must have been intended to recognize.

[4] For *Othello*'s elaborate play with ideas of 'place', see my 'Changing Places in *Othello*'.

unexpectedly consumed by his merely fugitive notion of seducing Desdemona—is no longer the psyche of the displaced husband, but the body of the aristocratic wife herself.

The idea of occupation or possession—the penetration and conquest of the private, inner self—symbolized by the presence of a citadel or castle is crucial to both tragedies.[5] But where in *Othello* fantasies of physical conquest and usurpation are merely the vehicle of a demonic stratagem whose aim is spiritual possession, in Middleton's fiercely material vision carnal occupation is all. The unsettling consequence is that De Flores becomes the real hero of the play; and his re-enactment of Othello's eroticized murder and suicide enforces, by its half-contemptuous self-satisfaction, the only claim to distinction that Middleton and Rowley's degraded world will allow. De Flores' ending is certainly shabbier and more soiled than the Moor's, but it is also less tainted by self-deception: he lacks the defiant swagger with which Webster's villain-heroes greet their deaths; yet, like everything he does, De Flores' dying is marked by the unblinking straightness of a self-inspecting gaze that compels not merely sympathetic involvement but grudging admiration from the audience.

The fantasy of secret occupation around which De Flores' ambition is woven is given startling dramatic life in the course of the brief soliloquy with which he ends the opening scene. Beatrice, in a gesture that the dramatist leaves deliberately obscure—perhaps it is intended for her new lover, Alsemero, perhaps it is designed to trap De Flores into fresh humiliation, or perhaps it is an unconscious revelation of the perverse physical fascination with this 'basilisk' (I. i. 116) at which her language progressively hints—has let fall her glove. Recoiling from the violation she feels when De Flores offers to return it, she throws down its pair: 'Take 'em and draw thine own skin off with 'em' (line 233). Flaying is no threat, however, to a man who has learned to see his skin in the distorting mirror of Beatrice's disdain ('Wrinkles like troughs, where swine-deformity swills | The tears of perjury that lie there like wash'; II. i. 42–3); and besides, De Flores is about to acquire a new skin:

> Here's a favour come, with a mischief! Now I know
> She had rather wear my pelt tanned in a pair

[5] Ibid. 117–18.

Of dancing pumps, than I should thrust my fingers
Into her sockets here. (I. i. 234–7)

What this gest displays is the very process of mutual penetration and occupation that constitutes the main action of the play—a process by which the ostensibly innocent and beautiful heroine and her lascivious, malformed adversary appear to change skins. At the same time it enacts the dialectical relation of inside and outside, secret and acknowledged, private and public which Middleton and Rowley's tragedy at once exploits and exposes to question.[6]

The glove is in some ways *The Changeling*'s equivalent for Desdemona's handkerchief—not because it has any equivalent structural significance in the play's erotic intrigues, but because of its metonymic suggestiveness. Like the handkerchief, it is flourished as if it were a favour—the badge of that 'mercy' for which De Flores begs in his travesty of chivalric 'service' (II. i. 63); and, like the handkerchief, it refers us to a hidden scene of desire that is once again a focus of compulsive fascination for audience and characters alike. To examine Middleton and Rowley's treatment of this naggingly absent scene, however, is to gain an unusually clear sense of the gulf that separates them from Shakespeare. The handkerchief, for example, however it may be usurped and abused, derives its symbolic power from a romantic myth of origin that make it seem a proper emblem of all that is unique about the love of Desdemona and Othello. What is striking about Beatrice's glove, by contrast, is its apparent interchangeability or repeatability—it is a token of sexual exchange that will fit any man's hand. Barely have we seen De Flores greedily thrusting his fingers into its sockets than the *double entendre* is transferred to the doddering Alibius (the cuckold-figure onto whom Middleton and Rowley displace Othello's anxieties about age):

I would wear my ring on my own finger,
Whilst it is borrowed it is none of mine,
But his that useth it.

[6] Cf. Frank Whigham, 'Reading Social Conflict in the Alimentary Tract: More on the Body in Renaissance Drama', *ELH* 55 (1988), 333–50: 'we ought to see the entire chain of glove/skin/pelt as marking an external boundary of the aristocratic body, already breached in prospect, just as blood will later signify its internalized and transferable essence' (p. 339).

—'You must keep it on still then,' replies his servant, Lollio, who aspires to be the De Flores of this other household, 'if it but lie by, one or other will be thrusting into't' (I. ii. 26–31). The ring, or rather the circle it describes, stands for the patriarchal 'secret' which Alibius is desperate to guard—a possession which his language carelessly identifies with the treasure between his wife's thighs. But this is a species of hidden wealth which, the bawdy commentary of Lollio (drawing on a repertory of familiar jokes about virginity) makes clear, can exist only for as long as no one possesses it: 'Fie, sir, 'tis too late to keep her secret, she's known to be married all the town and country over' (I. ii. 8–9). Like other kinds of discovery, sexual possession destroys what it desires, reducing the woman's treasure to the mere proverbial 'nothing' of a hole waiting to be filled and refilled.

Lollio's reductive gibes about sexuality and possession will be grotesquely confirmed in the climactic scene of the main plot when De Flores brings Beatrice ocular proof of his successful attempt on the life of her unwanted fiancé, Alonzo de Piracquo: 'I could not get the ring without the finger' (III. iv. 27). Standing impartially for the old bond with Piracquo that she has violated but can never obliterate, for the substitute bond with Alsemero that she is about to claim, and for the irresistible new bond that De Flores is about to enforce, this bloody token is also a grotesque reminder of the levelling interchangeability of sexual possession[7]—an idea which will be illustrated more conventionally in the performance of a bed-trick that permits Alsemero a rapturous consummation of his marriage to Beatrice upon the substituted body of Diaphanta. It is this symbolism more than any other, perhaps, which makes De Flores' disembodied member so shocking to the romantic sensibilities of Beatrice. Ring and finger, the very emblems of the sacramental distinction which wedding-rites confer upon animal desire, are translated into a brutal semiosis of Mercutio's idea of love as 'a great natural that runs lolling up and down to hide his ba[u]ble in a hole' (*Romeo and Juliet*, II. iv. 91–3).

At the same time, with its disturbing literalization of the imagery

[7] The effect is emphasized by the iteration of 'fingers' as a sign of erotic satisfaction (II. ii. 81, 148); and by the uncanny way in which the dazzling 'sparkles' from the diamond on the dead Piracquo's finger (III. ii. 20–2) recall Alsemero's blinding effect upon Beatrice: 'A true deserver like a diamond sparkles; | In darkness you may see him'; II. i. 15–16).

of dissection initiated by Beatrice's flaying gibe, the blood-stained finger is also a token of death, signifying its scandalous intimacy with sexuality in the assault upon distinction. In that sense it is the proper heraldry of De Flores, the badge of his levelling office; for in so far as he is the agent of a reductive transformation which 'blasts a beauty to deformity' (v. iii. 32), unforming form (beauty) itself, De Flores is the true plague of *The Changeling*, its active principle of indistinction. Beatrice loathes him 'As much as youth and beauty hates a sepulchre' (II. ii. 67); and Tomazo de Piracquo, contemplating the contrariety between his foul countenance and reputedly 'honest' character, reflects that

> honesty was hard beste[a]d
> To come there for a lodging, as if a queen
> Should make her palace of a *pest-house*.
>
> (v. ii. 11–13; emphasis added)

The progressive confusion of palace with pest-house or, to vary the metaphor in the play's own terms, castle with madhouse, is precisely what the action of *The Changeling* explores. It is a confusion which the denizens of Vermandero's castle try to account for with a rhetoric of arbitrary transformation—

> What an opacous body had that moon
> That last changed on us! here's beauty changed
> To ugly whoredom; here, servant obedience
> To a master sin, imperious murder
>
> (v. iii. 196–9)

—but one which the play itself sees as endemic to a society where, in Dekker's words, 'the Pest-house standeth everywhere'.[8] What to the innocent eye may appear as an inexplicable metamorphosis induced by some whimsical exterior influence, the informed gaze will discover as the manifestation of a secret infection, corroding from within—the tainted source of those 'lovers' plagues' of which De Flores speaks (III. iv. 151).[9] Death's arrest is manifested here as terminal disclosure, a symptomatic display as violent and sudden

[8] *Newes from Graues-end*, sig. E4.

[9] Ariès, *Hour of our Death*, remarks on how, in the wake of the plague, 'disease, old age, and death [came to seem] merely eruptions out of the rottenness within', death being something hidden 'in the inmost recesses of life' (p. 121).

as the plague-spots which announced the imminent death of the healthiest-seeming individual. The idea is introduced, almost casually, in the opening scene, where the love-struck Alsemero appears bafflingly altered to his friend Jasperino: 'have you changed your orisons?' (I. i. 34). Alsemero insists, however, despite his sense of odd dislocation, that he is still the same, 'Unless there be some *hidden malady* | *Within me* that I understand not' (line 24; emphasis added). The exchange serves as an early clue to an important discrimination: *The Changeling*, the audience are meant by the end to realize, has been only superficially concerned with 'change'; the shaping metaphor behind the whole action is not one of metamorphosis but of discovery—the penetration and display of morbid secrets. It is an idea worked out, in a fashion perhaps only possible in the conspicuously enclosed space of a private theatre, through a remarkable sequence of topographic metaphors.

The Castellated Body

At the centre of the dramatists' topographic scheme is Vermandero's castle itself—this play's equivalent for the Cyprus citadel in *Othello*. But Shakespeare's fortress existed only as a thinly sketched backdrop to the action, an almost abstract symbol of Othello's 'occupation', the remoter military counterpart, as it were, to the domestic symbol of the bed; Middleton's provides the locus for almost the entire main action. From the end of the first scene, the action of the high-plot is always 'inside' the castle, as that of the low-plot is 'inside' the madhouse. This location is imagined with a density and particularity unmatched in any play before the advent of the illusionistic proscenium stage transformed the theatrical representation of interior space. As so often in Renaissance art, however, this semblance of naturalism is misleading: Vermandero's is a 'real' castle, equipped with gatehouse, postern, sconces, stores of munitions, narrow winding passageways, cabinets, bedchambers, chimneys that need cleaning, a plethora of locked doors, a spacious park, and even a small pleasure-garden; but it is also, recognizably, an allegorical structure in the medieval tradition—a spatialized representation of the human subject that has as much in common with Spenser's Castle of Alma as with any actual military or domestic edifice.[10] The coincidence of this seemingly old-fashioned way of picturing the self with the psychological modernity that many readers have admired in the play is not as paradoxical as it might seem; for historians of private life have come to recognize the importance of such schematic representations, overlapping as they do with the new anatomy's spatialization of the human 'fabric', to the constitution of early modern subjectivity.[11] Moreover, as Jonathan Sawday has pointed out, Spenser's Castle of Alma was itself to provide a template for the human body explored at such length in the most Vesalian of English anatomical textbooks, Helkiah Crooke's *Mikrocosmographia* (1615).[12]

In the medieval tradition the subject was constructed in a double hierarchy—a horizontal hierarchy composed of concentric layers of increasing privacy, and a vertical hierarchy composed of ascending levels of social distinction.[13] One scheme, imagining the body as a great house, opposed a nest of secret inner spaces—bedchamber, closet, wardrobe, cabinet, study—to the enclosing walls of the grand public façade, just as it opposed the heart to the public persona of the clothed body; the other scheme, envisaging the body as tall donjon, set the site of lordly government at the top, against the sites of bodily grossness and decay, its kitchens and cesspits at

[10] For other readings which are sensitive to the architectural metaphors on which the play is structured—though with rather different emphases to my own—see Thomas L. Berger, 'The Petrarchan Fortress of *The Changeling*', *Renaissance Papers*, (1969), 37–46; Anne Lancashire, 'The Emblematic Castle in Shakespeare and Middleton', in J. C. Gray (ed.), *Mirror up to Shakespeare: Essays in Honour of G. R. Hibbard* (Toronto: University of Toronto Press, 1984), 223–41; and Mohammed Kowsar, 'Middleton and Rowley's *The Changeling:* The Besieged Temple', *Criticism*, 28 (1986), 145–64. For Berger the castle is a version of the traditional castle of the beloved, the object of erotic siege in Petrarchan love-poetry; for Lancashire it is 'simultaneously . . . the castle of female chastity (Beatrice-Joanna's) and of man-soul (Vermandero's and perhaps also Alsemero's), or of human virtue assaulted by internal enemies'—a fortress which she sees as transformed by the characters' sin into another version of Macbeth's hell-castle (p. 229); for Kowsar, on the other hand, it is a temple-fortress of patriarchal law and authority, and 'the alliance of Beatrice-Joanna and De Flores can be conceived as a powerful offensive machinery that penetrates, infects, and seeks to subvert the temple' (p. 156).

[11] See Danielle Régnier-Bohler, 'Imagining the Self', and Georges Duby and Philippe Braunstein, 'The Emergence of the Individual', in Ariès and Duby, *A History of Private Life*, ii. 311–93, 507–630; and Anne Ferry, *'Inward' Language*, 45–65.

[12] Sawday, *Body Emblazoned*, 167–70.

[13] See Duby and Braunstein, 'The Emergence of the Self', 522–5; and Dominique Barthélemy and Philippe Contarmine, 'The Use of Private Space', also in Ariès and Duby, *A History of Private Life*, 395–505: 420.

the bottom.[14] The two schemes frequently operated in tandem, as they do in a late example of this kind of architectural fantasy that is almost exactly contemporary with *The Changeling*, Samuel Purchas's *Microcosmus; or, The Historie of Man* (1619). Purchas's text combines an up-to-date interest in anatomy and the physiological discoveries of Harvey with an elaborate allegory in the medieval style, stretching across several chapters, in which 'Man's body [is] resembled to a palace':

We are first entertained with the manifold enclosures of this building (*cuticula*, *cutis*, *pinguedo*, *panniculus carnosus*, and the membrane of the muscles) as a five-fold wall encompassing the whole body throughout. . . . The trunk . . . is like to three spacious courts builded round, which as they are all admirable for their goodly, useful structure, so yield they a more stately magnificence in the ascent from the lowest venter to the middle, and thence to the supreme; as likewise in their form of government by those *Triumviri*, the LIVER, HEART, & BRAIN, as a sensible trinity in this unity. (pp. 32–4)

Prominent amongst the offices of the lowest venter are those which serve 'both for nutrition and generation, that is the *kitchen* . . . and the *bedchamber*' (p. 35). The middle venter is the domain of the Heart which is effectively walled off from potential rebels in the base court, there being only 'a few secret passages for private intelligence' (p. 47). This region also accommodates 'The LUNGS, [which] in this Palace are . . . the *chamber of presence*; as the space betwixt the division of the *mediastinum* may be termed the *privy chamber*; the *pericardium*, the *bedchamber*; the *wind-pipe*, the *great chamber*, of longer form, with so many *gristles*, as it were an *armed guard*, to secure the passages; and the *mouth* is the *hall*' (pp. 66–7). The mouth, in turn, provides the entrance-way to '*the tower*, *or highest venter and court*, *the head*' (p. 68), 'a *castle* annexed to this palace, the *capitol* of this city, the *senate-house of this state*, *the heaven* of this little universe' (p. 69), where the brain, '*great Emperor of this little globe, and General of the animal*

[14] Anne Ferry cites numerous examples in which heart and mind are figured as secret chambers: 'the most secret closet of his minde', 'his inward part, his privy chamber', '[what] lyeth secretly closed up within the closet of the heart', 'the secretest cabinet of our soules' , 'the cabinet and innermost withdrawing chamber of the soule' (*'Inward' Language*, 47, 59, 64). Cf. also Ford's *Broken Heart*, where Ithocles' heart is said to have 'crept into the *cabinet* of the princess' (IV. i. 118; emphasis added).

forces' (p. 74), is enthroned, 'not seated in a dark, obscure, melancholic room, as the *Heart*, but in open light and cheerfulness' (p. 69).

The two spatial schemes rather confusingly merged in anatomical blazons of this sort are figurations of two opposing notions of privacy, whose symbolic point of intersection, one might argue, is that most private of all spaces the 'wardrobe'—a name that originally denoted a specially private enclosure within the bedchamber, but that also euphemistically described the site of a different and more shameful kind of privacy—the garderobe or privy.[15] In Purchas, however, it is actually the bedchamber itself which acquires this double significance, by appearing twice in the topography of his palace. It is assigned first to the lowest court, where, as the place of reproduction, it is associated with the bodily grossness of the kitchen, and identified both as a site of forbidden spectacle—'As for the chamber of generation . . . there is nothing to be seen but secrets, and therefore not to be seen: the irrevocable Law of the Persians shall shut up this door unto us' (p. 44)—and as the source of that mortal corruption that is always already in those who are 'conceived in the midst of that privy lodging, betwixt and among variety of excrements' (pp. 177–8). But this privy space appears again in the middle court, where it belongs with the region of psychological privacy into which the soul (normally ensconced in the head) is said to withdraw 'when it is in some meditation, or deeper thoughts . . . as it were to go aside into some secret closet, or darker study, that it might bring forth counsel as out of a hidden treasury' (p. 59).

The scandalous interrelation of these apparently conflicting ideas of the private—that which is at once so valuable and so intrinsic to the self that it must be shut away and protected; and that which is so shameful, that it must be buried from view—is reflected in the culture's contradictory attitudes towards bodily secrets, especially those of the female body. Thus, for example, the misogynistic pamphlet *Hic Mulier* (1620) displays deeply ambiguous feelings about female concealment: on the one hand, women are denounced for the 'foul vizards' which make of their bodies a 'huge frame or mass of disguises'; on the other, they are urged to avoid 'immodest

[15] 'Privy' was itself, of course, liable to similarly ambiguous construction; and by the 1660s at least 'closet' had come to carry almost identical meanings.

discoveries' and to keep hidden everything that may 'inchant the weak passenger to shipwrack and destruction' (sig. B4). They are bound to 'discover unto men all things that are fit for them to understand', but commanded to 'hide . . . in the closest prisons of [their] strictest government' anything which is liable to excite 'wanton and lascivious delight and pleasure' (sig. B2ᵛ–B4). Face-painting is especially detestable since it is at once a mode of wicked disguise and a form of 'immodest discovery'—at once a kind of corrupt deceit and (as the pamphleteer earlier expresses it) a brand whose 'marks stick so deep on their naked faces, and more naked bodies, that not all the painting in *Rome* . . . can conceal them, but every eye discovers them almost as low as their middles' (sig. B1ᵛ).[16] Concealment, then, can be both reprehensible hypocrisy and a necessary engine of chastity—just as what is hidden is at one moment a source of contamination that must be contained, and at another a treasure or 'relique' that needs to be protected from thieves and usurpers.[17]

In terms of the traditional allegoric schemes which *The Changeling* at once exploits and transforms, Vermandero as the Lord of the Castle, is the head of its body, enthroned in the seat of patriarchal authority and reason. But his government is restricted by its implication with the lower, and typically female, domain of animality and passion: in Bakhtinian terms, the play introduces us to a world publicly constituted according to the language of the classical body, 'a language governed by the hierarchy and etiquette of "palaces, churches, institutions and private homes"'; but a world secretly marked by the instabilities of the grotesque body with its dangerously uncertain boundaries, its treacherous openings and orifices.[18] Considered as a social edifice, the castle–body exists to

[16] For Purchas, similarly, extravagance in dress only produces a kind of moral nakedness: 'since Man stripped himself of his best clothing, his very clothing makes him naked; and hard it is to say whether savage American nakedness, or curious fantastical attire do more deform him' (p. 255).

[17] Significantly John Banister's claim 'to set wide open the closet door of nature's secrets, to see clearly all the parts, and notable devices of nature in the body of man' is qualified by a modest refusal to inspect the secrets of the female body: 'From the female . . . I have wholly abstained my pen, lest, shunning *Charybdis*, I should fall into *Scylla* headlong' (*Historie of Man*, sig. B1ᵛ).

[18] Mikhail Bakhtin, *Rabelais and his World*, trans. Helene Ilswolsky (Cambridge, Mass.: MIT Press, 1968), as cited in Peter Stallybrass, 'Patriarchal Territories: The Body Enclosed', in Susan Snyder (ed.), *Othello: Critical Essays* (New York: Garland, 1988), 252. Stallybrass's application of Bakhtin's theory to Jacobean

encircle and protect that private domain; but what makes it so vulnerable is that its garrison is by definition given to passionate mutiny and shameful betrayal. 'Love', wrote Francis Bacon, 'can find entrance not only into an open heart, but to a heart well fortified, if watch be not kept.'[19] The protected secret is at once a source of mysterious power and the cause of deadly weakness. In this it reflects the ambiguous nature of female sexuality, as exhibited (or, more properly, *concealed*), according to Duby and Braunstein, in the female sex-organs themselves: 'Woman's body is a mirror of Adam's body; in particular, the female sex-organs are similar in structure, but turned around, introverted, more secret and thus more private but also, like anything hidden, suspect. ... her body is dangerous—both in danger and a source of danger.'[20]

Thus in *Hic Mulier*, published two years before the first staging of *The Changeling*, while women 'armed with the infinite power of virtue, are castles impregnable ... sentinels most careful' (sig. A3^{v}), the female body is generally a 'structure or frame' liable to sensual betrayal, unless care be taken to keep 'every window closed with a strong casement, and every loop-hole furnished with such strong ordnance that no unchaste eye may come near to assail them; no lascivious tongue woo a forbidden passage, nor no profane hand touch relics so pure and religious. Guard them about with counter-scar[p]s of innocence, trenches of human reason, and impregnable walls of sacred divinity' (sig. B4).[21]

drama is usefully extended in 'Reading the Body: *The Revenger's Tragedy* and the Jacobean Theater of Consumption', *Renaissance Drama*, NS 18 (1987), 121–48. See also Gail Kern Paster, 'Leaky Vessels: The Incontinent Women of Jacobean City Comedy', *Renaissance Drama*, NS 18 (1987), 71–86, repr. as ch. 1 of *The Body Embarrassed* (pp. 23–63).

[19] Francis Bacon, 'Of Love', in *Essays*, intro. Oliphant Smeaton (London: Dent, 1906), 29.

[20] Ariès and Duby, *A History of Private Life*, ii. 524.

[21] *Hic Mulier*'s metaphors neatly exemplify Mary Douglas's remarks in *Purity and Danger* about the body as 'a model which can stand for any bounded system ... [whose] orifices symbolise its specially vulnerable points' (pp. 115, 121). 'In a patrilineal system of descent,' she notes, the female body in itself constitutes a vulnerable point of entry into the social body, for 'wives are the door of entry to the group. ... Through the adultery of a wife impure blood is introduced to the lineage. So the symbolism of the imperfect vessel appropriately weighs more heavily on the women than on the men' (p. 126). In *The Changeling* and other texts of this period the female body is the door of entry for death itself.

Entering the Body

The Changeling is fascinated by the ambivalence of bodily secrets. Its final discovery—equated with the triumph of De Flores' plague, with mortality itself—is that the two kinds of secret are actually indistinguishable, that the secret treasure at the heart of the castle is only a kind of shame, a cistern of corrupted waste, a figuration of death:

> Oh come not near me, sir; I shall defile you.
> I am that of your blood was taken from you
> For your better health; look no more upon't,
> But cast it to the ground regardlessly;
> Let the common sewer take it from distinction.
>
> (V. iii. 149–53)

The play begins, as Alsemero is made to inform us, just outside the castle walls in the hallowed precincts of a church (''Twas in the temple where I first beheld her, | And now again the same'; I. i. 1–2)—a place which he associates with Beginning itself:

> The place is holy, so is my intent . . .
> And that methinks, admits comparison
> With man's first creation, the place blest,
> And is his right home back, if he achieve it.
> The church hath first begun our interview,
> And that's the place must join us into one;
> So there's beginning and perfection too.
>
> (I. i. 5–12)

Alsemero proposes for himself an ending which, in the manner of a divine comedy, must perfect this Edenic beginning; but the circular plot he envisages will be betrayed by the remorseless linearity of an action that merely recapitulates the primal tragedy of fall and expulsion—and that does so, moreover, in terms of an elaborate cloacal metaphor which reduces that spiritual history to the gross materiality of purgative evacuation.[22] The imminent necessity of such a purge is hinted at both in Alsemero's careless self-mockery concerning his 'hidden malady', and in Jasperino's bawdy

[22] Cf. Whigham, 'Reading Social Conflict', 340.

offer to provide Diaphanta with a physic that will 'tame the maddest blood' in their two bodies (line 147).

From the church, the action of the first scene moves to the gates of Vermandero's castle, a place whose 'chief strengths' the old man immediately identifies with its capacity to contain and protect secrets from the eyes of strangers:

our citadels
Are placed conspicuous to outward view,
On promonts' tops, but within are secrets.
(lines 167–9)

'Secrets', as Anne Ferry has observed, '[was] the commonest term in sixteenth-century English for the contents of the heart';[23] and the imagery of the scene expressly associates this secretive fortress with the aristocratic body of the female protagonist. Beatrice herself speaks of eyes as 'sentinels unto our judgements' (line 73);[24] and Alsemero's 'How shall I dare to venture in his castle, | When he discharges murderers at the gate?' (lines 225–6), while it may refer immediately to the unwelcome news of Beatrice's betrothal, is bound to recall the ocular cannonades of the conventional Petrarchan mistress. Vermandero's castle is, however, like Alibius' madhouse, a place rendered vulnerable by the very possession of those 'secrets' which make it a site of power; and as Alibius' domestic control is constantly threatened by the intrusions of Isabella's would-be seducers, so Vermandero's patriarchal realm is felt as a place constantly under siege.[25]

In both cases, however, the true threat proves to come from within rather than from without. Faced with the violated and dying body of his daughter, caught in the arms of her tempter, Vermandero breaks out, 'An host of enemies entered my citadel |

[23] Ferry, *'Inward' Language*, 8.

[24] The heavy irony of her misconception is underlined by Purchas's characterization of the eye as the port of error and the ear as the port of knowledge and piety: 'the EYE usually is an impediment (I mean in this our present corruption). . . . A good life begins at a good EAR, which, with a bad EYE, is usually corrupted' (p. 93); the eye he insists, in a whole chapter devoted to 'the manifold sins of the eyes' is 'a window for Hell, a loop-hole for Lust to shoot out, a look-hole for the Devil to shoot in himself and his fiery darts' (pp. 230–1).

[25] For discussion of the female body as a besieged fortress whose portals must be vigilantly policed, see Duby and Braunstein in Ariès and Duby, *A History of Private Life*, ii. 524–5; and Stallybrass, 'Patriarchal Territories', *passim*. Cf. also Douglas, 115–26.

Could not amaze like this' (v. iii. 147). The recognition is dawning in him that the castle has been mined from within, its peril having always lain in the very secrets it existed to guard. The source of defilement, which Beatrice discovers to him, the poisoned well from which the plague has spread, is after all in his own blood. The disturbing consequence is a subversion of the whole dialectic of inside and outside on which the constitution of subjectivity depends.

Much the same thing occurs in the subplot, where Alibius' household, like Vermandero's castle, is managed as a fortress-prison, protecting his secret, a 'knowledge . . . nearer, | Deeper, and sweeter' (I. ii. 12–13), from the 'shrewd temptations' and 'quick enticing eyes' of gallant visitors. The real menace to the body domestic, however, is once again an internal one—figured in the shrieking horde of madmen locked up in his asylum, incarnations of a passionate and turbulent animality that repeatedly demands to be 'fed'.

In a sense, of course, the madmen are both 'outside' and 'inside' (rather as early seventeenth-century medicine represented madness as both interior disorder and diabolical invasion)—they press from without upon the private space in which Alibius tries to protect his hidden treasure;[26] but, in a way that capitalizes on the ambiguous nature of Elizabethan theatrical space, they are also, as the stage directions remind us, 'within' (I. ii. 205), confined like other manifestations of the shameful body to a place of concealment.[27] They belong, that is to say, to the absent–present scene of forbidden desire which it is the play's business to discover. Release is permitted them only in the temporary carnivalesque licence of the 'wild distracted measure' they will dance for Beatrice's wedding revels—'an unexpected passage over | To make a *frightful pleasure*' (III. iii. 270–4; emphasis added)—which they rehearse at the

[26] For comment on the *topos* in which a wife is thought of as 'locked up amongst his other precious goods' in the private chamber of a wealthy man, see Orest Ranum, 'The Refuges of Intimacy', in Ariès and Duby, *A History of Private Life*, iii. 207–63: 218, and Stallybrass, 'Patriarchal Territories', 257.

[27] The madmen, one might suggest, stand in the same relation to the 'secrets' of the Vermandero's castle, as De Flores to the secrets of Beatrice's inner self. The nature of that relation is perhaps best expressed in a remark of Kenneth Burke's about Iago: 'What arises within, if it wells up strongly and presses for long, will seem imposed from without' (Kenneth Burke, '*Othello*: An Essay to Illustrate a Method', in Snyder (ed.), *Othello*, 128). See also Kowsar's essay 'Middleton and Rowley's *The Changeling*' for a reading which identifies the madmen as exemplifications of the Bakhtinian '"other side" of that which is denied. . . . the carnival truth of humans becoming animals' (pp. 160–1).

end of Act IV. But their offstage howlings serve as a constant reminder of how they must be disciplined to prevent a sudden wild irruption upon their keeper's private realm, such as occurs in Act III, scene iii. In this scene, which is strategically placed between the murder of Piracquo and Beatrice's *éclaircissement* with De Flores, the pretended lunatics begin their assault upon Isabella's virtue. The cries of the madmen serve as an intermittent chorus to the action, linking it to the myth of fall and damnation enacted in the main plot: 'Bounce, bounce, he falls, he falls! . . . Catch there, catch the last couple in hell!' (II. iii. 116, 172–3); and at the same time their presence 'within' ironizes the dialectic of outward show and inward reality on which the courtship of the counterfeit inmates, Antonio and Franciscus, depends. Antonio's 'shape of folly', he proclaims, is a demonstration of love's power of metamorphosis:

> Love has an intellect that runs through all
> The scrutinous sciences and, like
> A cunning poet, catches a quantity
> Of every knowledge, yet brings all home
> Into one mystery, into one secret
> That he proceeds in. (III. iii. 130–5)

Yet beneath 'these outward follies', he insists, an essential self remains unaltered—one that corresponds perfectly to the public persona that existed before his transformation: 'there is within | A gentleman that loves you' (lines 146–7); and this hidden sanity, Antonio suggests, is in the power of Isabella's vision to restore:

> Look you but cheerfully, and in your eyes
> I shall behold mine own deformity
> And dress myself up fairer. I know this shape
> Becomes me not, but in those bright mirrors
> I shall array me handsomely.
> (lines 194–8)

The speech provides the cue for the spectacular entry of the 'Madmen, *above, some as birds, others as beasts*', who indeed mirror with ironic exactitude his own deformity—one that he cannot, however, recognize, since it is confined 'within', out of his own sight. The madmen, by contrast, 'That act their fantasies in any shapes | Suiting their present thoughts' (lines 202–3) represent, in Isabella's description of them, an innocent conformity of the inward and the outward; but it is a conformity possible only in the case of creatures utterly 'out of form and figure' (line 274), whose demeanour confounds the must fundamental distinctions of human form:

> Sometimes they imitate the beasts and birds,
> Singing, or howling, braying, barking; all
> As their wild fancies prompt 'em.
>
> (lines 205–7)

It is as if what lies within, the hidden secret at the core of selfhood, amounts (in a disturbing reversal of the Aristotelian doctrine that the soul is the 'form' of the body) to a kind of formlessness, like the 'chaos' that comes again to Othello, a confusion of bestial desire; and this indeed (beyond its simple didactic point about the true and false vision of reason and desire) is what Isabella's own disguise plot in Act IV, scene iii demonstrates. Performing giddy changes on the dialectic of insides and outsides (lines 6–24, 51–5), it leads her through 'the lower labyrinth' of sexual desires to 'discover the [real] fool' and the true madman lurking beneath the disguises of madness and folly.

Private Passages

Meanwhile, the main plot is feeling its way towards similar disclosures. It, too, is increasingly preoccupied with secrets of the interior self. As if unconsciously paraphrasing Othello's characterization of Emilia, Alsemero imagines that Diaphanta will give him access to what he covets in Beatrice: 'These women are the ladies' cabinets; | Things of most precious trust are locked into 'em' (II. ii. 6–7).[28] His reflection metonymically announces the movement of the action deeper into the private spaces of the castle. The waiting-woman has brought him by a 'private way' to an assignation with Beatrice (line 55). But the real master of these private passages is De Flores, who turns out to have watched the whole meeting from some place of concealment; and it is he who will conduct the action into the most secret places of all.

From the beginning De Flores has been made to appear as

[28] Cf. 'This is a subtle whore; | A closet lock and key of villainous secrets' (IV. ii. 25).

Alsemero's dark Other: Beatrice's irrational aversion for him exactly corresponds to her equally irrational desire for her new lover. Alsemero's explanation, 'There's scarce a thing that is both loved and loathed' (I. i. 126), hints at the virtual interchangeability of loving and loathing in a paradox which Act II, scene ii begins to enact. 'Men of art', Beatrice reflects, 'make much of poison, | Keep one to expel another' (II. ii. 46–7); she has in mind using De Flores to purge her of the unwanted Piracquo, but the structure of the scene produces a different homology, in which it is Alsemero whom De Flores will in effect expel. Beatrice herself, careless of the implication, chooses him as the substitute for her lover, whose chivalric offer of 'service' in a duel with Alonzo de Piracquo (lines 21–8) De Flores is encouraged to take up in the form of murder (line 93). Beatrice privately intends 'service' in a purely menial sense (that is part of the 'secret' which she treasures; line 67), but she repeats the word with such caressing insistence that De Flores' knightly gesture seems perfectly fitted to the occasion: 'Put it not from me; | It is a service that I kneel for' (lines 116–17), and the bargain is sealed with a promise that recalls Alsemero's metaphoric cabinet of treasures: 'Thy reward shall be precious' . . . '[I] know it will be precious, the thought ravishes' (lines 130–2).

This scene concludes with a brief coda in which De Flores undertakes to introduce Alonzo to 'The full strength of the castle' by guiding him through 'the ways and straits' of its passages. The discarded lover is about to get a fatal glimpse of those secrets which the head of the house likes to keep from the eyes of strangers. In the remarkable series of short scenes which open Act III De Flores leads him into the very bowels of the fortress: 'you shall see anon | A place you little dream on' (III. ii. 1–2). De Flores' control over these inner reaches is symbolized by the bunch of keys that will unlock 'all' its doors (III. iii. 1–3); and by a remarkable metatheatrical coup that gains him access to the temporal no man's land between the acts, to hide a naked rapier '*in the act-time*' (III. i). As victim and murderer wind their way through increasingly cramped passageways and stairwells, recalling the 'labyrinthian gyres and winding revolutions' that Purchas discovered in the secret interior of the lower body (p. 39), it is apparent that their journey is downward as well as inward: 'The *descent* is somewhat narrow' (line 6). It brings them to a casement, from which Alonzo may see 'the full strength of all the castle' (III. ii. 7), including 'ordnance . . . will ring you a peal like bells | At great men's funerals' (lines 11–12); as he gazes, his guide performs his brutal 'work of secrecy' upon him (line 16). To complete the mortal purge, De Flores proceeds to 'clear the passages from all suspect and fear' (lines 24–5).

The labyrinthine descent acted out by De Flores and Piracquo in the murder scenes is re-enacted in psychological terms by De Flores and Beatrice in Act III, scene iv. A person's hidden thoughts, wrote Levin Lemmens in *The Touchstone of Complexions* (1581), are to be discovered in '[the] most secret corners and innermost places . . . conveyed by many crooked by-ways and windings'.[29] It is through such windings that De Flores is about to conduct his second victim: confronted with the shocking proof of her servant's 'work of secrecy', she finds herself 'in a labyrinth' (line 71) facing the blood-boltered minotaur of her own hidden desire.[30] For her, as De Flores instinctively realizes, killing is conceived not merely as an off-stage action, but as a way of permanently removing an unwanted object to the invisible off-stage setting: 'His end's upon him; | He shall be *seen no more*' (II. ii. 134–5; emphasis added). It is thus a 'work of secrecy' in a complex sense, both a secret action and a making of secrets. De Flores' display of the severed finger disgracefully flaunts what has been defined as invisible, so that murder is transformed to psychological assault: ''tis impossible thou canst . . . shelter such a cunning cruelty, | To make his death the murderer of my honour' (III. iv. 120–2); and Beatrice, like Piracquo, is brought to see a place she little dreamed of: 'thou'lt love anon | What thou so fear'st and faint'st to venture on' (lines 170–1). But this is also Middleton's equivalent for the temptation scene in *Othello*. Like that scene it establishes a bond of unholy wedlock: De Flores offers the uncanny bonding of finger to ring ('I could not get the ring without the finger . . . it stuck | As if the flesh and it were both one substance' (lines 28, 38–9) as a sign not merely of Beatrice's irrefragable betrothal to Piracquo,

[29] Ferry, *'Inward' Language*, 59.

[30] Like so many other details in the main plot, the labyrinth image is reflected in the distorting mirror of the lower plot, when Isabella, in her guise as madwoman, makes her sexual invitation to the horrified Antonio; the labyrinth here makes of the female genitalia the mortal passageway of death: 'Stand up, thou son of Cretan Dedalus, | And let us tread the lower labyrinth; | I'll bring thee to the clue' (IV. iii. 110–12).

but of the new intimacy which his remorseless innuendo slowly brings her to recognize: 'we should *stick together*. . . . Nor is it fit we two, *engaged so jointly*, | Should part and live asunder. . . . peace and innocency has turned you out | And made you *one with me*' (lines 84, 88–9, 139–40; my emphasis).

The moment of recognition is a kind of Fall:

> settle you
> In what the act has made you. . . .
> You must forget your parentage to me;
> Y'are the deed's creature; by that name
> You lost your first condition.
>
> (lines 134–8)

—and the Fall is always a discovery of Death.[31] This, for Beatrice, is the moment of mortal arrest, when De Flores, 'serpent', 'basilisk', 'sepulchre', and 'pest-house', unmasks himself as the mocking leveller of distinction and the avatar of her own end, speaking in the accents of a grim summoner from the *danse macabre*—'In death and shame my partner she shall be' (line 140)—as he leads her to a new 'work of secrecy', their fatal coupling, in words that disturbingly echo the Duchess of Malfi's reassurances to Antonio, with their ambiguous promise of eternal rest:[32]

> Come, rise, and shroud your blushes in my bosom;
> Silence is one of pleasure's best receipts;
> Thy peace is wrought for ever in this yielding.
>
> (lines 167–9)

At a less metaphysical level, however, this history of fall and expulsion can be reduced to the mere purging of corrupt matter. Desire begins in appetite, and proceeds through gorging to a purge and 'easing'. De Flores is 'as greedy of [Beatrice's body] as the

[31] The Fall motif becomes most explicit, perhaps, in the final scene of the play where Jasperino, who broke into Alsemero's meditation on 'man's first creation' at the beginning of the first scene, reveals his discovery of Beatrice's sin: 'The prospect from the garden has showed | Enough for deep suspicion' (v. iii. 2)—a revelation that leads immediately to Beatrice's confession, 'I have . . . stroked a serpent' (line 66).

[32] *Duchess of Malfi*, I. i. 467–8, 503–4: 'here upon your lips I sign your *Quietus est*. . . . let me shroud my blushes in your bosom | Since 'tis the treasury of all my secrets'. The echo highlights Middleton's deliberate inversion of Webster's scene: where the aristocratic woman once wooed the steward, now the steward woos his mistress.

parched earth of moisture' (III. iv. 107–8); and by the end he will have 'drunk up all' as insatiably as Diaphanta's 'greedy appetite' is said to '[devour] the pleasure' of Alsemero's flesh (V. ii. 170, V. i. 3). To imagine satisfaction is already to envisage its degraded consequence: 'I'm in pain,' De Flores tells Beatrice, with brutal directness, 'and must be eased of you' (lines 98–9)—just as murder eased Beatrice of the poison of Piracquo, and as Antonio promises that Isabella will be 'eased' of his rival Franciscus (IV. iii. 158). The last two acts of the play work out the metaphor of purging to its logical end in the indistinction of the common sewer.[33]

Discovering Death

> *Thou shalt bring every work to judgement, with every secret thing; and there is nothing covered that shall not be revealed.* ... As physic works, so it draws the peccant humour to itself, that, when it is gathered together, the weight of itself may carry that humour away.
>
> (John Donne, *Devotions upon Emergent Occasions*[34])

The plot of the virginity test, which takes up most of Act IV, is often regarded as a slightly embarrassing anomaly, a relic of superstitions incompatible with the 'psychological realism' admired elsewhere in the play. Indeed the risible triviality of the symptoms upon which its diagnostics depend—gaping, sneezing, and laughing—seems to be half-acknowledged in the description of the test as 'A merry sleight, but true experiment'. In theatrical terms, moreover, Alsemero's pretensions to physic are rendered even more ridiculous by the effortless pretence with which Beatrice outwits them. The mockery has a point, however: it is connected with the play's dialectic of inside and outside, and its associated metaphor of purging as dis-covery.

The fourth act begins with a dumb show that juxtaposes the 'great state' of Beatrice's marriage to Alsemero with the startling

[33] Purging, it may be worth remembering, 'eases' the body by reversing the humoral imbalance of 'dis-ease'.

[34] John Donne, *Devotions upon Emergent Occasions Together with Death's Duel* (Ann Arbor: University of Michigan Press, 1959), 66–7.

appearance of Alonzo's ghost before De Flores, 'showing him the hand whose finger he had cut off' (IV. i). It is a scene whose grim semaphore of bonds violated and reclaimed spectacularly enacts the contrast between outward display and hidden secrets in Vermandero's castle; and it acts as a prologue to a scene in which Beatrice contemplates the terror of a wedding-night that promises only the certainty of exposure. At the literal level her imagination fixes on the possibility of punishment in a way that suggests she has read *Othello*:

> There's no venturing
> Into his bed, what course so'er I light upon,
> Without my shame, which may grow up to danger;
> He cannot but in justice strangle me
> As I lie by him. (IV. i. 11–15)

But her language also plays on other, less articulate fears in which the penetration of the body becomes equivalent to the looting of its secrets, and so to a kind of unmaking of the inner self. 'This fellow has undone me endlessly,' Beatrice's soliloquy begins (IV. iii. 1), where *undoing* stands not merely for betrayal and sexual pillage, but (in a fashion that she herself can barely recognize as yet) for a radical unstitching of identity. To 'think upon th'ensuing night', she finds, is merely to 'dive | Into my own distress'; but that flight inwards offers 'no hiding', since its secret darkness is threatened by the dreadful illumination she attributes to Alsemero's understanding, whose impartial clarity recalls the ferocious indifference of plague—'That's my plague now' (lines 3–10). This tagging of Alsemero with the very imagery that is used to characterize De Flores' threat to difference and distinction matches the physical substitutions of the plot even as it helps to explain their significance.

The sequence which follows has something of the hallucinatory strangeness of a nightmare: at the very moment when Beatrice feels most exposed to the cunning of Alsemero's penetrating gaze, her eye falls upon the cabinet of his own secrets, a 'closet' with the key providentially left in it. As in the murder episode, and again in the final madhouse scene (IV. iii. 50–4), the key stands for control over private, inward spaces, the realm of the hidden, the precious, and the shameful:

> That key will lead thee to a pretty secret
> By a Chaldean taught me. . . .

It has that secret virtue, it ne'er missed, sir,
Upon a virgin (IV. ii. 111–12, 139–40)

Alsemero will inform the suspicious Jasperino. The deliberately pedestrian reminiscence of Othello's prophetic 'Egyptian charmer' in Alsemero's Chaldean tutor establishes an unexpected link between key and handkerchief as tokens of the hidden. Here the key enables Beatrice to uncover, concealed in Alsemero's closet, the thing that makes him 'The master of the mystery' (line 39), a manuscript entitled 'The Book of Experiment, | Called Secrets in Nature' (lines 24–5). As its name suggests, this volume is itself a kind of key, offering to unlock the truth of Beatrice's virginity—a secret which, in a variation on the metaphor of purging, will be expelled in the bizarrely concrete form of incontinent gaping, sudden laughter, and violent sneezing (lines 49–51).

Beatrice's usurpation of Alsemero's 'most admirable secret' (line 109), however, easily frustrates his police prerogative over her body. The intended purge becomes instead her own casting out of fear: 'Now if the experiment be true, 'twill praise itself | And *give me noble ease*' (lines 105–6; emphasis added)—a process symbolically completed in the murder of Diaphanta. This last phase of Beatrice's conspiracy is acted out by De Flores as a bizarre cleansing of the castle–body, another clearing of the passages. 'How this fire purifies wit!' he crows (line 55); and his newly physicked invention promptly turns fire into an emblem of bodily evacuation too, as he rushes with his 'piece', like some monstrous clyster-pipe, to scour the chimney of Diaphanta's private chamber (line 88). Just as Beatrice herself once used the poison of De Flores to expel the poison of Alonzo, so now De Flores uses fire to drive out fire—the conflagration of Diaphanta's lust (V. i. 107–8, 115) and Beatrice's burning fame (line 34).

This metaphoric linkage of maid and mistress, like the enacted pun of the bed-trick itself, suggests an uncanny interchangeability—one that is also implicit in Beatrice's railing against Diaphanta's treacherous blood ('This whore forgets herself', V. i. 23) with its echo of De Flores' bitter gibe, 'Push, *you forget yourself*! | A woman dipped in blood, and talk of modesty?' (lines 125–6). The fire is a brutally literalized metaphor, a purging of the lustful blood which to Beatrice is the vehicle of a secret that may otherwise leak out to betray her: 'No trusting of her life with such a secret, | That cannot rule her blood to keep her promise' (v. i. 6–7). But the real source of danger is her own blood; and tainted blood, as De Flores, haunted by the stench of murder about his victim's brother (IV. ii. 41), already knows, will find its own way out. 'That De Flores has a wondrous honest heart;' Tomazo reflects, 'He'll bring it out in time' (IV. ii. 57–8). The unconscious irony of that 'bring it out' is confirmed when they next meet, for it is as if De Flores were suddenly and unaccountably suffused with the signs of his secret wickedness:

> I find a contrariety in nature
> Betwixt that face and me . . .
> he's so foul
> One would scarce touch [him] with a sword he loved
> And made account of. So most deadly venomous,
> He would go near to poison any weapon
> That should draw blood on him . . .
> Some river must devour't; 'twere not fit
> That any man should find it. . . .
> He walks a'purpose by, sure to choke me up,
> To infect my blood. (v. ii. 13–25)

For Tomazo, De Flores is now a poison who must be flushed, together with everything that has been touched by his infection, from the body domestic ('Some river must devour't'). A strange reversal has occurred: Tomazo, who once professed to see through De Flores' foul exterior to his honest heart, now speaks the language which, at the beginning of the play, registered Beatrice's own violent antipathy to the manservant's 'dog-face'. Beatrice, on the other hand, though she finds that 'his face [still] loathes one', looks through it to a 'care' and 'service' that make De Flores into 'a man worth loving', beautiful in her sight (lines 70–2, 76). Both perceptions are in their way true, and each illustrates something about the biological imperative implicit in the play's metaphoric system.

The confession suddenly inscribed on De Flores' face serves as a reminder that one of the most common available senses of 'purge' was 'confess'. The diagnostic method of Alsemero's 'Book of . . . Secrets in Nature' amounts precisely to a species of purging-as-confession, compelling those hidden thoughts which, as Diaphanta observes, 'are so unwilling to be known' (line 65), to discharge themselves in infallible outward demonstrations—gaping, sneezing, violent laughing—rather as secret shame might manifest itself in the involuntary surfeit of blushing. Crudely and unreliably mechanical as his technique proves, there nevertheless seems to be at work in *The Changeling* a natural compulsion to purgative self-disclosure, which helps to account for the curiously anti-climactic plotting of Middleton and Rowley's denouement.

In plot terms Tomazo's moment of anagnorisis leads nowhere; but it follows hard upon De Flores' violent attempt at purging the castle; and it immediately precedes the utterly unexpected disclosure of Beatrice's perfidy. A curious irony, echoing the general logic of bodily substitution, seems to engulf De Flores' scheme at this point: barely has he made safe from discovery Diaphanta's scene of secret adultery than his own adulterous communion with Beatrice is laid bare—fittingly enough by Diaphanta's wooer, Jasperino. The garden where their crime is discovered, a *hortus conclusus* associated by both myth and literary convention with the satisfaction of transgressive desire, is another of the play's ambiguous private spaces[35]—suddenly as open to Jasperino's suspicious gaze as De Flores has become transparent to Tomazo. The discovery which now unfolds is presented in language which invites the audience to recognize in it the culmination of the play's most insistent metaphoric themes. It is a surgical disclosure of corrupted excrement ('Touch it home then: 'tis not a shallow probe | Can search this ulcer soundly; I fear you'll find it | Full of corruption'; (v. iii. 7–9); it is a curing of the mysterious 'hidden malady' of the opening scene (lines 15–18); and above all it is the final sack and slighting of the castellated body—a violent anatomy of the truth concealed in Beatrice's heart:

[BEATRICE] oh, you have ruined
What you can ne'er repair again.

[35] See Danielle Régnier-Bohler, 'Imagining the Self', in Ariès and Duby, *A History of Private Life*, ii. 322 for a discussion of the orchard or garden as a traditional site of amorous encounter, which, like other private, enclosed spaces, 'reflects an obsession with boundaries and their ambivalence'; and cf. Stallybrass, 'Patriarchal Territories', 254–60. For further discussion of violated boundaries in the play, see Kowsar, 'Middleton and Rowley's *The Changeling*' (156–9), who interprets Beatrice's final speech as a tactic of Kristevan 'abjection', covertly announcing a triumphant defilement of patriarchal territory.

ALSEMERO. I'll all demolish, and seek out truth within you,
If there be any left; let your sweet tongue
Prevent your heart's rifling; there I'll ransack
And tear out my suspicion.
BEATRICE. You may, sir,
'Tis an easy passage. (V. iii. 34–40)

The word that provokes Beatrice's outburst is the same word she applied to Diaphanta—'whore'. Beatrice feels it like a slap: 'What a horrid sound it hath!' Her wounded primness not only acts as a reminder that this is Middleton and Rowley's version of the brothel scene ('Am I that word?' *Othello*, IV. ii. 160), but also recalls her stunned reaction to De Flores' sexual demands:

Thy language is so bold and vicious,
I cannot see which way I can forgive it,
With any modesty. (III. iv. 122–4)

Just as the outrage of De Flores' vicious language lay in its abolition of social distinction ('the distance that creation | Set 'twixt thy blood and mine'; III. iv. 130–1), and its claim to make her 'one with [him]' (line 140), so the shock of Alsemero's insult lies in its contemptuous collapsing of differences, identifying her not merely with the corrupt animality of her own servant, but with the physical monstrosity of De Flores: 'thou art all deformed' (line 87). His insult is like the mortifying breath of a pestilence, whose power of absolute disfigurement threatens form itself:

What a horrid sound it hath!
It blasts a beauty to deformity;
Upon what face soever that breath falls,
It strikes it ugly. (V. ii. 31–5)

The terror of 'deformity' is the true secret of the pest-house over which De Flores presides, a place where, in Alsemero's words, 'The bed itself's a charnel, the sheets shrouds | For murdered carcasses' (lines 83–4).[36] Here the place of making is collapsed

[36] In *Hic Mulier* 'deformity', the unforming of the natural self, is the condition to which women are repeatedly said to be reduced by their violation of the laws of kind; it is a condition that threatens to level all 'difference' and 'distinction' of both gender and degree: 'It is an infection that emulates the plague, and throws itself amongst women of all degrees, all deserts, and all ages; from the Capitol to the cottage are some spots or swellings of this disease, yet evermore the greater the person is, the greater is the rage of this sickness, and the more they have to support the eminence of their fortunes, the more they bestow in the augmentation of their deformities' (sig. B1^{v}).

into the place of unmaking, where one piece of venereal carrion is indistinguishable from the next—as Diaphanta's bawdy paraphrase of Hamlet has already suggested: 'Earth-conquering Alexander, that thought | The world too narrow for him, in the end had but his pit-hole' (IV. i. 62–3). To it, in a last and brutally excremental variation upon the theme of purging, Beatrice consigns the very blood which once symbolized her distance from De Flores:

> I am that of your blood was taken from you
> For your better health; look no more upon't,
> But cast it to the ground regardlessly;
> Let the common sewer take it from distinction.
>
> (lines 150–53)

We have descended now into the very lowest regions of the castle to witness what Purchas called 'the washing of [the] kitchen', in which 'all wheyish and liquid superfluities' are swept 'down to the *grates*, that is, the *kidneys*, which lie hidden in the abstrusest parts of the whole body.... whence otherwise the *ureters*, as two *common sewers*, convey the same to the *sink*, or greater vault the *bladder*, thence to be exonerated (as by sweat and menstruous purgations ...) from the body's community' (pp. 42–3).

In this purge is disclosed the final secret of the citadel, for 'death', as Donne wrote, imagining his end as a grotesque evacuation, 'is a sordid *postern*, by which I must be thrown out of this world'.[37] From temple to sewer, from privileged head to forbidden anus, from idealized spiritual 'creation' to shameful bodily 'end', the 'issue' of Beatrice's corrupted blood—this has been the three-hour passage of *The Changeling*. In the form of tragedy, Kenneth Burke has suggested, it is possible to discern a survival of ancient purification rituals, such as those by which a city like Athens would seek to rid itself of plague by throwing into the sea a human scapegoat known as the *katharma*—literally, 'that which is thrown away in cleansing; the offscourings, refuse, of a sacrifice'.[38] Middleton and

[37] *The Sermons of John Donne*, ed. Evelyn M. Simpson and George R. Potter, 10 vols. (Berkeley and Los Angeles: University of California Press, 1954), vii. 14. 369: 359.

[38] Burke, '*Othello*', 128; in the light of this play's poison imagery it is worth noting that a synonym for *katharma*, as Burke observes, was *pharmakos* (literally *poisoner*, sorcerer, magician). Cf. also 'The Thinking of the Body', in Burke's

Rowley's tragedy may read as the extreme reduction, the ultimate degradation of such a rite of catharsis—one in which plague and city (castle), body and disease become indistinguishable, and cleansing is tantamount to self-annihilating convulsion.[39]

Yet, for De Flores at least, there is a kind of triumph to be salvaged from the very extremity of the degradation he has helped to produce. After his climactic exposure of their adultery, Alsemero contemptuously returns both Beatrice and De Flores to the scene of desire, the 'keeper's' closet 'within' (v. iii. 86–7), but it is a place which he imagines now as being so far from hidden that he casts himself as the virtual dramatist of its adulterate spectacle:

> ... get you in to her, sir.
> I'll be your pander now; rehearse again
> Your scene of lust, that you may be perfect
> When you shall come to act it to the black audience
> Where howls and gnashings shall be music to you.
> Clip your adult'ress freely; 'tis the pilot
> Will guide you to the Mare Mortuum,
> Where you shall sink to fathoms bottomless.
>
> (lines 113–20)

De Flores, however, remains so much Beatrice's real keeper and 'master of the mysteries' that even as Alsemero and the other voices of the classic body begin to parade their language of judicial closure, their domain, newly protected as they suppose from the invasive threat of enemies, is filled with 'horrid sounds', erupting like the madmen's howls from within. Alsemero's 'Come forth,

Language as Symbolic Action (Berkeley: University of California Press, 1966), 308–43. Compare Donne's *Sermons*, vii. 2. 277–80, where Cain is simultaneously plague and purgative scapegoat: '*Cains* own conscience tells him, *Catharma sum, Anathema sum, I am the plague* of the world, and I must dye to deliver it. *Catharma sum*, I am a *separated Vagabond* ... shut out from all, *Anathema sum*.' René Girard, *Violence and the Sacred* (Baltimore: Johns Hopkins University Press, 1977), 286–90, has a useful discussion linking *pharmakos*, *katharma*, and *katharsis* with 'the obsessive concern during the seventeenth century with clysters and bleedings, with assuring the efficient evacuation of peccant humors' (p. 289).

[39] For some interesting variations on the metaphor of spiritual purging, see Smith, *Perfection Proclaimed*, 60, especially Joseph Salmon's account of God's penetration of his inner self: 'Angry flesh being struck at heart with the piercing dart of vengeance, begins to swell, and contracting all the evil humors of the body into one lump ... at last violently breaks out, and lets forth the very heart or core of its pride and enmity.'

you twins of mischief' (line 142) marks, like the parting of the curtains to display Desdemona's corpse, a moment of shocking dis-covery is which the killing of Beatrice is revealed as the climax of their game of erotic barley-break ('Now we are left in hell'; line 163). De Flores announces his defiance in a language that satirically confounds Alsemero's rhetoric of infinite punishment ('you shall sink to fathoms bottomless'): this monstrous hybrid of Iago and Othello rejoices in nothing less than the experience of touching bottom, of making an end, writing a full stop,

> I thank life for nothing
> But that pleasure; it was so sweet to me
> That I have drunk up all, left none behind
> For any man to pledge me.
> (lines 168–71)

De Flores *is* his desire: to have 'drunk up all' is to have consumed himself. Vermandero longs to 'Keep life in him for further tortures': but there is nothing left in De Flores to reveal. By contrast with Iago's sneering retreat into the castle of enigmatic selfhood ('Demand me nothing. What you know you know'), De Flores seems to confound his questioners with a parade of absolute surface. Yet there is, after all, a paradoxical kind of privacy about a satisfaction so complete that he can hug it to himself like a secret, leaving nothing 'behind for any man to pledge me'. De Flores prevents his enemies' designs in what seems like a last ironic travesty of *Othello*: no heroic declamation, no hero's sword for him, but a penknife, that quaint, scalpel-like instrument of private inscription, does the trick.[40]

[40] Analysing the frontispiece portrait of Vesalius in the *Fabrica*, Jonathan Goldberg, *Writing Matter: From the Hands of the English Renaissance* (Stanford, Calif.: Stanford University Press, 1990), notices how the author's twin roles as anatomist and writer are linked by the instrument on the table before him, which may be either penknife or scalpel (p. 86). Cf. also my 'Amphitheaters in the Body: Playing with Hands on the Shakespearian Stage', in *Shakespeare Survey*, 48 (1995), 23–50.

PART II

Making an End: Death's Arrest and the Shaping of Tragic Narrative

5
Anxieties of Ending

Mid-night Death . . .
That end of all usurping ending powers.
(Thomas Newton, *The Death of Delia*[1])

This is one of the extravagances of Western thought: to regard death as the necessary companion of knowledge, as if without death to mark off the boundaries of what we are, there can be no interpretation, no 'meaning' of life.

(Joseph Leo Koerner[2])

Writing Finis

When De Flores contrives, with the aid of his penknife, to prevent the tortures that Vermandero has promised to inflict on him, he imitates one of the most famous episodes in high-Elizabethan drama, Hieronimo's suicide at the end of *The Spanish Tragedy*. His obdurate silence threatened with 'th'extremest kind of death | That ever was invented for a wretch' (IV. iv. 246–7), Kyd's hero stabs himself with the knife he has requested to 'mend his pen'. The choice of instrument to write *finis* to his tragedy is by no means fortuitous, of course; indeed Hieronimo makes its significance explicit by staging his death as the conclusion to the drama he has scripted for the bloody edification of the Spanish court:

And, princes, now behold Hieronimo,
Author and actor in this tragedy,
Bearing his latest fortune in his fist;
And will as resolute conclude his part

[1] Cited in Franco Moretti, 'The Great Eclipse: Tragic Form as the Deconsecration of Sovereignty', in *Signs Taken for Wonders: Essays in the Sociology of Literary Forms*, trans. Susan Fischer, David Fogacs, David Miller (London: Verso, 1983), 43–82: 65.

[2] Koerner, *Moment of Self-Portraiture*, 274.

As any of the actors gone before.
And gentles, thus I end my play.

(IV. iv. 145–50)

From the moment Hieronimo first introduced the play of 'Soliman and Perseda' to his cast by producing the manuscript 'book' of his masterpiece (IV. i. 77), and by distributing the several handwritten 'abstracts' from which the performers are to 'note [their] parts' (lines 140–1), Kyd has been at pains to draw attention to the text's concrete presence as the literal product of Hieronimo's pen. The playbook is introduced again at the beginning of the final scene, where its conveniently summarized 'argument of that they show' is expected to supply a useful guide to a production perplexingly couched in several 'unknown languages' (IV. i. 172). Castile, who is asked to undertake the duty of a 'book-holder', holds the manuscript in his hand and consults it during the performance—much as the real book-holder would have done with the prompt-book of *The Spanish Tragedy* itself; and the King twice asks his brother to elucidate obscurities in the action by 'look[ing] upon the plot' (lines 33–4, 72). To the frustration of the on-stage audience, however, the written key proves teasingly inadequate, leaving the 'mystery' of Hieronimo's tragedy still enfolded within its babel of conflicting tongues. Indeed, though 'Soliman and Perseda' ends in a conventional welter of blood, the tragic spectacle seems oddly incomplete, since the villainous Bashaw, played by the inventor of the piece, remains unpunished—'But now what follows for Hieronimo?' demands the King. The true answer, of course, is not to be found in the playbook; and before Castile can reply, Hieronimo chimes in with a lengthy explanatory epilogue. For all the apparent fullness of his confession, however, the old man is at some pains to make even this act of formal closure seem arbitrary and incomplete: 'I have no more to say. . . . Never shalt thou force me to reveal | The thing which I have vowed inviolate' (lines 151, 187–8). In this context the biting out of his own tongue is a gesture of finality that mockingly insists on unfinished business, expressing (as the author of the Fifth Addition has it) the violent 'rupture' rather than the proper conclusion of his part (line 239). The last secret of Hieronimo's theatre, the thing that still remains unrevealed and unwritten, is its ending. It is at this point that Castile, Hieronimo's manuscript in his hand, reminds the King with savage humour,

'Yet he can write' (line 244); and at Hieronimo's mute request, the Viceroy of Portugal supplies the old man with a penknife to sharpen his quill, advising him, as he does so, to 'write the truth' (line 249). The dumb eloquence of the truth he writes will be inscribed on the bodies of Castile and, above all, of Hieronimo himself as, in a fitting recollection of Bel-Imperia's sanguinary letter of disclosure (III. ii. 23–31), the tragedian pens his enigmatic conclusion in his own blood. The 'fist' that clutches the murderous pen–knife is the same that held the pen 'When in Toledo . . . It was my chance to write [this] tragedy' (IV. i. 76–7); and, by a characteristically ingenious pun, mending his pen turns out to mean emending the script, so that heroic act, histrionic 'action', and authorial pen-stroke are collapsed together in a single gesture of radical closure.[3]

The context for De Flores' equally bloody inscription is less elaborate and explicit; but the killing of Beatrice and his own suicide are once again identified as a kind of savage writing when the bereaved father reads in their corpses the scripture of his own disgrace:

VERMANDERO. Oh, my name is entered now in that record
Where till this fatal hour 'twas never read.
ALSEMERO. Let it be blotted out; let your heart lose,
And it can never look you in the face
Nor tell a tale behind the back of life . . .

(V. iii. 180–4)

As it happens, the link between writing, blood, and the violence of tragic catastrophe is by no means confined to these two texts: one may think of the letters written in blood which seem to script the endings of Chapman's *Bussy D'Ambois* (V. ii. 83.1 ff.) and (even more strikingly) of Ford's *'Tis Pity She's a Whore* (V. iii. 22–39)—where Giovanni's 'unripping' of the letter written in Annabella's heart-blood prefigures his subsequent unripping of her heart itself; or one may recall the extraordinarily painful scene in *Titus Andronicus* where Lavinia uses her mutilated mouth and bloody stumps to write the name of her ravishers in the dust, prompting her father in turn to the violent fantasy of inscription

[3] For some analysis of theatrical conceits linking the powers of the writing, acting, and speaking hand, see my 'Amphitheaters in the Body'.

that announces his implacable revenge ('I will go get a leaf of brass, | And with a gad of steel will write these words'; (IV. i. 102–3).

Jonathan Goldberg has provocatively examined the ways in which the Derridean association of violence with scene of writing is expressed in Renaissance texts by 'the very materials of [the writer's] craft'—above all by the close link (registered as a kind of visual pun) between penknife and pen: 'Writing is wielded as a weapon through a series of positions. The knife works: to produce the quill, to produce the writer.'[4] But there is, it seems to me, a more specific connection between these signs of writerly violence and the writing of tragedy. I have in mind not merely the psychological violence that characterizes the anatomical investigations of tragic drama—its ruthless opening up of hidden interiors—but a larger violence implicit in the narrative design of tragedy with its ferocious concentration upon mortal ends, and its need to mimic the arrest of death in its most sudden and brutal forms. The self-conscious metadrama of an episode like Hieronimo's suicide, in which a professing dramatist writes his own end in blood, allows an unusually sharp glimpse of the ambivalence attaching to such designs. The end is what the tragic dramatist most wishes to bring about, but it is also what (in common with his characters) he most dreads; it is both the end of his writing, and the very thing it wishes to defer. The narrative anxiety generated by that peculiarly tense contradiction is the subject of the present chapter.

This anxiety is perhaps only a subspecies of the generalized human nervousness about the aesthetics of closure that Frank Kermode has examined in *The Sense of an Ending*; and to that extent it is liable to infect any narrative enterprise. On the one hand, Kermode argues, narrative's insistence upon ending answers the fear of mere shapeless chronicity by gratifying the desire for significant form; on the other, it acts as a kind of structural *memento mori*, a figure of apocalypse, and a reminder of the imminence (and immanence) of our own end:

> Men, like poets, rush 'into the middest', *in medias res*, when they are born; they also die *in mediis rebus*, and to make sense of their span they need fictive concords with origins and ends, such as give meaning to lives and to poems. The End they imagine will reflect their irreducibly

[4] Goldberg, *Writing Matter*, 69.

intermediate preoccupations. They fear it, and as far as we can see have always done so; the End is a figure for their own deaths.[5]

But, if every ending is tainted with unease, it is necessarily in tragedy, the drama of death and apocalypse, that such anxieties about the teleological violence of narrative form become most acute.

It can be no accident that the characters of Renaissance tragedy so frequently envisage their ends in heavily narrativized terms. Brutus, for example, claims the mastery of his own death by imagining it as the deliberately orchestrated conclusion of a tragical narrative: 'Brutus' tongue | Hath almost ended his li[f]e's history' (*Julius Caesar*, v. v. 39–40). The entire point of such a history is to make a good end; and the failure to accomplish its proper consummation is always an occasion of extreme distress. Thus the horror of Macbeth's fate lies precisely in the sense of desperate narrative incoherence produced by the contemplation of his own death: when the end is recognized not as fulfilment but as an utter emptying out of meaning, then life is reduced to the senseless confusion of 'a tale told by an idiot'. Macbeth's 'last syllable of recorded time' announces no consummation, no apocalyptic revelation, but merely the arbitrary truncation of a repetitive mechanical series ('tomorrow, and tomorrow, and tomorrow'), 'signifying nothing' (v. iv. 19–28)[6]—an ending which perfectly expresses the principle of entropic undifferentiation that James Calderwood discerns in the battle with which the play opens.[7]

If *Macbeth* exhibits the moral vertigo that attends the inability to impose a shaping end upon the chaotic indigest of experience,

[5] Kermode, *The Sense of an Ending*, 7. Cf. also Spinrad, *Summons of Death*, pp. ix–x.

[6] For a suggestive treatment of the narrative motif in *Macbeth*, see Barbara Hardy, 'The Narrators in *Macbeth*', *Hilda Hume Memorial Lecture, 1986* (London: University of London, 1987).

[7] James L. Calderwood, *Shakespeare and the Denial of Death*, (Amherst: University of Massachusetts Press, 1987) 123: 'The battle . . . is a product of a rebellion against the most meaningful difference in Scotland, that between king and subjects; and in its efforts to elide that difference it is characterised by entropy. It dissipates meaningful human differences, even the differences between friend and foe, in a sea of blood.' Calderwood further notices how this blurring of difference frustrates Macbeth's longing for the definitive ending: 'death, perversely procreative, refuses to be terminal' (p. 124). In an elegant and penetrating account of the problems of ending in Shakespeare Stephen Booth makes much the same point in describing the play as 'all middle' (*'King Lear', 'Macbeth', Indefinition and Tragedy* (New Haven: Yale University Press, 1983), 91).

the deliberately abortive tragedy of *Troilus and Cressida* explores the fate of characters who seem permanently suspended 'in the middest', their psychological coherence repeatedly dissolved by the self-deconstructing narrative in which they float. When Hector, nettled by Ulysses' prophecies of a Trojan Armageddon, refers their quarrel to 'that old common arbitrator, Time', whose decision 'will one day end it', his gesture of abdication is curiously complicated by the familiar proverb that introduces it, *Finis coronat opus*—'The end crowns all' (IV. v. 223–6)—since the end which properly crowns the tragic masterpiece is one that heroic man fashions for himself. Such an end, aimed at transcending the casualties of time, is precisely what the 'monumental mockery' of this tragical satire denies its unheroic heroes—not least in the deliberately abortive design of the final scene. Here Shakespeare, as if recognizing the deconstructive logic of his design, at some point elected to superimpose on the closing couplet of Troilus' heroic peroration ('Strike a free march. To Troy with comfort go; | Hope of revenge shall hide our inward woe'; V. x. 30–1) the busy interruption of Pandarus ('But hear you, hear you') which he had originally intended to appear in V. iii.[8] The resulting bathos strips the play of the dignity of tragic closure, leaving the action as hopelessly intermediate as when the Prologue, in a sardonic parody of epic convention, announced its 'beginning in the middle'.

The way in which the unsettling effect of Shakespeare's hybrid tragedy is confirmed by this deliberate botching of its end seems well calculated to appeal to its presumptive audience of witty intellectuals. But such metatheatrical self-consciousness was by no means peculiar to coterie works like *Troilus*. From the very start, Elizabethan tragedy showed itself unusually knowing about the relation between mortal and narrative endings. This is true even of something as relatively crude as Thomas Preston's *King Cambyses*. The chorus of three Lords who organize Cambyses' funeral procession at the end of the play, for example, imagine the tyrant's death in the language of narrative closure: 'Yet a princely burial he shall have, according to his estate; | *And more of him here at this time we have not to dilate*' (x. 251–2; emphasis added). This

[8] Lines 32–4 of the present V. x appear twice in the Folio text—first at the end of V. iii, from where, as their absence from the Quarto shows, they were meant to be cancelled.

is exactly the 'end . . . decreed' (Epilogue, line 11) to the 'dilation' upon royal tyranny which the Prologue announced at the beginning of the play (line 34). For Preston, however, the shaping of a dramatic narrative seems largely unproblematic; and the shock of abruption created by the King's death can be completely contained by the ritual close of funeral. In the iconoclastic drama of Christopher Marlowe, by contrast, ending becomes an occasion of profound anxiety: in 2 *Tamburlaine* the ruthless end-direction of the hero's triumphal progress is finally revealed as being what the play's meteoric imagery already suggested in Part I, a process of furious self-consumption that can issue only in his own end—as the banally reductive language of the physicians, with its recollection of the Doctor's death in the *Totentanz*, insists:

> The humidum and calor, which some hold
> Is not a parcel of the elements,
> But of a substance more divine and pure,
> Is almost clean extinguished and spent;
> Which, being the cause of life, imports your death.
>
> (v. iii. 86–90)

What results is an ending in which the containing rites of coronation and funeral are undercut by the apocalyptic rant of Amyras' defiance:

> Meet heaven and earth, and here let *all things end*,
> For earth hath spent the pride of all her fruit,
> And heaven consumed his choicest living fire.
>
> (v. iii. 250–2)

In *Doctor Faustus*, where mortal limitation is an even more persistent theme, the anxiety of ending becomes proportionately more intense; but here it is compounded by a gathering horror of no-end.[9] What results is a frenzied climax in which longing for closure and dread of the end are almost evenly poised. In the big soliloquy that opens the play, the hero announces a beginning

[9] In my reading of *Faustus* I am considerably indebted to the seminal essays by Marjorie Garber ('"Infinite Riches in a Little Room": Closure and Enclosure in Marlowe') and Edward A. Snow ('Marlowe's *Dr Faustus* and the Ends of Desire'), both in Alvin Kernan (ed.), *Two Renaissance Mythmakers* (Baltimore: Johns Hopkins University Press, 1977), 3–21, 70–109.

fraught with the consciousness of ending, where every aim appears simply to define a limit, and every *telos* is realized as a *finis*:

> Settle thy studies, Faustus, and *begin*
> To sound the depth of that thou wilt profess:
> Having commenced, be a divine in show,
> Yet level at the *end* of every art . . .
> Is, to dispute well, logic's chiefest *end*?
> Affords this art no greater miracle?
> Then read no more; thou hast attained that *end*. . . .
> The *end* of physic is our body's health.
> Why, Faustus, hast thou not attained that *end*? . . .
> Yet art thou still but Faustus, and a man.
> Couldst thou make men to live eternally,
> Or, being dead, raise them to life again,
> Then this profession were to be esteemed.
> Physic, farewell! (I. i. 1–27; emphasis added)

At the furthest point of all his studies (an 'end' which is also the starting-point of the play) Faustus discovers not revelation but the ironic confinement of divinity, whose doctrine appears to promise him only the fearful oxymoron of ending without end:

> Why, then, belike we must sin,
> And so consequently die:
> Ay, we must die *an everlasting death*.
> (lines 45–7; emphasis added)

Not the least significant of the powers that Faustus attributes to magic is an ability to confound divinity by reversing this threat. For magic seems to hold out the promise of achieving ends without end—a teleological 'omnipotence' (line 55) capable of surpassing all limit. But the supposedly unconditional 'whatsoever' of Faustus' pact with Lucifer absurdly conflicts with the 'wheresoever' of the Devil's counter-claim, and is effectually nullified by the strict 'four and twenty years' of its 'conditions' (II. i. 95–111). The signing of the pact itself is accomplished in language that notoriously confuses two kinds of ending:

> Now will I make an end immediately.
>
> * * * * *
>
> *Consummatum est*, this bill is ended.
> (II. i. 71–3)

For *consummatum* read *finitum*. The writing of the bill in blood is meant to signal a new beginning, invoking a blasphemous analogy with the spiritual rebirth made possible by Christ's blood-sacrifice. Indeed in the following scene the born-again Faustus will compare himself to 'Adam [on] the first day | Of his creation' (II. ii. 116–17); but the parodic misapplication of Christ's last words on the cross ('Consummatum est') serves as a reminder that the magician is dooming himself to an end that excludes consummation.

Christ's words will be punningly echoed once more at the beginning of Faustus' passion in Act V, when Wagner announces the conclusion of his master's diabolic Last Supper: 'Belike *the feast is done*' (V. i. 9; emphasis added)—not *consummatum* here, but *consumptum*. The magic circle that is at once the symbol and the agent of Faustus' infinite desire now becomes the sign of his fatal limitation, marking his painfully human position 'in the middest' between the rival infinities of Heaven and Hell. 'Hell', Mephostophilis warns him, with a sardonic quibble, 'hath no limits, nor is *circumscribed*' (II. i. 121); and, as the protagonist's career 'draws towards a final end' (IV. iii. 24), the horror of an endlessness which he so easily dismissed ('I think hell's a fable'; II. i. 127) will come to embrace the dispensation of God himself—as in Faustus' tormented vision of the heavens, red with sacrificial blood at once infinitely abundant, infinitely potent, and infinitely unattainable ('See, see where Christ's blood streams in the firmament! | One drop would save my soul, half a drop'; V. i. 287–8). By this time, the various reminders of God's 'infinite' mercies, the 'eternal joy and felicity' of heaven, its 'Innumerable joys', 'Pleasures unspeakable, bliss *without end*' (lines 174, 203, 241, 248; emphasis added) serve only as reminders of eternal death, everlasting pain, and perpetual damnation (lines 165–6, 243, 258, 276). The language of Faustus' last speech is dense with apocalyptic suggestion, and in his panic the magus is made to quote the demented kings of the earth in Revelation as they face the terrors of the End: 'mountains and rocks, Fall on us, and hide us . . . from the wrath of the Lamb' (Rev. 6: 16). But in Faustus' case it is less the prospect of punishment and suffering than the vertigo of endlessness that is felt as so unbearable. He beats his head, like Lear, against those stony words that mark the unimaginable boundary between the mortal and the infinite, time and eternity:

> ... and must remain in hell *for ever*—hell, oh, hell *for ever*! Sweet friends, what shall become of Faustus, being in hell *for ever*?

> Now has thou but *one bare hour* to live,
> And then thou must be damned *perpetually*!
> Stand still, you *ever* moving spheres of heaven,
> That time may cease, and midnight *never* come;
> Fair nature's eye, rise, rise, again, and make
> *Perpetual* day ...

> Impose some *end* to my *incessant* pain;
> Let Faustus live in hell a thousand years,
> A hundred thousand, and *at last* be saved!
> No *end* is *limited* to damned souls!

> (v. i. 187–9, 275–80, 309–12; emphasis added)

In the *mise-en-abîme* of Faustus' last soliloquy the terror of ending is locked in struggle with the even greater terror of 'no end', just as in its final lines the fearful closure of midnight is poised against the ghastly opening of Hell.[10] The A text of the play seeks to resolve this tension by an act of violent scission—the sudden silencing of Faustus' cry as the devils drag him into the hell-mouth ('Ah, Mephostophilis!')—and by the intervention of an Epilogue that puts striking prosodic emphasis on the sudden abruption of his career ('*Cut* is the branch.... Faustus is *gone*'). But these gestures seem to have been insufficiently powerful to contain the anxieties let loose by Faustus' torment; for the author of the B text additions sought to allay them further in a coda that is full of the rhetoric of ceremonial closure. 'Faustus' end', for all its fearful signs of reprobation, is to be clad in the decencies of mourning:

> We'll give his mangled limbs due burial;
> And all the students, clothed in mourning black,
> Shall wait upon his heavy funeral.
>
> (lines 348–50)

[10] Faustus' paradoxical terror of and longing for the end is echoed in Tourneur's D'Amville, whose gathering terror of death comes to express itself in a similar longing for annihilation or unconsciousness: 'O were my body circumvolv'd | Within that cloud, that when the thunder tears | His passage open, it might scatter me | To nothing in the air!'; IV. iii. 248–51); 'I shall steal into my grave without | The understanding or the fear of death, | And that's the end I aim at' (V. ii. 174). Robert Watson's 'Duelling Death', in *The Rest is Silence*, 156–252, exposes similar contradictions in Donne's attitudes to ending.

The funeral pageant announced by the Second Scholar is designed to transform the arbitrary violence of ending into a ritual of consummation. But even these reduplicated signs of closure need to be reinforced in the printed text by the conclusive tolling of the motto that adorns both versions of the play: 'Terminat hora diem; terminat Author opus.' It is as if the vertigo of Faustus' dying moments, his dizzy gaze into the shapelessness of the infinite, had threatened the very form of drama itself; and only by an inscription which expressly returns us to the scene of writing, insisting on the dramatist's power to write an end to his own creation, can stability be restored.

Kyd and the Ends of Revenge

As its extraordinary emphasis on the violence of writing and its overdetermined elaboration of Hieronimo's role as playwright might suggest,[11] Kyd's *The Spanish Tragedy* is almost equally infused with the anxiety of ending. In this revenge play, however, it takes a rather different form—one that is shaped by the intense narrativity of the genre to which it belongs. Not only is the action of revenge tragedy typically set in train by an act of narration (the account of some hidden crime which the hero is bound to avenge); but the action is itself imagined as a particular kind of dramatic narrative—a story of action and reaction whose conclusion is utterly foreknown, but which nevertheless remains unnaturally suspended 'in the middest'. It is the revenger's task to steer this narrative to its necessary resolution; but that does not grant him any autonomous power—to the contrary, as the man 'born to set it right', he is in every sense the agent of plot, his life *a function of its prescribed end*. In Kyd's pioneering essay in the form, the Ghost's opening speech frames the action inside an elaborate narrative

[11] The self-reflexive and metadramatic aspects of the play are exceptionally well dealt with in Jonas A. Barish, '*The Spanish Tragedy*, or the Pleasures and Perils of Rhetoric', in John Russell Brown and Bernard Harris (eds.), *Elizabethan Theatre*, Stratford-upon-Avon Studies, no. 9 (London: Edward Arnold, 1966), 58–85; Scott McMillin, 'The Figure of Silence in *The Spanish Tragedy*', *ELH* 39 (1974), 203–17; and S. F. Johnson, '*The Spanish Tragedy*, or Babylon Revisited', in Richard Hosley (ed.), *Essays on Shakespeare and Elizabethan Drama in Honor of Hardin Craig* (Columbia: University of Missouri Press, 1963), 23–36.

whose completion remains suspended by the enigmatic verdict of the infernal lawcourts. Andrea himself is the victim of cruel abruption: treacherously killed, he is at first denied his proper burial rites (Induction, lines 20–6); and even when these have at last been accomplished, he finds his eternal fate mysteriously indeterminate. Referred by the judges of the Underworld to the appeal of Pluto and Proserpina, the dead man passes neither to the joys of Elysium nor to the pains of Tartarus, but along a 'middle path' (line 72) towards a judgement which, at the last minute, is withheld in the mystery of Proserpine's smile. The execution of justice will remain suspended until the 'tragedy' for which he and Revenge are to serve as 'chorus' has been played out—so completing the revenge story which his death at once began and, by virtue of its obscurity, left arrested *in medias res*.

In the final chorus Andrea takes grim satisfaction in a perfect symmetry of endings—'Ay, now my hopes have *end* in their effects, | When blood and sorrow *finish* my desires' (IV. v. 1–2; emphasis added)—and assumes the role of infernal justice, promising to lead his friends to Elysian happiness, while dooming his foes to Tartarean punishments (lines 13–44). The 'mystery', it seems, has found its proper and inevitable conclusion. Yet the rhetoric of closure undercuts itself by a curious stress on the beginning of that 'endless' torment to which Lorenzo (lines 33–4), Pedringano (lines 41–3), and the others are consigned: 'For here though *death* hath *end* their misery, I'll there *begin* their *endless tragedy*' (IV. v. 47–8; emphasis added). The intended effect of this epilogue is difficult to calculate with complete certainty; but the gloating tone of Andrea's judgements (like the murder and condemnation of the seemingly innocent Castile) appears designed to play on the profound ambivalence of Elizabethan attitudes to revenge. In such a context, there is something sinister in the vision of an afterworld which is to consist of endless re-enactments of the drama of retribution we have just seen enacted: it is as though Kyd were picking up the hint of infinite regression in *The Spanish Tragedy*'s Chinese-box design, to create another version of *Doctor Faustus*' horror of no-end.[12]

Within the play proper, it is the revenger, Hieronimo, who is

[12] This is the same horror that is awoken by Claudius' insistence that 'Revenge should have *no bounds*' (*Hamlet*, IV. vii. 127).

charged with accomplishing the end—in his own terms he must 'find relief' for the 'endless woe' threatened by the murder of his son (II. v. 41); and in accordance with the *regressus ad infinitum* of the play's structure, he brings it about in a play-within-the-play whose action precisely mimics his own tragedy. 'Soliman and Perseda' is presented as the vehicle of a little Apocalypse—a 'fall of Babylon' in Hieronimo's own words (IV. i. 194);[13] but in his elaborate epilogue, the hero is at pains to insist on his accomplishment of an end more absolute than any mere play can offer:

Haply you think, but bootless are your thoughts,
That this is fabulously counterfeit,
And that we do as all tragedians do:
To die today, for fashioning our scene,
The death of Ajax or some Roman peer,
And in a minute starting up again,
Revive to please tomorrow's audience.
No, princes, know I am Hieronimo,
The hopeless father of a hapless son,
Whose tongue is tuned to tell his latest tale,
Not to excuse gross errors in the play.

(IV. iv. 76–86)

Horatio's murdered body, formerly the sign of the broken narrative which the revenger was bound to complete, is now offered as a sign of ending, betokening (through the double sense of 'hope') the imminent consummation of Hieronimo's vindictive ends: 'See here my show, look on this spectacle. | Here lay my hope, and *here my hope hath end*' (lines 89–90; emphasis added). The speech, full of the language of death and ending (lines 95, 107, 121, 130, 140–3), climaxes on the triumphant couplet in which the hero announces his own death as a theatrical full stop:

And gentles, thus I end my play;
Urge no more words, I have no more to say.
[*He runs to hang himself.*

(lines 150–1)

The couplet is itself, of course, a conventional marker of dramatic closure; but, as we have seen, Hieronimo is held back from his

[13] See Johnson, '*The Spanish Tragedy*', for an analysis of this motif.

carefully prepared end by the King, whose attendants break in and seize the Knight Marshal, forcing him into the paradoxical gestures of narrative repudiation-in-consummation that begin with the biting out of his own tongue and end with the pen–knife suicide.

Oddly enough, however, Kyd's ending was not the end of the story. *The Spanish Tragedy* play was reprinted in 1602 (the same year, significantly, that *Hamlet* was entered on the Stationer's Register) with a number of Additions, some of which serve to tie up loose ends in the fiction, such as Hieronimo's previously unexplained gesture of biting out his own tongue. At certain points, the author of these Additions, who may well have been Ben Jonson, seems more sharply aware of the play's implications than the typically intuitive Kyd himself; and in the justly celebrated Painter scene, he created an episode which highlights, in a most striking fashion, the narrativity of revenge design, its ferocious concentration upon ending.[14] In this scene Hieronimo commissions the Painter to design him a picture—very much after the manner of the Darnley Memorial, the revenge painting executed for the infant James I[15] —whose complex but uncompleted narrative will act as a perpetual incitement to revenge: 'Draw me like old Priam of Troy, crying, 'The house is a-fire, the house is a-fire, as the torch over my head.' Make me curse, make me cry, make me mad, make me well again, make me curse hell, invocate heaven, and in the end, leave me in a trance—and so forth' (III. xii*a*. 160–5). As Hieronimo sketches the spectacle, his narrative frame begins to dissolve, rather as it does in his play-within-the-play, and the two Hieronimos, viewer and subject, become virtually indistinguishable; yet precisely at this moment of most intense identification, when the imagined

[14] The significance of this scene as embodying an acute contemporary reading of Kyd's play is well brought out in Donna B. Hamilton, '*The Spanish Tragedy*: A Speaking Picture', *ELR* 4 (1974), 203–17. The systematically applied intelligence which informs this and other revisions strengthens the case for supposing that Ben Jonson—who is known to have been paid by Henslowe for additions to the play in 1601 and 1602—was indeed their author. This case for Jonson has been powerfully restated by Anne Barton in *Ben Jonson, Dramatist* (Cambridge: Cambridge University Press, 1984).

[15] See Frye, *Renaissance Hamlet*, 29–37. It is curious, in the light of the complex historic interrelation of *The Spanish Tragedy*, *Hamlet*, and the Additions, that the portrait should include a fragment of the same narrative from which the Player quotes in the Hecuba scene.

consummation of revenge seems almost assured, a curious anti-climax supervenes. The Painter himself seems puzzled: 'And is this the end?' Hieronimo's reply anticipates the strange reduplications of the final scene and the 'endless tragedy' of the epilogue in its horrified glimpse of a hellish ending without end: 'Oh, no, there is no end; the end is death and madness' (III. 12*a*. 167–8).

6

'To know my stops': *Hamlet* and Narrative Abruption

> Only a madman or imbecile (in effect, those like Edgar or Malcolm who step in claiming to 'conclude' the tragedy) can think that [the protagonist's] story can be 'told', ordered on the basis of comprehensible meanings. . . . This is, in miniature, the lesson of tragic structure as a whole.
>
> (Franco Moretti[1])

Death and Narrative Desire

The connections between *Hamlet* and the work of Thomas Kyd are of a complex kind: Henslowe's commissioning of Jonson to revamp *The Spanish Tragedy* in the wake of *Hamlet*'s early success is a reminder that this play, in which Kyd had single-handedly reinvented Senecan revenge tragedy for the English stage, was not simply one of Shakespeare's 'influences': it remained part of the competition, something *against* which *Hamlet* was written. At the same time there are good reasons for supposing that *Hamlet* itself was conceived as a much more complete revamping of another well-worn revenge-play from the late 1580s, also attributed to Kyd—the now lost *Ur-Hamlet*, whose notoriously shrieking Ghost uttered the fearful command to which Shakespeare's design is at once obedient and obscurely resistant: 'Hamlet, revenge!'[2]

In its original context, then, *Hamlet* formed part of an elaborate three-way 'conversation' between dramatists, only fragments

[1] 'The Great Eclipse: Tragic Form as the Deconsecration of Sovereignty', in *Signs Taken for Wonders*, 43–82: 65.

[2] Cited in *Hamlet*, ed. G. R. Hibbard (Oxford: Oxford University Press, 1987), 13.

of which we can now reconstruct. In it Shakespeare exposes the problems of narrative and ending thrown up by *The Spanish Tragedy* to a scrutiny so exacting that it is possible to rethink the whole overworked question of Hamlet's delay in terms of the play's effort, as it were, to imagine an end for itself.[3] The difficulty of that effort has everything to do with the particular form taken by the fear of death in this play—a fear which, as C. S. Lewis once observed, is less concerned with the fear of dying than with the fear of *being dead*, and with the twin fears of ending and no-end which that involves.[4]

Death has two guises in *Hamlet*: it is both dreaded and longed for; it is that which renders life senseless, and that which completes and makes sense of life; it is at once end-as-termination and end-as-purpose, *finis* and *telos*. To Hamlet, in his most celebrated soliloquy, it is the desired point of rest, offering an 'end' to all the sufferings of the restless and tormented self—'a consummation devoutly to be wished' (III. i. 59–63). Hamlet's nightmare here is 'the dread of something *after* death'—the fear that it may prove only a false ending (lines 64–81). Yet, by the time he reaches the graveyard, death has become the mark of human futility, a last definement that abolishes all definition: 'is this the fine of his fines, and the recovery of his recoveries, to have his fine pate full of fine dirt' (V. i. 104–5). Both of these contradictory attitudes towards death can be accommodated in the hero's enigmatic final sentence, 'the rest is silence' (V. ii. 352); for the meaning of these words, whose terminating period enacts the abruption of which they speak, shifts with the degree of emphasis one gives to 'rest' or 'silence'. Spoken with one inflexion, they can signal the grateful release of a mind tired with the endless iteration of 'words, words, words'; spoken with another, they can express the frustration of a narrative voice cut short, like Hotspur's, by the 'stop' of death:

O, I could prophesy,
But that the earthy and cold hand of death
Lies on my tongue. No, Percy, thou art dust,
And food for—

(*1 Henry IV*, V. iv. 83–6)

[3] Michael Neill, '*Hamlet*: A Modern Perspective', in Barbara A. Mowat and Paul Werstine (eds.), *Hamlet*, The Folger Shakespeare (New York: Washington Square Press, 1992), 307–26.

[4] Cited in Watson, *The Rest is Silence*, 84.

From its very beginning, *Hamlet* manifests a fascination with and an anxiety about narrative more intense than in any other play of the period.[5] 'Speak', 'tell', 'tale', and 'story' are key words in the play—not surprisingly, since the action is punctuated by a series of inset tales and dramatic narratives, of which 'The Murder of Gonzago' is only the most elaborate example. The revenge plot is once again initiated by the story of a killing which is imagined as an unnatural abruption that leaves its narrator suspended in a state of tormenting incompletion—

Cut off even in the blossoms of my sin,
Unhous'led, disappointed, unanel'd,
No reck'ning made, but sent to my account
With all my imperfections on my head.

(I. v. 76–9; emphasis added)

And the revenger's task is once again construed as the only kind of reckoning that can perfect this broken narrative. In this case, however, the story is of a more than usually occulted kind, so that it is almost as hard to bring it to light as it is to bring it to completion: this, in fact, is a tale which has a great deal of difficulty getting itself told. More than that, there is the persistent suggestion that behind the ultimately rather conventional, if intractable, plot-narrative, there lie other stories which stubbornly resist telling—tales which remain either untold, or beyond completion even in the triumphant consummation of revenge.

At the same time as *Hamlet* is full of stories, it is also permeated with the most intense narrative and interpretative desire: Claudius' response to Polonius, when he promises to relate 'the very cause of Hamlet's lunacy', is echoed in one way or another by almost every significant character in the play: 'O, speak of that, that I do long to hear!' (II. ii. 50). Narrative is that kind of speaking which offers to put a form on the inchoate matter of experience; with its emphasis on cause and effect, on beginnings, middles, and ends, it is precisely a *making* of a sense.[6] But in *Hamlet* its strategies are

[5] For further discussion of narrative in this play, see Barbara Hardy, 'The Figure of Narration in *Hamlet*', in Robert Druce (ed.), *A Centre of Excellence: Essays Presented to Seymour Betsky* (Amsterdam: Costerus Rodopi, 1987), 1–14. I am grateful to Professor Hardy for supplying me with a copy of her essay.

[6] Watson ('Giving up the Ghost', 288) also recognizes how Hamlet's revenge quest is infused with a desire for 'narrative shape'.

always under question—as, for example, in the Prince's game with Polonius after the performance of that ambiguous dramatic narrative, the Mousetrap play:

HAMLET. Do you see yonder cloud that's almost in shape of a camel?
POLONIUS. By th'mass and 'tis, like a camel indeed.
HAMLET. Methinks it is like a weasel.
POLONIUS. It is backed like a weasel.
HAMLET. Or like a whale.
POLONIUS. Very like a whale. (III. ii. 376–82)

The game resembles a teasing parable of the vain interpretative fetches to which the action persistently drives both characters and audience. Allowing for his obsequious desire to please, Polonius' reading of the cloud is not unlike Claudius' attempts to 'open' the mystery of Hamlet's 'transformation' (II. ii. 4–18) or to 'translate' Gertrude's sighs (IV. i. 1–2); and it is closely mirrored in the desperate hermeneutics applied to what Laertes oxymoronically describes as Ophelia's 'document in madness' (IV. v. 178). Because her father is the victim of a murder which the state has chosen to keep 'hugger-mugger', Ophelia, like Hamlet, is tormented by a burden of narrative unspeakability. But just as Polonius detected 'method' in Hamlet's madness (II. ii. 205–6), so Laertes interprets the tessellation of incoherent speech and snatches of song in which Ophelia's story is at once uttered and silenced, discovering 'more than matter' (both 'narrative substance' and 'cause') in its apparent 'nothing' (IV. v. 174). The anonymous Gentleman explains the ambiguous power of this kind of dumb speaking even more eloquently: Ophelia, he says,

speaks things in doubt
That carry but half sense. Her speech is nothing.
Yet the unshaped use of it doth move
The hearers to collection; they [aim] at it,
And botch the words up fit to their own thoughts,
Which as her winks and nods and gestures yield them,
Indeed would make one think there might be thought,
Though nothing sure, yet much unhappily.
(IV. v. 6–13)

This speech epitomizes something disturbingly self-reflexive in the play's sceptical wit that repeatedly threatens the significance of its own story, holding up to mockery the desire it sedulously fosters to pluck out the heart of its mystery.

'Forbid to tell the secrets'

Hamlet begins, in ingeniously symmetrical fashion, with 'the counterfeit presentment of two brothers', the dead King Hamlet and the usurping King Claudius. The first two scenes introduce the rival narrative domains over which they preside. The Ghost's is a scene of narrative anxiety and frustrated telling, where the frustration is proportionate to that interrogative drive which Maynard Mack and Harry Levin long ago identified as crucial to the mood of the play. This scene is full of sudden abruption and aposiopesis, and all its energy is concentrated upon a story which the final breaking up of the watch leaves still uncompleted.[7] Barnardo begins it; after the unsettling confusion which surrounds the nervous changing of the guard, he seems to offer the reassurance of explanation:[8]

> Sit down awhile,
> And let us once again assail your ears,
> That are so fortified against *our story*,
> What we have two nights seen.
>
> (I. i. 30–3; emphasis added)

What we seem to be offered here is a kind of dramatized prologue—a familiar form of narrative exposition. But Barnardo has scarcely begun when he is interrupted by an uncanny repetition of the very events he is about to describe: the one o'clock bell sounds,[9] and the Ghost enters, pat on cue—

[7] See Maynard Mack, 'The World of *Hamlet*', *Yale Review*, 41 (1952), 502–23; and Harry Levin, *The Question of Hamlet* (New York: Oxford University Press, 1959).

[8] It is worth registering, however, the odd violence ('assail . . . fortified') with which the act of narration is already associated. Compare Gertrude's 'these words like daggers enter in mine ears' (III. iv. 95).

[9] There is no printed stage direction for the clock to strike, but since so much is made of the punctuality of the Ghost's reappearances at 'this dead hour' (I. i. 35–9, 65–6; I. iv. 3–4), we should probably assume an implied stage direction for both the scenes on the battlements, and probably again for the closet scene, where Hamlet's preceding soliloquy, ''Tis now the very witching time of night' (III. ii.

BARNARDO. Last night of all,
When yond same star that's westward from the pole
Had made his course t'illume that part of heaven
Where now it burns, Marcellus and myself,
The bell then beating one—
Enter the Ghost
MARCELLUS. Peace, *break thee off*. Look where it comes again.
(I. i. 35–40; emphasis added)

No sooner does it appear than the Ghost becomes the focus of insistent narrative curiosity: '*speak* to it, Horatio. . . . It would be *spoke* to. . . . *Speak* to it Horatio. . . . I charge thee, *speak*. . . . Stay. *Speak*, *speak*. I charge thee, *speak*' (I. i. 42–51; emphasis added).

But, apparently offended by these demands, the apparition vanishes without reply, its silence only intensifying Marcellus' longing for narrative resolution: 'Good now, sit down, and *tell me* he that knows' (line 70; emphasis added). Horatio offers a response, but his own telling (itself clouded by dubiety—'At least the whisper goes so'; line 80) is interrupted in turn by the Ghost's second entry: 'But soft, behold, lo where it comes again' (line 126). Once again this enigmatic revenant is assailed with urgently repeated demands: '*Speak* to me. . . . *Speak* to me. . . . O, *speak*! . . . *Speak* of it. Stay and *speak*' (lines 129–39; emphasis added); and this time it even seems 'about to speak' when it too is cut off, by the crowing of the cock. The scene ends indecisively with the promise that Hamlet's presence may finally induce the Ghost to deliver its repeatedly deferred narration: 'This spirit, dumb to us, will speak to him' (line 171). Before that can happen, however, Horatio will have to rerehearse Barnardo's unfinished tale to Hamlet, transferring the burden of narrative desire where it belongs—onto the shoulders of the revenger.

What immediately distinguishes the second scene of the play from its disjointed opening is the enormous narrative confidence of the King, the rhetorical contrast establishing an essential difference between the rival spheres of Claudius and the Ghost. The dead King's history is relegated to the margins of the Danish world, consigned to the obscurity and darkness of the battlements;

388 ff.), acts as an important temporal marker. The three times repeated tolling of the single hour would give particular dramatic emphasis to Hamlet's 'A man's life is no more than to say "one"' (V. ii. 74); see below, pp. 239, 302–3.

Claudius' story belongs to the brightly illuminated court, it issues from the 'state' that commands the emblematic centre of the political stage. If a King, in James I's celebrated formula, 'is as one set on a stage, whose smallest action and gestures all the people gazingly do behold',[10] his power derives also from his engrossment of their hearing: the throne, Claudius reminds us, is the fountainhead of public narrative, the edicts of official history. Usurpation of political power, therefore, involves the possession of narrative power; and at the heart of the revenger's project is the longing to supplant the usurper's fictions and to 'tell my story'. Authority (as Prospero will demonstrate once again in the opening scene of *The Tempest*[11]) is always a kind of authorship.

It is hardly surprising, then, that the dramatized prologue which Marcellus and Barnardo seemed unable to construct should be managed by Claudius with barely a flicker of hesitation: his economical exposition with its businesslike gestures of closure ('For all, our thanks. . . . So much for him'; lines 16, 25) shows official history in the making, challenged only by that silent mark of interrogation, the black-clad Prince, whose asides hint at a hidden but potentially subversive counter-narrative—'that within which passes show' (line 85). *Asides*, however, as their name suggests, are no more than marginalia: rhetorically, as in almost every other way, Hamlet belongs to the periphery of this court—it is not a position from which he can effectually speak, except in the private theatre of soliloquy. Hamlet's first soliloquy is in many ways the counterpart to Claudius' opening oration, with which it helps to frame the first half of the scene. It offers a rival version of the story of old Hamlet's death and Gertrude's remarriage. But it replaces the elegantly balanced antitheses in which Claudius speaks

[10] *The Political Works of James I*, ed. Charles Howard McIlwain (Cambridge, Mass.: Harvard University Press, 1918), 43.

[11] See Prospero's description of the usurping Antonio as

one
Who having into truth, by telling of it,
Made such a sinner of his memory
To credit his own lie.
(I. ii. 99–102)

In this scene, ironically enough, Prospero himself confirms his own authority in the island by asserting the power of his stories over those of the 'lying slave', Caliban, and even the 'malignant thing', Ariel, whom he has supplanted.

the order of his rule with a rhetorical mimesis of confusion: the speech is punctuated—in a fashion that significantly anticipates the wild, ejaculatory language of the Ghost (I. v. 41–91)—with rhetorical questions, exclamations, switches of direction, and breakings off (lines 132, 135, 137, 142–3, 145–6, 149–51, 156), culminating in sudden self-suppression, 'but break, my heart, for I must hold my tongue' (line 158). Even when he is alone, the suppressed history which so preoccupies him is something that the Prince cannot properly voice—a crucial part of it, indeed, remains hidden even from himself, locked away in the Ghost's occluded narrative.

Not until the last scene of the act is the Ghost allowed to break the silence that enshrouds it, and to command Hamlet's ear, as it has broken through cerecloth and coffin to compel the gaze of the watchers on the battlements. It is important to recognize that this is not just a device for theatrical suspense, but a way of dramatizing the pressure of oblivion under which memory labours wherever narrative authority is usurped. When it is at last allowed to speak, the Ghost proves in many ways the most powerful of all the play's story-tellers: indeed, like its partial model in *The Spanish Tragedy*, it speaks the master-narrative from which all others in the play in some sense derive; and whereas Andrea's prologue-history remains dramatically inert and detached from the main action, this one is granted an extraordinary transformatory power. Effacing all other histories from the mind of its hearer, it turns him from the passivity of mourning to the antic frenzy of a would-be revenger:

> Yea, from the table of my memory
> I'll wipe away all trivial fond records,
>
> * * * * * *
>
> And thy commandment all alone shall live
> Within the book and volume of my brain,
> Unmix'd with baser matter.
>
> (I. v. 98–104)

By one of those weird symmetries that characterize the drama of revenge, narrative here begins to act with something of the terrible efficacy of Claudius' poison, the 'leprous distillment' poured 'in the porches of [the] ears', which transforms its victim with 'a most instant tetter' (I. v. 63–71).[12] Yet for all its sinister power of psychic usurpation, the story is both limited in its immediate effect and, from the Ghost's own point of view, insufficient and incomplete. Unlike Andrea's choric narrative, which, by framing the action of the play, visibly constitutes its fate, this one has to compete with others for control; and, unlike Claudius, the dead King has no commanding platform from which to speak it. His voice is heard only once by anyone other than his son, and then it is a cry 'under the stage' barely distinguishable from an echo of Hamlet's own words. The Ghost's tale of fratricide may change Hamlet almost beyond recognition, as both Claudius and Ophelia sense (II. ii. 4–7; III. i. 150–61); but behind it, and still unspoken, the Ghost insists, lies another, forbidden narrative, detailing the spirit's painful travail in the 'undiscovered country' beyond the grave, beside whose violent transformations even Hamlet's startling metamorphosis would be as nothing:

> But that I am forbid
> To tell the secrets of my prison house,
> I could a tale unfold whose lightest word
> Would harrow up thy soul, freeze thy young blood,
> Make thy two eyes like stars start from thy spheres,
> Thy knotted and combinèd locks to part,
> And each particular hair to stand an end
> Like quills upon the fretful porpentine.
> But this eternal blazon must not be
> To ears of flesh and blood. (I. v. 13–23)

Meanwhile, even the story which the Ghost *is* licensed to tell must be related under the pressure of imminent abruption ('My hour is almost come. . . . methinks I scent the morning air. . . . The glowworm shows the matin to be near'; II. v. 2, 58, 89). The Ghost breaks into the narratives of others with an arrest as arbitrary as death's, yet is itself subject to such arrest, cut off from the tale of

[12] The point was strikingly made in Derek Jacobi's 1988 production for the Renaissance Theatre Company: as the Ghost told the story of his poisoning, Kenneth Branagh's Prince writhed upon the ground, clutching his ears as though the words alone were enough to make him relive his father's agonizing end. The play repeatedly attributes a violent transformatory power to language: not only do Hamlet's words strike Gertrude's ears 'like daggers', but the bereaved Laertes is surrounded by 'buzzers to *infect* his ear | With *pestilent* speeches of his father's death' (IV. v. 90–1); while Hamlet promises Horatio, 'words to speak in thine ear will make thee dumb' (IV. vi. 24–5).

purgatorial suffering it most longs to tell, and repeatedly summoned back to the speechless obscurity of its prison-house.

The idea, which the Ghost introduces, of the untellable tale—one so astounding and compelling that, could it only be told, it would leave its audience utterly changed—is a persistent motif in the play.[13] The hero himself, from when we first encounter him, tormented by memories ('that within which passes show') which he alone seems to acknowledge, is possessed by the unspeakable.[14] His encounter with the Ghost, while it redoubles the burden of memory, also reinforces the necessity of silence. Inscribed on the hidden tables of memory, the Ghost's tale is for the moment kept secret even from Horatio ('Good my lord, tell it.' 'No you will reveal it'; line 119), while his companions are all sworn 'Never to speak of this that you have heard' (line 160)—never indeed to admit even that they 'know aught' of Hamlet himself, whatever antic provocations they may suffer.

It is precisely at this critical juncture, when the audience's curiosity about the hero's inner state is at its most intense, that Hamlet is withdrawn from their gaze, rather as the story of occulted murder is withheld from Horatio's baffled enquiry. The hero disappears for nearly 300 lines (his second longest absence from the stage[15]). For this time the audience is permitted to glimpse him only through Ophelia's inset narrative, in which he appears as the very image of frustrated utterance, an uncanny replication of the Ghost itself, looking 'As if he had been loosed out of hell | To speak of horrors' (II. i. 83–4), yet able to find no expression beyond the inarticulate eloquence of

> a sigh so piteous and profound
> As it did seem to shatter all his bulk
> And *end his being*.
>
> (lines 94–6; emphasis added)

[13] Hamlet links this idea with the Ghost again in the closet scene: 'His form and cause conjoin'd, preaching to stones, | Would make them capable' (III. iv. 126–7); but the apparition remains invisible to Gertrude, its potential for metamorphic narration unrealized.

[14] Compare Laertes' reaction to the news of Ophelia's death: 'I have a speech a'fire that fain would blaze, | But that this folly drowns it' (IV. vii. 190–1).

[15] The second occasion is in the interval before the graveyard scene, another point of critical transformation in his character, when he is absent for about 500 lines; in that case he is once again visible only through a narrative medium—the letters read by Horatio and Claudius.

That indeed is the kind of story that Hamlet is now burdened with—one that threatens to end his being if he cannot complete it, and which will infallibly end it if he does. The sequence of scenes with the Players, who occupy a space so disproportionate to their function in the plot, is best understood as the hero's extended, but finally unsuccessful, attempt to find a method of telling this story.

'They'll tell all': Playing the End

Hamlet's suddenly exhilarated response to the Players' arrival is presented as a direct response to the failure of his narrative designs: he immediately begins to sketch out a story for them, registered in a tally of stock character-types and plot-situations whose loose ironic parallels seem to outline a comic version of *Hamlet* itself: 'He that plays the king shall be welcome—his Majesty shall have tribute on me, the adventurous knight shall use his foil and target, the lover shall not sigh gratis, the humorous man shall *end his part in peace*, the clown shall make those laugh whose lungs are tickle a'th'sere, and the lady shall *say her mind freely*' (II. ii. 319–25; emphasis added).

Against this, the next part of the scene will set a vision of tragic catastrophe, cast as a well-known story-within-a-story—'Aeneas' tale to Dido'. Hamlet's anxiety to begin this tale has him vying with the Player King in the art of declamation, but bringing it to a satisfactory end causes him greater difficulty. One can see why: it opens with an image of the bereaved Pyrrhus as black-clad revenger, lurking in concealment, which strongly associates him with Hamlet—

> The rugged Pyrrhus, he whose sable arms,
> Black as his purpose, did the night resemble
> When he lay couched in th'ominous horse . . .
>
> (II. ii. 452–4)

—and on this is imposed another, anticipating the successful consummation of his revenge:

> head to foot
> Now is he total gules, horridly trick'd
> With blood of fathers, mothers, daughters, sons.
>
> (lines 456–8)

But the significance of the metamorphosis from black to red, and the end it symbolizes, is immediately confused by that ambiguous 'blood of *fathers, mothers*', and further obscured by a 'tyrannous and damnèd light' illuminating a scene of king-murder that less resembles the punishment of a Macbeth than the butchery of a Duncan (lines 457–64). The more vividly 'the hellish Pyrrhus' and his frail victim, 'Th'unnerved father', are realized, the harder it becomes to decide whether the killer here is a model for Hamlet or for Claudius, and whether Priam is a cipher for Claudius or for Old Hamlet. The result is that the sudden transformation of Pyrrhus to 'a painted tyrant' and the arrest of his avenging sword in a truncated half-line ('And like a neutral to his will and matter | Did nothing'; lines 481–2) form a peculiarly revealing metaphor for Hamlet's own state of frozen inactivity—the suspension of his purpose between passive suffering and taking arms against a sea of troubles. This arrest of movement, fittingly enough, is imagined in the heroic simile which follows as a suppression of speech—it resembles a '*silence* in the heavens' which leaves 'The bold winds *speechless*' (lines 484–5; emphasis added). Here, of course, silence is only a prelude to the final storm of revenge; but it seems significant that the Player's speech is itself cut off in mid-line, before he can reach its appointed end in the fate of Hecuba-Gertrude—'Prithee no more', begs Polonius, overwhelmed by emotion, and Hamlet brings the performance to an abrupt halt: ''Tis well. I'll have thee speak the rest of this soon' (lines 520–2).

In the soliloquy that follows, the Prince returns to the motif of the untellable tale, as he contemplates the miraculous transformations that might be wrought by the Player's art, could it only be charged with the overwhelming force of his own suppressed narrative:

> He would drown the stage with tears,
> And cleave the general ear with horrid speech,
> Make mad the guilty, and appal the free,
> Confound the ignorant, and amaze indeed
> The very faculties of eyes and ears.
>
> (II. ii. 562–6)

But like the Ghost's 'eternal blazon' of hell, this is another story that obdurately resists telling—

> Yet I,
> A dull and muddy-mettled rascal, peak

Like John-a-dreams, unpregnant of my cause,
And can *say* nothing.

(II. ii. 567–9; emphasis added)

At this point the power to act seems completely identified with the power to speak, and revenge itself is imagined as precisely a form of (repressed) speaking; so that the soliloquy's erratic exclamatory progress, with its abrupt switches of direction, and choked half-lines (lines 557–8, 566, 571, 575–6, 580–2, 587–8), becomes a way of enacting the impotence it rails against. Yet paradoxically the nearer Hamlet comes to an expression of his vindictive frenzy, the more 'unpack[ing the] heart with words' is likely to seem like another kind of impotence (line 585):[16]

I should have fatted all the region kites
With this slave's offal. Bloody, bawdy villain!
Remorseless, treacherous, lecherous, kindless villain!
O, vengeance!
Why, what an ass am I! This is most brave . . .

(II. ii. 579–82)

The resolution of this rhetorical impasse takes the equally paradoxical form of choosing the dramatic narrative of a play as a surrogate for his own voice: 'For murther, though it have no tongue, will speak | With most miraculous organ' (lines 593–4). Murder will out, he means; but also, murder itself is a kind of utterance—the only kind that will serve.

In a more conventional revenge play, that identification of telling and acting would work itself out in a thoroughly literal and satisfactory fashion, as the play-within-the play became the actual vehicle of revenge. But Hamlet's 'Mousetrap' is allowed to operate only on a metaphoric level, and even then is sprung prematurely, before it can achieve its proper end. 'The Murder of Gonzago' is the most extended and spectacular of all the play's inset tales, a showing forth of 'that within which passes show', and a telling of the unspeakable:

[16] Patricia Parker has drawn attention to the play's association of the hero's dilatoriness with his propensity for rhetorical 'dilation' as signs of his womanish impotence (*Literary Fat Ladies*, 22–4). Arguably such 'dilation' is inseparable from the revenger's commitment to a narrative end which the contradictory nature of his role compels him to defer for as long as possible.

HAMLET. We shall know all by this fellow. The players cannot keep counsel. They'll *tell* all.
OPHELIA. Will 'a *tell* us what this *show* meant?
HAMLET. Ay, or any *show* that you will *show* him. Be not you ashamed to *show*, he'll not shame to *tell* you what it means.

... the *story* is extant, and written in very choice Italian.

(III. ii. 141–5, 262–3; emphasis added)

Partly rewritten by Hamlet himself, 'The Murder of Gonzago' is a story which replicates the suppressed history of Old Hamlet's murder, Claudius' usurpation, and Gertrude's adultery, and at the same time ominously hints at the prescribed ending of that history in its identification of the murderer as 'one Lucianus, *nephew* to the king' (line 244). But at its centre is a prolonged meditation on the disjunctions between impulse and remembrance, speaking and doing, aims, and ends, spoken by a character who is himself consciously under the shadow of his mortal end. The Player King's theme is that, in a world of mutability, the immanence of ending cruelly subverts all human ends:[17]

What to ourselves in passion we propose,
The passion ending, doth the purpose lose....
This world is not for aye, nor 'tis not strange
That even our loves should with our fortunes change.

(lines 194–201)

At the same time the structure of his speech is one which gestures at transcendence of this melancholy rule by flourishing the rhetorical illusion of a concinnity of ends:

But, *orderly to end* where I *begun*,
Our wills and fates do so contrary run
That our devices still are overthrown.
Our thoughts are ours, their *ends* none of our own.
So think thou wilt no second husband wed,
But *die* thy thoughts when thy first lord is *dead*.

(lines 220–5)

However, the consolations of rhetorical closure are conspicuously refused in the larger structure of 'The Murder of Gonzago',

[17] The importance of this theme in the play is suggested by the fact that the second Quarto version allows Claudius (in a moment of uncharacteristic pathos) to repeat it in his scene with Laertes (IV. vii. 110–23).

since the play is interrupted by the King's tempestuous departure before it can reach even the inconclusive conclusion foreshadowed in the dumb show ('She seems harsh awhile, but in the end accepts love'). Cut short at precisely the point where the Ghost's narrative stopped, as poison is poured in a sleeping ear, the story remains in suspension, conspicuously bereft of the inevitable reprisal prescribed by the didactic convention of Elizabethan tragedy. It is a Mousetrap which refuses to close. As a result, the performance remains fatally ambiguous—inviting misapprehension as the story of a nephew's murder and usurpation of his uncle. Yet one can't help noticing that Hamlet's excited chorus has actually seemed to encourage this misreading; and that as he teases Rosencrantz and Guildenstern with the promise of 'a whole history' (line 398), he exhibits a curious satisfaction in the obliquity of the performance. Murder, he promised, would speak 'with most miraculous organ', but in his game with the recorder he sardonically elaborates the conceit of an instrument which can at once sound and remain silent, whose most eloquent stops are, as it were, stopped:[18] 'You would play upon me, you would seem to know my *stops*, you would pluck out the heart of my mystery, you would sound me from the lowest note to the top of my compass; and there is music, excellent *voice*, in this little *organ*, yet cannot you make it *speak*' (lines 364–9; emphasis added).

Hamlet's defiance oddly mimics the triumphant Hieronimo's refusal to speak more, but in a context where the revenger's play has signally failed either to articulate his story or to provide the narrative determination conventionally expected of it. With characteristic obliqueness Hamlet identifies 'The Murder of Gonzago' as being, like Hieronimo's tragedy or Vindice's mask of revengers, an apocalypse in little: his chorus of 'That's wormwood' recalls the name of the ominous star in Revelation—the same that falls from the heavens before Vindice's masque in *The Revenger's Tragedy*.[19]

[18] Cf. also the deliberate incompletion of the snatches of verse and riddling with which the Prince signals his excitement—the excised rhyme at the end of 'Damon dear' (line 293), and the tautological inconclusiveness of 'For if the King like not the comedy, | Why then, belike he likes it not, perdy' (III. ii. 300–2). Anticlimax—even the literalization of the metaphor of revenge-as-narrative in the concluding soliloquy ('I will speak daggers to her, but use none'; line 396)—is always a kind of incompletion.

[19] 'And the name of the star is called Wormwood: and the third part of the waters became wormwood; and many men died of the waters, because they were made bitter' (Rev. 8: 11).

However, no such general slaughter ensues: it is true that the scene concludes with a soliloquy that seems to promise a change of direction, as though Hamlet now felt himself poised to supply the ending which 'The Murder of Gonzago' yaws away from; but this return to conventional revenger's bombast is once more cut off in mid-line—

> Now could I drink hot blood,
> And do such bitter business as the day
> Would quake to look on. *Soft*, now to my mother.
> (III. ii. 390–2; emphasis added)

In the face of the Mousetrap's abrupted performance, Hamlet is haunted by a continuing need to narrativize his future ('thinking too precisely on th'event'). It is this compulsion that visibly paralyses him in the prayer scene, where he no sooner imagines killing Claudius than he begins to tell the murder as yet another story—one which, once it finds an audience, will inevitably be subject to misprision:

> That would be scann'd:
> A villain kills my father, and for that
> I, his sole son, do this same villain send
> To heaven. (III. iii. 75–8)

Here (as at line 87) the prospect of such a reading once again cuts off the narrative flow with a violent aposiopesis; and in the pause the possibility of action is put aside (along with any prospect of making an end), to be replaced by a version of the revenge-as-speaking trope in which, however, words are acknowledged, and even welcomed, as a substitute for action, rather than a realization of it ('I will *speak daggers* to her, but use none'; III. ii. 396).

In many ways the closet scene, with its savage concentration upon story-telling and its power to transform an audience ('Peace, sit you down, | And let me wring your heart'; III. iv. 34–5), seems no more than a rather literal rerun of the play-within-the-play. Rehearsing for a third time the Ghost's tale of murder and adultery, Hamlet sets up a narrative 'glass' for Gertrude (III. iv. 19) as the Players had held 'the mirror up to nature' for Claudius (III. ii. 22); and just as the Players' performance was cut short by Claudius at its murderous climax, so Hamlet's narrative is interrupted by the appearance of the Ghost at its invective high-point:

A murtherer and a villain!
A slave that is not twentieth part the tithe
Of your precedent lord, a Vice of kings,
A cutpurse of the empire and the rule
That from a shelf the precious diadem stole,
And put it in his pocket. . . .
A king of shreds and patches—
Enter the Ghost in his nightgown
Save and hover o'er me with your wings,
You heavenly guards! What would your gracious figure?
(III. iv. 97–105)

If the play scene convinces Hamlet of his uncle's guilt, the closet scene appears to confirm Gertrude's innocence of the murder. But this apart, Hamlet's 'counterfeit presentment', like 'The Murder of Gonzago', seems to resolve nothing. Even if Hamlet's words are 'like daggers' to Gertrude's ears (line 95), he concludes his lecture with fresh adjurations to secrecy and silence (lines 185–96). Yet clearly something has happened here which, though treated by Hamlet as a mere marginal distraction, will alter the entire course of the play: the killing of Polonius. At the conclusion of the scene attention suddenly switches back to the counsellor's undignified corpse: in a wry, punning reversal of his vow to 'speak daggers . . . but use none', Hamlet dismisses the murder as the winding up of an interminable prating narrative ('Come, sir, to *draw toward an end* with you'; III. iv. 216), and then 'lug[s] the guts into the neighbour room' in a contemptuous burlesque of funeral closure.

At this point, without his intending (or even being aware of) it, Hamlet is suddenly exposed in the act and attitude of an orthodox Italianate revenger—as though the story he both longs for and resists had at last taken him over. And indeed the Prince who appears in the early scenes of Act IV, a black satirist, manipulating his emblems of mortality, is surprisingly like the hero of *The Revenger's Tragedy*. The stories he now tells are universal allegories of mortification, whose chains of ineluctable consequence lead to only one conclusion: 'a certain convocation of politic worms are e'en at him. Your worm is your only emperor for diet: we fat all creatures else to fat us, and we fat ourselves for maggots; your fat king and your lean beggar is but variable service, two dishes, but to one table—*that's the end*' (IV. iii. 19–25; emphasis added). This is his equivalent of Vindice's mockery of 'costly three-piled flesh'—or perhaps more precisely of Macbeth's idiot tale, since in it the name of 'King' itself is reduced to an empty signifier, 'a thing . . . of nothing'. It looks forward to Hamlet's last big story-telling scene in the graveyard with all its tumbled signs of 'peremptory nullification'.

'Every fool can tell that': Narrative in the Graveyard

The graveyard scene—whose significance as an emblematic epitome of the play is amply acknowledged in the history of *Hamlet* illustration—is ushered in by one of the most elaborately ornamented narrative exercises in Shakespeare, the pretty fantasy with which Gertrude, playing almost self-consciously the role of *nuntius*, decorates Ophelia's death with tokens of floral innocence. The speech is a kind of tragical pastoral in little, memorializing the story of Ophelia's death as Horatio will memorialize Hamlet's; yet, as Barbara Hardy has observed, its lyrical music is abruptly silenced by a half-line of singular, brutal directness:[20]

But long it could not be
Till that her garments, heavy with their drink,
Pull'd the poor wretch from her melodious lay
To muddy death. (IV. vii. 180–3)

The rhetorical violence of the contrast between 'melodious lay' and 'muddy death' has the effect of heightening the already self-conscious artificiality of Gertrude's narration;[21] and as though further to expose the hollowness of such consolatory artifice, the speech is immediately juxtaposed with the sordor and mockery of the grave-digging sequence—a theatrical oxymoron intensified by

[20] 'Figure of Narration in *Hamlet*', 9.

[21] In a private communication Peter Holland has registered his continuing discomfort with the violation of narrative probability and 'strange leap of styles' in Gertrude's speech: 'The other narratives . . . in the play are plainly within the competence of the teller but that traditional naive response to Gertrude's story—"if she knows about it someone must have watched it happen and could have saved Ophelia"—strikes strong chords in me, precisely because of the nature of the knowledge narrative confers [on its speaker] as observer or participator in the narrated events. This, a fully unfolded tale, is to be taken as beyond the competence of the teller or whoever told her. The jagged disruption of the play's narrative technique, or its technique with inserted narratives, is something that I still cannot resolve satisfactorily.'

the indecorum of this scene's eldritch variations on the theme of 'mirth in funeral and dirge in marriage'. Here the stage is presided over by a Clown who 'sings in grave-making' and a protagonist who himself mimics the levelling humour of death.[22] Its action culminates in a funeral whose 'virgin crants'[23] and 'maiden strewments' mark the funeral as a kind of grim marriage, the 'bringing home' of Ophelia as Death's bride (v. i. 232–3): 'I thought thy bride-bed to have decked, sweet maid, | And not have strewed thy grave' (lines 245–6).

The oxymoron serves as a reminder that a cemetery is itself the most paradoxical of locations: at once a place of oblivion, and a site of memory; a place which annihilates all distinction ('As if I never had been such'; line 74) and a site of monumental record; a place that both invites narrative and silences it.[24] To resist the cancellation of human forgetfulness, Hamlet asserted, a great man 'must build churches' (III. ii. 133), but, according to the grave-digger, 'the gallows is built stronger than the church' (v. i. 47–8); and if the players serve as 'abstract and brief chronicles of the time' (lines 524–5), 'the houses [the grave-digger] makes lasts till Doomsday' (line 59). The graveyard is the 'common' place where all stories end ('two dishes but to one table') and where all telling is ended ('That skull had a tongue in it, and could sing *once*'; lines 75–6; emphasis added); yet it is also noisy with recollections of the past, crowded with anecdotes for those who have the knack to scan them: 'Here's fine revolution, an we had the trick to see't' (lines 90–1). A skull, after all, as the deeply contemplative and enigmatic mood of *Et in Arcadia Ego* painting suggests—not least in Vesalius' wicked parody of the *topos*—is at once the most eloquent and empty of human signs. Simultaneously recalling and

[22] A superstitious fear attached to grave-diggers, as to hangmen, and in time of plague they were often seen as bringers of the devastation to which they catered, earning in some countries the sobriquet Death. See Deaux, *Black Death*, 164; Nohl, *Black Death*, 178–9; Chamberlin, *Black Death*, p. iv.

[23] The use of this rare German word for 'garlands' suggests an odd link with Rosencrantz (= 'garland of roses'), in a way that seems typical of a play whose names often generate a surplus of meaning: Polonius' name, for example, links tearingly with Fortinbras's scene of Polish conquest (the 'little patch of ground | That hath in it no profit but the name'; IV. iv. 18–19).

[24] Fly, in 'Accommodating Death', interprets the whole play in terms of the hero's 'passion for differences' and his struggle against 'a relentless force operating generally in the world of *Hamlet* to erode hierarchies of value and collapse systems of differentiation' (pp. 261, 263).

travestying the head which is the source of all meanings, the seat of all interpretation, the skull acts as a peculiar and sinisterly attractive mirror for the gazer, drawing endless narratives into itself only to cancel them, in very much the way that Ophelia's mad ramblings simultaneously invite and defeat interpretation, forcing hearers into narrative constructions which are instantly subverted. Hamlet tries stories on the anonymous skulls, rather as Vindice dresses Gloriana's skull in court finery, or as snatches of clothing are hung on the anonymous cadavers of a dance of death, parodying the identity of those they have come to summon—those whose stories they at once mimic and cut off. One skull, he suggests, might be Cain's 'that did the first murder', or it might be 'the pate of a politician . . . or of a courtier . . . [or] my Lord Such-a-one . . . [or] the skull of a lawyer . . . a great buyer of land' (lines 78–102). Another (on the grave-digger's unverifiable say-so) is even granted a specific identity: 'This same skull, sir, was Yorick's skull, the King's jester' (lines 180–1). Hamlet gratefully seizes on the pretext and (like a milder Vindice) immediately adorns its pate with the dress of memory. But it is hardly necessary to observe that there is no way of proving the Clown's claim; and his gestural 'this *same* skull' contains a mocking pun that returns us to the familiar truisms of *memento mori.* No sooner has Hamlet begun to evoke with such warmth the surrogate father who 'bore me on his back a thousand times', than the skull begins to reassert its horrible sameness; and as Yorick's familiar grin is collapsed into the alien 'grinning' of every skull, Hamlet recognizes in his reminiscence of the jester a familiar figure from the Dance of Death, the capering *transi* in his antic cap and bells: 'Now get you to my lady's chamber, and tell her, let her paint an inch thick, to this favour she must come; make her laugh at that' (lines 192–5). As the graveyard stories accumulate, they begin to point to an end beyond even the skull's sign of apparent finality—the absolute anonymity and severance from meaning which is glimpsed in Hamlet's travesty of biographic narrative:

> Why may not imagination trace the noble dust of Alexander, till 'a find it stopping a bunghole? . . . to *follow* him thither with modesty enough and likelihood to lead it: Alexander died, Alexander was buried, Alexander returneth to dust, the dust is of earth, of earth we make loam, and why of that loam whereto he was converted might they not stop a beer barrel?

Imperious Caesar, dead and turned to clay,
Might stop a hole to keep the wind away.

(lines 203–14)

In this jingling *reductio* of Ovidian metamorphosis, Hamlet's story-telling concludes; and as his imagination follows the stories of these classical heroes to their muddy end, it is as though he had followed his heroic father's ghost back to the grave from which, in the form of an appallingly insistent story, it first issued.

If the early scenes of the play are dominated by one messenger from the grave, the closing ones are overshadowed by another. Indeed Hamlet's quizzing of the skulls—in particular that of Yorick, the affectionately remembered father-figure—is the exact counterpart of his quizzing of the Ghost; except that all his tormented questioning is now reduced to a single familiar graveyard conundrum, 'Ubi sunt . . . ?' The skull is at once more eloquent and even more enigmatic in its answers: if there is a solution to the riddle, beyond the reductive materialism of the 'quintessence of dust' which stops a beer barrel, the play, as we shall see, finds it only in the uncertain reaches of memory. Hamlet imagines Yorick's skull carrying its levelling message of mortality (as it might be) to Ophelia's dressing-room. Yet the skull's tale, like Ophelia's document in madness, is one which is merely inscribed on its blankness by the horrified imagination of the spectator. 'Yorick' himself has *nothing* to tell: 'Where be your gibes now, your gambols, your songs, your flashes of merriment, that were wont to set the table on a roar? Not one now to mock your own grinning? Quite chop-fall'n?' (v. i. 184–91).

Bespeaking only an undifferentiated absence, the dumb eloquence of the skull presides over a scene in which language appears to fail before the nullity of death; and where Hamlet's scorn for the mouthing and ranting of Laertes' grief is matched by the collapse of his own attempts at self-explanation into sullen aposiopesis: 'Hear you, sir . . . I loved you ever. But it is no matter' (lines 288–90).

The only telling that matters here is the mechanical counting of the hours between cradle and grave, clocking the progress by which dust 'returns' to its 'base uses' (line 202):

[HAMLET]. How long hast thou been grave-maker?
FIRST CLOWN. Of all the days i'th'year, I came to't that day that our last King Hamlet overcame Fortinbras.

HAMLET. How long is that since?
FIRST CLOWN. Cannot you *tell* that? Every fool can *tell* that. It was that very day young Hamlet was born— (lines 142–7)

In this moment the Clown identifies himself as the Prince's mortal *Doppelgänger*, the sinister *Gefehrt* who has shadowed him, as the mysterious Lamord (La mort) seems to have shadowed Laertes.[25] He is the Sexton Death from the *danse macabre* who has been preparing Hamlet's grave from the moment of his birth. The grave-digger's work will no doubt end, 'of all days in the year', on the day that the second Hamlet lies prostrate at the feet of a second Fortinbras.[26] But it is not, after all, here in the graveyard, with its reduction of all narrative to the undifferentiation of the *Totentanz*, that the play ends; and it is proper to ask why.

'To tell my story': Hamlet and the Art of Ending

The scene shuts up with loss of breath,
And leaves no epilogue but death.
(Henry King, 'The Dirge')

'They say 'a made a good end' (IV. v. 185–6), sighs the distracted Ophelia, speaking of the father whom we have seen slaughtered like a rat. The hard truth behind her plangent fantasy is that Polonius has been as brutally 'cut off in the blossoms of [his] sin' as Old Hamlet had been. Her own end will come in the same way, pulling her with appalling suddenness 'from her melodious lay | To muddy death'; and in each case the shamefully unfinished quality of their ending is underscored by the disgraceful scanting of their funeral rites. The ancient horror of the *mors improvisa* awakened by these deaths is intensified by the fate of those 'indifferent children of the earth' (II. ii. 227), Rosencrantz and Guildenstern, hurried to their 'sudden death, | Not shriving time allowed' (V. ii. 46–7), of Gertrude, her voice silenced on a half-line, and, above

[25] The pun is pointed up by Laertes' exclamation 'Upon my life, Lamord' (IV. vii. 91).

[26] In *Julius Caesar*, Cassius, facing death on his own birthday, discovers a similar fatal circularity in the course of his life: 'time is come round, | And where I did begin, there shall I end' (V. iii. 24–5).

all, of Claudius, as he chokes on the poisoned wine of his parodic last Communion.

The Death that strikes 'so many princes at a shot' (v. ii. 366) scarcely troubles to distinguish between the innocent, the compromised, and the guilty. For all of them the end comes not as narrative consummation but as a violent aposiopesis. What is even more disturbing is that the hero's own death is haunted by a similar sense of fearful incompletion; and this in spite of the fact that he appears, against the odds, to have brought the revenge plot to its successful conclusion. Actually, of course, his agency in this consummatory process has been of an oddly equivocal kind.

The usual revenge catastrophe, with its wickedly elaborated symmetries of crime and punishment, is accomplished through an uncanny meshing of the revenger's will with the unfolding plot, to the point where the hero appears to author not merely the downfall of his enemies, but the very process of his own undoing. This is the self-annihilating authority figured in the pen–knife by which Hieronimo writes himself out of existence. In *Hamlet*, by contrast, the catastrophe occurs only when (and, we are almost made to feel, because) the hero abandons all attempts to script it for himself: 'There is a special providence in the fall of a sparrow' (lines 219–20). Even Rosencrantz and Guildenstern are killed not through the design of 'deep plots' but as a result of an impulsive 'rashness' in which the Prince sees himself as submissive to the designs of 'a divinity that shapes our ends' (lines 6–11). For Hamlet to believe this is to feel himself part of someone else's plot, one that he neither conceives, nor begins ('Or I could make a prologue to my brains, | *They* had begun the play'; lines 30–1; emphasis added), nor properly speaking ends—since the substitute letter that commands these deaths is expressly written in a hand not his own and given its counterfeit authority (and authorship) by 'my father's signet' (line 49). The odd gap between doer and deed registered in this performance, which ensures that the murders 'are not near my conscience' (line 58), is even more apparent elsewhere in the final scene.

Apologizing for his wrongs to Laertes, Hamlet insists on blaming a 'madness' somehow exterior to himself ('Hamlet does it not. Hamlet denies it'; line 236); and this slightly unnerving dissociation is enhanced by the contrast between the brutal content of the scene and the strange sweetness of tone that marks many of Hamlet's speeches. On the one hand, there is the repeated fideistic insistence on 'special providence', and the stoical resignation apparent in 'The readiness is all' (line 222); on the other, there is a spectacle of slaughter fit to rival that of the most primitive revenge drama. One key to this paradox may be found in Hamlet's compacted paraphrase of Montaigne's 'Wheresoever your life endeth, there is it all': 'A man's life is no more than to say "one"' (line 74).[27] When he repeats this pregnant 'one' at the beginning of a bout with Laertes that will bring both their lives to an end, it is as though he were pointing to his display of martial skill as belonging to a new kind of theatre of the self—one in which an improvisatory readiness in the art of self-presentation is everything, its end a matter of no concern.

Ironically, by abandoning himself to the hazard of a form of 'play' governed by strict rules but without a foreknown outcome, Hamlet surrenders to his enemies the revenger's prerogative of writing *finis* to his own story. But the conventional revenge narrative from which he thereby dissociates himself appears to have developed its own inexorable momentum: by turning their plots 'upon th'inventors' heads' (line 385), the duel reinstates one of the most insistent of all revenge *topoi*—that of the biter bit—but in a form that removes the revenger himself from the vindictive equation: 'I am justly killed with mine own treachery. . . . The foul practice | Hath turned itself on me' (lines 307, 317–18). It doesn't much matter whether we call the author of this ending 'providence' or 'Shakespeare'; what is more important is the sense of a plot-narrative having worked itself out in a fashion that leaves the hero strangely uncontaminated by the end he nevertheless helps to bring about—so that even Claudius' death is the product of 'a poison tempered by himself', as if the venom had its own 'work' to do (lines 328, 322). This effect is enhanced by what in coventional terms amounts to a curious narrative elision: for a stock revenge hero, like Hieronimo, the moment of revenge is also the occasion for an elaborate self-justificatory retrospect, vindicating murder as the necessary conclusion of his story. From Hamlet we get nothing more than a few dismissive adjectives ('incestuous,

[27] Since 'one' was the stroke that sounded at the beginning of the play to announce the arrival of the Ghost, it is as though the ending of the play were rolling itself up into its beginning.

murderous, damnèd Dane'). As a result the emotional focus of the scene is deflected from the problematic ethics of revenge to the hero's encounter with his own end.

This is an encounter that turns its back on the ancient dignities of ritual dying, whose loss so torments the Ghost, in favour of a theatrical aesthetic of self-presentation—an aesthetic embedded (as Anne Barton long ago made us see) in the reflexivity of a scene which, amalgamating play-goers and actors as 'mutes or audience to this act' (line 335), projects its own endless re-enactment on the 'stage' to which Hamlet's body is translated.[28] But *Hamlet* is too restless a play to remain content with that self-memorializing gesture; and its ending is disturbed by an unallayed narrative anxiety—an anxiety which only seems the more acute for the eloquent gestures of closure that so signally fail to contain it.

At the very point of death, the hero remains tormented by a sense of all that remains untold, as though his life were an unfinished story still struggling for expression. Horatio is saddled with the burden of articulating that tale, as Hamlet was once burdened with memorializing the Ghost's. Three times Hamlet insists on his friend's duty to tell it:

> *Report me* and my cause aright
> To the unsatisfied. . . .
> O God, Horatio, what a wounded name,
> Things standing thus unknown, shall I leave behind me!
> If thou didst ever hold me in thy heart,
> Absent thee from felicity awhile,
> And in this harsh world draw thy breath in pain,
> To *tell my story*. . . .
> Fortinbras . . . has my dying voice.
> *So tell him, with th'occurrents, more and less* . . .
>
> (lines 339–40, 344–9, 356–7; emphasis added)

Anne Barton has rightly protested the inadequacy of the bare catalogue of 'accidental judgements [and] casual slaughters' (line

[28] In this it partially recalls the metatheatrical confidence of Cassius in the play that immediately preceded it ('How many ages hence | Shall this our lofty scene be acted over | In states unborn and accents yet unknown'; III. i. 111–13), as well as anticipating the boast of Marston's *Antonio's Revenge*, where the hero's closing speech imagines a future author turning the story to 'immortal fame' in 'some black tragedy' (V. iii. 177–9).

382) which is all Horatio's stolid imagination can offer in response to these imprecations.[29] Yet if we ask what more Horatio *could* say, the answer is not readily apparent—especially since Hamlet's own attempts to tell his story are left hanging in frustrated aposiopesis:

You that look pale, and tremble at this chance,
That are but mutes or audience to this act,
Had I but time—as this fell sergeant, Death,
Is strict in his arrest—O, I could *tell* you—
But let it be. Horatio, I am dead.
(lines 334–8)

The coda which follows the Prince's death is full of telling and the promise of telling—from Horatio, from the Ambassadors, and, most magniloquently from Fortinbras, who insists upon the capacity of 'The soldier's music and the rite of war' to 'speak loudly' for the dead hero (lines 399–400); but a strongman's cannon are, if anything, even less well tuned to speak for this Prince than the player's pipe; and the ceremonious rhetoric of closure is inevitably ironized by its context of narrative collapse. Like Horatio's uninstructive plot-summary, Fortinbras's 'soldier's music' is really no more than a vain attempt to ventriloquize a voice that has been stopped for ever. With all its pomp, language here parades on the brink of silence: and the play remains full of the tension of unfinished business. It is no accident that *Hamlet*, almost uniquely in

[29] Barton describes it in her introduction to the Penguin edition as 'leaving out everything that seems important, reducing all that is distinctive about this play to a plot stereotype' (p. 52). Franco Moretti similarly argues that the mere 'plot summary' produced by Horatio's 'mediocre conscientiousness' exemplifies the impossibility in mature Renaissance tragedy of conferring significance upon the tragic errors of plot: 'what of the "rest", which is nothing if not the meaning of what has happened? On it falls Hamlet's prohibition [of silence]: let no-one presume to confer meaning on it' ('The Great Eclipse', in *Signs Taken for Wonders*, 55). Barbara Hardy, by contrast, finds Horatio's narrative entirely adequate to the occasion, for all its acknowledged externality ('who better to tell one's story truly?'), and takes its structural role as funeral oration entirely at face value: 'the function of such concluding assertion of narration is clear: it neatly and strongly binds retrospect with prospect, to strengthen closure' ('Figure of Narration in *Hamlet*', 13, 14). Similarly, Dennis Kay, in '"To hear the rest untold": Shakespeare's Postponed Endings', *Renaissance Quarterly*, 37 (1984), 207–27, accepts the adequacy of Horatio's story, while insisting that it looks forward to the consummatory performance of 'an official recognition scene' outside the confines of the play, which 'it is the responsibility of the audience to imagine' (p. 217).

Shakespeare, should end upon a half-line ('Go, bid the soldiers shoot');[30] for its whole form, one might say, is that of a great aposiopesis, whose 'sudden breaking off' is nothing less than the sign of Death's arbitrary arrest. The story of our lives, the play seems to suggest, is always the wrong story; but it also half-persuades us that somewhere on the other side of the silence imposed by abruption of death, Hamlet's true story remains, waiting to be told. This, however, of necessity, is a story that also lies on the other side of language, tantalizingly glimpsed only as Hamlet himself is about to enter the domain of the inexpressible.

[30] The only other instance (doubtful in view of the state of its text) is that of *Timon of Athens*.

7
Accommodating the Dead: *Hamlet* and the Ends of Revenge

Oh, no, there is no end; the end is death and madness.
(Hieronimo, in *The Spanish Tragedy*)

Remembrance and Revenge

Death assumes a variety of guises in *Hamlet*: the sinisterly named gallant, Lamord; the anonymous skulls of the graveyard; and the eldritch figure of the grave-digging Clown—all of them, in their different ways, can stand for the dis-guising leveller who, in Robert Watson's words, 'steals away the differences by and for which we live'.[1] In his suggestive essay on the Ghost, Watson argues that *Hamlet*, like all revenge tragedies, embodies a fantasy of overcoming death, its perennially compelling power deriving from 'the idea that revenge can symbolically restore us to life by defeating the agency of our death, conveniently localized in a villain'. For Watson, the undefined threat confronting the watchers on the battlements of Elsinore 'proves [for all its disguises] to be mortality itself, the foe against whom our weapons are futile'.[2] There is some truth in this; but to treat the agon of the play in such purely abstract terms is, I think, to dehistoricize the anxieties it explores. Nor is it possible to treat the Ghost itself simply as a figure for death; for, through the restless insistence of its yearning for remembrance, it expresses a desperate refusal of death's indifference, rejecting the insult (as it denies the consolation) of oblivion. More than anything, I have suggested, the Ghost embodies (or voices) a certain kind of story, one that begins and ends in death.

[1] Watson, *The Rest is Silence*, 98. [2] Ibid. 78.

Hamlet, I have been arguing, is a play that dramatizes its hero's resistance to the entrapment of this all-too-familiar narrative—a resistance which is also Shakespeare's, since the plot was among his givens, something with and against which he had to work. Ironically enough, however, *Hamlet* has become so much the best-known example of revenge tragedy, whose premisses it explores and questions, that it is difficult to recognize how significantly it reshaped the genre to which it belonged. Most of what we know about the original *Hamlet* amounts to educated guesswork; but one telling detail survives in Thomas Lodge's description of its Ghost, crying 'like an oyster-wife, "Hamlet, revenge!"'[3] This famous shriek is what the Globe audience must have expected; what they heard instead was the plangent injunction 'Remember me!' Behind this subtle adjustment lies the great discovery of the play, that revenge tragedy, at the deepest level, is less about the ethics of vendetta that it is about murderous legacies of the past and the terrible power of memory. If English Renaissance tragedy played out society's effort to reach a new accommodation with death, the drama of revenge showed how that must be contingent on the struggle to accommodate the dead themselves.

Among the more important contributory factors to the early modern 'crisis of death', as we have seen, was the effectual displacement of the dead as a distinct 'age-group' in Protestant societies. Its most crippling consequence was that it seemed to place the dead beyond the help or intercession of their survivors. The effect of this displacement, Natalie Davis speculates, was to load the Protestant conscience with an intolerable burden of remembrance:

> Especially, the living were left with their memories, unimpeded and untransformed by any ritual communication with their dead. Some memories bite the conscience. Paradoxically, in trying to lay all ghosts forever, the Protestants may have raised new ones. . . . the ending of Purgatory and ritual mourning, whatever energies were thereby freed for other work, may have left Protestants . . . less removed from their parents, more alone with their memories, more vulnerable to the prick of the past, more open to the family's future.[4]

[3] *Hamlet*, ed. G. R. Hibbard (Oxford: Clarendon Press, 1987), 13.

[4] Davis, 'Ghosts, Kin, and Progeny', 95, 96. Cf. also Gittings, *Death, Burial and the Individual*, 21–31; and Llewellyn, *Art of Death*, 27–8. Llewellyn notes how

But even as it exacerbated the guilt of the survivors, this change must have seemed likely to provoke the resentment of the deceased. Human cultures, as Elias Canetti reminds us, have always been haunted by a fear of the potential vindictiveness of the dead:

The first thing that strikes one is the universal *fear* of the dead. They are discontented and full of envy for those they have left behind. They try to take revenge on them, sometimes for injuries done them during their lifetime, but often simply because they themselves are no longer alive.... The spirits of the dead... [have] a hundred ways of meddling with life. Passionately and continually they seek to get hold of the living.... In the eyes of those who are still alive, everyone who is dead has suffered a defeat, which consists in *having been survived*. The dead cannot resign themselves to this injury that was inflicted on them, and so it is natural that they should want to inflict it on others.[5]

The envious malignity that Canetti describes is vividly apparent in the unholy glee with which the emaciated summoners of the *danse macabre* go about their work; but it can even be felt in the *memento mori* verses with which so many early modern gravestones arrest the attention of the careless passer-by: 'As you are now, so once was I: | As I am now, so shalt thou be.' Under the new Protestant dispensation there remained no institutionalized way of appeasing the indignation of the dead, whose stored-up malice might threaten the wholesale destruction of society.

More consistently than any other form, it is now possible to see, it was revenge tragedy that spoke to the anxieties produced by this painful transformation in relations with the dead:[6] its protagonists are haunted by ghosts because they are possessed by memory; the dead will not leave them alone, because the dead cannot bear to

'the theory of *memoria*, which stressed the didactic potential of the lives and deaths of the virtuous', developed 'to balance the traumatic effect of the loss of Purgatory' (p. 28). The poignant reflection of the *Acteur* in the *Grande Danse*, 'De gens mors nest plus nouvelle' ('There is no news about the dead'; *Danse Macabre of Women*, 124), suggests that such anxieties were not wholly confined to Protestant sensibilities.

[5] Canetti, *Crowds and Power*, 306.

[6] I have developed this argument at greater length in 'Remembrance and Revenge: *Hamlet*, *Macbeth*, and *The Tempest*', in Ian Donaldson (ed.), *Jonson and Shakespeare* (London and Canberra: Macmillan/HRC, 1983), 35–56, and 'Exeunt with a Dead March: Funeral Pageantry on the Shakespearean Stage', in David Bergeron (ed.), *Pageantry in the Shakespearean Theatre* (Athens: University of Georgia Press, 1985), 154–93.

be left alone. Alternately disabled by their inability to forget, and driven by their violent compulsion to remember, revenge heroes must wrestle to redeem their dead from the shame of being forgotten, even as they struggle to lay these perturbed spirits to rest, and thereby free themselves from the insistent presence of the past.

The terrible frenzies of the revenger, that berserk memorialist, can be understood as a fantasy response to the sense of despairing impotence produced by the Protestant displacement of the dead—a fantasy only slightly more grandiose than that represented by the ever more lavish funeral monuments which cluttered the churches of sixteenth- and seventeenth-century England.[7] Of course, the extraordinary imaginative stroke in Marston's *Antonio's Revenge*, whereby the hero is made to sacrifice the innocent Julio at Andrugio's tomb in a savage parody of the requiem mass, makes the connection between these two instruments of *memoria* as brutally and directly as possible;[8] and the bloodthirsty rites performed at the Tomb of the Andronici in the first act of *Titus Andronicus* (rites which initiate the remorseless sequence of revenge and counter-revenge that is to follow) have much the same significance. But it is *Hamlet* which, through its hero's preoccupation with memory, death, and decay, provides the most persuasive confirmation of the affective crisis Davis describes. What, after all, is its Ghost but an incarnation of those tormenting memories which 'bite the conscience'? And what are Hamlet's soliloquies but an expression of that unending 'inner dialogue with a parent who had reared one', the litany of resentment that no rite of passage could now erase?

What distinguishes *Hamlet* from all other revenge tragedies is this degree of conscious engagement with anxieties that often lie buried deep in the structures of the genre. This consciousness is registered through its self-reflexive preoccupation with story-telling on the one hand and its agitated concern with funeral rites on the other; and just as its inset narratives are typified by a desperate incompleteness, so its funeral rites are marked by their insultingly stunted or indecorous form. Indeed, in so far as funeral itself constitutes a form of symbolic narrative, maimed rites and interrupted

[7] On this point, see Ralph Houlbrooke, 'Death, Church, and Family in England between the Late Fifteenth and the Early Eighteenth Centuries', in Houlbrooke (ed.), *Death, Ritual and Bereavement*, 25–42.

[8] See G. K. Hunter's introduction to his Regents edition of the play (London: Edward Arnold, 1964), 8.

stories may be regarded as aspects of the same structural pattern; and the solemn obsequies that crown *Hamlet*'s last act are calculated to gratify the frustrated desire for closure produced by the play's many unfinished narratives. Of course, the military funeral orchestrated by Fortinbras is scarcely an unqualified triumph—in a play of such serpentine irony, so mockingly protective of its own 'mystery', how could it be? But, for the moment at least, it serves, in Seamus Heaney's marvellous phrase, to 'allay the cud of memory'.[9]

Since revenge drama shows vengeance to be no more than memory continued by other means, the role of the revenger is essentially that of a 'remembrancer' in two senses of that once potent word: he is both an agent of memory and one whose task it is to exact payments for the debts of the past. The familiar emblem of his double function is the *memento* that he typically treasures—a picture, a blood-soaked kerchief, a cadaver, or a skull—at once a warning to his enemies (a 'terror to fat folks', in Vindice's phrase) and a physical proof of the guilty history which they have sought to efface. In Kyd's *The Spanish Tragedy* and Marston's *Antonio's Revenge* the bereaved fathers, Hieronimo and Pandulpho, hoard up gory relics of their murdered sons against the day of revenge; Vindice in *The Revenger's Tragedy* sighs for nine years over 'death's vizard' (I. i. 50), the skull of his poisoned mistress; Chettle's Clois Hoffman preserves the cadaverous 'remembrance of my living father', hanging (like Horatio's body) in his arbour (I. i. 8); the more civilized Hamlet keeps only the memorial portrait of his father, but in the graveyard scene symbolically replaces it with Yorick's skull. The extreme emotion attaching to these various mementoes has to do with their function not merely as reminders of a past that has been shamefully 'throw[n] to earth' (*Hamlet*, I. ii. 106), but as signs of the imminent disclosure that will redeem that past from the grave—signs of a truly apocalyptic revelation that will expose the death at the core of the usurper's corrupt society.

[9] Seamus Heaney, 'Funeral Rites, III', in *Selected Poems, 1965–1975* (London: Faber, 1980), 103. A number of recent critics have stressed the importance of memory in the play: in addition to my 'Remembrance and Revenge', see John Kerrigan's brilliant 'Hieronimo, Hamlet, and Remembrance', *Essays in Criticism*, 31 (1981), 105–26, a version of which appears in ch. 7 of his *Revenge Tragedy: Aeschylus to Armageddon* (Oxford: Clarendon Press, 1996); James P. Hammersmith, '*Hamlet* and the Myth of Memory', *ELH* 45 (1978), 597–605; Richard Helgerson, 'What Hamlet Remembers', *Shakespeare Studies*, 10 (1977), 67–97.

Because it is precisely the *appearance* of facts that the revenger sets out to challenge, his emotions are always liable to seem (as Eliot famously complained about Hamlet) 'in excess of the facts as they appear'.[10] The intolerable tension between his duty to articulate what has been rendered (literally) unspeakable and his politic need to conceal his emotions is one reason why madness, real or feigned, is important to the action of so many revenge-plays ('break my heart, for I must hold my tongue'); for madness is typically imagined as a linguistic breakdown which bespeaks an inner disintegration, while nevertheless allowing a kind of inarticulate utterance to the unutterable.[11] Of the many examples (Kyd's Hieronimo, Marston's Antonio and Malevole, Webster's Ferdinand, Ford's Penthea, Shakespeare's Titus, and Hamlet himself) it is perhaps Ophelia who most clearly displays the connection between madness and the repressed past. Her collapse follows the obscure death and interment of Polonius, both of which have been kept 'hugger-mugger' for the political convenience of the King. Tormented by the contemptuous indistinction of her father's end, Ophelia calls Claudius, the agent of oblivion, to account with a significant heraldic pun: 'You must wear your rue *with a difference*' (IV. v. 183–4; emphasis added). As she distributes the herbal emblems of memory and repentance, Ophelia gives a kind of paradoxical substance to the annihilated past, symbolically redeeming it from the indifference of death to provide what Laertes calls a 'nothing . . . more than matter. . . . A document in madness: thoughts and remembrance fitted' (IV. 5. 174–9). Characteristically, the disjointed laments that her brother interprets as persuasions to revenge are filled with desperate yearning for the irrecoverable: 'He will never come again.'[12]

[10] T. S. Eliot, *Selected Essays* (London: Faber, 1961), 145 (emphasis added); ironically Eliot's is exactly Claudius' complaint.

[11] The connection between madness, linguistic breakdown, and social disintegration is most forcefully displayed in *The Spanish Tragedy*, where it culminates in Hieronimo's bizarrely emblematic biting out his own tongue. For relevant discussion of this episode, see Johnson, '*The Spanish Tragedy*'; McMillin, 'The Figure of Silence in *The Spanish Tragedy*'; and Barish, '*The Spanish Tragedy*'. Cf. also the recurrence of the mutilated-tongue motif in *Titus Andronicus*, *Antonio's Revenge*, and *The Revenger's Tragedy*.

[12] In Ford's *The Broken Heart* Penthea's nostalgic pastoral ('Remember, | When we last gathered roses in the garden, | I found my wits; but truly you lost yours'; IV. ii. 119–21) is similarly interpreted by Orgilus as an oracular 'inspiration' to revenge (line 125).

The pastoral sweetness briefly evoked by Ophelia's herbal emblems is not a mere sentimental indulgence: like the 'fantastic garlands' with which Gertrude decorates the picture of Ophelia's death, it serves to link her violated innocence with the garden motif that in *Hamlet*, as in other revenge-plays, is an important vehicle for a peculiar anxiety about the past. In all of them the initial crime is imagined as a kind of primal pollution that has marked a whole society with death—rather as the usurpation and murder of Richard II is seen to do in the grand revenge scheme of Shakespeare's histories: 'Exton, thy fierce hand | Hath with the king's blood stain'd the king's own land' (v. v. 109–10). As a result, the hero's individual passion for retribution is complicated and intensified by a profound nostalgia for a vanished prelapsarian order. *The Spanish Tragedy*, in so many ways the model for later revenge tragedy, is dominated by the image of a violated garden, Hieronimo's 'sacred bower' (II. v. 27), where Horatio is hanged in Act II, scene iv, and where his body must once again appear hanging in the 'spectacle' with which Hieronimo rounds off his tragedy of 'Soliman and Perseda'. Drawing the curtain (in the manner of Clois Hoffman after him) to reveal the bloody cause which has brought him to this end, the old man shows his son once again 'hanging on a tree' in an accursed 'garden plot' (IV. iv. 88–113). The echoes of the Genesis garden myth and of its New Testament counterpart in Gethsemane–Golgotha[13]—the archetypes of narrative beginning and ending—are apparent here, as they are in *Hamlet*, where the story of the old King's murder in the 'orchard' and the visual detail of the 'bank of flowers' on which the Player King lies in 'The Murder of Gonzago' (I. v. 59; III. ii. 135) serve to body forth the 'unweeded garden' of Hamlet's imagination. In the scheme of images to which the Prince's highly traditional metaphor belongs, Denmark is figured as a formerly Edenic garden which the 'serpent' Claudius has turned to wilderness, leaving it to the possession of 'things rank and gross in nature' (I ii. 135–6; I. v. 35–40).[14] It is thus particularly appropriate that

[13] These two sites of Christ's passion are habitually conflated in biblical typology, in order to stress the correspondences between the scenes of Fall and Redemption.

[14] The First Quarto (1603) specifies that the Player King 'sits down in an Arbour' during the dumb show, making the visual resemblance to *The Spanish Tragedy* even more striking. The image of the violated garden is one that links *Hamlet* with the histories, notably *Richard II*; see Maynard Mack, Jr., *Killing the King* (New

Claudius should identify his crime with the first death recorded in Genesis—the killing of Abel by his brother Cain, in which the mortal curse of Eden is confirmed: 'It hath the primal eldest curse upon it, | A brother's murther' (III. iii. 37–8).[15]

The revenger's task is essentially backward-looking—in his end he is to rediscover his beginning; but this attempt to restore the prelapsarian innocence of mythic origins entrammels him in hopeless contradictions. In *The Spanish Tragedy*, for example, Hieronimo's purging of the corrupted garden-state is prefigured in Isabella's frenzied reduction of her husband's garden to a Babylonic wasteland, as she 'cuts down the arbor' where her son was hanged:

Down with these branches and these loathsome boughs
Of this unfortunate and fatal pine;
Down with them, Isabella, rent them up
And burn the roots from whence the rest is sprung.
I will not leave a root, a stalk, a tree
A bough, a branch, a blossom, nor a leaf,
No, not an herb within this garden plot—
Accursèd complot of my misery.
Fruitless forever may this garden be,
Barren the earth, and blissless whosoever
Imagines not to keep it unmanured!
An eastern wind commixed with noisome airs
Shall blast the plants and the young saplings;
The earth with serpents shall be pesterèd . . .

(IV. ii. 6–19)

Isabella's *gestus* symbolically repeats the original violation of the garden, as her language berating Hieronimo's procrastination makes plain:

Ah, nay, thou dost delay their deaths,
Forgives the murderers of thy noble son,

Haven: Yale University Press, 1973), 83–4, and John Wilders, *The Lost Garden* (London: Methuen, 1978). In *Macbeth* a comparable nostalgia for a lost garden-world is suggested by the brief lyricism of Duncan's arrival at Macbeth's castle, and Macbeth's own yearning for the style of kingship embodied in 'the gracious Duncan'.

[15] In *The Revenger's Tragedy*, where nostalgia for an idealized past is emblematized in a skull named 'Gloriana' (after the dead Elizabeth), the violated garden is secularized in the satiric evocation of a countryside pillaged to feed the corrupted appetites of a court where women 'Walk with a hundred acres on their backs— | Fair meadows cut into green fore-parts' (II. i. 214–15).

And none but I bestir me—to no end!
And as I curse this tree from further fruit,
So shall my womb be cursèd for his sake.

(lines 32–6)

The terrible circularity implied here ('to no end') is confirmed in the following scene. Hieronimo 'knocks up the curtain' over the desecrated arbour, and then, at the climax of his re-enactment of Horatio's murder, draws it to show his son's mutilated body, the obscene 'fruits of love' (II. iv. 55) once again hanging on a tree.

The contradiction displayed in such repetitions is exacerbated by the uncanny precision with which the revenger's obsession with the past leads him to imitate the enemy he detests. So in 'Soliman and Perseda' Hieronimo takes the part of the murderous Bashaw, corresponding to Lorenzo, while casting Lorenzo as the Horatio-like victim, Erasto. Similarly, in *The Revenger's Tragedy*, Vindice's witty variation on the theme of the biter bit ('Those that did eat are eaten'; III. v. 160) exactly reverses the Duke's poisoning of Gloriana by inducing him to kiss her poisoned skull. Clois Hoffman announces the achievement of his vindictive ends by hanging a second cadaver, its skull identically scarred with a burning crown, beside that of his father. Revenge, as the fiercely exacting irony of such moments insists, is an action which, through its very attempt to revive and atone for the violated past, finishes by re-enacting the crime of violation. Vindice will end up stabbing the corpse of an arch-enemy dressed as his own double: ''Tis time to die', as his last speech ruefully has it, 'when we are ourselves are foes' (V. iii. 110).

'Must I remember?'

The action of revenge tragedy, then, involves a system of tormenting paradox. The dream of re-membering the violated past and destroying a tainted order is fulfilled only at the cost of repeating the violation and spreading the taint. Increasingly infected with the corruption of his antagonist, the revenger courts his own destruction, and his claims upon the audience's sympathy are disturbingly compromised. He is the agent of that remembrance upon which a restored social order is felt to depend; but he has ceased to be a social man, for in his willed surrender to the claims of the dead he invariably 'loses' or 'forgets' himself (*Revenger's Tragedy*, IV. iii. 201; IV. iv. 24–5, 84–5); and in the process his actions threaten to produce an apocalypse of indifference such as we see played out in the farcical confusions, piling corpse on corpse, at the end of *The Revenger's Tragedy*.

In *Hamlet* the deep moral, as well as emotional, ambivalence of memory is signalled early in the play by the tormented 'Must I remember?' of the hero's first soliloquy (I. ii. 143). The psychological focus of this tragedy is almost exclusively upon the revenger's suffering: condemned as he is to sweat under the 'fardels' of memory in a world of 'bestial oblivion', he is riven by the maddening disparity between the version of the past known by the mind and the version propagated by the lies of official history. If the Ghost is the 'cherub' of remembrance (IV. iii. 48) then Claudius is the archdemon of oblivion, whilst Polonius (with his bland connivance in usurpation), Gertrude (with her public unconcern for Old Hamlet's death), Ophelia (with her ill-timed repudiation of Hamlet's 'remembrances'; III. i. 92–4), and those 'indifferent children of the earth' Rosencrantz and Guildenstern (with their betrayal of old friendship) are all, from Hamlet's point of view, the pliant accessories in a plot to violate the truth of their common past. Claudius' first speech, even as it pays lip-service to the 'memory' of his brother's death, characteristically perverts the very meaning of 'remembrance' by attaching it resolutely to present interest—'remembrance of ourselves' (I. ii. 1–7).[16] The bland obliquity of the King's rhetoric occludes his incest by stretching a curtain of magniloquence between past and present fact, separating the fatal phrases 'sometime sister' and 'taken to wife' with nearly six lines of ingeniously embroidered syntax (lines 8–14). The passage perfectly epitomizes the surreptitious violence which the usurper has done to time, rendering it radically 'out of joint' (I. v. 188). His usurpation simultaneously dislocates the political law of 'fair sequence and succession',[17] and the moral law of consequence ('thinking too precisely on th'event'; IV. iv. 41). By contrast, what Claudius

[16] Compare his final degradation of the word in II. ii. 26, where 'a king's remembrance' is merely a lofty euphemism for a cash bribe. Cf. also the usurping Piero's attempt to corrupt Maria, Gertrude's counterpart in *Antonio's Revenge*: 'O that you could remember to forget!' (II. ii. 167).

[17] The phrase is York's in *Richard II*, II. i. 199.

dismisses with a contemptuous quibble as 'obsequious sorrow' (I. ii. 92) commits Hamlet to brood obsessively on temporal chains of cause and effect. In so far as he is his father's son, he represents the future of a past that Claudius has 'cut off'. His repeated determination to 'follow' the Ghost in Act I, scene iv becomes an enactment of his commitment to due sequence, to the claims of the past upon the present and the future, to memory, consequence, and succession.[18] But such a commitment to the re-jointing of time is also a commitment to the completion of a certain all-too-familiar kind of plot-narrative, and one that risks the radical disjointing of the self whose only imaginable end is death.

Even before the Ghost saddles him with its terribly repeated obligation to remember (I. v. 91–111), Hamlet's memories of his father resemble a haunting ('My father—methinks I see my father'; I. ii. 184). He will escape the net of Claudius' narrative, only to become entangled in that of the Ghost. In this sense the Ghost, too, is a kind of usurper—as indeed Horatio's challenge to it suggests:

What art thou that *usurp'st* this time of night,
Together with that fair and warlike form
In which the majesty of buried Denmark
Did sometimes march?

(I. i. 46–97; emphasis added)

[18] I. iv. 63, 68, 79, 86. 'Follow' has some claim to be considered a key word in *Hamlet*, where it is reiterated more frequently than in any other play in the canon except *King Lear*. In Act I, scene ii, for example, the memory of Gertrude 'following' old Hamlet's coffin in the due order of funeral set against the marriage that so disgracefully 'followed hard upon' that funeral (lines 148, 179) helps to define the disjointing of time and state. For Hamlet, Denmark is a world where 'thrift may follow fawning' (III. ii. 62), but where nothing else properly 'follows': his mad logic-chopping with Polonius enforces this point ('Nay, that follows not'; II. ii. 413). Polonius himself constructs a world where things complacently 'follow, as the night the day' (I. iii. 79): but the Denmark described in the opening scene, which 'makes the night joint-labourer with the day' (I. i. 78), will scarcely accommodate his proverb. In Act V the spectacle of another funeral procession 'following' Ophelia's hearse into a graveyard whose unspoken motto is the 'All must follow' of the *memento mori* tradition (V. i. 218, 220), together with Hamlet's mockingly ambiguous promise to 'follow the king's pleasure' (V. ii. 200–1), ushers in a series of mortal followings in which Claudius is dispatched to 'follow' Gertrude (line 327) and Hamlet himself 'follows' Laertes (line 332). With the solemn funeral march that ends the play, these last followings in effect knit up the broken sequences from the beginning of the play. Patricia Parker fascinatingly extends this idea of 'sequence' to make the idea of *non sequitur* a kind of rhetorical analogue for the play's design in *Shakespeare from the Margins: Language, Culture, Context* (Chicago: University of Chicago Press, 1996) 45–7, and *Literary Fat Ladies*, 119–20.

It is not only the 'form' of the dead King that the Ghost usurps, but Hamlet's, transforming 'That unmatch'd form and [feature] of blown youth' (III. i. 159) to the uncanny simulacrum of a revenant, 'loosed out of hell | To speak of horrors' (II. i. 80–1), who haunts Ophelia's bedchamber. The instrument of possession, as we have seen, is the tale it pours in Hamlet's ear, 'usurping' his 'wholesome life' as surely as the poisons of Claudius and Lucianus do those of Old Hamlet and Gonzago (III. ii. 260). In this context it is significant that Hamlet's solemn rite of memory after his first encounter with the Ghost should also be an act of oblivion, in which the memories installed by the Ghost expunge 'all forms, all pressures past' with their oppressive scripture (I. v. 100).

Thus the Ghost contains in itself the unjointing contradictions by which the revenger's consciousness is torn asunder. On the one hand, as the embodiment of a usurped past that must be restored, it represents a force of indestructible memory, an uncanny return of the repressed; on the other, it is itself the usurping instrument of a dangerous oblivion. Remembrance and oblivion are the insistent theme of its own laments; indeed this Ghost distinguishes itself from its proliferating sixteenth- and seventeenth-century kin precisely by its melancholy yearning to be remembered: 'Adieu, adieu, adieu! Remember me!' (I. v. 91). More even than the history of Claudius' iniquity, it is the desperate pathos of this appeal (with its poignant echoes of the *memento mori* tradition[19]) that possesses Hamlet's imagination (lines 92–111): and his revenge itself is conceived less as a piece of retributive justice than as a proof of remembrance.[20] It is as though only such an act, absolute and irreversible, can escape the transience of feeling, the hollowness of mere words and gestures, to provide an unequivocal demonstration of a love that is capable of surviving the grave:

[19] Marjorie Garber ('"Remember me": *Memento Mori* Figures in Shakespeare's Plays', *Renaissance Drama*, 12 (1981), 3–25) sees the Ghost's 'Remember me' as a deliberate recollection of the speaking skull in the *memento mori* tradition, and thus 'directly proleptic to Hamlet's literal interview with a skull in the graveyard, and later transmuted to his dying request to Horatio . . . "To tell my story" ' (p. 4).

[20] On this point, see Kerrigan ('Hieronimo, Hamlet, and Remembrance', 113–14), who notes the striking fact that 'Hamlet never promises to revenge, only to remember' (p. 114). Cf. also the terms of Francisco's self-dedication as Isabella's revenger in *The White Devil*: 'Believe me, I am nothing but her grave, | And I shall keep her blessed memory | Longer than a thousand epitaphs' (III. ii. 341–3); 'What have I to do | With tombs, or death-beds, funerals, or tears, | That have to meditate upon revenge' (IV. i. 110–12).

[GHOST.] If thou didst ever thy dear father *love* . . .
Revenge his foul and most unnatural murder. . . .
HAMLET. Haste me to know't, that I with wings as swift
As meditation, or the thoughts of *love*,
May sweep to my *revenge*.
(I. v. 23–31; emphasis added)

Memory in these lines ('meditation [and] the thoughts of love') becomes the very pattern of swift revenge.

When the Ghost returns in the closet scene (almost as though conjured up by Hamlet's attempts to reawaken Gertrude's forgotten love for her dead husband), its first words once again evoke its unappeasable longing for love and remembrance: 'Do not forget!' (III. iv. 110). Significantly, this is the same emotion which seems to possess the Player King in Hamlet's revised version of *The Murder of Gonzago*, when he begins to brood on the state of things after his own death (III. ii. 186–215).[21] There is no limit to the love which the remorseless dead seek to exact from the living; and consequently (as Hamlet's 'Hecuba' and 'How all occasions' soliloquies insist) no impiety more dreadful than forgetfulness—stigmatized as '*bestial* oblivion', because here it is only memory and the pain which memory begets that is allowed to distinguish man from beast. Ironically enough this will be exactly the foundation of Claudius' appeal when he tries to work Laertes to revenge for *his* lost father:

Laertes, was your father dear to you?
Or are you like the painting of a sorrow,
A face without a heart?

* * * * * *

Not that I think you did not *love* your father,
But that I know love is begun by time,
And that I see, in passages of proof,
Time qualifies the spark and fire of it.

* * * * * *

[21] Whether or not one accedes to the tempting suggestion that the 'dozen or sixteen lines' which Hamlet promises to insert into the play are to be found in the Player King's big speech, 'The Mousetrap' remains Hamlet's version of 'The Murder of Gonzago' if only because the context to which he transfers it endows the play with entirely new meanings.

What would you undertake
To show yourself in *deed* your father's son
More than in words?

(IV. iii. 110–26; emphasis added)

This insistence that the proofs of love and remembrance are to be found in deeds alone is made for the last time in the quarrel between Hamlet and Laertes over Ophelia's grave; but this time it is given a bitterly ironic twist:

I *lov'd* Ophelia. Forty thousand brothers
Could not with all their quantity of love
Make up my sum. What wilt thou *do* for her?

* * * * * *

'Swounds, show me what thou't *do*.
Woo't weep, woo't fight, woo't fast, woo't tear thyself?
Woo't drink up eisel, eat a crocodile?
I'll *do*'t. (V. ii. 269–77; emphasis added)

By now, in the face of death, the Herculean deeds themselves seem as empty as words, barely distinguishable from the drab's bombast of the Hecuba soliloquy: 'Nay, an thou'lt mouth, | I'll rant as well as thou' (lines 283–4). In the end, as the graveyard seems to have brought home to the Prince, there is nothing to be *done* for the dead: we can no more sate their importunate desire for love than they can answer our impertinent questions about death.

As the Ghost makes demands that nothing (short of death) can fully satisfy, so it arouses a curiosity that nothing (short of death) can answer. For, apart from its restless longing for remembrance, this apparition's most striking feature is its enigmatic, even secretive, nature. It can disinter the past, but of its own present it can reveal almost nothing. At best it makes the vague claim to issue from a Purgatory which, for most of Shakespeare's audience, was no longer supposed to exist; and as if this were not suspicious enough, it is singularly reticent about its place of suffering. Traditionally the pains of Hell and Purgatory, far from being secret, had been graphically paraded as a warning to the living; and to sense the full oddness of the prohibition under which it claims to labour, it is only necessary to look at one of Shakespeare's models, the Ghost of Andrea in Kyd's *The Spanish Tragedy*, whose eloquently embellished account of his Underworld experiences takes up nearly seventy lines of the Induction. Kyd's is a classic Renaissance exercise in the art of *paragone*, rising to the challenge of Virgil's Underworld, as the Friar in Ford's *'Tis Pity She's a Whore*, for example, rises to that of Dante's *Inferno*—or as we might expect Shakespeare himself to rise to that of Kyd. Instead what we are given is an elaborate *occupatio* (that devious figure of speaking and not speaking) cut short by what amounts to a sudden aposiopesis:

> But that I am forbid
> To tell the secrets of my prison-house,
> I could a tale unfold whose lightest word
> Would harrow up thy soul, freeze thy young blood....
> But this eternal blazon must not be
> To ears of flesh and blood. (I. v. 13–22)

It is often supposed that, given his apparent acceptance of the Ghost's bona fides, there is something inconsistent about Hamlet's description of death as 'The undiscover'd country, from whose bourn | No traveller returns' (III. i. 78–9). But unlike Kyd's ghost of Andrea, that voluble Hakluyt of the Underworld, this strangely secretive Ghost barely qualifies as such a 'traveller'—its reticences helping to ensure that its true origin and nature ('spirit of health or goblin damn'd') remain uncertain to the very end. The Ghost can do nothing, therefore, to alleviate those puzzles of the will which attend the obscure dread of 'something after death': it exists, perhaps, only as a force of discarnate longing. Yet there are other suggestions which make it appear surprisingly substantial, and hint that it comes, if anywhere, quite literally 'from the grave', as Horatio says (I. v. 125). When Hamlet calls it 'dead corse' (I. iv. 52) the phrase suggests that (for all its sometimes startling resemblance to the living Old Hamlet) this ghost is cadaver-like, resembling one of those *transi* tomb effigies in which the signs of mortal decay have already appeared:[22]

[22] For evidence that 16th-century lore commonly presented ghosts as 'solid corpses up out of their graves to walk again', see Morris, *Last Things in Shakespeare*, 25–6; and compare Macbeth's response to Banquo's Ghost: 'If charnel-houses and our graves must send | Those that we bury back, our monuments | Shall be the maws of kites' (*Macbeth*, III. iv. 71–3).

Let me not burst in ignorance, but tell
Why thy canoniz'd bones, hearsed in death,
Have burst their cerements; why the sepulchre
Wherein we saw thee quietly inurn'd
Hath op'd his ponderous and marble jaws
To cast thee up again. What may this mean,
That thou, *dead corse*, again in complete steel,
Revisits thus the glimpses of the moon.

(I. iv. 46–53; emphasis added)

This ghostly rising, drawing on the old resurrection iconography of the Last Judgement, is a kind of funeral in reverse, in which the corpse successively throws off cerecloths and coffin to break through the marble doors of its sepulchre and return to the palace from which it was ceremoniously transported.[23] When referred to this charnel image, Hamlet's reiterated determination to 'follow it' develops large and potentially sinister resonances—it amounts to a purposeful redirection of that 'obsequious sorrow' which kept him (as though locked for ever in the ritual following of the funeral procession) seeking his noble father in the dust; and it reaches its inevitable conclusion in the graveyard of Act V, where actual bones take the place of the ghostly cadaver.

'Chronicles of the time': Hamlet and the Performance of Memory

If the revenger's obsession with the past contains its own nemesis, so too does his protagonist's greed for the future. Not even Claudius

[23] The play is full of such repellently literal reminders of mortal decay; from the first appearance of the Ghost and Horatio's recollection of the broken cemeteries of Caesar's Rome (I. i. 115–16), Elsinore is overhung with that sense of putrefaction which filled every 16th-century church and graveyard (see Ariès, *Hour of our Death*, 56–9, 481–3; and Stone, *Family, Sex, and Marriage*, 78). Hamlet's charnel vision of the world as a 'foul and pestilent congregation of vapours' (II. ii. 293–303), his invocation of 'the very witching time of night, | When churchyards yawn, and hell itself breathes out | Contagion' (III. iii. 388–90), his mockery of the dead Polonius as a cadaver already in advanced decay (IV. ii. 6, IV. iii. 19–37), all give an unpleasantly literal dimension to that sense of 'something . . . rotten' beneath the state and majesty of Denmark, which the Ghost stirs up. Significantly the ghost of Andrugio in *Antonio's Revenge* introduces himself in terms that suggest a similarly repulsive physicality: 'Thy pangs of anguish rip my cerecloth up; | And lo, the ghost of old Andrugio | Forsakes his coffin' (III. i. 32–4).

can permanently free himself from the 'heavy burden' of remembrance (III. i. 53); and the prayer scene forces him to acknowledge an inexorable logic of moral consequence—his fault is 'past' and yet, by virtue of its 'effects', unremittingly present (III. iii. 51–6), 'done' but not ended. Together the revenger and his antagonist illustrate the poor condition of humankind as Montaigne had described it: 'We are never in our selves, but beyond,' he wrote; for either 'Our Affections are Transported beyond our Selves' to an unreal future, or we become denizens of an equally unreal past —'Death possessing what ever is before and behind this moment, and also a good part of this moment'.[24]

Hamlet, like other revengers, seeks to escape from this mortal impasse by contructing a particular kind of memorial that will reunite the fractured joints of time. In revenge tragedy such memorials typically take the form of theatrical fictions whose images of the occluded truth, by making re-enactment the witty instrument of revenge, magically compact together the original crime and its requital. What results is a kind of enacted pun that works 'tropically' to redefine the present in its representation of the past. By such inventions (whether we think of Hieronimo's ingeniously cast 'Tragedy of Soliman and Perseda', or Vindice's fiendishly equivocal puppet-play with the painted skull) the revenger, plotting for himself the very course of time, contrives a brilliant contraction of that very process of 'consequence' which his antagonist has sought to deny. As his re-creation of the past begins to possess the creatures of the present, his play acquires a double function as both memorial and fatal *memento mori*. In this way the revenger-dramatist successfully mediates between those antitypes of the *Hamlet* world, the grave-diggers and the players—those whose task is to inter the dead, and those whose office is to resurrect them.[25]

But Hamlet's own play-memorials are at once more ingenious and more elaborate than others of their kind. The first of them, 'Aeneas' tale to Dido', is an elaborate memorial oration which 'lives' in Hamlet's memory partly because it contains in Hecuba an idealized image of his bereaved mother, and in the avenging

[24] Montaigne, *Essays*, i. 25; ii. 232.

[25] Helgerson, in 'What Hamlet Remembers', has argued that Hamlet as 'antic' fulfils the role of Death in medieval 'summoning plays' like Everyman (pp. 85–93); cf. also Hammersmith, '*Hamlet* and the Myth of Memory', 599–602, for a discussion of memory and the graveyard.

Pyrrhus a model for himself.[26] Its equivocal representation of 'the hellish Pyrrhus', however, is telling: when combined with the contradictory function of Priam as *both* Old Hamlet and Claudius, it points to the way in which every revenger becomes his antagonist's double. Precisely that sort of doubling confuses the meaning of 'The Murder of Gonzago', whose poisoner is at once a representation of Claudius-as-murderer and of Hamlet-as-revenger—a figure of self-annihilation, that is to say. As a result, the magical re-jointing of past and present is aimlessly deferred. Significantly perhaps, in this context, the centre-piece of his play is a speech from the Player King (arguably of Hamlet's own composition) which meditates upon the connections between 'memory', 'purpose', and 'enacture', and upon the melancholy disjunction between 'thoughts' and 'ends'. Hamlet's play, then, remains, like the Player's Trojan apocalypse, a mere 'fiction, [and] a dream of passion' (II. ii. 552), ultimately ineffectual, because its inventor confines himself (an Andrea when he should be a Hieronimo) to the purely passive role of 'chorus' (III. ii. 245)—just as in the Hecuba speech his true surrogate was not Pyrrhus, but Aeneas, the mere *nuntius*, or narrator.

As critics have often observed, however, the metatheatrical dimension of Shakespeare's tragedy is scarcely confined to the scenes involving the players; and the revenger's 'dream of passion', so furstratingly cut short in the 'Murder of Gonzago' performance is brought to a kind of completion in the self-consciously theatrical 'play' of Hamlet's exhibition bout with Laertes. Here is another transformed fiction, a scene of pretended violence that becomes the real thing, and that concludes in the prescribed fashion with the ironic compacting of past and present, as Hamlet pours into the King's mouth the same poison that Claudius had once poured into Old Hamlet's ear. Yet, though it superficially conforms to the conventional ending of revenge tragedy, there is a certain incongruity about this eruption of histrionic violence. For, unlike the perfectly theatrical revenges of, say, Hieronimo and Vindice, it is a piece (as Hamlet's fatalistic self-abandonment to the 'shaping' hand of

[26] The layering of memory in this episode is particularly striking: Hamlet introduces the speech with a detailed recollection of its first performance ('I remember . . . I remember'), calls on the player ('if it live in your memory') to recite it, and exhibits the power of his own memory in a declamation of its first thirteen lines. The speech itself recounts Aeneas' memories of an episode whose central character is a son inspired to revenge by the promptings of his own memory.

'divinity' is made to emphasize) conspicuously not of the hero's own composition. On the level of mere plot, it supplies the expected end to one kind of memorializing narrative; but in terms of the disturbing questions about memory and death that are posed in the graveyard scene it can seem as frustratingly inconclusive as that litany of 'casual accidents' whose violent 'upshot' is proclaimed by Horatio. In this context it is necessary to recognize that if their play has its structural counterpart in the duel of Act V, scene ii, the players themselves have their symbolic antitype in the clownish grave-digger of v. i. The rites of funeral, as that correspondence reminds us, are perhaps the most conspicuous form through which memory is performed (or suppressed) in the *Hamlet* world.

PART III

'Rue with a difference': Tragedy and the Funereal Arts

8
'Death's triumphal chariot': Tragedy and Funeral

Man is a Noble Animal, splendid in ashes, and pompous in the grave.

(Sir Thomas Browne, *Urn Burial*[1])

Distinguishing the Dead: The Role of Heraldic Funerals

As we might expect in a drama centrally concerned with the accommodation of the dead, the action of revenge tragedy often manifests acute anxieties about the proprieties of burial. It is from the initial failure to honour Andrea's obsequies that the vindictive action of *The Spanish Tragedy* appears to spring (Induction, 21–6); just as it is the dangerous persistence of unburied human remains in *Hoffman* and *The Revenger's Tragedy* that helps to produce their catastrophic holocausts; while in *Hamlet* the hero's vindictive rage against the King and Queen is triggered by the disgraceful 'mirth in funeral' that has disrupted the mourning ceremonies due to his dead father and that seems directly related to the restless presence of the Ghost. Such preoccupations help to reveal how, as Ariès has shown, the Renaissance continued to preserve the ancient pagan superstition that happiness beyond the grave was somehow contingent upon proper disposal and preservation of one's mortal remains[2]—a belief that is probably reflected in the formulaic curse protecting Shakespeare's own tomb from disturbance. The power of such belief animates the bitterness of the early quarrel in *Titus Andronicus* over Mutius' right to proper interment in the family tomb, just as it helps to explain the contemptuous

[1] In *Religio Medici and Other Writings*, 137.
[2] Ariès, *Hour of our Death*, 31.

treatment meted out to the bodies of Tamora and Aaron at the end of the play. But its operation is by no means confined to revenge-plays: one may feel it in Pericles' distress at his failure to give proper burial to Thaisa (*Pericles*, III. i. 58–64); or in the determination of Kyd's distraught heroine in *Cornelia* to go on living solely to ensure decent interment for her father and husband (*Cornelia*, V. 431–65). Nor is the classical setting of such works sufficient to explain the intensity of emotion attaching to the proper performance of funeral rites, since in Massinger's *The Fatal Dowry*, for example, with its wholly contemporary subject, the entire plot is actually put in train by the filial Charalois's decision to commit himself to prison rather than see his father denied burial in the monument of his ancestors (I. ii. 211–13). In this context one can begin to see how the wretchedness and despair of Dr Faustus' death are mitigated by the care with which his students dispose his funeral:

> Well, gentlemen though Faustus' end be such
> As every Christian heart laments to think on,
> Yet for he was a scholar, once admired
> For wondrous knowledge in our German schools,
> We'll give his mangled limbs due burial;
> And all the students, clothed in mourning black,
> Shall wait upon his heavy funeral.
>
> (*Doctor Faustus*, V. i. 344–50)

By the same token the silent oblivion to which Shakespeare consigns the corpses of villain-heroes like Richard III and Macbeth, by denying them any concluding rite of burial, can be as much the sign of their damnability as the grotesque anti-funerals accorded to Aaron and Tamora.

However, as most of these examples also show, superstition alone will not account for the dramatic prominence given to funeral rites in so many Renaissance plays. In *Hamlet*, Laertes' extraordinary rage at the shameful scanting of both his father's and his sister's obsequies is enough to demonstrate that the proprieties of funeral are at least as important to the living as they are to the dead. The proper performance of such ceremonies has, that is to say, an essential social role. At this level they have a demonstrably larger importance in tragic design, for tragedy habitually signalled its role as the drama of death by a wholesale appropriation of the socially loaded iconography of funeral. To understand how this functioned in the theatre it will be necessary to give some attention to the cultural function of Renaissance funeral practice.

The appropriation was perhaps made easier by the fact that in Tudor and Stuart England the funerals of the great themselves belonged to a species of public theatre, for they were self-consciously designed as pieces of street-pageantry or 'triumph'. Thus the herald Sir William Segar, Garter King of Arms, took it for granted that funeral 'shows' belonged to the same order of spectacle as coronations, royal weddings, entries, and progresses: 'Triumphs have been commonly used at the inauguration and coronation of emperors, kings and princes; at their marriages, entry of cities, interviews, progresses and funerals. Those pompous shows, were first invented and practised by the Romans, whom divers other princes have imitated . . . according to the measure of their empires.'[3] Indeed of all the many forms of triumphal display that adorned the streets of early modern England, the funerals of princes, great nobles, powerful gentry, and wealthy merchants were, of disagreeable necessity, the most common.[4] Reminders of their pomp, in the form of hearses (Fig. 23), hatchments, and heraldic acoutrements decorated every church in the land, where the tombs of the great themselves formed a kind of permanent funeral show, rivalled only (in the case of Westminster Abbey) by the collection of wooden and wax portrait effigies originally displayed on princely coffins.[5]

As their triumphal aspect might suggest, heraldic obsequies were,

[3] Sir William Segar, *Honor Military, and Civill, Contained in Foure Bookes* (London, 1602), 138. In effect Segar simply gives a heraldic cast to the Christian tradition described by Panofsky, according to which 'every one of [the Christian dead] was an Anointed, and, in a sense, a *triumphalis*'; see Panofsky, *Tomb Sculpture*, 46. The triumphalist thrust of Renaissance funerals was frequently reflected in the architecture of tombs; thus Francis I's tomb was designed as a triumphal arch, its reliefs celebrating battles and victories, and featuring a formal triumph *all'antica* (ibid. 80; cf. also pp. 83–5). The tomb, indeed, stood in the same relation to the funeral pageant as the triumphal arch to the military triumph, a permanent memorial of its splendours.

[4] For a discussion of the development of funeral rites through the late Middle Ages and Renaissance, see Malcolm Vale, *War and Chivalry* (London: Duckworth, 1981), 88–99; Ariès, *Hour of our Death*, 164–8; Paul S. Fritz, 'From "Public" to "Private": Royal Funerals in England 1500–1830', in Joachim Whalley (ed.), *Studies in the Social History of Death* (London: Europa, 1981); and Lawrence Stone, *The Crisis of the Aristocracy 1558–1641* (Oxford: Oxford University Press, 1965), ch. 10, sect. 7. For a detailed analysis of the ideological function of Renaissance funerals, see Ronald Strickland, 'Pageantry and Poetry as Discourse: The Production of Subjectivity in Sir Philip Sidney's Funeral', *ELH* 57 (1990), 19–36.

[5] See Ariès, *Hour of our Death*, 170–1; and below, Ch. 10, p. 339 and n. 19.

23. *Prince Henry's Hearse*, engraving by William Hole, printed in George Chapman, *Epicede or Funerall Song; on the death of Henry Prince of Wales* (London, 1612).

in spite of their religious context, primarily exercises in secular ostentation; 'symbolic justifications of rank and status', they were organized according to elaborate rules by the College of Heralds in a fashion that owed more to Feudal antiquarianism than to the rituals of Christianity, looking to one sceptical observer 'as if Duke Hector, or Ajax, or Sir Lancelot was buried'.[6] For Sir Thomas More, indeed, the shameless worldly pomp of such processions identified them as one of 'The Devil's Temptations at the Time of Death':

> instead of sorrow for our sins and care of heaven, he putteth us in mind of provision for some honourable burying—so many torches, so many tapers, so many mourners laughing under black hoods, and a gay hearse, with the delight of goodly and honourable funerals: in which the foolish sick man is sometimes occupied as though he thought that he should stand in a window and see how worshipfully he shall be brought to church.[7]

Every detail of the funeral procession, from the display of knightly arms, banners, and heraldic devices to the arrangement of successive groups of paupers, yeomen, household servants, serving gentlemen, client gentry, and noble mourners, was designed to proclaim not just the power, wealth, and status of the defunct, but their place inside a fixed and unassailable social order,[8] to which the rituals of the Church gave ultimate sanction and the inscription and iconography of the tomb bore lasting testament (Figs. 24–5).[9] Segar, who devotes an entire chapter of his treatise on honour to the 'order to be . . . kept' in funerals, gives a particularly clear sense of this social symbolism. He even proposes that, to avoid inappropriate expense and to preserve a proper decorum, the Sovereign or her Earl Marshal should 'prescribe a certain number of mourners

[6] Stone, *Crisis of the Aristocracy*, 586, 573. Two finely illuminated manuscript rolls in the British Library (Add. MSS 45131 and 35324) illustrate the heralds' practice of drawing up 'remembrances' of these events in order to instruct their successors in the proper order to be kept in marshalling the procession and in the niceties of its heraldic pageantry. MS 45131 includes sketches which show how the heralds' part in designing the funeral procession and hearse naturally extended to include the more permanent forms of display on monuments and tombs.

[7] More, *Four Last Things*, in *Works*, i. 470.

[8] For a useful account of the organization of heraldic funerals and the accoutrements assigned to various ranks, see Litten, *English Way of Death*, ch. 7.

[9] For a discussion of the strong family emphasis in 16th- and 17th-century funerary monuments (many of which were family tombs), see Ariès, *Hour of our Death*, 74–7, 254–8, 288–93; and Stone, *Family, Sex, and Marriage*, 135, 225–6.

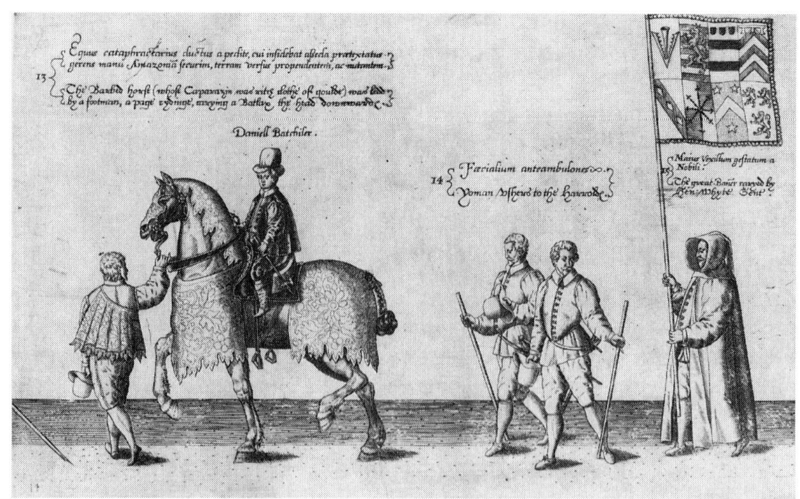

(*a*)

(*b*)

24(*a–c*). Part of the funeral procession for Sir Philip Sidney, from a funeral roll designed by Thomas Lant and engraved by Theodore de Bry, 1587 (Aldrich Collection, Christ Church, Oxford). By permission of the Governing Body of Christ Church, Oxford.

(c)

25

25. *Portrait of Sir Henry Unton* (NPG 710), anon., *c.*1596. By courtesy of the National Portrait Gallery, London.

to every degree, and that no man of greater title than the defunct should be permitted to mourn, so as the chief mourner may ever be *in pari dignitate* with the defunct, and all the rest of meaner quality'.[10] In addition to this somewhat bureaucratic preoccupation with the minutiae of hierarchical ordering, the heralds must exhibit a proper care for celebrating the defunct's personal honour and exalted rank—the funeral procession should constitute, in effect, a kind of heraldic biography:

> *Nota*, that an Officer of Arms weareth the King's coat at th'interments of noblemen and others of dignity and worship, not only for the ordering of the funerals, and marshalling of the degrees . . . but to the intent that the defunct may be known to all men to have died honourably in the Kings allegiance, without spot or infamy, or other disworship to his name, blood & family: and that this heir, if he have any, or next of whole blood, or someone for him (which commonly is the chief mourner) may publicly receive in the presence of all the mourners, the coat armour, helm, crest, and other achievements of honour belonging to the defunct: whereof the King of Arms of the Province is to make record, with the defunct's match, issue and decease, for the benefit of posterity.[11]

The well-known portrait of Sir Henry Unton, now in the National Portrait Gallery, London, provides an eloquent pictorial gloss on Segar's funeral instructions (Fig. 25). The portrait, commissioned by Unton's widow after his death in 1596, is both a *memento mori* and a memorial.[12] The domestic equivalent of that magnificently embellished church monument towards which its narrative leads, it enshrines the history of an entire life, seen retrospectively—as it might be, the narrative of the funeral sermon being preached in Faringdon Church on the left of the painting. The composition is dominated by an outsize portrait-figure of Sir Henry: the protagonist

[10] Segar, *Honor Military, and Civill*, ch. 27, p. 253. [11] Ibid. 254.

[12] For invaluable analyses of this portrait, see Roy Strong, *The Cult of Elizabeth: Elizabethan Portraiture and Pageantry* (London: Thomes & Hudson, 1977), ch. 3; and Llewellyn, *Art of Death*, 13–16. Strong describes memorial portraits of this kind as occupying 'a curious hinterland between the living portrait and the funeral or tomb effigy', and sees the Unton picture as both 'a *memento mori* . . . [and] a Triumph of Fame' (p. 84). The important interrelationships between monumental art, portrait-painting, and literature in the Renaissance are explored by David Rosand, 'The Portrait, the Courtier, and Death', in Robert W. Hanning and David Rosand (eds.), *Castiglione: The Ideal and the Real in Renaissance Culture* (New Haven: Yale University Press, 1983), 91–129; Rosand's arguments are supported by the close connection which Ariès discerns between the emergence of realistic tomb sculpture in the late 14th and 15th centuries and the development of the portrait genre in painting (*Hour of our Death*, 257–63). See also Mercer, *English Art*, 162–5; and Stone, *Family, Sex, and Marriage*, 226.

of the funeral drama is presented as he was in life—the diplomatist at his desk, seemingly caught at the instant of composing a dispatch to his royal mistress. But the semblance of frozen life is misleading: for the image, though it may suggest the moment of death's arrest,[13] is superimposed on the biographical narrative, not a part of it; the funeral black of Sir Henry's costume and of the drapes behind him remind us that it is the portrait of a man already dead. Like the bust-effigies of tomb sculpture that it deliberately resembles,[14] it is an ideal image, summarizing a life already lived—a point emphasized by the flanking figures of Fame and Death making their rival claims for the dead hero, as they might in some church monument (and as Fame indeed does in the lunette of Unton's arched tomb below). The hangings that frame the portrait also seem to draw upon the vocabulary of memorial sculpture, where parted curtains often functioned as a symbol of resurrection.[15]

This central figure has the effect of dividing the picture space into two—a sunlit world of light and business, and a night-world of death, its darkness, silence, and emptiness broken only by the crowded funeral service and the brightly illuminated tomb. Strictly speaking, however, this division affects only the upper two-thirds of the painting; cutting off one narrative sequence at its height, it leaves another, visually more compelling, intact. For the foreground asks to be read in terms of a single ineluctable movement from cradle to grave, only fleetingly diverted by the harmonious circling of the wedding masquers in Sir Henry's hall at Wadley. To this

[13] Compare Raphael's *Portrait of Tommaso Inghirami*, repr. in Rosand, 'The Portrait, the Courtier, and Death', 118, where the sitter looks up from his desk as though summoned in the very instant of writing.

[14] Strong (*Cult of Elizabeth*, 85) compares it with the half-figures on the tombs of Shakespeare and Stow—both of whom are also presented in the act of writing. Formally speaking, the table seems to be an adaptation of the frontal parapet common to so many Renaissance *en buste* portraits, a motif which expressly drew attention to the type's inspiration in ancient Roman stelae and tombstones, and served 'as a sign . . . of the commemorative context of the image'; see Rosand, 'The Portrait, the Courtier, and Death', 97.

[15] See George R. Kernodle, *From Art to Theatre: Form and Convention in the Renaissance* (Chicago: University of Chicago Press, 1944), 53–8, 151, and Mercer, *English Art*, 246, 251; the emblematic significance of the drawn curtains is relevant to the 'resurrection' scenes of *The Winter's Tale* (where Paulina draws the curtain to reveal the living monument of Hermione) and *The Tempest* (where Prospero similarly discloses the living figures of Ferdinand and Miranda); it may also have an ironic bearing on the parallel 'discoveries' by revengers like Hieronimo and Hoffman of corpses symbolically revived by their acts of vengeance—just as it has on the repeated drawing of the bed-curtains in the final scene of *Othello*.

grim progress the major events of Unton's life, as scholar, traveller, soldier, and diplomat, appear to form no more than a picturesque but remote background: they become in the strict sense marginalia, ornaments of a life properly comprehended in death. The effect is emphasized by a continuous line of masonry, beginning as the outer wall of the house in Ascott-under-Wychwood where Unton was born, continuing through the house and park wall at Wadley, to the walls of Faringdon churchyard and the vault beneath Unton's monument in the Unton chapel. Arrayed along the wall are spectators—witnesses of a life whose meaning is concentrated in the funeral pageant before them.[16] The procession itself stretches fully two-thirds of the picture's length, emerging from the porch at Wadley even as the wedding revels continue in the hall above. By virtue of the mourning black worn by most of the principals in the action—including Unton's mother as she cradles the infant Sir Henry, and even his bride at their wedding-feast—the procession can even seem to include the life:[17] it is as though funeral provided the occasion for biography.[18]

[16] These witnesses (others of whom sit under trees to which are attached escutcheons bearing epitaphs and mottoes) act as a surrogate for viewers of the painting. In this sense their function is not unlike that of the scholars in *Doctor Faustus*, a play whose curiously compressed time-scheme has something in common with that of the Unton portrait. In Marlowe's Prologue the hero's entire life from birth to untimely death ('Now is he born . . . heavens conspired his overthrow'; lines 11–12) is visibly conflated in the figure of the doomed scholar at his desk ('And this the man that in his study sits'; line 28): the Prologue, of course, introduces a play in which the twenty-four years of Faustus' career as a conjuror are wittily contracted to the twenty-four hours classically allowed to the action of a play. This telescoping is made theatrically possible by the fact that the action (as in the Unton portrait) is established as seen retrospectively—from the perspective of a damnation already achieved.

[17] Strong (*Cult of Elizabeth*, 104) challenges the view that this scene is intended to represent Unton's wedding-feast, on the grounds that no Elizabethan bride would wear black. But the traditional identification has been cogently reasserted by Edward Berry in *Shakespeare's Comic Rites* (Cambridge: Cambridge University Press, 1984), 215–16 n. 40. My own belief is that the young Dorothy Unton wears black for the same reason that her mother-in-law seems to be in mourning in a birth-chamber already hung with funeral blacks. The life is seen from the perspective of the funeral; it is as though the bride were already the black-clad 'figure cut in alabaster | Kneels at my husband's tomb' (*Duchess of Malfi*, I. i. 458–9). In this sense the painting responds to the elaborate aesthetic of mourning established by Unton's widow, and observed by Dudley Carleton: 'Her black velvet bed, her cypress veil, her voice tuned with a mournful accent, and her cupboard (instead of perfume sprinklers) adorned with prayer books, and epitaphs makes her chamber look like the house of sorrow' (cited in Llewellyn, *Art of Death*, 14).

[18] On the connection between biography and burial custom, see Ariès, *Hour of our Death*, 222–30.

Death, Montaigne wrote,

> is the condition of your creation: death is part of your selves. . . . The first day of your birth doth as well address you to die, as to live. . . . The continual work of your life is to contrive death; you are in death during the time you continue in life; for you are after death when you are no longer living . . . and death doth more rudely touch the dying than the dead, and more lively and essentially.[19]

Thus the day of death became 'the master-day, the day that judgeth all other'.[20] The Unton portrait interprets this familiar sentiment pictorially; but, because of its heraldic perspective,[21] the 'master-day' on which its action is focused is that of the funeral, rather than the day of death itself. Sir Henry was buried, according to a College of Arms memorandum, 'with a baron's hearse, and in the degree of a Baron, because he died Ambassador Lieger for France'.[22] The portrait (recording the family's pride in the distinction) gives some idea of what this 'degree' entailed: the cortège winds its way into a church hung with blacks, emblazoned with the Unton escutcheon; the coffin, placed at the symbolic centre of the procession, is preceded by a sombre parade of mourners in ascending order of rank; immediately before the pall-bearers marches the heralds'

[19] Montaigne, *Essays*, I. xix. 87; Cf. also 'Death's Duel', the sermon Donne preached in anticipation of his own funeral: 'from the womb to the grave. . . . we pass from death to death. . . . Our critical day is not the very day of our death, but the whole course of our life'; *Devotions*, 177–80. Herbert's poem 'Mortification' methodically analogizes the whole progress of a man's life to a funeral—beginning with the dressing of the infant in those 'little winding sheets', his swaddling-clothes, and concluding with the 'hearse' that awaits his bier in the church. For further discussion of this motif, see Spencer, *Death and Elizabethan Tragedy*, 59 ff., and 146 ff.

[20] *Essays*, I. xviii. 72.

[21] Strong (*Cult of Elizabeth*, 85) makes the attractive suggestion that the painting may actually have been commissioned from one of the heralds involved in the obsequies: 'The meticulous rendering of the funeral procession and of the numerous and complex coats of arms suggests that the picture may well be the work of a herald, whose task it would have been to supervise the correct rendering of his achievements, both during the funeral ceremonies and upon his monument.' An inscription above the nursery scene, deciphered by Strong, continues the heraldic emphasis by carefully tracing Sir Henry's descent from the Seymour family and his consequent connection with the royal house.

[22] Quoted in Strong, *Cult of Elizabeth*, 99. The term 'hearse' may require some explanation: it refers here to the elaborate temporary structure (resembling a tester-tomb) decorated with heraldic banners and devices, with candles, and with epitaphs, on which the coffins of the great were placed while they lay in the church (Fig. 23). In theatrical stage directions, however, it more commonly refers to the bier or to the coffin itself.

party. Black-clad figures who carry great banners ('streamers') displaying the armorial bearings of Unton's family and the cross of St George, the three heralds are distinguished from the rest of the company by their resplendent coat-armour, and the last of them carries Unton's achievements, including the great crested helm which is to be mounted above the tomb, adorned with the heraldic proof of his descent from Edward Seymour, Duke of Somerset; behind the bier walk the chief and principal mourners with their friends and servants in descending order of rank, a long line that stretches back to Wadley. Such a funeral is a conclusive statement, the abstract record of a life achieved, a Triumph of Fame whose meaning is blazoned for ever in that illuminated marble monument of which the picture itself provides a kind of exegesis. On the personal level it celebrates, as George Wither's elegy on the death of Prince Henry insists, a 'triumph over death'.[23] But this triumph stood for more than individual transcendence: as both its proclamations of family honour and its intense concern for the proprieties of degree reveal, it was also a piece of propaganda—the symbolic celebration and justification of an entire social order.[24]

The Unton painting necessarily works in a kind of shorthand, of course; but an early sixteenth-century 'ordinance and guiding' for 'the worshipful burying of any estate' gives some notion of the pompous ritual of offering which provided the climax of the funeral procession:

> 1. FIRST to be offered a sword by the most worshipful man of the kin of the said estate. . . .
>
> 2. ITEM in like wise his shield, his coat of worship, his helm and crest.
>
> 3. ITEM to be had a banner of the Trinity, a banner of our Lady, a banner of Saint George, a banner of the saint that was his advower, and a banner of his arms. Item a pennon of his arms. ITEM a standard and his best therein. ITEM a geton [?guidon] of his device with his word.
>
> 4. ITEM a double valance about the hearse both above and beneath with his word and his device written therein.

[23] George Wither, Elegy 42 (on Prince Henry's Funeral), in *Juvenilia* (London, 1622; Scolar Press facsimile, 1970), 374.

[24] Llewellyn (*Art of Death*, 15) notes how the opposition between the personal and social meanings of death is implied in the juxtaposition of Unton's sculptured monument with the representation of his 'body natural', sprawled beside the tomb. For treatment of the social and individualist implications of heraldic funeral rites, see Gittings, *Death, Burial and the Individual*, 13–15, 102, 175–9.

5. ITEM xii scutcheons of his arms to be set upon the bars without and within the hearse, and iii dozen pensels [small pennons] to stand above upon the hearse among the lights.

6. ITEM to be ordained as many scutcheons as be pillars in the church; and scutcheons to be set in the four quarters of the said church, as best is to be set by discretion.

7. ITEM as many torches as the said estate was of years of age. And on every torch a scutcheon hanging. And the bearers of the torches in black.

8. ITEM it is to be ordained standing v officers of arms about the said hearse, that is to say, one before the said hearse bearing the coat of worship . . . the second standing on the right side . . . in the forefront bearing his sword, the third standing on the left side . . . bearing his helmet and crest, the fourth on the right side . . . in the nether part of the hearse bearing his banner of arms, and the vth standing on the left side in the nether part, he bearing his pennon . . . And the banners . . . to be set above in iii parts of the said hearse and his standard also.

9. ITEM to be ordained certain cloths of gold for the ladies of his kin being within the said hearse, and they to offer the said cloths of gold.

10. ITEM a certain [number] of innocents all clothed in white, every innocent bearing a taper in his hand.

11. ITEM the horse of the said estate trapped with his arms, and a man of arms being of his kin upon the same horse . . . having in his hand a spear, sword, or axe, so to be presented to the offering in the church with ii worshipful men, [on each side] of the horse, and a man leading the same horse.

12. ITEM the heir of the said estate, after he hath offered, shall stand upon the left side of the priest receiving the offering of the sword, helm and crest, banner of arms, coat of worship, and pennon.[25]

The funerals of great nobles and princes were even more splendid: Mary Queen of Scots, for example, despite the disgrace of her execution, was accompanied to her burial in Peterborough Cathedral by elaborate procession suitable to her rank:

On Tuesday, being the first of August, in the morning, about eight of the clock, the chief mourner, being the Countess of Bedford, was attended upon by all the lords and ladies, and brought in the presence chamber within the bishop's palace, which all over was hanged with black cloth; she was by the Queens Majesty's gentlemen ushers placed somewhat under a cloth of estate of purple velvet, where, having given to the great officers their staves of office . . . she took her way into the great hall,

[25] Cited from *Archaeologia; or, Miscellaneous Tracts relating to antiquity*, i (London: Society of Antiquaries, 1770), 346–8.

where the corpse stood; and the heralds having marshalled the several companies, they made their proceedings as followeth.

Two conductors in black, with black staves.
Poor mourners to the number of 100. 2 and 2.
Two yeomen harvengers [? harbingers].
The standard of Scotland borne by Sir George Savile, knight.
Gentlemen in cloaks to the number of 50, being attendants on the lords and ladies.
Six grooms of the chamber. . . .
Three gentlemen sewers to the Queen's Majesty . . .
[7] Gentlemen in gownes.
Scots in cloaks, 17 in number.
A Scottish priest.
Mr. Fortescue, Master of the Wardrobe to the Queen's Majesty.
The Bishop of Peterborough.
The Bishop of Lincoln.
The great banner, borne by Sir Andrew Knowell, knight.
The Comptroller . . .
The Treasurer . . .
The Lord Chamberlain . . .
The Lord Steward.
Two ushers.
Achievements of honour born by heralds . . .
Clarenceaux king of arms, with a gentleman usher . . .
The corpse born by [6] esquires in cloaks . . .
Eight bannerols borne by esquires . . .
The canopy, being of black velvet fringed with gold, borne by four knights . . .
Assistants to the body, four barons which bore up the corners of the pall of velvet.
Mr Garter, with the gentleman usher, Mr Brakenbury.
The Countess of Bedford, supported by the Earls of Rutland and Lincoln, her train born up by the Lady St John of Basing, and assisted by Mr. John Manners, Vice Chamberlain.
The Countess of Rutland, Countess of Lincoln.
The Lady Talbot, Lady Mary Savile.
The Lady Mordant, the Lady St. John of Bletsho.
The Lady Manners, the Lady Cecil.
The Lady Montague, the Lady Knowell.
Mrs Alington, Mrs. Curle.
Two ushers.
Eight Scottish gentlewomen.

The gentlewomen of Countesses and Baronesses, according to their degree, all in black.

Servants in black coats.
The Countess of Bedford, 10.
Countess of Rutland, 8.
Countess of Lincoln, 8.
Lady St John of Basing, 5.
All lords and ladies, 5.
All knights and their wives, 4.
All esquires, 1.

The body being thus brought into the choir, was set down within the royal hearse, which was 20 feet square, and 27 feet in height, covered in black velvet, and richly set with escutcheons of arms and fringe of gold; upon the body, which was covered with a pall of black velvet, lay a purple velvet cushion, fringed and tasselled with gold, and upon the same a close crown of gold set with stones.

After the body was placed in the hearse, the Bishop of Peterborough preached a sermon, which was followed by 'certain anthems ... sung by the choir' which accompanied the offering of Mary's heraldic achievements by the Earls of Rutland and Lincoln to the Bishop and Garter, King of Arms.

In which offering every course was led up by a herald, for the more order; after which, the two bishops and the Dean of Peterborough came to the vault, and over the body began to read the funeral service; which being said, every officer broke his staff over his head, and threw the same into the vault to the body; and so every one departed, as they came, after their degrees, to the bishop's palace, where was prepared a most royal feast, and a dole given unto the poor.[26]

A great Elizabethan funeral of this kind was both biographical drama and political theatre, designed (as Nigel Llewellyn puts it) to insist upon 'the continuity of the social body' in the face of Death's subversive challenge;[27] and since funeral pageantry belonged to the public language of power, its splendours were vigorously promoted by the state. The encouragement (often amounting to blackmail or naked compulsion) which the Queen and Burleigh gave to the maintenance of this costly form of display reveals the importance they attached to it as a symbolic accompaniment to their

[26] *Archaeologia*, i. 356–60. [27] Llewellyn, *Art of Death*, 60.

systematic underpinning of place and prerogative;[28] and Elizabeth's own funeral was not surprisingly among the most magnificent spectacles of her reign. The list of participants from paupers, grooms, and porters to heralds, prelates, and noblemen, all 'in their place and order' runs to six pages in Nichols' *Progresses*; at the centre of the procession, preceded by 'the great embroidered banner of England', carried by the Earl of Pembroke and Lord Howard of Effingham, and a group of heralds bearing the Queen's achievements, came '[t]he lively [waxwork] picture of her Majesty's whole body, in her parliament robes, with a crown on her head, and a sceptre in her hand, lying on the corpse enshrined in lead and balmed; borne in a chariot drawn by four horses, trapped in black velvet. . . . A canopy over the corpse, borne by six knights'; the funeral-car was accompanied by 'gentleman ushers with white rods . . . six earls, assistants unto the body', while on each side of the corpse were displayed six great bannerols each carried by a nobleman.[29]

The ideological content of such performances was well understood by a man like John Weever, the historian of funerary monuments, for whom the proper ordering of funerals and 'sepulture' according to the 'state and dignity' of the deceased was to 'make a difference of personages' in spite of the blank indifference of death.[30] For Weever, the declining popularity of heraldic obsequies in the 1620s amounted to a flouting of decorum that must pose a serious threat to the order of society itself.[31] The pamphleteer Peter Wentworth made much the same point when he joined the

[28] See Stone, *Crisis*, 578. Significantly, the careful Walsingham, who appears to have thought the erection of a monument to Sir Philip Sidney a superfluous expense, nevertheless 'spared not any cost to have [Sidney's] funeral well performed' (Wallace, *Life*, 394).

[29] Nichols, *Progresses and Public Processions*, 621, 625.

[30] Weever, *Ancient Funerall Monuments*, 11.

[31] Ibid. 17–18; Lady Unton's desire in 1634 to be buried 'without any pomp or solemnity, and with as small charge as may be, in the night' (cited in Stone, *Crisis of the Aristocracy*, 108) is an example of the changing fashion which Weever decried. Cf. also Segar, *Honor Military, and Civill*, ch. 27 *passim*. Weever (pp. 10–11, 37–41) and Segar (ch. 28) show a common concern for the social meaning of monuments, which, they urge, an ordered society must be careful to preserve—'A matter of more consequence than everyone marketh,' as Segar puts it, 'yet necessary to be looked unto, both for public and private respects' (p. 254). Their anxiety echoes that of Queen Elizabeth herself, who in 1560 issued a proclamation against the defacing of church monuments in order to prevent 'the extinguishing of the honourable and good memory of sundry virtuous and noble persons deceased. . . . [and to ensure that] the true understanding of divers families in this realm . . . [shall

chorus of voices in the last years of Elizabeth's reign, begging the Queen to address the dangerous matter of her succession. In addition to the usual political arguments, his *Pithie Exhortation*, urged upon the Queen a number of more personal considerations, warning her that, in the absence of an heir, 'it is to be feared, yea, undoubtedly to be judged, that your noble person shall lie upon the earth unburied, as a doleful spectacle to the world. . . . The shame and infamy hereof, we beseech your grace to be careful of . . . . [for] if your noble person . . . should come to that shame as to lie unburied. . . . you shall leave behind you . . . a name of infamy throughout the whole world.'[32]

The 'shame and infamie' which might result from the scanting of the funeral ceremonies was something that Elizabeth, who had devoted much energy both to preserving church monuments and to enforcing the proper observance of heraldic funerals, was well equipped to appreciate. What was at issue was not merely the fame of the deceased and the honour of both immediate family and lineage, but the stability of the social system—hence the money impartially lavished by the normally frugal James I in securing suitable monuments both for his predecessor and for his own mother, whom Elizabeth had executed a decade and a half earlier. As *Hamlet* amply testifies, the infamy of degrading burial could cause more pain than the death itself, however disgraceful that might have been; and the tomb of Mary Queen of Scots remains as an eloquent testimony to the strength of such feelings.

Funeral Rites and Tragic Ending

Both tragedy and comedy made dramatic capital from the spectacular possibilities of funeral pageantry.[33] But tragedy did much more than simply incorporate funeral episodes in its action, for

not be so] darkened, as the true course of their inheritance may be hereafter interrupted' (cited in T. S. R. Boase, *Death in the Middle Ages: Mortality, Judgement and Remembrance* (London: Thames & Hudson, 1972), 87.

[32] Peter Wentworth, *A Pithie Exhortation to her Majestie for establishing her successor to the crowne* (Edinburgh, 1598), 102–3.

[33] See Michael Neill, '"Feasts put down Funerals": Death and Ritual in Renaissance Comedy', in Linda Woodbridge (ed.), *True Rites and Maimed Rites: Ritual and Anti-Ritual in Shakespeare and his Age* (Urbana: University of Illinois Press, 1992), 47–74.

the very decor of the tragic stage was determined by the conventions of funeral, effectively framing it with the social assumptions inherent in this form of display. A particular tragedy might challenge or subvert these assumptions, but it could never detach itself from them.

The self-conscious use of this convention is apparent in plays such as *1 Henry VI*, where Bedford's opening proclamation, 'Hung be the heavens with black! yield, day, to night!' (I. i. 1), is designed to draw attention to the actual dressing of the stage for what Marston called the 'black-visaged shows' of the 'sullen tragic scene' (*Antonio's Revenge*, Prologue, lines 20, 7). The players decked their stage with black hangings and curtains derived from the 'blacks' of funeral custom and calculated to attune the audience's emotions to the ensuing drama of death: 'The stage is hung with black; and I perceive | The auditors prepared for tragedy.'[34] A casual pun in Dekker's *Lanthorne and Candlelight* (1608) even suggests that, for the principal players at least, black costumes may have formed part of the expected funereal decor of tragedy: 'And now, when the stage of the world was hung with black, they *jetted* up and down like proud tragedians.'[35] The effect of this

[34] [?Thomas Heywood], *A Warning for Fair Women*, ed. Charles D. Cannon (The Hague: Mouton, 1975), Induction, lines 82–3. Chambers (*Elizabethan Stage*, iii. 79) gives a full list of contemporary references to this practice, making it clear that it was standard in both public and private playhouses, as well as in the court theatres. Cf. also M. C. Bradbrook, *Themes and Conventions of Elizabethan Tragedy*, 2nd edn. (Cambridge: Cambridge University Press, 1980), 16–17; and Michael Hattaway, *English Popular Theatre* (London: Routledge & Kegan Paul, 1982), 20. The black hangings, as several of the passages cited by Chambers suggest, had the effect of consigning tragedy to an imaginative night-world—a fact that helps to account for the popularity of 'night-pieces', or 'nocturnals', in tragic drama. In Marston's *The Insatiate Countess*, for instance, the onset of night immediately evokes the tragic spectacle of blackness: 'The stage of heaven, is hung with solemn black, | A time best fitting to act tragedies' (cited from *The Plays of John Marston*, ed. W. Harvey Wood, 3 vols. (Edinburgh: Oliver & Boyd, 1934–9), iii. 65); similarly, in Chapman's *Bussy D'Ambois* when King Henry seeks a metaphor for tragic ending, he looks to the decor of the stage: 'I see . . . the sky | Hid in the dim ostents of tragedy' (IV. i. 110–12); while in Tourneur's *The Atheist's Tragedy* D'Amville imagines the black hangings as the 'sable garment' assumed by Heaven to mourn the murder of Montferrers (II. iv. 30–3). Vindice's invocation of Night in *The Revenger's Tragedy* makes explicit the triple connection of nocturnals, black hangings, and funeral decor: 'Night, thou that lookest like funeral herald's fees | Torn down betimes i' the morning, thou hangest fitly | To grace those sins that have no grace at all' (II. ii. 133–5).

[35] Cited in Chambers, *Elizabethan Stage*, iii. 79 (emphasis added).

proleptic announcement of catastrophe was to supply a continuous visual commentary on the action, often creating (particularly in scenes of romantic intrigue and comic by-play) a sharply ironic effect—as, for example, in the first half of *Romeo and Juliet* where the playing out of an action that strongly resembles a romantic tragicomedy on a stage hung with funeral blacks will have created a powerfully emotive contrast to match the oxymoronic patterns of the play's rhetoric and design.

At the same time the use of black hangings must have fostered a sense of funeral as the proper and expected end of this kind of drama, so that the final parade of mourners with its accompanying 'dead march' came to occupy in tragedy precisely the place accorded in comedy to wedding revels and the final dance of reconciliation. As early as 1583, indeed, we find Sir Philip Sidney using 'hornpipes' and funerals' as natural metonymies for the opposing genres which 'mongrel tragi-comedy' grafted so indecorously together.[36] If in comic endings feasting, music, and circulating movements of the dance reasserted that transcendent harmony of the universe which the follies of mankind had temporarily disguised, then the 'dead march' and solemn procession of tragic ending served to reaffirm the hierarchic sense of 'fair sequence and succession' which the disorders of sin and rebellion had temporarily disrupted.[37]

At a deeper level, it might be argued, these two rituals of order correspond to metaphoric meanings embedded in the very structure of these opposing genres. For if the dance of comedy enacts the 'whirligig of time' in which all things turn and return as though governed by the seasonal patterns of rotation and renewal, the

[36] Sir Philip Sidney, 'An Apology for Poetry', 46. The plausibly balanced antitheses of Claudius' opening oration in *Hamlet* create a tragicomic paradigm in which 'marriage' and 'funeral' have the same metonymic function:

with a defeated joy,
With an auspicious, and a dropping eye,
With mirth in funeral, and with dirge in marriage,
In equal scale weighing delight and dole.

(I. ii. 11–13)

Tourneur crowns *The Atheist's Tragedy* with an enacted version of such 'dirge in marriage' by combining the funeral of D'Amville and his sons with the marriage of Charlemont and Castabella, while 'The drums and trumpets interchange the sounds | Of death and triumph' (V. ii. 296–7).

[37] The phrase is from York's rebuke to the King (*Richard II*, II. i. 199).

processional endings of tragedy answer to the alternative sense of time as an ineluctable linear process. Indeed the whole action of a tragedy moved from its opening spectacle of blackness to its concluding ritual of death rather as a funeral moved from the defunct's house with its black-swathed rooms, windows, staircases, and deathbed to the graveside at the black-draped church; and because in tragedy the anticipated obsequies were almost invariably those of the hero himself, the final procession became a re-enactment in little of the plot's remorseless progress to the grave. Beyond the grave lies judgement; and as *Tamburlaine* with its rhetoric of universal desolation, *The Spanish Tragedy* with its babylonical catastrophe, *King Lear* with its horrified glimpse of 'the promised end', and *Doctor Faustus* with its tormented paraphrase of Revelation variously remind us, the endings of tragedy are haunted by intimations of apocalypse.[38]

The funeral procession itself helped to confirm those intimations, since while it was structured as a demonstration of earthly order, its narrative movement simultaneously mimicked the very teleological process that would ultimately sweep this order away for ever: and against the elaborate parading of degree so essential to its processional design, it set the levelling anonymity of mourning blacks, symbolically confounding the meticulous hierarchy of costume enshrined in what Keith Thomas has called 'the vestimentary system'. Indeed the emotional power of the heraldic funeral depended on its ability to contain, within its ceremonial enactment of triumph *over* Death, the ominous lineaments of a triumph *of* Death, so that Samuel Purchas could describe Queen Elizabeth's funeral as the spectacle of 'Death riding in triumph on that wonder to men, and miracle of women, our gracious *Deborah*'.[39] This fundamental ambivalence is even more beautifully caught in the rhetorical *occupatio* that frames Purchas's reminiscence of the 'funeral pomp' for Anne of Denmark:

[38] Compare Faustus' desperate appeal, 'Mountains and hills, come, come and fall on me, | And hide me from the heavy wrath of God' (*Doctor Faustus*, v. i. 292–3) with the desperation of humanity at the opening of the Sixth Seal: 'And [they] said to the mountains and rocks, Fall on us and hide us from the face of him that sitteth on the throne, and from the wrath of the Lamb' (Rev. 6: 16). For the idea of individual death as a private Day of Judgment, see Kermode, *Sense of an Ending*, 25–8; and Ariès, *Hour of our Death*, 106–10.

[39] Purchas, *Microcosmvs*, 193.

I say not [he begins] that this was Death's trophy, the prince of whatsoever is mortal in princes; and that all those *Blacks*, in all degrees, did there perform a ceremonial . . . suit and service, accompanying her funeral (nay, Death's triumphal) chariot, both it & them suited in Death's livery; and all the spectators no less by their presence presenting Death a homage, than obsequious duties to the exequies and memory of that worthy and glorious name: this I say, that Death could not then forbear, in the busy and pompous celebration of his late exploits, but (as fearing the vulgar would conceit, that greatness might seem to insult over him by such state and magnificence) proves an actor, and makes this funeral show a true tragedy and funeral.[40]

The figure draws attention to the way in which the pageant-language of funeral itself works by a kind of insistent *not saying* to equivocate upon its own triumphalism, reminding the spectator that all its pompous rituals are only a mask for that same fool's pilgrimage to dusty death that haunts Macbeth's imagination. The funeral procession enacts a line of tragic succession which indeed stretches out to 'the crack of doom', beyond the immediate catastrophe to 'the promised end'; each of us, great or humble, it tacitly insists, must follow.

The convention of funeral ending seems already to have been well established by the time Thomas Preston composed his *Lamentable Tragedy of Cambyses, King of Persia* (*c.*1558–69) at the very beginning of Elizabeth's reign. In the final moments of Preston's play three Lords are left to moralize in the dramatist's inimitably jigging vein over the corpse of their unlucky monarch:

1 LORD. A just reward for his misdeeds the God above hath wrought,
For certainly the life he led was to be counted naught.
2 LORD. Yet a princely burial shall he have, according to his estate;
And more him here at this time we have not to dilate.
3 LORD. My Lords, let us take him up and carry him away.

(x. 249–53)

[40] Ibid. 191–2. According to Purchas, Death converted the show to a 'true Tragedy' by 'suddenly bringing one spectator (even before he could be a spectator) upon the stage to act his own tragedy; and he which came to see the pomp of another's, is now really adjudged, and by the fall of a stone from an house, executed to his own funeral' (pp. 192–3); a woman was then so overcome by the ghastly looks of the dead man that she too 'falls into [Death's] unexpected snare' (p. 193).

At first sight these lines may appear to do little more than provide a fairly predictable solution to one of the most basic practical problems of an uncurtained stage—that of clearing away the corpses after a scene of climactic butchery. For an audience schooled in the idiom of Renaissance pageantry, however, this simple processional exit—two men bearing a corpse and a third following in an attitude of mourning—will have had an eloquence beyond Preston's limping fourteeners. For the actors are to compose, as the Second Lord makes clear, a rudimentary version of a funeral cortège—reminding the audience of those rites of 'princely burial' that partly offset God's levelling judgement with a symbolic reassertion of earthly rank ('according to his estate'). The wickedness ('naught') of Cambyses' life has fittingly reduced him to nothing ('nought'), and all the dilatory rhetoric of 'King Cambyses' vein' will no longer serve to postpone his end;[41] but the ceremonial ordering of his regal obsequies, at which the simple processional exit gestures, amounts to a symbolic reassertion of the proprieties of difference and degree[42]—a defiant enactment of the human power to impose significance upon nothingness itself.

Among other things, this funeral ending serves, in its hieratic fashion, to return the play from the morality world of Ambidexter's mocking farewell to the social reality proper to that realm of 'tragical history' proclaimed by the Epilogue. For all the crudeness of its execution, it works in a fashion fundamentally indistinguishable from the more elaborate pageant that crowns the action of Kyd's infinitely more sophisticated *Spanish Tragedy* (*c.*1587–90) twenty or thirty years later: 'The trumpets sound a dead march, the KING of Spain mourning after his brother's body, and the KING of Portingale bearing the body of his son' (IV. iv. 266).[43] Often the stage funeral was no more elaborate than this—two pall-bearers,

[41] For a dazzling treatment of the word-play that associates rhetorical 'dilation' with 'deferral' of the end, see Patricia Parker, 'Literary Fat Ladies and the Generation of the Text', in *Literary Fat Ladies*, 8–35.

[42] For funerary rites and monuments as a response to 'death's assaults of social differentiation', see Llewellyn, *Art of Death*, 50–4, 102–5.

[43] The stage direction is incomplete, since the bodies of Hieronimo, Bel-Imperia, Lorenzo, and perhaps Horatio have also to be removed. Presumably they too are carried in the procession—though one or more might conceivably be concealed behind the curtain of the 'arbour' where Horatio's body was discovered hanging. For a general discussion of the method of removing bodies from the stage, see Chambers, *Elizabethan Stage*, iii. 80.

a token mourner or two, and the corpse carried off to the doleful sounding of a funeral march; at other times the companies would be asked to stretch themselves to the full in order to create as nearly as possible the illusion of a magnificent public funeral.[44] In either case, the power and meaning of the stage spectacle drew on a major tradition of street pageantry, whose rituals and conventions bore a complex and interesting relation to those of tragedy itself. If Renaissance tragedy was above all a dramatization of the human encounter with death, then funeral obsequies provided its natural and fitting conclusion. The heraldic funeral, after all, was itself a kind of drama, as George Wither reminds us in his Elegy 42 on Prince Henry's funeral:

> Say why was *Henry's* hearse so glorious?
> And his sad *funeral* so full of state?
> Why went he to his tomb as one victorious:
> Seeming as blithe as when he lived of late?
> What needed all that ceremonious show? . . .
> What was it but some antic curious rite,
> Only to feed the vain beholders' eyes,
> To make men in their sorrows more delight,
> Or may we rather on it moralize?
> Yes, yes, it show'd that though he wanted breath,
> Yet could he ride in triumph over death.[45]

What Wither described was a pageant of fame and worldly pomp, a 'triumph over death' that symbolically cancelled the universal Triumph of Death, and enabled its principal performer, like the 'only Roscius' of Thomas Dekker's defiant scene of dying, to prolong his performance beyond the moment of extinction itself.

Given its relation to such 'Ceremonious show' a dramatized funeral can never have been merely a neutral piece of stage business; as with other forms of pageantry, its gestures and decor carried with them a freight of social and political meanings on which dramatists were bound to draw. It is not, of course, always easy to determine how far the players sought to match the pompous

[44] Early examples of full pageant funerals occur in the Inns of Court tragedies *Gorboduc* (1562) and *Jocasta* (1566), though in neither case is the funeral incorporated in the action, being confined to allegorical dumb shows before the acts. The *Jocasta* procession, involving two coffins and sixteen mourners, is particularly elaborate.

[45] Wither, *Juvenilia*, 374.

dignity of these shows in the funeral processions that moved across their stages. But theatrical companies, if only by virtue of their nominal status as servants of a great household, would have been directly acquainted with the protocol of such events—Shakespeare's troupe, for instance, will have had their allotted place in the grand funeral of their patron, Lord Hunsdon, in 1596. In some plays we can see this experience being turned to striking theatrical account. In Marston's *Antonio's Revenge*, for example, the unusually full stage directions (evidently deriving from an autograph manuscript used in the playhouse[46]) show a dramatist, ambitious to evoke the magnificence of an actual rite, mobilizing all the resources of his company to that end:

The cornets sound a sennet. Enter two mourners with torches, two with streamers, CASTILIO and FOROBOSCO with torches, a Herald bearing Andrugio's helm and sword, the coffin, MARIA supported by LUCIO and ALBERTO, ANTONIO by himself, PIERO and STROTZO talking, GALEATZO and MATZAGENTE, BALURDO and PANDULPHO; the coffin set down, helm, sword, and streamers hung up, placed by the Herald, whilst ANTONIO and MARIA wet their handkerchiefs with their tears, kiss them, and lay them on the hearse, kneeling. All got out but PIERO. Cornets cease and he speaks. (II. i)

Clearly very few of the more or less improvised processions into which the ceremonies of mourning are telescoped at the end of most tragedies cannot have been so splendidly mounted. Nevertheless, however curtailed and hieratic their treatment, they must always have been constructed with an awareness of the rich significance of funeral pageantry.

Displaced Funerals

The audience's sensitivity to the decorum of such endings meant that playwrights were able to produce powerful dramatic meanings from the displacement, stinting, or abruption of funeral ceremonies. Part of the effectiveness of Andrugio's funeral depends upon its unexpected appearance so early in the tragedy. Similarly

[46] See Reavley Gair's introduction to his Revels edition of the play (Manchester: Manchester University Press, 1978), 2.

in 2 *Tamburlaine* the disturbing effect of Zenocrate's death and funeral is greatly enhanced by the staging of a scene of mourning so early in the play, at the very height of Tamburlaine's triumphs. An even more expressive example of this kind of displacement occurs in the beginning of *1 Henry VI* where Bedford's opening oration ('Hung be the heavens with black') immediately marks the stage's resemblance to a funeral church. By starting the play with this black pageant, Shakespeare creates the disconcerting impression that we are actually watching the end of another (unwritten) tragedy and the burial of its hero-prince, Henry V. It is one of the many devices by which, throughout this tetralogy, the dramatist reinforces the sense of a plot larger than that of any single play; but it has the effect, too, of plunging the audience into a world whose significant history is already past, a world intensely conscious of ending; and it ushers in a tragical history whose first four acts are structured around a series of funeral episodes: the carrying out of Gargrave, Mortimer, and Bedford's bodies in I. iv, II. v, and III. ii; the dead march for Salisbury in II. I; and the degradation and carrying out of the Talbots' corpses in IV. vii. The last of these in effect constitutes the play's tragic catastrophe; but it is denied any structural dignity by the coda of Act V, which climaxes in the travesty of a comic romance ending created by Henry's betrothal to Margaret of Anjou.

The unsettling funeral opening of *1 Henry VI* is revisited in two other early plays, *Richard III* and *Titus Andronicus*. *Richard III* indeed announces a kind of full circle from the beginning of the tetralogy, by building its second scene around the funeral of the murdered Henry VI. Here the displacing of funeral is complicated by the stunted nature of the rites afforded the dead king, and by Richard's contemptuous abruption of them—a black-comic anticipation of Claudius' blasphemously indecorous mingling of 'mirth in funeral and dirge in marriage'.[47] Even more arresting is the funereal opening of *Titus Andronicus*, whose entire first act is dominated, iconically and dramatically, by the family monument of the Andronici. After what amounts to a brief dramatized prologue, sketching in the political background to the action, the stage is filled

[47] Compare the effect created by the substitution of a wedding for the funeral rites which we might expect at the end of *Henry V* (whose tragical issue is glanced at in the Epilogue).

with a procession which is simultaneously a military triumph *all'antica* and a funeral:[48]

Sound drums and trumpets, and then enter . . . two of Titus's sons [MARTIUS and MUTIUS]; and then two MEN bearing a coffin covered with black; then two other sons [LUCIUS and QUINTUS]; then TITUS ANDRONICUS; and then TAMORA, the Queen of the Goths, and her [three] sons, [ALARBUS], DEMETRIUS and CHIRON, with AARON the Moor, and others as many as can be; then set down the coffin,[49] and Titus speaks. (I. i. 69)

The spectacular intention of the entry is underlined by that optimistic-sounding 'as many as can be'. Neither the spectacle nor its displacement of conventional sequence are arbitrary effects: they are designed to imprint a key image on the mind of the audience. The rites performed at the tomb, the sacrifice of Alarbus, and the interment of Titus' sons amount to a symbolic enactment of those values of piety and order for which Titus stands and which epitomize the play's idea of 'Roman' civilization; but they are also an intimation of the latent barbarity by which this civilization will be consumed.

The 500-year-old tomb itself is an embodiment of this contradiction: described by Titus as 'sacred receptacle of my joys, | Sweet cell of virtue and nobility' (I. i. 92–3), it is the monumental repository of Roman honour and familial piety; but it is also, by its quenchless thirst for human life, an anticipation of that 'detested, dark, blood-drinking pit' which takes its place in Act II.[50] The dumping of Bassianus' body and the entrapment of Quintus and Martius

[48] Marcus' speech, later in the scene, spells out the double nature of this pageant:

Long live Lord Titus, my beloved brother,
Gracious triumpher in the eyes of Rome! . . .
But safer triumph is this funeral pomp,
That hath aspired to Solon's happiness
And triumphs over chance in honour's bed.
(I. i. 169–78)

[49] Although only one coffin is specified in the stage direction, the action properly calls for several; at line 149 the folio text emends the direction to read 'coffins'; actual stage practice was probably contingent on how 'many' the company could assemble in a given production.

[50] Passages that establish an imaginative association between the 'blood-drinking pit' and the tomb include II. iii. 176–7, 198–202, 210, 222–4, 226–36, 239–40; the association would be visually reinforced by the conventional use of the stage trap as a grave.

are presented as ghastly mock-interments; so that the pit becomes a second burial vault, and tomb and pit together can be seen to represent that destructive grip of the past upon the present which is the ruling theme of revenge tragedy. By the end of the play the monument will have swallowed Titus and most of his kin as surely as the 'swallowing womb' of earth will have devoured Tamora and most of hers. There is an awful kind of congruence between their conditions, for both become the destroyers of their own kin: Titus' obsessive preoccupation with family honour makes him the murderer of his own children; Tamora's consuming passion of revenge leads her to the final reductive enactment of her desire in Titus' banquet, where 'Like the earth [she] swallow[s] her own increase' (V. ii. 191).

Where the action of *Titus* is carefully framed by two sets of obsequies, Shakespeare's second Roman tragedy, *Julius Caesar*, follows the pattern of *2 Tamburlaine* by falling into two halves, each of which is rounded with a funeral.[51] But in this case the division is one that corresponds to the play's double nature as both the Tragedy of Julius Caesar and the Tragedy of Marcus Brutus. With the entry of Caesar's funeral procession and the delivery of Antony's oration over the dead body, the play reaches the natural conclusion of its titular tragedy. But the decorum of ritual closure is overturned by Antony's rhetoric; and in place of a processional reassertion of order, the scene issues in the anarchic violence of the mob, recapitulating in a more violent fashion the mood of the opening scene, with its desecration of Caesar's images:

[1 PLEBEIAN.] We'll burn his body in the holy place,
And with the brands fire the traitors' houses.
Take up the body.

(*Julius Caesar*, III. ii. 254–6)

It is a wild travesty of civilized funeral custom which marks not the expected end but a destructive new beginning:

2 PLEBEIAN. Go, fetch fire!
3 PLEBEIAN. Pluck down benches!
4 PLEBEIAN. Pluck down forms, windows, anything!

(III. ii. 257–9)

[51] The two halves of Tourneur's *Atheist's Tragedy* are similarly marked by funeral endings—the obsequies of Montferrers and the supposedly dead Charlemont in III. i being balanced by those of D'Amville and *his* dead sons in V. ii.

After such a scene, the epitaph and funeral instructions uttered by the victorious Antony and Octavius over the body of Brutus ('According to his virtue let us use him, | With all respect and rites of burial. | Within my tent his bones tonight shall lie, | Most like a soldier, ordered honorably'; v. v. 76–9) can begin to sound, for all their magnanimity, more like the theatre of political interest than the restoration of traditional pieties. Those 'rites of burial' which are represented for the audience by the parting procession of soldiers are exposed as the conservative public face of a social order founded upon violent innovation. A similar ambivalence complicates Octavius' funeral tribute to his antagonists in *Anthony and Cleopatra*,[52] where the 'solemn show' promised for Cleopatra's obsequies, compromised as it is by association with the triumphal display of the living Cleopatra he had promised himself in Rome, inevitably sends us back to the eminently politic 'triumph' of Ventidius at the beginning of Act III, with its display of Pacorus' degraded corpse. A similar suspicion of opportunism colours Aufidius' parade of generosity to his butchered rival at the end of *Coriolanus*:

My rage is gone,
And I am struck with sorrow. Take him up.
Help, three o'th'chiefest soldiers; I'll be one.
Beat thou the drum, that it speak mournfully;
Trail your steel pikes. Though in this city he
Hath widowed and unchilded many a one,
Which to this hour bewail the injury,
Yet shall he have a noble memory.
Assist.
[*Exeunt, bearing the body of Martius. A dead march sounded.*
(v. vi. 146–54)

What, after all, can we make of a tribute to heroic fame contrived by a man whose own actions appear to have destroyed the last remaining shreds of those values on which it might rest?

Maimed Rites

As the travesty-funeral of Caesar shows, the *form* of stage funerals can be as crucial to their dramatic meaning as their placement. As

[52] See below, Ch. 9, pp. 325–7.

we have seen, it was the cancellation of the consolatory rites of burial in time of plague that was responsible for the most terrible of its psychic wounds; and by the same token the mounting of carefully hierarchized funeral processions, whose pomp was later crowned by the erection of lavishly ornamented tombs, has to be recognized as a principal mode of resistance to the aggressive commonness of death. But ironically enough if the elaboration of funeral arts sought to contain the threatened chaos of mass extermination, it also served, in a society almost neurotically obsessed with stabilization of the social order, to make any disruption or displacement of funeral proprieties seem even more dangerous and offensive than it had done before.

Henry V's funeral at the beginning of *1 Henry VI* is designed both to memorialize a heroic past and to enact the forms of political order that the subsequent action will shatter. Shakespeare clearly intended that it be staged in an appropriately spectacular fashion: the coffin, it would appear, was meant to be placed on a funeral-car, recalling the pageantry of King Death:

> [EXETER.] Upon a wooden coffin we attend,
> And death's dishonourable victory
> We with our stately presence glorify,
> Like captives bound to a triumphant car.
>
> (*1 Henry VI*, I. i. 19–22)

The retinue of mourning nobles in their funeral blacks (line 17) pass over the stage to the sombre music of a dead march (I. i. 1), accompanied by the Heralds in their glittering coat-armour (line 45) displaying, in the prescribed fashion, the arms and chivalric achievements of the dead hero. In accordance with its memorializing function, the ceremony is to culminate in the formal offering of knightly arms to the shade of the King. The ceremonies, however, are violently interrupted by the arrival of a Messenger announcing (in fittingly heraldic terms) the imminent collapse of Henry's empire in France: 'Cropp'd are the flower-de-luces in your arms, | Of England's coat one half is cut away' (I. i. 80–1). The interruption is followed by Bedford's formal repudiation of mourning ('Give me my steeled coat. I'll fight for France. | Away with these disgraceful wailing robes!' lines 85–6) with its reminiscence of Tamburlaine's disdainful uncasing from his shepherd's weeds (*1 Tamb.* I. ii. 41–3); and the breaking of ceremonial order becomes a prophetic anticipation of the disastrous course of the play's action.

In *Richard III*, by contrast, the pathetically stunted retinue of Henry VI's corpse—guarded by 'Halberds' and accompanied only by Lady Anne ('being the mourner') and her two attendants (I. ii. 1)—is a ritual of debasement (carried to its comic extreme by Richard's wooing over the hearse) that announces an already shattered frame of order. In a similar way, Bolingbroke's attempt to cobble together a proper ceremony for the casually produced coffin of the murdered Richard II ('March sadly after, grace my mournings here, | In weeping after this untimely bier'; V. vi. 51–2) perfectly enacts his need to restore those very forms of sequence and succession which his own hand has destroyed.[53] The hopeless inadequacy of the gesture is apparent as soon as one compares the studied decorum of the funeral commanded for his father by the pious young Edward III at the end of Marlowe's rival deposition tragedy *Edward II*: 'Go fetch my father's hearse, where it shall lie; | And bring my funeral robes . . . Help me to mourn, my lords' (V. vi. 94–8)—though Marlowe makes his characteristically sardonic comment on the rites by having the new King adorn the hearse with the severed head of his father's murderer, Mortimer, placed where the crown would normally sit.

The attempts of politicians like Henry IV and Octavius Caesar to pageant out a vision of restored order in the funeral processions of their rivals draw on a vocabulary of political theatre that other plays make entirely explicit. Tamburlaine, for instance, crowns the contemptuous killing of his cowardly son, Calyphas, by devising for him a cruel burlesque of military burial:

> Ransack the tents and the pavilions
> Of these proud Turks, and take their concubines,
> Making them bury this effeminate brat,
> For not a common soldier shall defile
> His manly fingers with so faint a boy.
>
> (2 *Tamb.* IV. i. 162–6)

Similarly, in *Titus Andronicus*, the grisly farce of revenge is carried through a series of increasingly grotesque mock-funerals, finding its climax in the banquet scene of Act V. The first of these is

[53] The broken and violated funeral ceremonies of *1 Henry VI*, *Richard III*, and *Richard II* are briefly discussed in somewhat similar terms by David Bevington in *Action is Eloquence: Shakespeare's Language of Gesture* (Cambridge, Mass.: Harvard University Press, 1984), 147.

the procession arranged by Titus at the end of Act III, scene i, where the Andronici solemnly bear off the severed heads of Quintus and Martius together with Titus' severed hand, in a shocking re-enactment of the funeral rite of Act I, scene i, with its sacrificial 'lopping' of Alarbus limbs; the second is the 'funeral' mockingly prescribed for the Nurse by Aaron in Act IV:

Hark ye, lords, you see I have given her physic,
And you must needs bestow her funeral.
The fields are near, and you are gallant grooms.

(*Titus Andronicus*, IV. ii. 162–4)

Then in Act V, scene ii, Titus is made to preface his sacrifice of Demetrius and Chiron with a speech whose hideous word-play converts his forthcoming banquet into the most atrocious parody of all:

Hark, villains, I will grind your bones to dust,
And with your blood and it I'll make a paste,
And of the paste a *coffin* I will rear,
And make two pasties of your shameful heads,
And bid that strumpet, your unhallowed dam,
Like to the earth swallow her own increase.

(V. ii. 186–91; emphasis added)

'Coffin' here (quibbling shamelessly on the Elizabethan term for pie-crust) makes it clear that Titus' entry with members of his household in V. iii, bearing these cannibal pasties, was meant to be staged as a full burlesque re-enactment of the funeral procession for Titus' own sons in the opening scene:[54] 'Trumpets sounding. Enter TITUS like a cook, placing the dishes, and LAVINIA with a veil over her face, [young LUCIUS, and others]' (V. iii. 25).

Finally, in the closing episode of the play, the triumphant Lucius defines his new order by setting forth, with methodical grimness, the funeral arrangements for the victims and perpetrators of this Roman holocaust; the Emperor, with careful deference to his rank, is to be honoured with 'burial in his father's grave' (V. iii. 192); Titus and Lavinia, more solemnly, 'shall forthwith | Be closed in

[54] Davenant repeats the pun in *The Wits*, where the Elder Palatine, undergoing his mock-burial in a chest, feels 'coffin'd up, like a salmon pie' (cited from A. S. Knowland (ed.), *Six Caroline Plays* (London: Oxford University Press, 1962), 409). This usage is still preserved in French, where 'sarcophages' are pastry-cases.

our household's monument' (lines 193–4); Aaron, in a vicious mock-interment that mirrors his treatment of Titus' sons, will be 'set . . . breast-deep in earth [to] famish' (line 179); while the barbarous Tamora's corpse will be cast into the wilderness where it belongs: 'No funeral rite, nor man in mourning weed, | No mournful bell shall ring her burial' (lines 196–7). If Aaron is to be starved in the hungry maw of the earth, Tamora, who has come to embody the greed of its swallowing womb, will now be left 'not where [she] eats, but where' (in Hamlet's phrase) 'a is eaten'—as 'prey' for 'beasts and birds' (line 198).[55]

Very different in their effect are the equally unorthodox endings of *Troilus*, *Timon*, *Othello*, and *King Lear*. In the first of these, the fact that both the nominal hero and the heroine remain alive reinforces the play's sense of ending, despite the death and funeral of Hector, much as it began, irremediably 'in the middle'. In *Timon*, on the other hand, the hero chooses to inter himself in an 'everlasting mansion', placed 'upon the beached verge of the salt flood'; deliberately exposed to the destructive battery of the 'turbulent surge' and engraved with characters too cryptic for any but Alcibiades to decipher, his tomb seems designed to court an enigmatic oblivion. For this sardonically contrived anti-monument where 'language ends' conspicuously reverses the conventional epitaph's appeal to memory: 'Seek not my name. . . . Pass by and curse thy fill, but pass and stay not here thy gait' (v. i. 215–20; v. iii. 5–8; v. iv. 71–3). Significantly, in the final scene Alcibiades is driven, even in the absence of a body, to improvise a funeral rite of sorts to revive the memory of a man he wants to think of as 'noble Timon' (v. iv. 75–85).

In *Othello*, by contrast, both the profoundly private quality of the tragedy and its degrading cruelty are signalled by Lodovico's horrified attempt to efface the spectacle of death, as he orders the curtains drawn upon the bed of slaughter: 'Let it be hid' (v. ii. 365). This tragedy is shorn of the funeral dignities that serve to

[55] Bevington (*Action is Eloquence*, 147) discusses the ironic parallels between the opening funeral procession of Titus' sons and that which closes the play. In 2 *Tamburlaine* the corpse of the renegade Sigismund is refused burial by Orcanes, and surrendered, like Aaron's and Tamora's, to the mercies of wild beasts. Cf. also Alexander Iden's contemptuous consignment of Jack Cade's body 'Unto a dunghill, which shall be thy grave, | . . . Leaving thy trunk for crows to feed upon' (2 *Henry VI*, IV. x. 81–4).

put a form of order upon such spectacles of ruin; and in the absence of any witness sympathetic enough to tell his story, the disgraced Othello has to speak what amounts his own funeral oration—one whose lofty rhetoric is arrested in mid-line by the 'bloody period' of his own suicide (line 357). 'All that's spoke is marred,' observes Gratiano, but no memorializing tributes ensue. Yet the violent aposiopesis cannot altogether efface the fact that Othello, whose Venetian history began with the exotic magic of his story-telling to Desdemona, is allowed to confer something of the grace of fictional closure upon the 'chaos' of his life through this last act of story-telling. Moreover, even in the terrible image of the murdered Desdemona there are hints of memorial grandeur: Othello's picture of his sleeping wife with her skin 'smooth as monumental alabaster' (v. ii. 5) plays on the audience's recollection of those great tester tombs where the effigies of husbands and wives lie as though frozen upon their beds of state—a suggestion intensified when at last Othello's body lies beside hers.

No such ritual consolations however, are allowed to modify the starkness of *Lear's* ending—the brutal termination that James Calderwood calls its 'un-end'.[56] Although the final 'Exeunt with a dead march, carrying the bodies' bespeaks a funeral procession of sorts, it is one which requires to be staged with a bareness fitting to a world laid waste. There is no talk here of 'princely burial' or 'degree', no attempt at the formal magnanimity of a funeral oration, only Albany's terse 'bear them from hence', and Edgar's painfully insufficient 'Speak what we feel, not what we ought to say' (v. iii. 318, 325).[57]

If such scanted ceremonies speak of a kingdom made wilderness, elsewhere, in the tragicomic world of *Cymbeline*, a wilderness is made civil in the careful orchestration of burial rites for Innogen-Fidele and Cloten in the false tragic ending of Act IV, scene ii. It is Belarius' firm sense of the ceremonious marks of distinction due even to a Cloten which shows him, cave-dweller though he is, as the play's true champion of courtly values—just as it is Guiderius' and Arviragus' decorous improvisation of a pastoral equivalent of church obsequies for 'Fidele' that helps to confirm their princely

56 Calderwood, *Shakespeare and the Denial of Death*, 164.

57 Riverside here follows the Folio text—the first Quarto assigns the closing speech to Albany.

natures. It shows their instinctive feeling for that 'very good order' emblematized in the funeral with which the pious Charalois restores the memory of his disgraced father in Massinger's *The Fatal Dowry*.

By contrast, in the drama of playwrights like Dekker, Marston, Tourneur, and Webster, with their ingrained suspicion of courtly values, the pageantry of heraldic obsequies may come to stand for the empty pride and hypocrisy of the court world. The strikingly elaborate funeral procession which opens Dekker's *1 Honest Whore*, with its hearse, coronet, scutcheons, and garlands, is merely a tyrannical prince's device to keep his daughter from an 'unworthy' lover; while in Marston's *Antonio's Revenge*, the high pomp of Andrugio's funeral at the beginning of Act II is intended to point up, with bitter irony, Duke Piero's barely concealed contempt for its ceremonial meanings:

Rot there, thou cerecloth that enfolds the flesh
Of my loathed foe; moulder to crumbling dust;
Oblivion choke the passage of thy fame!
Trophies of honoured birth drop quickly down;
Let naught of him, but what was vicious, live.

(II. i. 1–5)

The double funeral of Montferrers and Charlemont orchestrated by the villainous D'Amville in Tourneur's *The Atheist's Tragedy*, together with the extravagant mourning ceremony he conducts at their monuments, is turned to much the same effect: 'Thus fair accomplishments make foul | Deeds gracious' (III. i. 49–50). Here, however, D'Amville's cynical appropriation of the rites is punished in the symmetrical irony that crowns the last act with a second double funeral, that of his own two sons, whose hearses he leads on (V. ii. 68); and the proper function of exequy is restored in the decorous sequence announced by Charlemont:

When those nuptial rites are done,
I will perform my kinsmen's funerals....
Thus by the work of Heav'n the men that thought
To follow our dead bodies without tears
Are dead themselves, and now we follow theirs.

(V. iii. 294–301)

In Webster's radically anti-court tragedy *The White Devil*, on the other hand, the pomp of noble funerals becomes one of the ruling metaphors of glittering falsehood—a grimly ironic epitome of 'courtly reward and punishment': 'Be thy life short as are the funeral tears | In great men's—[?obsequies]' (I. ii. 302–3).[58] Cornelia's curse, in Webster's characteristic fashion, is woven into the action of the play—first through the dumb-show processions and Brachiano's sardonic commentary following the deaths of Isabella and Camillo (II. ii. 24, 38–9), and then through Vittoria's short-lived 'howling' at Brachiano's own deathbed. The last act begins with a scene in which Francisco and his fellow conspirators enter 'bearing their swords and helmets' and hang them up (as Brachiano announces) 'For monuments in our chapel' (V. i. 43, 51); on the black-draped stage this piece of business will have irresistibly recalled the ceremonial dedication of knightly arms and achievements above the tomb in Renaissance funerals. Ironically the funeral being announced is Brachiano's own. Webster goes on to contrast the pompous black farce of his death (climaxing in a grotesque parody of extreme unction carried out by revengers in the guise of Capuchin friars; V. iii. 121 ff.) with the lyric simplicity of Marcello's funeral preparations (V. iv. 66–112). The contrast is emphasized by the visual resemblance of the two tableaux, each of which (perhaps making use of the same bed-property) is revealed by the drawing of a curtain (V. iii. 83; V. iv. 65), and each of which presents a group of mourning women around a dead, or dying, body. But where Marcello's corpse, in what becomes a moving secular *pietà*, remains at the centre of the composition, Brachiano's is relegated contemptuously to the background by the courtship of Zanche and Francisco. Webster's choice of a scene of domestic grief to replace the public ostentation of funeral in the final act of his play is deliberate and revealing: it speaks of a world where the forms of ritual display, no longer answering to any profound intimation of social order, are felt to be inadequate, or even inimical, to the intensity of private emotion. By the end, the elaborate decorum of courtly ceremonial is reduced to the curt command of a slaughterhouse: 'Remove the bodies' (V. vi. 300).[59]

[58] Cf. also III. ii. 92–3; V. iii. 50–1, 167–8; V. vi. 153–7.

[59] A similar casualness of tone marks the end of *The Revenger's Tragedy*, where Antonio's perfunctory clearing of the royal shambles, 'Bear up | Those tragic bodies' (V. iii. 127–8), contrasts pointedly with the elaborate tableau of mourning he assembled around his wife's corpse (presumably lying on its fixed hearse) in Act I, scene iv. At the end of Middleton and Rowley's *Changeling* the funeral exeunt is

Hamlet's Rites of Memory

No play is more obsessively concerned with funeral proprieties than *Hamlet*.[60] The action begins a mere two months after the death of King Hamlet, and little more than a month after his interment; but we are introduced to a court that has so rapidly abandoned the decencies of mourning for the revelry of wedding that, to Hamlet's imagination at least, it is as if these symbolically opposed rites have been collapsed together, so that 'the funeral bak'd meats | Did coldly furnish forth the marriage tables' (I. ii. 179–80). The prince alone maintains his 'inky cloak [and] customary suits of solemn black', proclaiming an 'obsequious sorrow' which keeps him like the downcast follower of some interminably rolling funeral-car, forever seeking his 'noble father in the dust' (I. ii. 68–92).

On Shakespeare's stage the propriety of Hamlet's mourning display would have been affirmed by the conventional black hangings of the tragedy, even as it was challenged by the splendid court costumes appropriate to royal nuptials.[61] For Claudius, however, Hamlet's wilful ostentation of these 'trappings' of grief is not merely an insult to his wedding celebration, but an implicit denial of the due succession meant to be affirmed in the pageantry of funeral custom—this is what the elaborately sequential figures and pious exhortation of his rhetoric are intended to proclaim:[62]

> But you must know your father lost a father,
> That father lost, lost his, and the survivor bound
> In filial obligation for some term
> To do *obsequious* sorrow. But to persever

replaced by a dramatized stage direction inviting De Flores and Beatrice-Joanna to rise for the audience's applause—an effect partially anticipated in Chapman's *Bussy D'Ambois*, where the murdered Bussy stands up to speak the epilogue.

[60] Apart from Frye's *Renaissance Hamlet*, recent work which touches on the importance of funeral in the play includes Michael MacDonald, 'Ophelia's Maimèd Rites', *Shakespeare Quarterly*, 37 (1986), 309–17; and James V. Holleran, 'Maimed Funeral Rites in *Hamlet*', *ELR* 19 (1989), 65–93.

[61] For a discussion of the scene which places the behaviour and appearance of both Hamlet and the court in the context of 16th-century mourning and wedding customs, see Frye, *Renaissance Hamlet*, 82–103.

[62] For further discussion of the linked ideas of 'following', 'sequence', and obsequies, see Ch. 7 n. 18.

In obstinate condolement is a course
Of impious stubbornness; 'tis unmanly grief....
A fault against the dead, a fault to nature,
To reason most absurd, whose common theme
Is death of fathers, and who still hath cried,
From the first corse till he that died to-day,
'This must be so.' We pray you throw to earth
This unprevailing woe.

(I. ii. 89–107; emphasis added)

For Claudius, tellingly, sorrow is not something to feel, but something to 'do' (line 92)—a thing to be paraded in public, and then to be discarded like a funeral posy. Ritual, for him, serves as a way of burying the past. But for Hamlet the rites of burial have already been rendered void by his mother's violation of them ('A little month, or ere those shoes were old | With which she followed my poor father's body'; lines 147–8), and by that perverted 'thrift' in which marriage 'followed hard upon' the heels of mourning, creating the obscene confusions of 'mirth in funeral' and 'dirge in marriage' that Claudius' elegant antitheses can barely conceal.[63]

It is important to recall that Hamlet's distress at his father's contemptuously huddled obsequies is by no means unique. It will be mirrored later in the play by Ophelia's and Laertes' bitter reaction to the 'hugger-mugger' interment of Polonius. Indeed Laertes'

[63] In the Players' dumb show Gertrude's infidelity is telescoped in the wooing-over-the-corpse motif already encountered in *Richard III* and used again by Webster in *The White Devil*. That this may actually have been part of the old Hamlet play is suggested by its recurrence in another *Ur-Hamlet* offspring, Marston's *Antonio's Revenge*, where Piero successfully woos Maria over the tomb of her murdered husband, Andrugio (III. i). Marston went on to rework the episode a second time in the opening scene of *The Insatiate Countess*, where (in an episode full of echoes of *Hamlet*) the opening tableau of mourning gives way to the Countess's passionate wooing of Roberto:

What think'st thou of this change?
A player's passion I'll believe hereafter,
And in a tragic scene weep for old *Priam*,
When fell revenging *Pyrrhus* with supposed
And artificial wounds mangles his breast....
The tapers that stood on her husband's hearse,
Isabel advances to a second bed.

(Cited from *The Plays of John Marston*, ed. Wood, iii. 8)

Chapman carries the device to marvellously parodic extremes in the tomb seduction of *The Widow's Tears*; see my 'Feasts put down Funerals', 61–2.

rhetoric suggests that this insult to honour and degree, with its contemptuous refusal of due remembrance, gives him even more pain than the murder itself:

> His means of death, his obscure funeral—
> Nor trophy, sword, nor hatchment o'er his bones,
> No noble rite, nor formal ostentation—
> Cry to be heard. (IV. v. 214–17)

The full intensity of his bitterness is comprehensible only once it is recognized that this neglect amounts to an act of calculated public oblivion—the wilful silencing of a narrative of honour that then cries 'to be heard' in the barbaric commemoration of revenge. Laertes' anger recalls Hamlet's savage girds to Ophelia: 'O heavens! die two months ago, and not forgotten yet? Then there's hope a great man's memory may outlive his life half a year, but, by'r lady, 'a must build churches then, or else 'a shall suffer not thinking on, with the hobby-horse, whose epitaph is, "For O, for O, the hobby-horse is forgot!"' (III. ii. 130–5).

It is not only Hamlet's and Laertes' dead fathers who are exposed to the ridicule of such forgetfulness. In Act V both of these vindictive memorialists will be compelled to witness the degradingly 'maimed rites' of Ophelia, denied the requiem and full service of the dead which Laertes insists is her due (V. i. 219–42), her obsequies exposed to the humiliating interruptions of the quarrelling Hamlet and Laertes, and her body laid (like her father's) not in the church tomb to which her rank would entitle her, but in the common graveyard, to be commemorated only by the vaguely promised 'living monument' with which Claudius tries to appease his queen's distress (line 297).[64]

Life, the graveyard scene seems to declare, is merely a procession to the grave: the grave-digger began his work on 'that very day that young Hamlet was born' (line 147), and in this violently

[64] The strict rules governing the place and mode of burial are analysed by Ariès (*Hour of our Death*, 45–62, 71–92): 'There was a hierarchy of honour and devotion that extended from the confession of the saint or the high altar to the edge of the cemetery' (p. 50). Although Ariès suggests that this was less rigidly observed in Protestant England than in Catholic France, Weever (*Ancient Funerall Monuments*, 10–11, 17–18) certainly thought in terms of a strict gradation of rank that encompassed not only the place of burial but the style of monument to which the deceased was entitled. Since burial *ad sanctos* was popularly supposed to improve one's chances of salvation, more than merely family honour was involved here. Cf. also Litten, *English Way of Death*, 220; Frye, *Renaissance Hamlet*, 50–1.

foreshortened temporal perspective a man's life is indeed 'no more than to say "one"' (v. ii. 74). Nevertheless, that grim procession can also become a species of triumph, which finds its proper extension in the rites of memory and the monuments of art. It should be clear by now that the carefully orchestrated funeral decreed for Hamlet in the closing moments of the play is a crowning gesture that will make complete sense only in the context of the play's sequence of broken and truncated funerals and the violent emotion attaching to them.

For all the irony that haunts Hamlet's last efforts to give voice to his story, it clearly matters that the Prince's body should not only be granted the formal dignity of funeral orations from both Horatio and Fortinbras, but that it should be honoured with the pomp of full military obsequies, 'the soldier's music and the rite of war' (v. ii. 391). Of course, the music may sound oddly for him, and Fortinbras's generosity can hardly escape the taint of a conqueror's interest; but then the metatheatrical ingenuities of the play ensure that it is not strictly with this ambiguous marital ritual itself that Hamlet's progress ends. The curiously moving self-reflexiveness which insists that this triumphal pageant is to be performed on a 'stage' before an 'audience' (v. ii. 335, 378, 387, 396) seems calculated to remind us that the last rite of memory is the play itself; and whilst the play's sceptical interrogation of narrative may expose the efficacy of such gestures to question, it would be a mistake to underestimate their consolatory power. They endow the ending with a sense of ritual consummation that, as David Bevington has observed, 'completes something left unfinished in the abortive rites of passage for old Hamlet, Polonius, Ophelia and others who have died'.[65] Not for nothing does Horatio's farewell ('Good night, sweet prince . . .') so conspicuously echo the *In paradisum* antiphon from the Sarum funeral rite.[66] More powerfully

[65] The doubts which the play creates about the ambiguous character of the military adventurer Fortinbras are borne out, Bevington suggests, by a serious indecorum in the ceremony he contrives: its martial character amounts to 'a disruption of the nominal ceremony of reconciliation with which the play's climatic scene begins'; so that for all its panoply of order, this funeral becomes yet another of the many 'inversions of ceremony' which function as 'signs of disorder in the play' (Bevington, *Action is Eloquence*, 186–7).

[66] The antiphon's words, sung as the body was carried from requiem mass to churchyard, were as follows: 'May the angels lead thee to paradise. . . . May the choir of angels receive thee, and . . . mayst thou now have eternal rest' (cited in Litten, *English Way of Death*, 150).

than in any other play, funeral pageantry functions here as a sign of human order rescued from the jaws of chap-fallen death itself—not simply the social order enacted in the military procession, but the monumental ordering of art. For beyond the rather barren plot narrative that Horatio offers by way of epitaph is the larger 'story' of the play itself. *Hamlet, Prince of Denmark* puns sublimely on Fortinbras's boasted 'rights of memory' in a rite of ending that supplies its hero with a genuinely 'living monument'.[67] For, if anything truly remains 'to tell [his] story', as Anne Barton long ago observed, it is the play itself[68]—a monument which, like Shakespeare's sonnets, defiantly offers to 'wear this world out to the ending doom', issuing its own challenge to the undifferentiating 'havoc' of those charnel-houses which the grave-digger mockingly claims must 'last till doomsday' (v. i. 59).

[67] Properly speaking, a 'living monument' (*tombe animée*) was a tomb with sculptured effigies (Ariès, *Hour of our Death*, 229), but such structures did not normally belong in open cemeteries: Claudius perhaps has in mind only the coming 'hour of quiet' between the feuding families as a memorial to Ophelia's sweetness. For further discussion of the idea of the play-as-monument, see Spencer, *Death and Elizabethan Tragedy*, 42 ff. D. J. Gordon's outstanding essay 'Name and Fame: Shakespeare's *Coriolanus*', in Stephen Orgel (ed.), *The Renaissance Imagination* (Berkeley and Los Angeles: University of California Press, 1975), 203–19, is also relevant. It is partly the familiar association of tragedy and fame that Hamlet has in mind when he describes the Players as the 'abstract and brief chronicles of the time', and warns that '[a]fter your death you were better have a bad epitaph than their ill report while you live' (II. ii. 524–6). Compare also the metatheatrical irony at the end of Massinger's *The Duke of Milan*, where the villain Sforza falls silent just as he is about to speak his own epitaph.

[68] See her intro. to the Penguin edition, 54.

9
Finis coronat opus: The Monumental Ending of *Anthony and Cleopatra*

> Not marble nor the gilded monuments of princes
> Shall outlive this pow'rful rhyme,
> But you shall shine more bright in these contents
> Than unswept stone, besmear'd with sluttish time.
>
> (Shakespeare, Sonnet 55)

'Fame's eternity'

When Laertes rails so bitterly against his father's 'obscure funeral', it is not merely the want of 'noble rite' that enrages him, but the King's failure to honour Polonius' bones with a 'trophy' or monument, crowned with 'sword [and] hatchment', fitted to the dignity of his rank and office. For Laertes the provision of such a memorial is an essential part of the 'formal ostentation' of noble obsequies; and to look at the Unton portrait in this context is to be reminded that it was neither the funeral sermon, nor even the rites at the graveside, that wrote *finis* to the performance of a heraldic funeral; for the true consummation of such triumphal ceremonies was supplied by the extravagantly ornamented tomb, conceived as a kind of perpetual pageant, in which the splendours of the funeral ceremony were frozen for all posterity. Unton's tomb with its coats of arms, its emblems of fame and grief, its laudatory inscriptions and records of lineage, all surrounding the figure of the deceased lying upon his burial casket with his mourning wife kneeling beside him, seems to condense the entire heraldic ceremony, and its freight of personal and social meanings, into a single powerfully expressive image (Fig. 25). If the funeral procession itself encapsulated a whole life, idealized as an ineluctable but splendid progress towards death, the monument emblematizes the consummatory goal at which such a life is directed.[1]

The overwhelmingly secular significance of such edifices did not escape the observation of contemporaries.[2] When John Weever observed that 'every man . . . desires a perpetuity, after death, by these monuments', he acknowledged a motive scarcely compatible with the pious inscriptions with which many tombs were adorned.[3] Webster's Bosola complains that 'Princes' images on their tombs do not lie, as they were wont, seeming to pray up to heaven . . . but as their minds were wholly bent upon the world' (*Duchess of Malfi*, IV. ii. 156–61); but the worldly gaze of monumental sculptures was entirely appropriate, for, like funeral pageants themselves, they had become as much instruments of social propaganda as expressions of piety or tokens of family grief.

Perhaps the clearest sense of the ideological investment in memorial art can be gathered from Weever's treatise *Ancient Funerall Monuments* (1631). Weever's definition of what constitutes a monument is a permissive one—'a thing erected, made, or written, for a memorial of some remarkable action fit to be transferred to future posterities'; broadly interpreted it can extend to all the substantial material remains of the past—'thus generally taken, all religious Foundations, all sumptuous and magnificent structures, cities, towns, towers, castles, pillars, pyramids, crosses, obelisks, amphitheatres, and the like, as well as tombs and sepulchres are called monuments'.[4] But his principal interest is in those edifices, like the funeral monuments of his title, whose express purpose was to preserve the honourable mention of the dead—'remembrances, by which men have endeavoured, even in despite of death, to give unto their fames eternity'.[5] In Weever's eyes, however, even their role as memorials of personal fame, or signs of humanist transcendence, is secondary to their indispensable function as documents of genealogy and social history. For he believes that the continuity and stability of his hierarchical society are crucially dependent upon the preservation of such records.

[1] Whilst Unton's tomb was not completed until ten years after his death, effectively prolonging the death ritual for an entire decade, funeral monuments were often erected in the defunct's own lifetime, serving as objects of *memento mori* contemplation for their proprietors (Llewellyn, *Art of Death*, 15, 17).

[2] On the increasing secularization of funeral monuments in the early modern period, see ibid. 118–21.

[3] Weever, *Ancient Funerall Monuments*, 18.

[4] Ibid. 1.

[5] Ibid. 2.

Weever's introductory address 'To the Reader' offers a lengthy excursus on the dangerous consequences of the post-Reformation vandalism of church monuments by Protestant iconoclasts, 'by which inhumane, deformidable act, the honourable memory of many virtuous and noble persons deceased is extinguished, and the true understanding of divers families in these realms is so darkened, as the true course of their inheritance is thereby partly interrupted'.[6] The human folly of iconoclasm assists the assault of 'eating time's ruins' in undoing the originary records of distinction; and Weever's purpose, in what is at once a work of history and an exercise in heraldic conservation, is to arrest the march of oblivion in the interests of securing the foundations of the inherited social order.[7]

In its conservative ambitions *Ancient Funerall Monuments* necessarily replicates the function of memorials themselves. Weever, indeed, draws considerable satisfaction from the self-reflexiveness of a project which promotes itself as a prime example of the very monumental art whose cause it serves, justifying his enterprise with the reflection that 'for worthiness and continuance, books or writings have ever had the preeminence'.[8] In a world of notorious mutability, books can claim to be the most effective of all memorials because 'the Muse's works are of all monuments the most permanent; for of all things else there is a vicissitude, a change both of cities and nations'[9]—literary works, as Webster's motto to *The White Devil* has it, are monuments which do not know how to die.[10] Launching his treatise by tracing a whole series of *loci classici* for the idea of literature-as-monument, Weever declares common cause with the Renaissance writers who, in innumerable variations upon the Horace's *Exegi monumentum aere perennius*,[11]

[6] Ibid., 'To the Reader', [p. i].

[7] On the role of funeral ritual and monuments in preserving both 'continuity and differentiation' in the face of 'Death's roughshod ride over the fine distinctions of social difference [and] his challenge to continuity', see Llewellyn, *Art of Death*, 103–4.

[8] Weever, *Ancient Funerall Monuments*, 1.

[9] Ibid. 3. Compare also Amyot's address 'To the Readers' in *The Lives of the Noble Grecians and Romanes* [Plutarch's *Lives*], trans. Sir Thomas North (London, 1579), p. iii: 'history . . . is the surest, safest, & durablest monument that men can leave of their doings in this world to consecrate their names to immortality. For there is neither picture, nor image of marble, nor arch of triumph, nor pillar, nor sumptuous sepulchre that can match the durableness of an eloquent history'.

[10] *Non norunt haec monumenta mori*. Webster borrows the tag, which concludes his epistle dedicatory, from Martial, 2. 2. 12.

[11] Horace, *Carmina*, 3. 30.

had turned the Roman poet's conceit into the most popular of all tropes for literary fame.

Perhaps the best-known treatment of the trope is in the remarkable series of Time sonnets in which Shakespeare pitches the fragile artifice of poetry against the encroachments of 'sad mortality', the power of 'Time's injurious hand', and the 'fell arrest' of Death. The encomiasts who wrote commendatory verses for the first Folio must have had these sonnets in mind when they praised Shakespeare's works as providing him 'a monument without a tomb' (Jonson) asserting that

> This book,
> When brass and marble fade, shall make thee look
> Fresh to all ages.
>
> (Digges)

—but like Middleton, Ford, and Rowley, celebrating *The Duchess of Malfi* as its author's true monument, they may also have been remembering the self-referential wit with which several of his plays signal their own monumentalizing ambition. Nowhere, in fact, was the trope of poem-as-monument more ingeniously developed than in the theatre, where dramatists regularly exploited the iconic potential of tombs and monuments in a reflexive celebration of their own art that went far beyond Weever's rather wooden manipulation of commonplaces; and no account of how tragedy incorporated the rites of funeral into its dramatization of the human encounter with death can be complete without some consideration of the use of tombs and monuments as stage properties. In tragic drama, I shall suggest, the monument with its artifice of eternity stands in the same relation to play-as-finished-artefact as the funeral to the play-as-unfolding-plot; and typically it has much the same emblematic relation to the whole action as the tomb in Sir Henry Unton's portrait to the narrative it completes.

Triumphant Graves

The prominence of tombs among the standard properties of the Elizabethan playhouse is indicated by Henslowe's famous inventory, which lists no fewer than three in its oddly heterogeneous catalogue:

Item, 1 rock, 1 cage, 1 tomb, 1 Hell-mouth.
Item, 1 tomb of Guido, 1 tomb of Dido, 1 bedstead . . .[12]

That so notoriously thrifty an entrepreneur should have felt it necessary to multiply his investment in a large item of this sort is in itself remarkably suggestive; and the continuing popularity of tombs and funeral monuments in Elizabethan and Stuart theatres is reflected in an extraordinary range of plays from Greene's *James IV* (*c.*1590) to Ford's *Love's Sacrifice* (*c.*1630): prominent examples include *Titus Andronicus* (1589–1603), *Romeo and Juliet* (*c.*1595), *The Widow's Tears* (1603–9), *Anthony and Cleopatra* (*c.*1606–8),[13] *The Atheist's Tragedy* (1607–11), *The Second Maiden's Tragedy* (1611), *The Winter's Tale* (1610–11), *The Duchess of Malfi* (*c.*1613). In most cases the action appears to call for the use of a distinct tomb-property; but the discovery space could be used to represent the interior of a burial vault, as it probably was in *Romeo and Juliet*, while the architecture of the tiring-house façade, with its formal resemblance to a triumphal arch, made it a natural image for the kind of grandiose funeral monument that Shakespeare envisages in the final scene of *Anthony and Cleopatra*.[14]

Like a number of other properties, the tomb was a survival from the mystery cycles, where it had featured in plays of *The Raising of Lazarus* and *The Resurrection*; and it is possible to read the final scenes of *Romeo*, *Anthony*, and *The Winter's Tale* as reworkings of the *visitatio sepulchri* motif—creating, in the case of *The Winter's Tale*, a secular equivalent of the old resurrection motif.[15] In the medieval theatre the tomb had been a sign of spiritual triumph,

[12] Cited in Gurr, *The Shakespearean Stage*, 123.

[13] Although quotations from this play are keyed for ease of reference to the Riverside edition, the spelling of names follows those adopted in my edition of the play; see *Anthony and Cleopatra*, ed. Michael Neill (Oxford: Oxford University Press, 1994), pp. 131–5.

[14] On the ability of the façade to combine in one emblem elements of 'castle, throne, pavilion, tomb, altar, and triumphal arch', see Kernodle, *From Art to Theatre*, 172. The relationship between theatrical architecture and the 'architectural settings' of Elizabethan and Jacobean monuments, 'against which the frozen dramas of the dead are acted out', is usefully discussed and illustrated by Jean Wilson in *The Archaeology of Shakespeare* (Stroud: Alan Sutton, 1995), 81–95. For the controversial staging of the two scenes in Cleopatra's monument, see app. B in my edition, pp. 363–7.

[15] See Glynne Wickham, 'Romance and Emblem: A Study in the Dramatic Structure of *The Winter's Tale*', in David Galloway (ed.), *The Elizabethan Theatre*, 3 (Toronto: Macmillan, 1972), 82–99: 97.

the Christian victory over death; but in the new popular theatre it quickly developed an extended range of secular meanings,[16] influenced by the classical idea of the monument, and reflecting the increasingly temporal bias of Renaissance funeral art. Depending on whether their memorial or *memento mori* aspects were more heavily stressed, monuments could function as symbols of humanist transcendence, as they do in *Anthony and Cleopatra* and *The Duchess of Malfi*, or as emblems of human transience, as they do in *James IV* or *The Atheist's Tragedy*. Alternatively, exploiting the obvious melodramatic appeal of tombs as accoutrements of the tragedy of blood, dramatists might capitalize on both aspects of their meaning to convert them into signs of the deadly grip of the past upon the present. Thus in Marston's *Antonio's Revenge* the tomb of Andrugio becomes a physical embodiment of the hero's vindictive mission: from it issues the Ghost, who loads Antonio with the fearful commandment to remember and revenge (III. i. 32–73, 174); and it serves as the altar on which he sacrifices the helpless child Julio in a savage act of commemoration that parodies the requiem mass:

> Ghost of my poisoned sire, suck this fume;
> To sweet revenge, perfume the circling air
> With smoke of blood. I sprinkle round his gore,
> And dew thy hearse with these fresh-reeking drops.
>
> (III. i. 208–11)

The tombs which adorn the action of Shakespeare's two earliest tragedies, *Titus Andronicus* and *Romeo and Juliet*, are endowed with similar significance—complicated, in the case of the latter, by an ending which in some ways looks forward to the monument of *Anthony and Cleopatra*.

In retrospect, the strategic placement of a family sepulchre in the first scene of Shakespeare's earliest tragedy acquires, as we have seen, a proleptic appropriateness. In *Titus Andronicus* (*c.*1593–4) the rites performed at the 'sumptuously re-edified' monument of the Andronici mark the consummation of the funeral 'triumph' that is the spectacular centre-piece of Act I. To this mausoleum the hero brings the body of the latest of his 'five and twenty valiant sons' to die for Rome. Addressed by Titus as 'sacred receptacle of my joys, | Sweet cell of virtue and nobility' (I. i. 92–3), the tomb

[16] Glynne Wickham, *Early English Stages* 1300–1600, 3 vols. (London: Routledge & Kegan Paul, 1959–72), i. 244 and pl. xvi; vol. ii, pt. i, pp. 318 ff.

is the focus of a religious awe which depends less on distant recollections of a very different kind of tomb-opening than on the play's self-consciously classicizing attempt to reimagine Roman ideas of *virtus* and *pietas* through the lens of Renaissance funeral practice. With its 500-year history, it stands not merely as the expression of a great family's honour and fame, but as the physical symbol of those ideas of continuity and distinction on which the stability of the Roman state depends. It is as much the epitome of the city and its civil order as the 'blood-stained hole' into which Bassianus' body is thrown is an epitome of the chaotic wilderness of Act II. Ironically enough, however, the monument's role as a place of human sacrifice tends to collapse the opposition between the two, just as Shakespeare's language seems to equate the tomb's 'earthy prison' (I. i. 99) with the 'gaping hollow of the earth' in which Titus' sons find themselves entrapped (II. iii. 249). Similarly, if Martius' description of 'this fell devouring receptacle, | As hateful as [Cocytus'] misty mouth' identifies the pit as a secular equivalent of the medieval hell-mouth, its 'ragged entrails' also resemble 'some monument . . . poor Bassianus' grave' (II. iii. 228–40), so that tomb and hell-mouth, the typological opposites of the old religious drama, also become conflated. Moreover, in the light of the revenge action initiated by the sacrificial butchery before it, the sepulchre's appetite for blood comes to seem little different from that of 'this detested, dark, blood-drinking pit' with its 'swallowing womb' and blood-stained mouth (II. iii. 199–200, 224, 239). The result is that the splendid monument of the Andronici, with all its eloquent symbolism of caste pride and social continuity, comes to stand for nothing more than the dead hand of memory, the murderous tyranny of the past over the present so characteristic of revenge drama.

Shakespeare's second tragedy, *Romeo and Juliet* (*c.*1595–6), takes over from his first the stage image of a family sepulchre, emblem of a pride so consuming that it devours its own progeny. Echoing *Titus*, Old Capulet salutes this vault as the

> ancient receptacle,
> Where for this many hundred years the bones
> Of all my buried ancestors are pack'd.
>
> (IV. iii. 39–41[17])

[17] Cf. also IV. i. 110–12.

—and, like the equally hallowed tomb of the Andronici, it becomes a visible sign of the tyrannous past to which the lovers have fallen victim. As Romeo's 'detestable maw [and] womb of death' (v. iii. 45) it is also an emblem of mortality and death's inevitable triumph: Juliet imagines herself there, demented by the company of the latest sacrifice on the altar of family pride, 'the bloody Tybalt, yet but green in earth . . . festering in his shroud' (IV. iii. 42–3), and driven to a suicide that seems to enact the ancestral greed for propitiatory blood: 'And, in this rage, with some great kinsman's bone . . . dash out my desperate brains' (lines 53–4). But, as the site of an erotic consummation that paradoxically cheats Death of his desire, the Capulet tomb becomes a 'triumphant grave' (v. iii. 83) in another, more positive sense; for by the end of the scene the lovers on their bed of death have begun to resemble figures of tomb sculpture, anticipating the 'statue[s] of pure gold' which the penitent fathers promise to raise to the memory of their children (line 299). When such a spectacle is set against the self-referential flourish of the Prince's concluding couplet, 'Never was a *story* of more woe . . .', the effect is to turn it into a figure for the play itself, reminding the audience of the monumentalizing power of poetry in a way that anticipates the much more elaborately reflexive dramaturgy of *Anthony and Cleopatra.*

Marble Constancy

The final scene of *Anthony and Cleopatra*, like that of *Romeo and Juliet*, is played out in a tomb, which is once again a site of erotic consummation. Here, however, it is no longer a family sepulchre full of grotesque reminders of mortality, but a royal mausoleum consecrated to a queen's immortal fame; and the tragic catastrophe is transformed by the daring generic stroke that yokes the conventions of love-tragedy with those of heroic drama, staging Cleopatra's suicide not merely as a replay of Juliet's *liebestod*, but as a ceremonious tableau of constancy that recalls the marmoreal transfiguration of the dying hero in Chapman's *Bussy D'Ambois*. Cleopatra's show of 'marble-constancy' derives a particularly potent suggestiveness, however, from its monumental setting; and the histrionic self-consciousness of her performance works to remind the audience that her true monument is, after all, the play itself—a suggestion underlined by the use of the entire stage to embody the Queen's resplendent monument.

In its richly metatheatrical play with monumental tropes *Anthony and Cleopatra* (1606–7) belongs with a group of Stuart tragedies, including Webster's *The Duchess of Malfi* (1613), and Ford's *The Broken Heart* (*c.*1631), in which political defeat is transformed into moral or aesthetic victory, as death becomes an occasion for triumphant self-definition. All three plays construct their endings as elaborate variations upon the favourite Renaissance tag, *finis coronat opus*; and all three use the figure of art-as-monument to develop the Senecan aesthetic of the good death in strikingly new directions. In the case of *Anthony and Cleopatra*, however, the notorious doubleness of vision encoded in its very title and played out in its 'divided catastrophe'[18] gives the tropes a shimmering ambivalence; and, in accordance with this inherent paradoxy, the power of Cleopatra's performance proves to be oddly inseparable from the fragility of its artifice.[19] It is a tragedy that carries the self-monumentalizing gestures of heroic dramas like *Bussy D'Ambois* to a magnificent extreme, yet exposes the masculine values of the genre to a stubborn interrogation that makes Chapman's (or even Marlowe's) ironies seems casual by comparison.

Anthony is Shakespeare's characteristically decentred version of the Herculean hero—one whose attempts at the self-affirming singularity of a Bussy paradoxically render him even more vulnerable to mutability and the dissolution of differences. This is never more intensely felt than at the instant of death, in what he feels as 'the miserable change now at my end' (IV. XV. 51). What Anthony glimpses here is the terminal self-loss that was symbolically announced in the mysterious desertion of the same divine patron, Hercules, with whom Bussy's triumphant end united him (*A&C* IV. iii; *Bussy*, V. iii. 270). At the same time, in Cleopatra, whose transformation to 'fire and air' (V. ii. 289) recalls Bussy's fiery apotheosis, the play creates an equally paradoxical female hero—one whose

[18] For a brilliant analysis of the play's double ending, see Anne Barton, 'Nature's Piece 'Gainst Fancy: The Divided Catastrophe of *Antony and Cleopatra*', *Bedford College Inaugural Lecture* (London: Bedford College, University of London, 1973).

[19] The classic treatment of paradox in *Anthony and Cleopatra* is Janet Adelman's *The Common Liar* (New Haven: Yale University Press, 1973). On the Renaissance tradition of paradox generally, Rosalie Colie's *Paradoxia Epidemica* (Princeton: Princeton University Press, 1966) is indispensable.

dizzying capacity for metamorphosis mocks Anthony's desire for heroic singularity and yet becomes the means enabling her to imitate so splendidly the marble-constancy that eludes her Roman lover.

The play accommodates this symmetrical reversal in its two contrasted endings: in one, death is an experience of absolute indeterminacy, an annihilation of identity ('Here I am Anthony, | Yet cannot hold this visible shape'; IV. xiv. 13–14); in the other, it is an occasion for resolute self-determination, the last display of a virtuoso art of self-fashioning. Cleopatra's art is not confined to the performance of her own end: before her death, in the great aria of celebration that serves as Anthony's funeral oration, she reshapes her lover in the colossic image of the Herculean hero whom the play has invoked so often but never allowed us to see:

> His legs bestrid the ocean; his rear'd arm
> Crested the world. . . . realms and islands were
> As plates dropp'd from his pocket.
>
> (V. ii. 82–92)[20]

The monumental icons created in Cleopatra's theatre of death work as symbols of consummation, not because they ignore the ironies which undercut such posturing in *Julius Caesar*, for example ('How many ages hence | Shall this our lofty scene be acted o'er'; III. i. 111–12), but because they confront, with an unblinking gaze, the most reductive possibilities of the theatrical mode itself:

> The quick comedians
> Extemporally will stage us, and present
> Our Alexandrian revels: Anthony
> Shall be brought drunken forth, and I shall see
> Some squeaking Cleopatra boy my greatness
> I'th'posture of a whore. (V. ii. 16–21)

The dramatic and emotional weight given to the monumental ending of *Anthony and Cleopatra* is proportionate to the play's preoccupation with the fearful indistinction of death. No tragedy is more shot through with such anxiety. In contrast to (say) *Hamlet*, however, *Anthony* does not articulate it directly; instead the

[20] Jonathan Dollimore also discovers here 'an image of the commemorative statue, that material embodiment of a discourse which . . . skilfully overlays (without ever quite obscuring) obsolescence with respect' (*Radical Tragedy*, 215).

fear of undifferentiation and self-loss is characteristically displaced onto the self-abandon and dissolution of Anthony's sexual infatuation and the feminization of masculine identity which it entails. 'Beneath the surface of this tragedy', writes Anne Barton, 'lies one of the great Renaissance wish-dreams: the dream not only of harmony but of exchange and union between the masculine and feminine principles.'[21] But such a dream, the play shows us, can also be a nightmare of generic and gender confusion, whose violent assault upon the boundaries of identity and kind closely resembles death.

The sense that Anthony's entanglement with Cleopatra involves an undoing of his essential self is registered time and again, especially by its Roman voices: by Philo, for whom 'this dotage of our general's', by stripping him of self-defining 'property', produces the self-cancelling paradox of an Anthony who 'is not Anthony', (I. i. 1, 57–9);[22] by Scarrus, for whom the 'doting mallard' of Actium is the very type of radical self-violation (III. x. 17–23); by Enobarbus, for whom Anthony's heroic rededication to Cleopatra shows only how 'valour . . . eats the sword it fights with' (III. xiii. 198–9); and even by Iras and Charmian, to whom the defeated Roman seems 'unqualitied with very shame' (III. xi. 44), or split asunder like soul and body at the point of death (IV. xiii. 4–5). But the anxiety of self-loss is above all Anthony's theme; and there is a sense in which these other characters are merely reflectors of his inner crisis, which, because of the play's deliberate avoidance of soliloquy, has to be explored largely from without. We get a glimpse of Anthony's gathering crisis as early as Act I, scene ii, when the hero's queasy sense that he is about to 'lose [him]self in dotage' (line 117) is used to justify abandonment of Cleopatra—a rationale ironically echoed in Act III, scene iv, when he defends his desertion of Octavia with the equivocal assertion that to 'lose [his] honour' is to 'lose [him]self' (lines 22–3). In the wake of Actium the feeling of self-loss becomes obsessional: 'I | Have lost my way for ever. . . . My very hairs do mutiny . . . let that be left | Which leaves itself . . . for indeed I have lost command' (III. xi. 3–4, 13, 19–23), 'Authority melts from me. . . . I am | Anthony yet' (III.

[21] Barton, 'Nature's Piece 'Gainst Fancy', 5.

[22] The question of what it means for Anthony to 'be himself' or to appear 'like himself', in the terms that Cleopatra, Enobarbus, and Canidius, as well as Philo, so carelessly employ (I. i. 57; II. ii. 4; III. x. 26; III. xiii. 185–6) is repeatedly problematized in the play—see my intro. to the Oxford edition, 100–7, 123–30.

xiii. 90–3); and again after the final débâcle at Alexandria: 'this grave charm . . . hath at fast and loose | Beguil'd me to the very heart of loss' (IV. xii. 25–9); 'Here I am Anthony, | Yet cannot hold this visible shape' (IV. xiv. 13–14).

Anthony's sense that his true, heroic identity is melting or leaking away—leaving him just as his heroic ancestor 'the God Hercules. . . . Now leaves him' (IV. iii. 16–17)—is figured precisely as a loss of distinction or (to use Philo's term) of 'property':[23] he feels himself becoming 'indistinct as water is in water' (IV. xiv. 10–11). Water is that which always threatens (in Philo's characteristically Roman phrase) to 'o'erflow . . . the measure'; and water, for Anthony, is associated impartially with the self-dissolving excess of sexual infatuation, and with the unboundedness of death. Water is the metamorphic, unpropertying element into which, in his most dissolute Egyptian mood, he can imagine Rome itself dissolving (I. i. 33); and it is, of course, the substance with which Cleopatra, the 'serpent of old Nile' (I. v. 25), is most closely identified, especially in Anthony's imagination. Thus there is a complex appropriateness in the language with which Anthony responds to the desertion of Cleopatra's fleet in the waters off Alexandria ('The hearts | That spanieled me at heels . . . do discandy, melt their sweets | On blossoming Caesar'; IV. xii. 20–3), echoing as it does the striking neologism of Cleopatra's protestations to him after her flirtation with Thidias:

Dissolve my life! The next Caesarion smite,
Till by degrees the memory of my womb,
Together with my brave Egyptians all,
By the *discandying* of this pelleted storm,
Lie graveless . . .[24]

(III. xiii. 162–6; emphasis added)

Like Cleopatra's paraphrase of Anthony's 'Let Rome in Tiber melt', it is a reminder of how the same language can respond to entirely different constructions of the world. When the Queen rages against Anthony's desertion, 'Melt Egypt into Nile!' (II. v. 78), the curse

[23] For a more extensive treatment of this motif, see the section 'Properties of the Self' in my Oxford intro., 112–23.

[24] The echo is made especially striking by the rarity of the coinage: 'discandy' appears twice in this play and nowhere else in Shakespeare.

reflects only her final indifference to public values; Anthony's asseveration, on the other hand, is a boast that voices his sense of just how *much* his love will drive him to surrender—it anticipates an absolute dissolution of his Roman selfhood and makes that the measure of his desire.

The badge of that selfhood, and the property as overwhelmingly associated with Anthony's heroic masculinity as water is with Cleopatra's feminine instability, is his sword. Conceived both as an instrument of aggressive *measurement* and *boundary-making* ('I, that with my sword | *Quartered* the world'; IV. xiv. 57–8, emphasis added) and as an emblem of distinction ('He at Philippi kept | His sword e'en like a dancer, while I struck | The lean and wrinkled Cassius'; III. xi. 35–7), Anthony's sword is the sign not merely of his heroic difference from Caesar, but the weapon with which he will challenge the undifferentiating rage of King Death himself: 'I'll make death love me, for I will contend | Even with his pestilent scythe' (lines 192–3). Inevitably, therefore, the unpropertying of the hero, his dissolution into a state that seems, if possible, to undo him more than death itself could do, is represented as the enfeeblement and loss of this potent stage-property:

You did know
How much you were my conqueror, and that
My sword, made weak by my affection, would
Obey it on all cause. (III. xi. 65–8)

O, thy vile lady!
She has robb'd me of my sword.
(IV. xiv. 23–4)

—a loss which is ironically literalized in Dercetus' cynical theft of the blade after his master's botched suicide ('This sword but shown to Caesar . . . Shall enter me with him'; IV. xiv. 112–13).

Yet the sword is also an instrument of paradox and contradiction. For Anthony, falling on his sword is an attempt to reassert what is 'proper' to his essential self, a conclusive demonstration of the absolute authority of the instrument in which his heroic identity is invested. To claim the right to '[s]ubdue my worthiest self' (IV. xii. 47), to show himself 'conqueror of [him]self' (IV. xiv. 62), 'a Roman by a Roman | Valiantly vanquished', his valour 'triumph[ing] on itself' (IV. xv. 58–9, 15), is to claim, in the language of Roman Stoicism, the conquest of Death itself. Thus the sword attempts a harsher, Roman version of the mysterious paradox of Cleopatra's fans that do what they undo (II. ii. 205)[25]. But the reflexive antinomies in which Anthony repeatedly attempts to write his own epitaph subtly undermine the self-sufficiency of his gesture, recalling Caesar's ironic manipulation of their last battle, in which Anthony was forced 'to spend his fury | On himself' (IV. vi. 9–10), and making his death seem less the resolution than the inevitable expression of the self-annihilating contradictions that have afflicted his problematic identity from the opening scene. Suicide, after all—the 'decision to undo, to unmake, to eliminate oneself by one's own act'—is, as Rosalie Colie has remarked, nothing less than 'the paradox of self-contradiction at its irrevocable extremity'.[26]

In this respect it is significant to find the image of self-destructive excess, with which Philo had evoked the wild energy of Anthony's heroic past ('his captain's heart . . . hath burst | The buckles on his breast'; I. i. 6–8), recast as a metaphor of willed disintegration—one that helps to mark Anthony's last unarming as a ritualized dismantling of heroic identity:

Off, pluck off!
The sevenfold shield of Ajax cannot keep
The battery from my heart. O, cleave, my sides!
Heart, once be stronger than thy continent,
Crack thy frail case! Apace, Eros, apace.
No more a soldier. Bruised pieces, go,
You have been nobly borne.
(IV. xiv. 37–43)

The heavy contrapuntal stress on 'Crack' will be echoed in the even more strenuous 'Splitted' of Dercetus' equivocal effort at the heroical sublime

that self hand
Which writ his honor in the acts it did
Hath, with the courage which the heart did lend it,
Splitted the heart. (V. i. 21–4)

The masculine assertiveness implicit in the consonantal muscularity of such language only emphasizes the self-cancelling violence of 'labour [that] | Mars what it does' and 'force [that] entangles |

[25] On this paradox, see the sections 'Doing and Undoing' in my Oxford intro., 100–7, 123–37.

[26] Colie, *Paradoxia Epidemica*, 486.

Itself with strength' (IV. xiv. 47–9). On one hand, suicide can be celebrated as a sublime folding in of the self upon itself, an assertion of integrity in the very act of disintegration; on the other, it represents the extreme of paradoxical self-division. Thus Dercetus' eulogy serves (particularly in the mouth of this cynical opportunist) as a reminder that Anthony's last act of self-affirmation may actually amount to nothing more than the very collapse into indistinction that he most wishes to avert.

For Anthony, sexual appetite is invariably a temptation to self-abandonment—losing oneself in dotage. Where Othello discovers his love for Desdemona as the very foundation of his identity ('and when I love thee not, | Chaos is come again', 'Othello's occupation's gone'; *Oth.* III. iii. 91–2, 357), Anthony knows his passion for Cleopatra only as the flood that dissolves that foundation. To have made 'this grave charm', Cleopatra, 'my chief end', he comes to believe, is to have betrayed himself to 'the very heart of loss' (IV. xii. 25–9). For Anthony, desire turns out always to have been the desire for annihilation. Thus his welcoming of death, which reverses the familiar *danse macabre* trope of Death as a Bridegroom to cast an unexpectedly erotic glow over his display of Roman fortitude, remains profoundly ambivalent:

I will be
A bridegroom in my death, and run into't
As to a lover's bed.

(IV. xiv. 99–101)

He will die, he proclaims (in words that play significantly upon a name that Shakespeare found in Plutarch), the 'scholar' of his servant Eros; and the resonant phrasing of the lines in which he falls on his sword suggests a deliberate attempt to reconcile the heroic and the erotic: '*To do thus* | I learnt of thee' (lines 102–3; emphasis added). The words echo both his first great aria of love to Cleopatra ('the nobleness of life | Is *to do thus*'; I. i. 36–7, emphasis added) and his reassertion of heroic selfhood in the chivalric embrace of Caesar ('Were we before our armies, and to fight, | I should *do thus*'; II. ii. 27, emphasis added). But the art of erotic dying fails Anthony, and he must vainly beg his own guards to 'make an end' of his pain and humiliation (line 105). Although Cleopatra, in her turn, tries to paint his death with the colours of erotic consummation ('Die when thou hast lived, | Quicken with kissing'; IV. xv. 38–9), while Anthony seeks to dress it in the language of heroic authenticity ('A Roman by a Roman | Valiantly vanquished'), the scene of his ending in the monument can never wholly escape the taint of this botched attempt at reaffirming distinction. Indeed the elegiac power of Cleopatra's grief comes precisely from her overwhelming sense of death as the annihilator of all differences:

> The crown o'th'earth doth *melt* . . .
> O, wither'd is the garland of the war,
> The soldier's pole is fall'n! Young boys and girls
> Are *level* now with men; the *odds is gone*,
> And there is *nothing left remarkable*
> Beneath the visiting moon. (IV. xv. 63–8)

In a more conventional tragic structure this scene would mark the ending of the play. The last two scenes of Act IV are indeed full of the language of finality—'Ourselves to end ourselves', 'The long day's task is done', 'Seal then, and all is done', 'make an end | Of what I have begun', 'the star is fallen', 'time is at his period', 'The miserable change now at mine end' (IV. xiv. 22, 35, 49, 105–6; IV. xv. 51); and, in the prescribed fashion, the hero's death is followed by a long speech of lament, which concludes in instructions for a funeral procession. Cleopatra's oration is adorned with the usual rhetorical signs of closure, including a terminal rhyme upon the word 'end' itself:

> We'll bury him; and then, what's brave, what's noble,
> Let's do't after the high Roman fashion,
> And make death proud to take us. Come, away.
> This case of that huge spirit now is cold.
> Ah, women, women! Come, we have no friend
> But resolution, and the briefest end.
> *[Exeunt . . . bearing off Anthony's body*
> (IV. xv. 86–91)

As if in defiance of this carefully orchestrated scene of ending, however, the play begins again with the entry of Caesar's council of war. The disruption of closure together with Octavius' disappointed response to the news of Anthony's death revives the sense of anticlimax created by Anthony's botched suicide. It is as if Caesar were cheated of the apocalyptic end that would properly usher in the millennial 'time of universal peace' he anticipated before the final battle at Alexandria (IV. vi. 4–6):

The breaking of so great a thing should make
A greater crack. The round world
Should have shook lions into civil streets,
And citizens to their dens. The death of Anthony
Is not a single doom, in the name lay
A moiety of the world. (V. i. 14–19)

Caesar's final council scene winds up on a note of conspicuous incompletion with a half line ('Go with me, and see | What I can show in this'); and the action of the long scene that ensues turns upon his unsuccessful struggle to 'determine' Cleopatra's fate (V. i. 59), and so to orchestrate the ending of the play. What Caesar envisages is a politicized form of comic catastrophe ('her life in Rome | Would be eternal in our triumph'; V. i. 65–6), which from Cleopatra's point of view can only amount to a brutally indecorous parade of mirth-in-funeral: 'The quick comedians | Extemporally will stage us' (V. ii. 216 ff.). Rather than be part of the trappings of Caesar's monumentalizing ambition—'Your scutcheons and your signs of conquest' (line 135)—she proposes to become her own monument. In the process her death reverses the transformation suffered by the dying Anthony, becoming the act of supreme distinction at which Anthony can only gesture.

For most of the play Cleopatra, the 'serpent of old Nile' (I. v. 25), appears like the metamorphic water-creature evoked in Anthony's teasing portrait of that 'strange serpent', the crocodile, which he makes a monster so resistant to definition, yet so utterly distinct from all others, that it can be described only by tautology: 'It is shap'd, sir, like itself, and it is as broad as it hath breadth. It is just so high as it is, and moves with it own organs. It lives by that which nourisheth it. . . . Of it own colour too. . . . and the tears of it are wet' (II. vii. 42–9). Anything so singular as to be beyond comparison is, paradoxically enough, beyond description—language, that is to say, cannot adequately distinguish it. Furthermore, while this creature is so sublimely like itself that it resembles nothing else, nevertheless 'the elements once out of it, it transmigrates' (line 45), metamorphosing upon the instant into something not itself.[27] But the death Cleopatra now proposes is an action which will translate her out of the mutable world of doing and

[27] For metempsychosis as a species of metamorphosis, see Leonard Barkan, *The Gods Made Flesh: Metamorphosis and the Pursuit of Paganism* (New Haven: Yale University Press, 1985), 86–8.

becoming into the region of absolute being—a paradoxical change to end change:

> And it is great
> To do that thing that ends all other deeds,
> Which shackles accidents and bolts up change.
> (v. ii. 4–6)

For the pragmatic Proculeius her suicide would be merely a self-destructive 'undoing of yourself' (line 44); but for Cleopatra it is to be an act of transcendent self-fashioning, transforming mortal flesh to marmoreal sculpture in a fashion wholly fitted to its monumental setting:[28]

> My resolution's plac'd, and I have nothing
> Of woman in me; now from head to foot
> I am marble-constant; now the fleeting moon
> No planet is of mine. (v. ii. 238–41)

Like her celebration of the dead Anthony, this is an attempt, as Anne Barton sees it, to defeat time through rewriting her own history; by thus transforming herself she is at once able to 'remake past time' and to deny death.[29] A double paradox is involved here, since the turning of human flesh to stone is conventionally a sign of death's arrest, an 'essential metaphor for the body's undoing'.[30] But Cleopatra makes it the sign for a different kind of arrest, the shackling of accident and bolting up of the arbitrary change associated not just with her infinite variety, but with mutability and death itself.[31]

Just as her rhetorical apotheosis seeks to restore the panoply of heroic difference to her dead lover (lines 77–100), so all the resources of Cleopatra's artifice are devoted to the performance of her own end as a pageant of royal distinction. As a rite of coronation, the scene is contrived as a ceremonial realization of the ancient

[28] For a discussion of the funerary iconography of the scene which compares the figure of the dead Cleopatra to a piece of mortuary sculpture in a chantry chapel, see John M. Bowers, '"I am marble-constant": Cleopatra's Monumental End', *Huntington Library Quarterly*, 46 (1983), 283–97.

[29] Barton, 'Nature's Piece 'Gainst Fancy', 11, 17, 20.

[30] Barkan, *Gods Made Flesh*, 90.

[31] Cf. Barton, 'Nature's Piece 'Gainst Fancy', 20: 'It is Cleopatra who finally arrests the eddying of the vagabond flag, who gives to the swan's down feather an immutable poise . . . by creating a tableau, "still and contemplative in living art".'

motto that for the Renaissance best expressed the aristocratic art of dying: *finis coronat opus*. Where Anthony performed the ritual unmaking of his martial self as Eros removed his armour, Cleopatra enacts the formal reassumption of her regal identity as Iras invests her with robe, crown, and sceptre.[32] The rich and self-conscious theatricality of the occasion (emphasized by the iteration of words like 'show', 'play', 'act', 'perform'), on which critics often remark, draws attention to the scene as an exhibition of the monumentalizing power of art.

'Finish, good lady,' urges Iras; 'the bright day is done, | And we are for the dark' (lines 193–4); but 'to have done' here is no longer to surrender to the indifference of what *Troilus and Cressida* calls 'monumental mockery'.[33] In *Anthony and Cleopatra* 'doing' becomes itself the rhetorical site of transcendence. 'Is this well done?' the guard demands of Charmian: 'It is well done, and fitting for a princess | Descended of so many royal kings' (v. ii. 326–7). Charmian's reply, with its delicate echo of Anthony's amatory hyperbole 'The nobleness of life is to do thus', catches up Cleopatra's recollection of Cydnus (lines 228–9), and even her playful eroticization of the aspic's bite, into a fully accomplished aesthetic of dying that proclaims the decorum of an entire life.

In her essay 'Nature's Piece 'Gainst Fancy: The Divided Catastrophe of *Antony and Cleopatra*', Anne Barton argues that the play's double ending, 'in its unpredictability, its very untidiness . . . seems to reflect not the dubious symmetries of art but life as we normally experience it in a world where events invariably straggle on beyond the point that art would regard as climactic'.[34] If she were right, then Cleopatra's end would have to be accounted a failure, since a sense of life 'straggling on' is precisely what her rhapsodic artifice is designed to arrest. But it is Anthony's death, surely, that seems 'untidy', compromised by an embarrassing sense of life's

[32] The parallel between the two episodes is emphasized by the protagonists' exclamations of impatience: 'Apace, Eros, apace' (IV. xiv. 41) and 'Yare, yare, good Iras; quick' (v. ii. 283).

[33] In the world of *Troilus* the verb 'do', by virtue of both its ferocious temporal concentration and its obscene suggestiveness ('Things won are done, joy's soul lies in the doing', I. ii. 287; 'to have done is to hang | Quite out of fashion', III. iii. 151–2; 'All's done, my lord', v. ii. 115), is one of the most treacherous words in the lexicon. No wonder that Thersites uses it to spit abuse at that man of empty action, Ajax ('Do! Do! . . . Do, rudeness! Do, camel, do, do!' II. i. 42–54).

[34] Barton, 'Nature's Piece 'Gainst Fancy', 4.

indifference to the ordering distinctions of art. The double ending has less to do with any resistance to the formal satisfactions of literary closure than with the play's concern to dramatize contrasting ways of encountering death.

In his first exchange with Anthony, Enobarbus had mocked Cleopatra's erotic hyperbole with his own sardonic version of Death and the Maiden: 'I do think there is mettle in death, which commits some loving act upon her, she hath such a celerity in dying' (I. ii. 142–4). Now the Queen produces her own strangely metamorphosed version of this well-worn conceit, endowing it with an astonished (and astonishing) literalness: 'The stroke of death is as a lover's pinch, | Which hurts, and is desir'd' (lines 295–6). The agent of that stroke, the asp, is delivered by a Clown whose eldritch humour identifies him as the antic voice of mortality;[35] and the Clown's description of his 'worm' that feeds on woman's flesh associates it with the maggots of vermiculation. From this perspective, the image of a queen with a worm at her breast resembles a portrait in the *macabre* tradition. Nevertheless, for Cleopatra herself the asp is 'the pretty worm of Nilus' (line 243), a diminutive or infant version of her personal emblem 'the serpent of old Nile', and so identified as 'the baby at my breast, | That sucks the nurse asleep' (lines 309–10); it is even a surrogate for Anthony himself: 'As sweet as balm, as soft as air, as gentle— | O, Anthony!—Nay, I will take thee too!' (lines 311–12). The combined effect of Cleopatra's aposiopesis and the dying fall of a feminine ending is to emphasize the complex word-play on 'gentle' here: picking up the soothing suggestions of 'balm', it also seems to send her mind back to the 'gentle' Anthony; applied to a worm, however, 'gentle' must recall her fantasy earlier in the scene of her own fly-blown corpse in a 'gentle grave' (line 38), with its grotesque play on *gentle* as a word for maggot. What results is a rhetorical metamorphosis in which the worm of corruption becomes itself the balm of preservation.

[35] Barton identifies the Clown as representing Comedy, 'the last obstacle Cleopatra faces on her way to death'; the Queen is thus exposed to a kind of trial by ordeal involving 'ridicule, the thing she most dreads, and potentially most deadly to her' (ibid. 18). I find Bowers's identification of the Clown as an antic Death-figure, analogous to the Grave-digger in *Hamlet* or the Mower in Marlowe's *Edward II*, more persuasive—though the two readings are not, of course, mutually exclusive.

The play does not, of course, end on a note of unambiguous triumph. Whatever her imagination makes of it, 'the worm will do his kind', and the fulfilment of Cleopatra's 'immortal longings' is dependent on an '[immortal] biting' (lines 262–3, 246–7) that cuts off her speech upon an enigmatic half-line whose incompletion marks the sudden arrest of death ('What should I stay—'; line 313). Cleopatra may choose to think of Octavius as the relict of her transformation, a cast-off creature of sublunary Fortune (lines 2–4); but even if he is bilked of his triumphal centre-piece, the closing moments of the play seem to belong to him. However Anthony and Cleopatra may seem to elude the ends their conqueror designs for them, the ending is nevertheless practically at his disposal. It is Caesar's rhetoric which forces the Queen's monumental spectacle to submit to one of those potentially self-cancelling oxymorons familiar from the earlier part of the play: 'O noble weakness' (line 344). The phrase is curiously reminiscent of Cleopatra's dismissal of Anthony's 'excellent falsehood' and 'excellent dissembling' (I. i. 40; I. iii. 79); and a kind of excellent falsehood—'lies, | Alas, unparallel'd', in the pun that Charmian's fine tribute cannot quite exclude (lines 315–16)—is all that Caesar tempts us to see in the exquisite dissembling of Cleopatra's end. By the same token, however, dissembling of another kind is what we are bound to recognize in a 'solemn show' that expresses the victor's 'pity' for the defeated only in so far as it proclaims 'his [own] glory which | Brought them to be lamented' (lines 362–3). In its meticulous rendering unto Caesar of that which is his, *Anthony and Cleopatra* is careful to acknowledge the limitations attendant on its poetry of transcendence. But paradoxically its power to move us is at every point dependent on such awareness of the fragile nature of the artifice on which it stakes everything—an awareness that is never more beautifully registered than in the gesture of extraordinary tenderness with which Charmian registers her allegiance to the end that crowns the masterpiece: 'Your crown's awry; | I'll mend it, and then play—' (lines 318–19).

Cleopatra's self-monumentalization is a triumph that presses even Octavius Caesar into the reluctant service of her fame:

> She shall be buried by her Anthony;
> No grave upon the earth shall clip in it
> A pair so famous. (lines 357–9)

This valedictory tribute turns upon a word-play of uncharacteristic delicacy: 'clip' first hints at the arbitrary cutting off, the sudden arrest of death, only to reveal itself as a word from Anthony's amatory vocabulary ('clip your wives'; IV. viii. 8) which serves to prolong the erotic glow that the lovers' own rhetoric has cast over their end. In this it recalls the ending of *Romeo and Juliet*, where the statues promised by the grieving fathers will enshrine for ever the erotic embrace of the lovers' death ('As rich shall Romeo's by his lady's lie'; V. iii. 303). The parallel serves as reminder of another aspect of the play's double nature—the generic irregularity that allows this political history-play to preserve, in the teeth of its own scepticism, the qualities of both heroic drama and love-tragedy. The 'fame' of which Octavius speaks attaches the dead to his public realm of 'high events' and 'solemn shows'; but the embrace of the grave belongs to that conspicuously private domain in which Caesar is rendered 'ass | Unpolicied' (V. ii. 307–8).

Anthony and Cleopatra ends in the prescribed fashion with instructions for a funeral:

Take up her bed,
And bear her women from the monument.
She shall be buried by her Anthony;

* * * * * * * *

Our army shall
In solemn show attend this funeral,
And then to Rome. Come, Dolabella, see
High order in this great solemnity.
(V. ii. 356–66)

For the last time in this urgently demonstrative play, we are being asked to 'behold and see'; by now, however, we should be accustomed to discovering that *what* we see is seldom what the presenter intends. The projected funeral show, for all its public display of magnanimity, is too much the substitute for that military triumph, adorned with the captive figures of Anthony and his Egyptian queen, of which Caesar has been cheated.[36] The most compelling

[36] Compare the ending of Marston's *Sophonisba*, where a spectacular scene, beginning as a military triumph *all'antica* for the victorious Scipio (V. iv), is ritually converted into a funeral triumph for Sophonisba, when Massinissa 'all in black' transfers to his dead Queen 'this crown | This robe of triumph, and this conqueror's

image, when all is said, remains that of Cleopatra's monument and the tableau of marble-constancy that she composes within it. Here the monument is not confined to one of those tomb-properties that appeared in so many plays, but has expanded to encompass the entire stage—dominated by that façade which bore more than a passing resemblance to a Roman triumphal arch. It is a setting that embodies, more completely than in any other play, the idea of poetry-as-monument.[37] To the extent that it stands for a kind of transcendence, a mortal triumph over the destructive agencies of Time and Death, it is also this spectacle that most contributes to the often felt connection between *Anthony and Cleopatra* and the tragicomic romances that followed it. It suggests (as the tombs and monuments of *Pericles* and *The Winter's Tale*, those dramas of resurrection, can also suggest) a bridge between dirge and marriage, funeral and revels.

wreath, | This sceptre, and this hand' (v. iv. 44–6). Ford surely had both tableaux in mind when he composed the extraordinary ceremonial ending of *The Broken Heart*, a white-clad ritual of marriage-in-funeral that resolves itself as a monumental display of Love's triumph over Death.

[37] The trope is fittingly turned on its head in *Troilus and Cressida*, where the 'monumental mock'ry' of 'rusty mail' (i.e. the knightly achievements hanging over a tomb) serves Ulysses as a metaphor for the ephemerality of fame (III. iii. 151–3)—of which the play itself (as an anti-chronicle of infamy) constitutes a sardonic demonstration. For further comment on this motif, see Duncan Harris, 'Tombs, Guidebooks, and Shakespearean Drama: Death in the Renaissance', *Mosaic*, 15, special issue on Death and Dying (1982), 13–28; and Bowers, 'I am marble-constant'.

10

'Fame's best friend': The Endings of *The Duchess of Malfi*

> But to subsist in bones, and be but pyramidally extant, is a fallacy in duration. . . . *pyramids*, *arches*, *obelisks* were but the irregularities of vain-glory, and wild enormities of ancient magnanimity.
>
> (Sir Thomas Browne, *Urn Burial*[1])

Monuments and Ruins

The ending of *Anthony and Cleopatra* confounds expectation in a remarkable way. By setting the mire and blood of Anthony's bungled suicide against the high rhetoric, erotic intensity, and ritualized splendour of Cleopatra's death, and by measuring both against Caesar's calculating political determinations, Shakespeare's tragedy preserves to the last that paradoxical yoking of opposites on which its whole design is founded; but by stripping the heroic male protagonist of his consummatory act of self-fashioning, and transferring it (in a subtly altered form) to his female co-rival, the divided catastrophe abets her in a species of generic usurpation. It can hardly be coincidental that two other great Stuart tragedies which monumentalize specifically feminine versions of the heroic, Webster's *The Duchess of Malfi* and Ford's *The Broken Heart*, also deploy alternative endings of this kind.

In *The Duchess of Malfi* the tragic action once again appears to conclude with the death of the nominal protagonist at the end of Act IV. Repeated prolepses have prepared us for just such a catastrophe, starting with the very first scene, where her brothers' lecture upon the iniquity of remarriage viciously inverts the familiar

[1] In *Religio Medici and Other Writings*, 133, 139.

conceit of eroticized death-as-wedding to make of widow's marriage a kind of death:[2]

[FERDINAND]. Such weddings may more properly be said
 To be executed than celebrated.
CARDINAL. The marriage night
 Is the entrance into some prison.
FERDINAND. And those joys,
 Those lustful pleasures, are like heavy sleeps
 Which do forerun man's mischief.
CARDINAL. Fare you well.
 Wisdom begins at the end: remember it.

(I. i. 330–5)

The same ominous concatenation of beginnings and ends is apparent in the Duchess's wooing of Antonio, where wedding-sheets are identified with winding-sheets and courtship is conducted under the ominous pretence of making a will—a conceit that will find its mortal echo in the Duchess's pronouncement of her 'last will' and Bosola's promise to execute it at the end of a murder scene that has itself been orchestrated as a grotesque nuptial travesty (IV. ii. 200, 368).[3] Like the fourth act of *Anthony and Cleopatra*, this one concludes with a mimesis of tragic closure, as Bosola, who earlier in the scene has brought the Duchess her coffin as 'a present from your princely brothers' (line 166), begins the preparations for her funeral:

Come,
I'll bear thee hence,
And execute thy last will; that's deliver
Thy body to the reverend dispose
Of some good women.

(IV. ii. 366–70)

The seeming finality of this gesture is undercut, however, by the conclusion of Bosola's valedictory lament, in which he turns away

[2] The sexual innuendo of Ferdinand's threats is underlined by the explicitly phallic menace of his father's poniard (lines 337–47)—a weapon which, significantly, he will flourish again in the bedchamber scene (III. ii), where it serves as a bloodthirsty pointer to his monitory fable of Reputation, Love, and Death. For a more extensive discussion of the poniard, see my 'What Strange Riddle's This?' in my *John Ford* 153–79: 169–72.

[3] Gittings, *Death, Burial and the Individual*, 111–12.

from the Duchess's corpse to point the course of his own future action, anticipating his emergence as the tragedy's second protagonist. Not for nothing is his speech left prosodically suspended on a half-line; for another whole act—one so full of deaths that Bosola expects to 'grow the common bier for churchyards' (v. ii. 309)—must unfold before the action can be terminated. The deferred ending recalls *Anthony and Cleopatra*, but, in a significant departure from Shakespeare's plan, Webster has reversed the order of the double catastrophe, producing a final act that much more exactly illustrates Anne Barton's notion of the unpredictability and untidiness of mortal endings. In this case, however, the resistance to ordered closure has less to do with some abstract notion of life's essential irregularity than with the social and moral didacticism of the play. The notorious shapelessness of the final act, epitomized in the near-farcical mistake of Antonio's death 'in a mist' and the confused 'scuffle' in which the Cardinal, Bosola, and Ferdinand receive their death-wounds, contrasts with the ceremonial formality of the Duchess's death to exhibit the helpless subjection of these characters to the arbitrary power of death.

Often dismissed by critics as a long-drawn-out and anticlimactic coda to a work whose real interest concludes with the Duchess's death, Act V has always presented difficulties to directors of the play. Yet it would be unwise to assume that so painstaking a craftsman arrived at this design out of dramatic incompetence, merely following his sources with unthinking fidelity. Indeed, as I intend to show, the full significance of the Duchess's death is hardly comprehensible outside the context created by the fifth act, and in particular by the crucial third scene, in which Antonio and Bosola visit the site of her tomb. Often regarded as one of the Gothic extravagances of a 'Tussaud laureate', and generally neglected in the study and the theatre alike, it is an episode which (like the murder scene superbly anatomized by Inga-Stina Ekeblad[4]) will yield its meaning only to an attentive and sympathetic visual reading; for it relies on that favourite Websterian device the 'figure-in-action'[5] to create

[4] Inga-Stina Ekeblad (Ewbank), 'The "Impure Art" of John Webster', in G. K. and S. K. Hunter (eds.), *John Webster*, Penguin Critical Anthologies (Harmondsworth: Penguin, 1969), 202–21.

[5] See Hereward T. Price, 'The Function of Imagery in Webster', in Hunter, *John Webster*, 194–202.

a powerful iconographic effect that reveals the play as a dramatized pageant of Fame, bringing its monumental theme to life in a richly enacted metaphor.

At the conclusion of Webster's first great tragedy, *The White Devil*, Death had been left in unchallenged possession of the stage, as even the brilliant Flamineo, briefly resurrected from his mock-death, sank into the 'mist' of mortal ending: 'I recover like a spent taper, for a flash, | And instantly go out' (v. vi. 363–4); but in *The Duchess of Malfi*, which forms a kind of diptych with the earlier play, the reign of Death is challenged by Fame, in a pattern that reverses the triumphal sequence established by the two parts of Marlowe's *Tamburlaine*. In place of *The White Devil*'s despairing emblems of mortality—'A dead man's skull beneath the roots of flowers!' (v. iv. 136)—*The Duchess of Malfi* places at the centre of its symbolic system a monument of fame which stands, as Webster's own encomiasts implicitly acknowledge, for the eternizing artifice of the play itself.

A monument properly speaks for those whom the grave has silenced; but in this play the dramatist allows his murdered heroine herself to speak, in the accents of the monitory echo which sounds, according to the opening stage direction in Act V, scene iii, 'from the Duchess's grave'. As his wife's voice overcomes the deathly 'quiet' to which her brothers have consigned her (IV. ii. 236; V. iv. 33), Antonio has a vision of 'a face folded in sorrow', illuminated by the 'clear light' whose beams, in contrast to the ephemeral 'flash' of Flamineo's spent taper, emblematize the transcendent power of Fame and its agent Poetry. For the staging of this extraordinary spectacle, as John Russell Brown has shown, Webster must have intended to make use of a specially adapted version of the tomb-property which the King's Men had already employed in *The Second Maiden's Tragedy*, two years before. In the fourth act of that play the hero Govianus visits the cathedral to offer his 'grief's devotion' (IV. iv. 11) at the family tomb, 'richly set forth', where '[his] Lady lies buried' (IV. iii)—unaware that her body has been stolen by the Tyrant whose violent lust compelled her suicide. A mysterious voice sounds from the tomb declaring 'I am not here' (IV. iv. 40); and then, as if in answer to his astonished questioning, 'On a sudden . . . the tombstone flies open, and a great light appears in the midst of the tomb; his LADY, as went out, standing just before him all in white, stuck with jewels, and a great crucifix on her breast' (IV. iv. 42).[6]

But what in the earlier play is mainly a sensational contrivance in Webster's tragedy contributes to a subtle transformation of the monumental motif. The monuments of plays such as *Titus Andronicus*, *Romeo and Juliet*, *Anthony and Cleopatra*, and *The Second Maiden's Tragedy* are all, in their different ways, embodiments of a kind of fame that is inseparable from caste pride and the honour of blood. The Duchess's tomb, by contrast, surrounded as it is by ruins that express the frailty of mere worldly greatness,[7] is the instrument of a radical, anti-courtly aesthetic: it stands for the individual renown, dissociated from the accidents of rank, earned by a woman whose unbreakable 'integrity of life' is celebrated in the play's final couplet.

'Non norunt haec monumenta mori'

Tombs, graves, and decaying ruins are recognizable staples of Webster's imagery, routinely dismissed as the melodramatic trappings of a morbid imagination. But their controlling significance in *The Duchess of Malfi* seems to have been perfectly apparent to Webster's contemporaries—or at least to the three fellow dramatists who supplied encomiastic verses for its published text—Thomas Middleton, William Rowley, and John Ford. Their contributions are distinguished by a preoccupation with endings, both literary and mortal; and, as is frequently the way in such occasional pieces, all four spin conceits around the governing ideas and images of the play,[8] drawing in each case upon the ancient trope of

[6] Act V, scene ii of this play, in which the Lady's ghost appears beside her corpse, presumably required the services of the same waxwork artist who provided the figures for Webster's play. For further discussion of the *Second Maiden's Tragedy* tomb, see David M. Bergeron, 'The Wax Figures in *The Duchess of Malfi*', *Studies in English Literature*, 18 (1978), 331–9: 331–2.

[7] The emblematic significance of the ruined abbey on which Antonio's melancholy imagination so lingers (lines 9–19) may well indicate that it was intended to be a part of the scene's spectacular staging—but this need have presented no great problems for a theatre whose stock properties could include architectural effects as elaborate as 'ii steeples . . . and the city of Rome' (Henslowe, cited in Gurr, *Shakespearean Stage*, 123).

[8] Among *Malfi*'s encomiasts, Ford was to make elaborate use of the tomb motif in his own tragedy, *Love's Sacrifice*, while Middleton was in all probability the

poetry-as-monument. Ford, most simply, declares that in *Malfi* Webster 'to memory hath lent | A lasting fame, to raise his monument' (lines 8–9). Middleton elaborates the metaphor:

Thy monument is rais'd in thy life time;
And 'tis most just; for every worthy man
Is his own marble; and his merit can
Cut him to any figure, and express
More art than Death's cathedral palaces,
Where royal ashes keep their court: thy note
Be ever plainness, 'tis the richest coat:
Thy epitaph only the title be,
Write, *Duchess*, that will fetch a tear for thee . . .[9]

(lines 9–17)

Even more strikingly, the Latin couplet that concludes his verses recalls the symbolic chiaroscuro of the moment in Act V, scene ii when the light of the Duchess's memory shines out over the ruin that surrounds her grave:

Ut lux et tenebris ictu percussa Tonantis,
Illa, ruina malis, claris fit vita poetis.

(lines 20–1)

[As light springs from darkness at the stroke of the Thunderer,
So [Tragedy], while bringing ruin to the wicked, brings life to illustrious poets.[10]]

Rowley's rather clumsy encomium varies the conceit by reminding the reader that the tragedy is also a monument to the Duchess herself, a device which (like the stage property of the echo scene)

author of *The Second Maiden's Tragedy* itself (see Lancashire's introduction to the Revels edition, 19–23).

[9] Interestingly, in view of the connections between *Malfi* and *The Second Maiden's Tragedy*, Middleton's reference to 'Death's cathedral palaces | Where royal ashes keep their court' seems to echo the Tyrant's description of the glistering monuments in his cathedral as 'death's palaces' (*The Second Maiden's Tragedy*, IV. iii. 83). But for Webster's readers it will surely have evoked Henry VII's Chapel at Westminster Abbey, where the King had recently interred his mother and eldest son. Middleton may have been responding to the play's own oblique allusion to these royal tombs; see below, p. 343. Cf. also Henry Vaughan's 'An Elegy on the Death of Mr R. W.', with its elevation of poets' monuments above those of 'all those *lordly fools* which lock their bones | In the dumb piles of chested brass, and stones' (cited in Llewellyn, *Art of Death*, 105).

[10] The subdued pun on *clarus* (clear–famous) picks up the significance of Webster's own 'clear light'.

enables her voice to sound beyond the grave: 'my opinion is, she might speak more; | But never in her life so well before' (lines 8–9).

In his own epistle dedicatory, Webster, who had ushered in his first tragedy with a tag from Martial proclaiming art's resistance to death—*Non norunt haec monumenta mori* ('Monuments such as these do not know how to die')—extends his colleagues' conceits by asserting the power of poetry to include the patron in its immortalizing transformations: 'by such *poems* as this', he reminds Lord Berkeley, 'poets have kissed the hands of great princes, and drawn their gentle eyes to look down upon their sheets of paper, when the poets themselves were bound up in their winding sheets. The like courtesy from your Lordship shall make you live in your grave, and laurel spring out of it; when the ignorant scorners of the muses . . . shall wither, neglected and forgotten' (lines 18–23). Like Middleton's verses, the dedication links the monumental function of poetry to the themes of reputation and true greatness: 'I do not altogether look up to your *title*, the ancientest *nobility* being but a *relic* of time past, and the truest *honour* being indeed for a man to confer *honour* on himself' (lines 13–15; emphasis restored from original). Expressed with that sturdy independence of spirit which finds another voice in the satiric scorn of Bosola, this too is to be a theme of the play, whose female hero becomes a figure cut (as Middleton expresses it) with her own merit from enduring marble, while the mighty edifice of her brothers' pride is reduced to a 'great ruin', an empty relic of time past:

[BOSOLA]. I do glory
That thou, which stoodest like a huge pyramid
Begun upon a large and ample base,
Shalt end in a little point, a kind of nothing.
(V. v. 76–9)

These wretched eminent things
Leave no more fame behind 'em than should one
Fall in a frost, and leave his print in snow;
As soon as the sun shines, it ever melts
Both form and matter. (V. v. 113–17)

As it happens, the themes highlighted by the play's prefatory material are also central to a long funeral poem which Webster is known to have composed at about the same time as *The Duchess of Malfi*—his elegy for King James's eldest son, entitled *A Monumental*

Columne. The two are very much companion pieces. Like the play, the poem is a meditation on the transience of worldly pride, and a celebration of the Fame that the memorializing genius of poetry alone can render immortal:

> And though he died so late, he's no more near
> To us, than they that died three thousand year
> Before him; only memory doth keep
> Their *Fame* as fresh as his from death or sleep.
>
> (lines 120–3)[11]

The elegy expresses a contempt for worldly greatness in lines strikingly reminiscent of Delio's epitaph for *Malfi*'s 'wretched eminent things':

> O greatness! what shall we compare thee to?
> To giants, beasts, or towers fram'd out of snow,
> Or like wax-gilded tapers, more for show
> Than durance? Thy foundation doth betray
> Thy frailty, being builded on such clay.
> This shows the all-controlling power of Fate,
> That all our sceptres and our chairs of state
> Are but glass-metal, that we are full of spots.
>
> (lines 109–16)

If play and poem share important themes and images, that is perhaps only because Prince Henry's death—which the dramatist still recalled with painful nostalgia twelve years later in his civic pageant *Monuments of Honour*—seems to have supplied the emotional impulse for this most elegiac of Jacobean tragedies.[12] But, since *A Monumental Columne*, entered on the Stationers' Register in late December 1612, and published in 1613, was almost certainly in print by the time of *The Duchess of Malfi*'s first performance,[13] it is even possible that more-discriminating members of the audience were expected to pick up echoes of Webster's elegy in his new tragedy. The melancholy ambiguity of the Duchess's betrothal kiss ('Being now my steward, here upon your lips | I sign

[11] Citations from *A Monumental Columne* are to F. L. Lucas's edition of Webster's *Works*, 4 vols. (London: Chatto & Windus, 1927), iii. 267–92.

[12] For a similar view, see M. C. Bradbrook, *John Webster, Citizen and Dramatist* (London: Weidenfeld & Nicolson, 1980), 3, 144, 147, 163.

[13] See *The Duchess of Malfi*, ed. John Russell Brown, The Revels Plays (London: Methuen, 1964), pp. xvii–xviii, for discussion of the dating of the two works.

your *Quietus est*'; I. i. 467–8) would have had a deeper and more ominous resonance for those who remembered Webster's picture of a dying Prince who

> in such joy did all his senses steep
> As great accountants (troubled much in mind)
> When they hear news of their *Quietus* sign'd.
> (*A Monumental Columne*, lines 218–20[14])

Even more strikingly, when the admiring Antonio says of the Duchess in the play's opening scene 'She stains the time past, lights the time to come' (I. i. 119), it is almost as though he were being made to quote prophetically from a poem whose vision of transcendence he will help to fulfil; for his line is directly borrowed from the visionary passage in *A Monumental Columne* which salutes the Prince as

> Young, grave *Maecenas* of the noble arts,
> Whose beams shall break forth from thy hollow tomb,
> Stain the time past, and light the time to come!
> (lines 276–8)

The intertextual homage marks the Duchess and Antonio with the language of epitaph—as if their love were inscribed from the beginning with the signs of mortal ending. But it also anticipates the symbolism of transcendence associated with that strange moment in the Echo scene when indeed 'beams . . . break forth from [the Duchess's] hollow tomb' to announce the persistence of her fame amid the darkness of time's ruin.[15] The odd sense that *Malfi* is in

[14] A further parallel with *The Duchess of Malfi* occurs at lines 162–5, where the presentation of Sorrow as a banished galley-slave and a victim of 'court delays' recalls both Bosola's condition at the beginning of the play and the Duchess's speech at IV. ii. 27–30.

[15] Recent historicist readings of Shakespeare's *The Winter's Tale*, linking its statue scene to the circumstances of both Henry's investiture and his death two years later, may point to even more publicly accessible connections between the play and the dead Prince. Glynne Wickham, in 'Romance and Emblem', for example, has proposed that *The Winter's Tale* should be read as an entertainment for the investiture of the Prince, arguing that Hermione's statue alludes to the monument for Mary, Queen of Scots, which James installed in Westminster Abbey to complete his emblematic celebration of the Union; alternatively, David Bergeron's 'The Restoration of Hermione in *The Winter's Tale*', in Carol McGinnis Kay and Henry M. Jacobs (eds.), *Shakespeare's Romances Reconsidered* (Lincoln: University of Nebraska Press, 1978), 125–33, argues that the resurrection of Hermione

part an extension of Webster's monumentalizing tribute to the hero of English Protestants seems to be confirmed by the way in which the ruling conceit of the Echo scene is borrowed from his fellow elegiast George Wither; for among the poems in Wither's *Prince Henry's Obsequies* is one in which the allegorical figure of 'Great Britain' summons the dead Prince to 'rise' from his tomb, and is answered, exactly as Antonio is, by the Prince's spirit in the form of '*Echo's* most unperfect voice'.[16]

As its title suggests, *A Monumental Columne* offers itself, like *Malfi*, as a chaste alternative to the pompous memorials of 'wretched eminent things':

> And by these signs of love let great men know,
> That sweet and generous favour they bestow
> Upon the Muses, never can be lost:
> For they shall live by them, when all the cost
> Of gilded monuments shall fall to dust.
>
> (*A Monumental Columne*, lines 317–21)

Just as the Duchess's tomb is located amid a prospect of ruins, so Henry's burial, in the poet's fancy, reduces the architecture of worldly pride to ruinous collapse:

> Time was when churches in the land were thought
> Rich jewel-houses, and this age hath b[r]ought

was added in the course of revision in 1613 and was meant as a response to the public grief surrounding Henry's death. Bergeron even argues that Hermione's statue was probably mounted 'on some kind of tomb device' (p. 129). *The Winter's Tale* may have been revised for its performance at Princess Elizabeth's Wedding in the spring of 1613; and the connection between the two plays is strengthened by the possibility that Webster's Masque of Madmen in IV. ii drew on wedding masques written for the same occasion; see Brown's intro. to the Revels edition, pp. xxxvi–xxxvii. Bergeron's description of the pageant-resurrection of Lord Mayor Farringdon in Munday's *The Triumphs of Golde* (1611) provides an interesting analogue for both plays. A link between Hermione's statue and the waxwork figures of *Malfi* is suggested by both David Bergeron, 'The Wax Figures', 332–3, and Joan M. Lord, '*The Duchess of Malfi*: "The Spirit of Greatness" and "of Woman"', *Studies in English Literature*, 16 (1976), 305–17: 312–13. In the light of these readings it becomes attractive to see *The Duchess of Malfi* as a specific response to the death of Webster's hero, in which the monument of a murdered prince is once again mysteriously animated, but this time in a setting more fitted to funeral than to revels.

[16] George Wither, 'A Supposed Inter-locution between the Spirit of Prince *Henry and Great Britain*', in *Juvenilia*, 378–9. The parallel is noted by Brown (intro. to the Revels edition, p. xxxv).

That time again—think not I fain—go view
Henry the Seventh's Chapel, and you'll find it true.
The dust of a rich diamond's there enshrin'd
To buy which thence, would beggar the *West-Inde.*
What a dark night-piece of tempestuous weather
Have the enraged clouds summon'd together,
As if our loftiest palaces should grow
To ruin, since such highness fell so low!

(lines 289–98)

The brilliance of this 'rich diamond' set against a 'dark night-piece'—an image for the Prince that recalls a key line from Webster's self-proclaimed theatrical 'night-piece' *The White Devil*: 'Through darkness diamonds spread their richest light' (V. vi. 299; III. ii. 294)—helps to elucidate the chain of associations that link the image of the Duchess as diamond (*Malfi*, I. i. 308–9) with the symbolic chiaroscuro of the night scene at her tomb.

'The figure cut in alabaster'

If the straightforward social didacticism of *A Monumental Columne* provides a particularly useful gloss on *Malfi*'s double catastrophe, it is important to recognize that the emblematic power of the final act is not significantly dependent upon its recollections of the elegy, for it builds upon an internal system of imagery, both linguistic and theatrical, whose remarkable density and consistency was long ago demonstrated by Hereward Price.[17] In particular, the central contrast between the Duchess's living monument and the ruinous 'dead walls [and] vaulted graves' of Bosola's despairing imagination, between her illuminated tomb and his 'shadow, or deep pit of darkness' (V. v. 97–8, 101), completes a pattern of figurative prolepsis which can be traced back to the very beginning of the play.

On the level of theatrical spectacle, this pattern includes two pageant properties—the waxwork figures, representing the dead bodies of Antonio and his children, with which the Duchess is tormented in prison (IV. i), and the altar of Our Lady of Loreto, which is the setting for the Cardinal's ominous rite of military

[17] 'The Function of Imagery in Webster'.

initiation and the ensuing banishment of the Duchess and her family (III. iv). These displays are associatively linked to the Duchess's tomb, not only because of the morphological resemblance between altars and Renaissance funeral monuments,[18] but because the 'sad spectacle' of the waxworks will inevitably have recalled the waxwork figures (themselves resembling the painted marbles of tomb sculpture) which were displayed on hearses at important funerals and subsequently put on display in 'death's cathedral palaces' as companion attractions to the tombs of the great.[19] But, as we have already seen, the proleptic pattern is initiated much earlier—on the verbal level at that moment in I. i when Antonio's eulogy of the Duchess supplies what will amount to a prophetic motto for the Echo scene ('She stains the time past, lights the time to come'). The funereal resonances of this quotation from *A Monumental Columne* are given startling emphasis by the mood of morbid anticipation in which the Duchess's courtship of Antonio is conducted.

The apparent caprice that prompts the young widow to disguise her wooing as the making of a will (I. i. 383) may be read as an attempt to laugh off the anxieties aroused by her brother's threats, but it activates a sequence of nervous badinage whose suggestiveness only renders the anxieties more intense. When Antonio attempts to redirect her conceit, urging her to 'provide for a good husband' by giving herself in marriage (line 394), she turns the jest back on him with the query 'In a winding sheet?' (line 396), playing with

[18] Although the author ostentatiously 'disclaim[ed] this Ditty to be his', the song sung at the altar underlines the connection by making the Cardinal's installation as a soldier into a pageant of Fame: 'Arms and honour deck thy story, | To thy fame's eternal glory. . . . Victory attend thee nigh, whilst fame sings loud thy powers, | Triumphant conquest crown thy head, and blessing pour down showers' (*Malfi*, III. iv. 7–22).

[19] For the possibility that the King's Men made use of the same waxwork sculptor, Abraham Venderdorf, who provided the 'very curiouslie wrought' wax funeral effigy for Prince Henry's hearse, see Bergeron, 'The Restoration of Hermione', 132. The popularity of these waxwork figures, along with tombs and monuments, as objects of resort is evidenced later in the century by Walter Pope's *The Life of Seth Lord Bishop of Salisbury* (London, 1697), 1557: 'It is a custom for the servants of the church upon all holidays, *Sundays* excepted, betwixt the sermon and evening prayers, to shew the tombs, and effigies of the Kings and Queens in wax, to the meaner sort of people, who then flock thither from all the corners of the town, and pay their twopence to see *The Play of the Dead Volks*, as I have heard a *Devonshire* Clown not improperly call it' (cited by John Barnard, in his New Mermaid edition of George Etherege, *The Man of Mode* (London: Ernest Benn, 1979), 42).

the familiar imagery of erotic death in a way that, like Desdemona's request to Emilia, disturbingly recalls the contemporary fashion for women to be buried in their wedding-sheets.[20] The emotional climax of this episode is reached in a speech that not only prefigures the ritualized kneeling of the Duchess's death but directly anticipates the monumental spectacle of Act V, scene iii:

> Make not your heart so dead a piece of flesh
> To fear, more than to love me. Sir, be confident,
> What is't distracts you? This is flesh, and blood, sir,
> 'Tis not the figure cut in alabaster
> Kneels at my husband's tomb. (I. i. 455–9)

Antonio himself picks up her impassioned comparison and gives it an elegant complimentary twist—'I will remain the constant | Sanctuary of your good name' (lines 464–5)—presenting himself as a kind of living memorial to her fame. But this courtly gesture is subtly discomposed by a second ominous echo of *A Monumental Columne* in the quietus which his mistress signs upon his lips—a gesture that anticipates the '*perfect peace*' signed for the Duchess herself in the dirge with which Bosola announces her death at the terminal hour of midnight: ''Tis now full tide 'tween night and day, | End your groan, and come away' (IV. ii. 185, 194–5). In a scene of spousals, whose ceremonial language is often closer to that of funeral than of holy matrimony, even small verbal details—such as when the Duchess begs to 'shroud' her blushes in her husband's bosom—can develop baleful overtones; while gestures such as Antonio's kneeling before his mistress (I. i. 420, 477) acquire quite new meanings when set beside the Duchess's invocation of the kneeling statuary on tombs (Fig. 25).

One effect of this patterning is to highlight the way in which the scenes of the Duchess's torture and murder (IV. i–ii), with their dirges, charnel imagery, and clustered allusions to tombs and monumental sculpture, are at once a reversal and an ominous consummation of the wooing. To Cariola, at the beginning of the death scene, the Duchess resembles 'some reverend monument | Whose ruins are even to be pitied' (IV. ii. 33–4), as if her sufferings had already begun her metamorphosis into that effigy of pious widowhood whose cold embrace she had sought to escape in the wooing

[20] See Gittings, *Death, Burial and the Individual*, 111–12.

scene—a metamorphosis which will be symbolically completed at the point of death when she self-consciously mimics the alabaster figure's kneeling posture:

> heaven gates are not so highly arch'd
> As princes' palaces; they that enter there
> Must go upon their knees.
>
> (IV. ii. 232–4)

'Heaven gates' here are literally the portals of the grave, the tomb which the Duchess must exchange for the high-roofed palace to which she once elevated her steward-husband; and her lines hark insistently back to the complimentary flourish with which she first raised the kneeling Antonio to her side:

> Sir,
> This goodly roof of yours is too low built,
> I cannot stand upright in't, nor discourse,
> Without I raise it higher.
>
> (I. i. 415–18)

By its exact and ceremonious reversal of the earlier ritual, her dying gesture becomes more than a sign of simple Christian humility; it is an emblematic recapitulation of one of the play's most insistent themes, the opposition of the monuments of true fame to the ephemeral architecture of worldly greatness.[21]

'Hearts are hollow graves'

In themselves, of course, tombs and monuments are deeply equivocal devices; and Webster's imagery constantly exploits their doubleness. While they may serve as images of fame's triumph over death, they can equally (as their inscriptions frequently remind us) act as warnings against the instability of all worldly achievement. In *Ancient Funerall Monuments*, John Weever expatiated at length upon the calculated ambiguity through which epitaphs could simultaneously offer love to the deceased, tributes to their

[21] Ironically enough Ferdinand, in his parable of Reputation, Love, and Death, ends by implicitly identifying himself with Reputation (III. ii. 130–6). The memorial function of the play is also noted by Bradbrook: 'If an overarching fable were to be sought for the whole play, it could be called a Masque of Good Fame' (*John Webster*, 164). Cf. Bergeron, 'The Wax Figures', 336.

fame, and comfort to friends, whilst putting the reader 'in mind of human frailty'. The very Latin name for a tomb, he claimed, pointed to its double aspect, since *sepulchra* was to be derived from *semi-pulchra*—'half fair and beautiful: the external part or superficies thereof being beautified and adorned, and having nothing within, but dreadfull darkness, loathsome stink, and rottenness of bones'; yet at the same time tombs were 'called by S. Paul, *Seminatio*, in the respect of the assured hope of resurrection'.[22] This was part of the point made by those strange double-decker monuments which juxtaposed their splendid portrait sculptures with hideous *transi* cadavers; and Webster produces a similar effect by constantly switching attention from the 'fair marble colours' (V. ii. 294) of funerary monuments to the rottenness concealed in the grave beneath them. In accordance with this scheme of imagistic contrast, even the Duchess's gorgeous palace, transformed by turns to prison and madhouse, is reduced to a kind of charnel. The 'inconstant | And rotten ground of service' which Antonio finds in it (III. ii. 198–9) suggests a graveyard; while for the Duchess it becomes a kind of reliquary for her living remains—

Why should only I,
Of all the other princes of the world
Be cas'd up, like a holy relic?
(III. ii. 137–9)

—an image which springs to grotesque life in her description of Antonio's farewell kiss as 'colder | Than that I have seen an holy anchorite | Give to a dead man's skull' (III. v. 85–7).

The sudden appearance of Ferdinand's waxworks in Act IV, scene ii makes of her prison a bizarre funerary chapel, amongst whose crumbling memorials the Duchess herself, with her 'deal of life in show, but none in practice', might find a fitting place 'like some reverend monument | Whose ruins are even pitied' (IV. ii. 32–4). In such a context it is wholly appropriate that among the

[22] Weever, *Ancient Funerall Monuments*, 9. These ambiguities, for Weever, make the tomb especially valuable as an object of pious contemplation; and he even suggests that the contemporary taste for visiting not just the splendid royal monuments in Westminster Abbey, but the ruined and broken tombs in old monasteries, should be construed as a spiritual exercise calculated to 'strike . . . a religious apprehension into the minds of the beholders [and so put them] in mind of . . . mortality, and consequently bring [them] to unfeigned repentance' (p. 41). It is in exactly this spirit that Antonio visits the ruined monastery and its graves in Webster's play.

charivari of madmen sent to her by Ferdinand there is one who was formerly the lecherous sacristan of a royal chapel ('a snuffling knave, that while he shows the tombs will have his hand in a wench's placket'; lines 102–4); and hardly has this morbid grotesque left than Bosola himself enters in the guise of a tomb-maker, an expert in the monumental arts, who satirically instructs the Duchess in the marble fashions of the grave:

> Princes' images on their tombs
> Do not lie, as they were wont, seeming to pray
> Up to heaven, but with their hands under their cheeks,
> As if they died of the tooth-ache. They are not carved
> With their eyes fixed upon the stars, but as
> Their minds were wholly bent upon the world,
> The self-same way they seem to turn their faces.
>
> (IV. ii. 156–62)

With her brothers' gifts of 'coffin, cords and a bell' and Bosola's 'talk fit for a charnel' (lines 165–6), the palace is converted to a place of 'mortification' in its most literal sense:

> Call upon our dame, aloud,
> And bid her quickly don her shroud.
> Much you had of land and rent;
> Your length in clay's now competent.
> A long war disturbed your mind;
> Here your perfect peace is signed.
>
> (IV. ii. 180–5)

This dirge speaks the language of epitaph, as though the Duchess were already dead. But, like Weever's epitaphs, Bosola's weirdly alienated performance is ambivalent, its hallucinatory sequence of transformations, from tomb-maker, to bellman, to executioner, reflecting the profound inner conflict of a murderer who has insisted that his last business with his victim 'shall be comfort' (IV. i. 136). It serves to confer a kind of ritual dignity upon the Duchess's murder that is essential to the monumentalizing of her end. The tableau which Bosola helps the Duchess to compose at her death is modelled upon the images of those pious Princes whom he describes as 'seeming to pray | Up to heaven . . . with their eyes fixed upon the stars'. Ceremoniously putting off her 'last woman's fault' to welcome her end ('Come, violent death, | Serve for mandragora to make me sleep'; lines 234–5), the Duchess comes to resemble a Christianized version of Cleopatra, subsuming her own murder in an artifice of self-fashioning whose magnificence is inseparable from its humility ('they that enter there | Must go upon their knees'; lines 233–4). Where Bussy D'Ambois dies standing, in the attitude of a Roman statue, and Cleopatra's 'marble' self is fittingly disposed upon a regal bed, the Duchess faces her martyrdom in the kneeling posture of the obedient wife carved upon her first husband's tomb, but converts that image of domestic piety into a martyr's gesture of heroic singularity. It is a gesture whose full meaning, as we shall see, will be disclosed in the monumental apotheosis of the Echo scene.

If the Duchess is associated with the eternizing artifice of tombs, Webster's imagery with equal insistence links Bosola and the Aragonian brothers to the corruptions of the grave. For Bosola in his vein of melancholy satire, the body is not the lofty palace the Duchess's metaphor made of it, but a vessel of mortal corruption, given the false semblance of life by the bravery of its decoration:

> Though we are eaten up of lice, and worms,
> And though continually we bear about us
> A rotten and dead body, we delight
> To hide it in rich tissue: all our fear,
> Nay, all our terror, is lest our physician
> Should put us in the ground to be made sweet.
>
> (II. i. 62–7)

And this conceit gives a peculiarly concrete nastiness to his moral denunciations of Ferdinand and the Cardinal: 'You have a pair of hearts are hollow graves, | Rotten and rotting others' (IV. ii. 317–18). The heart is as secret as the grave; but, like the secrets of the grave, the mysteries contained in its fleshly casket are, in the last analysis, only the grim truths of vermicular corruption. The Cardinal, with sadistic irony, finds in the painted body of his mistress, Julia, 'a grave dark and obscure enough' to keep the secret of his complicity in the Duchess's murder (V. ii. 270). For Ferdinand, his sister's remarriage is a stroke which reduces his own body to a sepulchre in which his heart is concealed:

> thou hast ta'en that massy sheet of lead
> That hid thy husband's bones, and folded it
> About my heart. (III. ii. 113–5)

As that telling 'hid' suggests, this is an image of secrecy as well as of morbidity: and what is hidden will not be fully revealed until, after the Duchess's death, 'The wolf shall find her grave, and scrape it up' (v. ii. 307).

The wolf is to be none other than the demented Ferdinand himself, and the grave he violates is a figure for his own morbid psyche. The symptoms show his lycanthropy to be a monstrous literalization not just of his passionate animality, but of his terrifying compulsion to exhume the secret corruptions of his hidden self:

In those that are possessed with't there o'erflows
Such melancholy humour, they imagine
Themselves to be transformed into wolves,
Steal forth to churchyards in the dead of night
And dig dead bodies up: as two nights since
One met the Duke, 'bout midnight in a lane
Behind St Mark's church, with the leg of a man
Upon his shoulder; and he howled fearfully,
Said he was a wolf; only the difference
Was, a wolf's skin was hairy on the outside,
His on the inside. (v. ii. 8–18)

The inverted wolfskin is an image both of secret viciousness and (in its recollection of the penitent's hair shirt) of the inward suffering that ensues from it. The imaginative connection between the horrors hidden in the grave and those concealed within himself is underlined in the anatomical grotesquerie of the Duke's injunction to his followers, bidding them 'take their swords, | Rip up his flesh, and try' (lines 18–19).

In *Troilus and Cressida* appetite was figured as a 'universal wolf' doomed in the end to 'eat up himself'. Ferdinand's incestuous desire for his sister issues in a similarly wolfish frenzy of self-cancellation, enacted for the audience in a bizarre stage action, when he throws himself upon his own shadow in the conviction that it is following him with malign intent: 'I will throttle it' (line 38). 'My lord,' Malateste rebukes him, 'you are angry with nothing,' making his fury seem like an uncanny realization of Antonio's melancholy reflection 'Heaven fashioned us of nothing; and we strive | To bring ourselves to nothing' (III. v. 79–80). If Ferdinand tries to strangle his dark shadow self, the Cardinal discovers his own reflection menacing him from the garden fishponds, a mortal double armed with the diabolic rake that parodies his pastoral crozier

(v. v. 5–7).[23] In each case the *Gefehrt* becomes a figure for the self-devouring appetite whose logic Ferdinand glimpses in the instant of clarity before his death: 'Whether we fall by ambition, blood, or lust, | Like diamonds we are cut with our own dust' (v. v. 72–3). 'Dust' here is primarily a metonymy for the sinful nature of humanity, but uttered as Ferdinand's last word it is bound to suggest the dust to which his body is about to be consigned; it signals that same ignoble collapse into the undifferentiation of the grave that Bosola, with grim satisfaction, announces for the Cardinal:

I do glory
That thou, which stoodest like a huge pyramid
Begun upon a large and ample base,
Shalt end in a little point, a kind of nothing.
(v. v. 77–80)

Bosola's irony is fiercely exacting, since a pyramid was the conventional type of those proud monuments by which the mighty sought to rescue themselves for ever from the indistinction of death: but his neat inversion turns the pyramid's aspiring top into a sign for the annihilation of a man whose dearest longing is now oblivion: 'I pray, let me | Be laid by, and never thought of' (lines 89–90). The 'fortification' which embodies the Cardinal's worldly power 'grew', we are told, 'from the ruins of an ancient abbey' (v. iii. 1–2); and those ruins (as well standing for the pious ecclesiastical history that provides the ironic foundation for his vicious authority) emblematize both the decayed 'relics of time past' on which 'the ancientest nobility' depends, and the dusty nothing to which his pomp must be reduced. As for Bosola—himself unable to distinguish, in the 'deep pit of darkness' to which the world is reduced by the Duchess's death, between hated enemies and 'The man I would have saved 'bove mine own life' (v. iv. 52)—he has already begun to see himself as no better than the 'common bier' of a universal graveyard (v. iii. 309). The heroic tautology in which he takes refuge after the inadvertent killing of Antonio ('I'll be mine own example'; v. iv. 81) is only a desperate prelude for his surrender to the utter indifference of the earth: 'We are only like dead walls, or vaulted graves | That ruined, yields no echo' (v. v. 97–8).

Ironically enough, however, 'echo' here is itself an echo of a

[23] See above, Ch. 1 n. 61.

most potent kind. It reminds us that just before the final apocalyptic slaughter, the action of *The Duchess of Malfi* (like that of *Hamlet*) has come to a brief meditative rest in an actual cemetery. But, where in Hamlet's graveyard the dead remained obstinately silent, animated only by the desperate ventriloquy of the Prince, here they speak: in Antonio's charnel the liveliest presence is the voice of Echo, issuing like the 'clear light' of fame from his Duchess's tomb. Antonio's and Delio's pilgrimage of melancholy reflection amongst the graves and ruins is clearly designed in symbolic counterpoint to Ferdinand's wild desecration of the churchyard. Both are grave-openings of a kind, anxious reworkings of the *visitatio sepulchri* in the Mystery Plays, in which the idea of resurrection is successively parodied and then (in a new secular fashion) triumphantly enacted. To the 'dazzled' Ferdinand, with his 'cruel sore eyes' (IV. ii. 263; V. ii. 62) the grave offers up images of darkness and horror, tokens of that violated past which so haunts him; to Antonio it shows a luminous image of compassionate sorrow which 'lights the time to come'. For him then, if not for Bosola, it is as if the Duchess's 'fair soul' is indeed able to 'return . . . from darkness' to lead him 'Out of this sensible hell' (IV. ii. 340–1).

The full meaning of the Echo scene is shaped by Antonio's moralization on the ruined abbey—a setting whose poignant spectacle of violated glories and defaced memorials belongs not to the play's nominal Italian setting, but to a peculiarly English post-Reformation context (the same that produced Shakespeare's Sonnet 73 and John Weever's anxious reflections on the decay of funeral monuments):

I do love these ancient ruins.
We never tread upon them, but we set
Our foot upon some ancient history.
And, questionless, here in this open court,
Which now lies naked to the injuries
Of stormy weather, some men lie interred
Loved the church so well, and gave so largely to't,
They thought it should have canopied their bones
Till doomsday. But all things have their end:
Churches and cities, which have diseases like to men,
Must have like death that we have.

(V. iii. 9–19)

Here images of ruin and tomb come together to provide an emblem of vanity ('all things have their end'), its ironies redoubled (as in the *Hamlet* graveyard scene) by Antonio's ignorance of who lies buried in this cemetery. When the mysterious Echo strikes into his thoughts with 'Like death that we have', it rings the admonitory note of an epitaph ('As I am now so shalt thou be . . .'); yet paradoxically its 'deadly accent', in sounding to Antonio 'like my wife's voice' (line 26), challenges the simple *memento mori* with its grim annihilation of differences, and, by restoring the memory of the Duchess, translates the signs of mortal corruption into the transcendental symbolism of monument.

Finis coronat opus

In *The Duchess of Malfi*, then, the encounter with death becomes an occasion for working out the defiant social attitudes articulated in Webster's dedicatory epistle—his disdain for a 'nobility' founded on nothing more than the decayed relics of 'time past'; his insistence on an art of moral self-fashioning through which (in Middleton's phrase) 'every worthy man [becomes] his own marble'. The subversive inflexion which Webster's careless tone ('I do not altogether look up . . .') gives to what otherwise might seem merely a reformulation of an ancient debate—whether birth or virtue is the true foundation of honour—is borne out (and complicated) by the decision to make the principal vehicle of his argument a woman who self-consciously dresses her defiance of both rank and gender norms in the heroic rhetoric of male chivalry:

as men in some great battles
By apprehending danger, have achieved
Almost impossible actions: I have heard soldiers say so,—
So I, through frights and threatenings, will assay
This dangerous venture. . . .
Wish me good speed,
For I am going to a wilderness,
Where I shall find nor path, nor friendly clue
To be my guide. (I. i. 351–5, 365–8)

At one extreme of its social argument, the play sets the caste pride of the Aragonian brothers, for whom their sister's marriage of disparagement unpardonably taints 'our blood | The royal blood of Aragon and Castile' (II. iv. 21–2); at the other extreme it places the sardonic levelling of Bosola, who (like many an alienated Jacobean intellectual) has made his Montaigne into a bible of degraded scepticism:[24]

a duke was your cousin-german, removed. Say you were descended from King Pippin, or he himself, what of this? Search the heads of the greatest rivers in the world, you shall find them but bubbles of water. Some would think the souls of princes were brought forth by some more weighty causes than those of meaner persons. They are deceived, there's the same hand to them; the like passions sway them; the same reason that makes a vicar go to law for a tithe-pig and undo his neighbours makes them spoil a whole province, and batter down goodly cities with the cannon. (II. i. 104–15)

Setting aside its openly contemptuous tone, this is remarkably close to the attitudes of Webster's dedication, but Bosola's cynicism is like Thersites': in its insistence on the sameness of motive behind all human behaviour it threatens a plague of indistinction. It is in part Bosola's activity which brings Antonio to the despairing perception that 'The great are like the base; nay, they are the same' (II. ii. 136); just as it is Bosola who undercuts the Duchess's last attempts to proclaim her royal self, with its echo of Anthony's heroical 'I am | Anthony yet' (*A&C* III. xiii 92–3):

DUCHESS. Am not I thy Duchess?
BOSOLA. Thou art some great woman sure; for riot begins to sit on thy forehead (clad in grey hairs) twenty years sooner than on a merry milkmaid's . . . .
DUCHESS. I am Duchess of Malfi still.
BOSOLA. That makes thy sleeps so broken:
Glories, like glow-worms, afar off shine bright,
But look'd to near, have neither heat nor light.

(IV. ii. 259–60)

Yet it is precisely at this moment that Bosola chooses to cast himself in the ambiguous role of a tomb-maker whose 'trade is to flatter the dead' (line 147). And there is another side to Bosola's satiric malice, which emerges, curiously enough, in the course of

[24] Brown's edition (p. 45) identifies the borrowing from Florio's translation of the *Essays* (II. xii).

his attempt to persuade the Duchess to betray the identity of her husband. When she seeks to parry his effusive praise of Antonio with an evasive 'But he was basely descended' (III. ii. 258), Bosola comes back with what at first appears to be a piece of stock moralization, culled from the pages of Sidney's *Arcadia*: 'Will you make yourself a mercenary herald, | Rather to examine men's pedigrees than virtues?' (III. ii. 260–1). But the sentiment answers closely to a rankling sense of neglect in the world of courtly reward which is not at all feigned; and it is this which fuels his subsequent reflections upon Antonio's fate with an emotion powerful enough to overwhelm the Duchess's natural caution. Her confession—'Oh, you render me excellent music . . . | This good one that you speak of is my husband' (lines 275–6)—while it tells the court informer exactly what he wants to know, at the same time deals a crippling blow to his cynical composure. His reply registers genuine wonder, an emotion compounded of astonishment at this profound shock to his habitual construction of the world, as well as the simple excitement of discovery:

> Do I not dream? can this ambitious age
> Have so much goodness in't as to prefer
> A man merely for worth, without these shadows
> Of wealth, and painted honours? possible?
>
> (III. ii. 277–80)

It is true that there is a degree of comic exaggeration in what follows, as though the old sardonic Bosola were reasserting his ironic control:

> You have made your private nuptial bed
> The humble and fair seminary of peace.
> No question but many an unbeneficed scholar
> Shall pray for you, for this deed. . . .
> The virgins of your land,
> That have no dowries, shall hope your example
> Will raise them to rich husbands. Should you want
> Soldiers, 'twould make the very Turks and Moors
> Turn Christians, and serve you for this act.
>
> (III. ii. 282–91)

But it is important, if Bosola's subsequent conversion is to seem convincingly motivated, that the irony be understood for what it is—self-mockery directed at an emotion as dangerous as it is unfamiliar.[25] Perhaps the clearest pointer to such a reading is the way in which Bosola is made to end his speech with a version of the very theme announced in Webster's dedication:

> Last, the neglected poets of your time,
> In honour of this trophy of a man,
> Raised by that curious engine, your white hand,
> Shall thank you in your grave for't; and make that
> More reverend than all the cabinets
> Of living princes. For Antonio,
> His fame shall likewise flow from many a pen,
> When heralds shall want coats, to sell to men.
>
> (III. ii. 291–8)

For the audience, the irony is disarmed by Webster's pen; for heraldry in this play is the art and property of madmen:

FIRST MADMAN. I have skill in heraldry.
SECOND MADMAN. Hast?
FIRST MADMAN. You do give for your crest a woodcock's head, with the brains picked out on't. You are a very ancient gentleman.

(IV. ii. 85–90)

That 'spirit of greatness' for which, in Cariola's eyes, her mistress seems to stand (I. i. 505) is best defined, perhaps, in the fable which the Duchess offers to Bosola in the course of her arrest. Her persecutor, in the bitterness of his already divided emotions, turns on Antonio, denouncing him as 'this base, low fellow . . . | One of no birth' (III. v. 116–18); the Duchess responds with a recapitulation of Bosola's own theme:

> Say that he was born mean,
> Man is most happy, when's own actions
> Be arguments and examples of his virtue. . . .
> I prithee, who is greatest? Can you tell?
>
> (III. v. 118–22)

[25] Compare Flamineo's puzzled glimpse of an emotion he has systematically repressed in *The White Devil*: 'I have a strange thing in me, to the which | I cannot give a name, without it be | Compassion (V. iv. 113–15)—where the line-break perfectly represents the slow dawning of reluctant comprehension. Webster's interest in the consequence of unacknowledged or repressed feeling is of course most apparent in his treatment of Ferdinand's incestuous passion for his sister.

She answers her own question with the parable of the salmon and the dogfish; though offered as a defence of Antonio's low birth, it is also a deliberately humble paraphrase upon the old tag *finis coronat opus*; and it looks forward to her own death as the master day by which her life will be judged:

> 'Our value never can be truly known,
> Till in the fisher's basket we be shown;
> I'th'market then my price may be the higher,
> Even when I am nearest to the cook, and fire.'
> So, to great men, the moral may be stretched:
> Men oft are valued high, when th'are most wretched.
>
> (III. v. 135–40)

In fact her moral is precisely that with which Delio, confronted with the 'great ruin' of the house of Aragon, will end the play: 'Integrity of life is fame's best friend, | Which nobly, beyond death, shall crown the end' (V. v. 120–1).[26]

The visible sign of these values, of this ethos of ending, is the Duchess's tomb, whose light of fame illumines the dark world of 'these wretched eminent things'; while the vanity of their illusory 'quest of greatness' is expressed in the 'dead wall, or vaulted graves' of the surrounding ruins, figuring forth the empty pride of that vast pyramid to which Bosola compares the cardinal.[27] But the Duchess's tomb is itself only a theatrical cipher for the true monument which, Webster defiantly asserts, will overtop and outlast all the vain architecture of courtly grandeur. Just as *A Monumental Columne* was meant as a 'shrine' for that 'rich diamond' his beloved

[26] The play's connection with Prince Henry is further strengthened by Webster's paraphrase of these lines in an epitaph attached to the final section of *Monuments of Honour*, the Monument of Gratitude, which is dedicated to the dead Prince:

> Such was this Prince, such are the noble hearts,
> Who when they die, yet die not in all parts:
> But from the *integrity* of a brave mind,
> Leave a most clear and eminent fame behind.
>
> (*Works*, 327)

[27] Lord, '*The Duchess of Malfi*', 316, makes a similar point: 'It is only from the Duchess's grave that an echo is heard . . . for her memory still reverberates in the minds of those who are left.'

Prince Henry, so his *Duchess of Malfi* becomes the finely embellished tomb from which the echo of his heroine's memory sounds:[28] 'For they shall live by them, when all the cost | Of gilded Monuments shall fall to dust' (lines 320–1).

[28] Compare Webster's afterword to *The White Devil*, where the *finis coronat opus* trope is said to have been embodied in the very performance of the tragedy through the 'industry' of the actor Perkins, 'the worth of [whose] action did crown both the beginning and end'.

11

'Great arts best write themselves in their own stories': Ending *The Broken Heart*

> Our present life is but the entrance and end of a tragedy, a perpetual issue of errors, a web of unhappy adventures, a pursuit of divers miseries enchained together on all sides... The day of death is the master day, and judge of all other days, the trial and touchstone of all the actions of our life. Then do we make our greatest assay, and gather the whole fruit of all our studies. He that judgeth of the life of a man, must look how he carrieth himself at his death; for the end crowneth the work, and a good death honoureth a man's whole life.
>
> (Pierre Charron, *Of Wisdome*[1])

John Ford was among the small group of theatre poets who expressed their admiration for Webster's tragic 'monument' in the encomiastic verses that greeted the publication of *The Duchess of Malfi* in 1623; and a few years later he was to return to its controlling metaphor in what was probably the earliest of his own tragedies, *The Broken Heart* (*c.*1627–31).[2] Like *Malfi*, *The Broken Heart* was written for the King's Men; but in its celebration of courtly values it represents a marked ideological shift from the play that helped to inspire it. In Ford's play funereal art is reinvested with all its traditional hierarchic symbolism:

> lastly
> We slip down in the common earth together.

[1] Charron, *Of Wisdome*, 121, 345–6.

[2] *The Broken Heart* was published exactly ten years after *Malfi*, in 1633; its exact date of composition is uncertain, but it appears to be the latest of three plays that Ford wrote for the King's Men between 1627–31.

And there our beds are equal, save some monument
To show this was the king, and this the subject.

(IV. iii. 137–9[3])

But here, where the plangent elegance of the poet's style becomes a figure for the emotional restraint of the aristocratic culture it celebrates, the monumental idea is no longer represented by an actual stage property. Thus the grave self-referential wit with which Webster transforms the Duchess's miraculously illuminated tomb into a figure for his own tragic design has no exact equivalent in Ford's tragedy. Instead it is matched by an even more self-conscious preoccupation with the eternizing artifice of poetry: it is as if the characters themselves can already discern, in the carefully ritualized spectacles through which they fashion their own ends, the lineaments of that 'high-tuned poem' through which their heroic endurance will be preserved for all posterity. Their self-perfecting aesthetic of death is given peculiar emphasis through the carefully graduated sequence of endings that crowns the play's action. *The Broken Heart* vies with the carefully divided catastrophes of *Anthony and Cleopatra* and *The Duchess of Malfi* by offering no fewer than four 'final' scenes, each one treating with weight and dignity the death of a major character who has some claim to be regarded as the protagonist of the play—Penthea, Ithocles, Orgilus, and Calantha.

For all the ceremonious solemnity of the Ford's style, there is a deliberate virtuosity about this parade of contrasting ends, which is wholly consistent with the dramatist's experimental approach to the orchestration of tragic closure. The last scene of *'Tis Pity She's a Whore*, for example, is a bizarrely extravagant reworking of the Jacobean revenger's apocalypse, in which the demented emblem that Giovanni makes of his sister's eviscerated heart brutally deconstructs the Websterian figure-in-action.[4] The tainted theatricality of Giovanni's 'last and greater part' (*'Tis Pity*, V. v. 106) contrasts powerfully with the heroic histrionism of the pretender, Perkin Warbeck, whose constancy-in-performance paradoxically turns pretence into the ground of a genuinely regal transcendence which the play itself exemplifies ('So illustrious mention | Shall

[3] All citations are from *The Broken Heart*, ed. Brian Morris, The New Mermaids (London: Ernest Benn, 1965).

[4] See my 'What Strange Riddle's This?', 169–74.

blaze our names, and style us kings o'er death'; *Perkin Warbeck*, v. iii. 207–8)—as though Ford were determined to put the Senecan metaphors of theatrically performed dying to their ultimate test.

Yet another kind of formal extremism is exhibited in the ending of *Love's Sacrifice*, which remodels the tomb scene from *Romeo and Juliet* with a disconcerting combination of emotionalism and witty ingenuity reminiscent of Marston's mannerist style. This play makes use of a species of divided catastrophe in order to increase the sensational effect of its final scene: Duke Caraffa's murder of Biancha early in Act V is followed by an elaborate scene of confrontation scene with her lover, Fernando, which leads (in the Fletcherian fashion) through a series of violent peripeties to the apparent reconciliation of these former friends. This is followed by the denunciation of the 'arch-arch-devil' D'Avolos (whose machinations have helped to produce the crisis), and the Duke's penitent announcement of Biancha's funeral rites:

order straight, Petruchio,
Our Duchess may be coffin'd; 'tis our will
She forthwith be interr'd with all the speed
And privacy you may, i'th' College Church
Amongst Caraffa's ancient monuments.
Some three days hence we'll keep her funeral....
No counsel from our cruel wills can win us;
But ills once done, we bear our guilt within us.

(v. [ii]. 2676–84[5])

In this case, however, the carefully prepared semblance of closure is delusive: for the Iago-like D'Avolos remains on stage to make his sardonic commentary upon the Duke's conclusive gestures, ushering in a further sequence full of surprising reversals. The final scene opens with the 'strange miracle' of Roseilli's undisguising, and the unexpected granting of his erotic suit by the Duke's sister Fiormonda. Roseilli greets this transformation as a metaphoric resurrection ('In death you have reviv'd me'; line 2713); and his conceit is promptly literalized in the course of the spectacular peripety that ensues. The stage direction announces 'A sad sound of soft music. The tomb is discovered'; the Duke enters at the head

[5] Cited from *John Fordes Dramatische Werke*, ed. W. Bang, Materialen zur Kunde des älteren Englischen Dramas, ser. 1, vol. 23 (Louvain: A. Uystpruyst, 1908).

of a torchlit mourning procession to do penance at Biancha's grave, 'making show of ceremony' (lines 2735–40). Ordering the monument opened, in order 'that I may take | My last farewell, and bury griefs with her' (lines 2761–2), he is confronted by the macabre figure of Fernando rising out of the tomb, like the famous portrait of Dr Donne, 'in his winding-sheet, only his face discovered'. With a sly glance at the necrophile excitements of *The Second Maiden's Tragedy*, Fernando denounces Caraffa as a tyrant come 'To practice yet a rape upon the dead',[6] and claims the tomb for his own:

> this place
> Is pointed out for my inheritance:
> Here lies the monument of all my hopes.
>
> (lines 2769–72)

Then, in a final gesture of defiance, he performs his imitation of Romeo's *Liebestod*:

> O royal poyson! trusty friend! . . .
> Feast on, do! Duke, farewell. Thus I—hot flames
> Conclude my love—and seal it in my bosom, oh—
>
> (lines 2804–10)

In this he is instantly followed by Caraffa himself, who makes himself an amatory sacrifice on the 'altar' of his wife's tomb ('Biancha, thus, | I creep to thee—to thee—to thee Bi-an-cha'; lines 2840–41). It remains only for Roseilli to honour their double wedding-in-death with the solace of monumental record:

> we'll rear a tomb
> To those unhappy lovers, which shall tell
> Their fatal loves to all posterity.
>
> (lines 2871–3)

Thus in bewildering succession a funereal ending is followed by a mock-resurrection drawn from the conventions of Jacobean comic catastrophe, only for this resurrection to be undone in turn by a

[6] Ford seems to be building on Act IV of this anonymous tragedy, where the mourning Govianus visits his wife's tomb to find it empty, her corpse having been spirited away by the necrophile Tyrant; Govianus is surprised at his devotions by the entrance of his wife's ghost in a scene touched with echoes of the Resurrection. No doubt the author of this play was himself familiar with Chapman's irreverent treatment of the same motif in *The Widow's Tears*, five years earlier; see my 'Feasts put down Funerals', 47–74.

pair of erotic suicides. This pattern of self-conscious reversals is completed in a solemn anti-wedding, as Roseilli formally dissolves his own betrothal and banishes the conniving Fiormonda from 'the mutual comforts of our marriage-bed' to the austerity of 'the *Bride-bed* in [her] soul' (line 2885).[7]

Written in Ford's chaster Blackfriars style, *The Broken Heart* is more restrained in its approach to the conventions of tragic closure, but makes even more elaborate use of the marriage-in-funeral trope. Like *Romeo and Juliet* and *Anthony and Cleopatra*, it seems peculiarly aware of its anomalous status as a love-tragedy: the plot is framed around the impediments to fulfilment of three love affairs; and in the Bassanes–Penthea–Orgilus triangle it plays with the traditionally comic January and May motif of jealous age misallied to reluctant youth, in a fashion that owes a conspicuous debt to the ridiculous frenzies of Corvino in Jonson's *Volpone*. Moreover, the plot follows the convention of romantic comedy to the extent of frequently seeming to propose marriage as the proper end of its action, even as its central characters seem driven by a kind of death-wish towards the tragic catastrophe. By the end of the play this *nostalgie de la bout* has consumed even the violently jealous Bassanes, whose sad retirement will resound to the mournful notes of funeral:

> Give me some corner of the world to wear out
> The remnant of the minutes I must number,
> Where I may hear no sounds but sad complaints . . .
> of fathers
> Weeping upon their children's slaughtered carcasses;
> Or daughters groaning o'er their father's hearses:
> And I can dwell there, and with these keep consort
> As musical as theirs. (v. iii. 25–35)

In this he has learnt to echo the plaintive tones of his dead wife, Penthea, filled with her yearning for the end:

> In vain we labour in this course of life
> To piece our journey out at length, or crave
> Respite of breath: our home is in the grave.
> (II. iii. 146–8)

[7] For discussion of the curious games with convention involved in this scene, and elsewhere in the play, see the essays by Kate McLuskie and Martin Butler in my *John Ford*, 97–127, 201–31.

Every hair of Penthea's head feels 'like a leaden plummet . . . [which] sinks me to the grave' (IV. ii. 76–8); and her idea of 'comely music' is a part-song of unhappy lovers singing 'one another's knell' (IV. ii. 70–1). Her brother Ithocles, guilty over having forced her loveless marriage and despairing of his own love for Princess Calantha, is touched by similarly morbid fantasies—

> I could wish
> That the first pillow whereon I was cradled
> Had proved to me a grave. . . .
> Death waits to waft me to the Stygian banks,
> And free me from this chaos of my bondage.
>
> (III. ii. 36–8, 90–1)

—whilst Penthea's frustrated lover, Orgilus, instinctively associates the marriage-bed itself with the grave:

> The bed?
> Forfend it Jove's own jealousy!—till lastly
> We slip down in the common earth together.
> And there our beds are equal, save some monument
> To show this was the king, and this the subject.
>
> (IV. iii. 135–9)

Almost from the beginning, indeed, Ford links the ideas of death and wedding, marriage and funeral, as if consciously elaborating the oxymoronic yoking of tragic 'pity' with comic 'delight' that characterizes his prologue.[8] Ithocles' forcing of his sister's marriage to Bassanes makes him, for the disappointed Orgilus, 'a brother | More cruel than the grave' (I. iii.63–4), and leaves Penthea (as Crotolon sees her) 'buried in a bride-bed' (II. ii. 38); Penthea herself thinks of the marriage as a kind of death, since it amounts to a 'Divorce betwixt my body and my heart' (II. iii. 57)—by it she is as if 'turned to marble' (line 62), while Orgilus' appeal to their past love is '*buried* in an everlasting silence' (line 69; emphasis added).[9] The mid-point of the action (in a conspicuous reversal of

[8] For discussion of oxymoron and paradox in the play, see Anne Barton, 'Oxymoron and the Structure of Ford's *The Broken Heart*', *Essays and Studies*, 33 (1980), 70–94; and my own 'Ford's Unbroken Art: The Moral Design of *The Broken Heart*', *Modern Language Review*, 75 (1980), 249–68.

[9] Her figure is echoed in Orgilus' description of the disguise in which he conceals his grief as 'the shroud, in which my cares | Are folded up from view' (II. iii. 49–50).

the tragicomic hourglass structure of Shakespeare's romances) is marked by the ceremonious betrothal of Euphranea and Prophilus and the performance of their 'bridal song' by Orgilus (III. iv. 69 ff.).[10] However, the semblance of comic closure produced by this piece of ritualized action is immediately contradicted through the morbid counter-ritual of the 'will' which Penthea lays out before Calantha. A much more elaborate version of the will conceit that opens the Duchess of Malfi's wooing, this one finds its own way of linking death and marriage: for the last of the three 'jewels' Penthea disposes of, before seeking out the remedy of 'a winding-sheet, a fold of lead, | And some untrod-on corner of the earth' (III. v. 32), is the hand of her own brother Ithocles to be taken by the Princess 'in holiest rites of love' (line 77).

In terms of theatrical convention, Penthea's will has a power of obscure prediction comparable to the prophecies of the Delphic oracle, in whose riddles the destinies of the characters are mysteriously enfolded. With its double stress on funeral and wedding, it sets the play simultaneously on course for a tragic and for a comic end, just as Tecnicus' gnomic gloss upon the oracle's 'dark sentences' invites reading both as a prophecy of Calantha's death, and as the promise of 'Her marriage with some neighbouring prince' (IV. iii. 33)—paradoxes that are only rendered more enigmatic by the philosopher's oracular vision of marriage-in-death, 'The lifeless trunk shall wed the broken heart' (IV. i. 134). In accordance with this pattern, Act IV, scene iii, in which the truth of Tecnicus' riddles is partially disclosed, concludes with 'soft sad music' from Penthea's lodgings, a 'deathful air' which proves indeed to have been her 'funeral song' (IV. iii. 139, 155; IV. iv. 7), though it might easily be mistaken for a love lyric describing the 'little death' of erotic consummation:

now Love dies,
Now Love dies,—implying
Love's martyrs must be ever, ever dying.

(IV. iii. 151–3)

[10] Ford used the same pattern again, this time with a particularly bitter twist, in *'Tis Pity She's a Whore*, where Act IV begins with a feast to celebrate the marriage of Annabella and Soranzo—revels which are bloodily interrupted by Hippolita's masque of revenge.

Penthea's death is quickly followed by those of Ithocles and the King, confirming the imminence of a tragic ending; but it is one that will nevertheless be played out within the convention of romantic comedy. News of all three deaths are brought to Calantha in the course of the celebrated dance scene which crowns the wedding revels of Prophilus and Euphranea; for the Princess's iron insistence upon carrying the dance through to its '*last change*', before ordering immediate preparations for her own coronation, seems designed as much to shape her performance to the poetic decorum of comic closure as to preserve the social decorum of courtly ceremony. The one, indeed, becomes a figure for the other; and the strange formal tensions of the scene are exacerbated by Orgilus' attempt to reshape the 'revels' with 'some new device ... wherein ... Lord Ithocles and he himself are actors (v. ii. 3–5). The successive interventions of Armostes, Bassanes, and Orgilus himself as 'messengers of death' allow the audience to identify this courtly dancing as a weirdly displaced *danse macabre* which only Calantha's defiant 'bravery' transforms into a 'triumph over ruin', matching the heroic 'last act' of her betrothed (v. ii. 41–3):

Oh, my lords,
I but deceived your eyes with antic gesture,
When one news straight came huddling on another
Of death, and death, and death. Still I danced forward;
But it struck home, and here, and in an instant.

(v. iii. 67–71)

If Calantha's last big speech confesses the frailty of the 'antic gesture' with which she confronted the repeated summons of her true dancing-partner, she is as far from repudiating the consolations of artifice as Hans Hug Kluber, the self-monumentalizing painter of the Basel *Tod*. In the play's final scene she goes on to stage her own death as the supreme enactment of the play's theme of dirge-in-marriage, making it at once a rite of coronation, a wedding, and a funeral obsequy:

An altar covered with white; two lights of virgin wax, during which music of recorders; enter four bearing ITHOCLES on a hearse, or in a chair, in a rich robe, and a crown on his head; place him on one side of the altar. After him enter CALANTHA in a white robe and crowned; EUPHRANEA, PHILEMA, CHRISTALLA, in white, NEARCHUS, ARMOSTES, CROTOLON, PROPHILUS, AMELUS, BASSANES, LEMOPHIL, and GRONEAS. CALANTHA goes and kneels before the altar, the rest stand off, the women kneeling behind. Cease recorders, during her devotions. Soft music. CALANTHA and the rest rise, doing obeisance to the altar. (V. iii)

In this unusually elaborate stage direction, Ford's anxiousness about the detail of his setting is apparent even in the telling hesitation of 'on a hearse, or in a chair': while the hearse would clearly be appropriate to the funeral aspect of Calantha's ritual, the chair, as well as recalling the regal chair to which the ailing King Amyclas was confined in IV. iii, would also recall the moment of Ithocles' paradoxical triumph over death, 'catch'd in the engine' which Orgilus ironically describes as 'thy throne of coronation' (IV. iv. 23).[11]

The gravely ceremonious catastrophe of the play is built around a last ingenious variation upon the oxymoronic scheme introduced by Penthea's will, in which Calantha lays down the articles of a nuptial treaty which sound to Bassanes more like 'a testament [than] conditions on a marriage' (V. iii. 53–4)—and fittingly so, since the wedding she intends is not with the Prince of Argos, as all suppose, but with the dead Ithocles, whose hand she will presently claim:

Bear witness all,
I put my mother's wedding-ring upon
His finger; 'twas my father's last bequest.
Thus I new marry him whose wife I am;
Death shall not separate us.
(V. iii. 63–7)

This is Calantha's ceremonial version of Cleopatra's claim to consummation-in-death, 'Husband, I come' (*Anthony and Cleopatra*, V. ii. 86), announcing, in defiance of Petrarch's triumphal sequence,

[11] The chair appears to have been suggested to Ford by the same play that influenced Webster's Echo scene; indeed Calantha's ceremonial entry seems to be closely modelled on the elaborate dumb show early in the final scene of *The Second Maiden's Tragedy*. There the Lady's richly attired corpse is carried into the Tyrant's presence 'in a chair' while music plays, followed by a song ('O, what is beauty that's so much adored?' V. ii. 14–19), whose *memento mori* theme anticipates the song which Calantha has fitted to her end. During the song the soldiers 'make obesiance to [the Lady]' and the Tyrant 'himself makes a low honour and kisses her hand' (line 13) in a gesture that anticipates the last kiss that Calantha plants on Ithocles' cold lips before the performance of her song. At the end of the scene, moreover, the triumphant Govianus honours his wife's body with a ritual that, like Calantha's, combines elements of coronation, wedding, and funeral: 'Here place her in this throne; crown her our queen, | The first and last that ever we make ours. . . . That honour done, let her be solemnly borne, | Unto the house of peace from whence she came | As queen of silence' (V. ii. 200–5).

that the arrest of Death is nothing less than the Triumph of Love: 'Love only reigns in death' (line 93). From Bassanes, torn between grief and admiration, it produces a salute to a new kind of mirth-in-funeral: 'I must weep to see | Her smile in death' (lines 97–8), a version of that 'Excellent misery' to which he himself aspires (v. ii. 66).

Calantha's art of dying writes itself in a language of enacted oxymoron ('Let me die smiling'; line 76) that triumphantly combines the contradictions of her being (antic gesture and silent griefs) and proclaims her own defiant authorship of her last and greatest 'part'. But the Princess's death, with its rite of coronation, is only the play's most elaborate variation on the great theme of aristocratic dying, *finis coronat opus*, which we have already seen explored in *Anthony and Cleopatra* and *The Duchess of Malfi.* All of Ford's Spartans cultivate a similar aesthetic of death, and the ends of Penthea, Ithocles, and Orgilus are marked by the same transcendent paradoxy. Penthea's starvation reclaims the 'noble shame' forfeited in her polluted marriage (IV. ii. 150); Ithocles' death is marked by the strange sympathy between murderer and victim reflected in the revenger's determination to be 'gentle even in blood' (IV. iv. 61). Orgilus' ensuing execution is performed as a tableau of 'Desperate courage' and 'Honourable infamy' (v. ii. 123). The oxymoronic language reminds us that each death is, in its own way, self-authored and hence a kind of suicide—Rosalie Colie's 'paradox of self-contradiction at its irrevocable extremity'.[12] Like Octavius' ambivalent tribute to Cleopatra's 'noble weakness', these clustered oxymorons have a characteristically double function in a world where, as in *Anthony*, paradoxy can express both annihilating self-contradiction and mysterious transcendence. For if the characters of *The Broken Heart* find in performance a successful stratagem against flux, a way of fixing their identity in a single attitude of marmoreal constancy, it is also true that the tragedy of the play springs directly from their attempts to impose a formal mask of manners upon the refractory inner self.[13]

[12] Colie, *Paradoxia Epidemica*, 486.

[13] In 'Ford's "Waste Land": *The Broken Heart*', *Renaissance Drama*, NS 3 (1970), 167–87, R. J. Kaufmann anatomizes *The Broken Heart* as a 'tragedy of manners' in which unbending allegiance to a moral code of inhuman severity creates an emotional desert; by contrast Hariett Hawkins, while equally sceptical about the absolute demands of the Spartan moral code, reads the play as a tragedy of

The world of *The Broken Heart*, as Bassanes sees it, is a mere gallery of tragic divisions, a spectacle

> Of virgins who have lost contracted partners;
> Of husbands howling that their wives were ravish'd
> By some untimely fate; or friends divided
> By churlish opposition. (V. iii. 28–31)

Physical divisions lead to divisions of the self: above all in Penthea, who is equally divided from her husband, her contracted partner, and her brother ('Alas, sir, being children, but two branches | Of one stock, 'tis not fit we should divide'; III. ii. 112–13), what results is the 'Divorce betwixt my body and my heart' (II. iii. 57) that reduces her to the paradoxical condition of 'a ravish'd wife | Widowed by lawless marriage' (IV. ii. 146). But in their own fashion Ithocles, Calantha, and Orgilus all suffer from what the latter calls 'the leanness of a heart *divided* | From intercourse of troth-contracted loves' (II. iii. 38; emphasis added).

This pervasive split between inner desires and outward demeanour produces the play's characteristic preoccupation with secrets. 'Heaven', Euphranea reminds her brother in the first scene, 'Does look into the secrets of all hearts' (I. i. 113), a claim which is echoed in Tecnicus' rebukes:

> Tempt not the stars, young man; thou canst not play
> With the severity of fate. This change
> Of habit, and disguise in outward view,
> Hides not the secrets of thy soul within thee
> From their quick-piercing eyes, which dive at all times
> Down to thy thoughts. (I. iii. 1–7)

The privacies of the human heart may be accessible to the gods, but for mortals they remain lapped in silence, concealed in the casket or 'cabinet' (IV. ii. 118) of the 'inward' self, to be 'read' only through impossible scrutiny of the bosom (IV. iii. 121–2):

> Our mortal eyes
> Pierce not the secrets of your hearts; the gods
> Are only privy to them. (III. i. 10–12)

incompatible moral and emotional extremes which embroils the audience's sympathies on both sides of the argument ('Mortality, Morality, and Modernity in *The Broken Heart*: Some Dramatic and Critical Counter-Arguments', in my *John Ford*, 129–52).

Our eyes can never pierce into the thoughts,
For they are lodg'd too inward.
(IV. i. 17–18)

Ithocles typically imagines his passion for Calantha as 'a secret . . . I dare not murmur to myself' (III. ii. 95–6); while Orgilus hyperbolically supposes that his love for Penthea remains hidden even from the gods:

The deities
Themselves are not secure in searching out
The secrets of those flames, which, hidden, waste
A breast made tributary to the laws
Of beauty. (I. iii. 36–40)

—and he makes the 'unmatched secret' (V. i. 37) of his revenge a kind of challenge to the omnipotence of Fate. Secrecy becomes for Orgilus a way of preserving inviolate the mysteries of the self, a magical substitute for the outward action by which a conventional hero should work out his own destiny; so that when he greets death it is as the final guarantor of that 'privacy' he urges upon Bassanes, 'as strong in silence | As mysteries locked up in Jove's own bosom' (V. i. 49–50). In death Orgilus consciously adopts the role of 'surgeon . . . well-skilled in letting blood' (V. ii. 100–1) whose dagger becomes the 'skilful instrument' (line 103) of medicinal bleeding: 'thus I show cunning | In opening of a vein too full, too lively' (V. ii. 121–2). But this surgical display is so far from the self-anatomizing 'opening' it seems to mimic that it serves only to confirm the closed, gnomic circularity of Tecnicus' riddle ('Revenge proves its own executioner'; (line 147). Death for Orgilus is simply the final sovereign preservative of the occluded inner self: 'Welcome, thou ice, that sitt'st about my heart; | No heat can ever thaw thee' (V. ii. 154–5). Art may find no comfort for a broken heart, but its fragments are sealed up for ever in that icy cabinet.

When Bassanes consents to Orgilus' oath of privacy he gives himself to an emotional silence which is also a kind of burial: 'A skull hid in the earth a treble age | Shall sooner prate' (V. i. 51–2). Remembering the brutally eloquent silence of Hamlet's ventriloquized skulls, the figure also echoes Penthea's metaphor for the self-suppression of her love for Orgilus: ''Tis buried in an everlasting silence | And shall be, shall be ever' (II. iii. 69–70). Her own submission to Bassanes takes the form of a 'silent duty' (III. ii. 159), and it is the strain of that silence, like the torture of Calantha's 'silent griefs', which drives her to madness and death. Emotional silence is so much the rule of this society that even the carefully contrived privacy of Penthea's scene with Calantha does not license the articulation of her 'Private thoughts'; the princess's stern rebuke 'Your check lies in my silence' (III. v. 108) is not merely a refusal to answer but an appeal to an irrefragable moral norm.

Behind these consciously guarded secrets are others even more inward, the psychological counterparts of Delphic mysteries, obscure even to their possessors. In his bitter riddling at Euphranea's wedding, Orgilus speaks of virginity as 'A trifle maids *know only that they know not*' (IV. iii. 62; emphasis added). Concealed in his familiar bawdy is a gnomic sentence that recalls Penthea—her ambiguously motivated intercession with Calantha on Ithocles' behalf,[14] and the profound obliquity of her words and gestures in the mad scene (IV. ii). To Orgilus her meanings seem tragically clear: 'If this be madness, madness is an oracle' (IV. ii. 133); but oracles being what they are, his confidence is ironic: his 'inspiration' amounts only to the opening of his own repressed secrets—for though he has constantly adopted the devious and threatening manner of a revenger, Orgilus has never, until this moment, acknowledged the meaning of his obsession: that he must kill Ithocles.

The secrets of *The Broken Heart* prove, then, to be doubly destructive: locked away, they are responsible for the 'hidden wast[ing]' felt by Orgilus (I. iii. 39), for Penthea's pining away, and for the cracking of Calantha's heart-strings; released, they may issue in the anarchic violence of revenge. The symbol for those secrets of the heart is the sealed-up casket which contains the secrets of fate, in the form of the Oracle's prophetic utterances. The casket is a peculiarly appropriate emblem, since the imagery of the play associates it with the even more equivocal figure of 'Pandora's box' (III. ii. 167), variously interpreted by the Renaissance as the source of all evils, the source of all heavenly gifts, or a paradoxical compound of the two.[15] The locking up of

[14] Kaufmann, for instance, thinks this a malevolent 'act of vengeful contagion' ('Ford's "Waste Land"', 174).

[15] For a comprehensive treatment of this motif, see Dora and Erwin Panofsky, *Pandora's Box: The Changing Aspects of a Mythical Symbol* (New York: Pantheon Books, 1956). Bocchi's use of Pandora's husband, Epimethus, the opener of the box, to represent 'Miseria honorata' (cited p. 67) interestingly anticipates the typing of Ford's Orgilus ('honourable infamy' and 'noble sorrow'), Bassanes ('excellent misery'), and Penthea ('noble shame').

the passional self in Ford's Sparta is equally ambivalent: it is at once a necessary restraint upon the anarchy of emotion, and a disastrous constriction of being—in effect a kind of 'burial' whose consequence is emotional death. It is as a sign of that radical self-suppression that Penthea announces the moment of her end by drawing a veil across her face, as if deliberately reversing the trope of death as apocalyptic unveiling (IV. iv. 10).

In a world where the pressures of society persistently drive a wedge between inner and outer, between the obsessive 'secrets' of the hidden self, and the 'actions' of the public persona, there is always a divorce, like that felt by Penthea 'betwixt my body and my heart'. In one sense physical death is only the final confirmation of that divorce: Orgilus imagines his own end as a last severing of his inner and outer selves, in which 'I' will be forever 'divided | From this my humble frailty' (V. ii. 86–7). Yet death is also imagined as a knitting up of divisions: not only does Calantha's marriage-in-funeral restore her bond with Ithocles, but Penthea, Orgilus, and Ithocles are ceremonially united by the three chairs of the latter's death scene; and Orgilus in his final extremity punningly acknowledges that link—'On a pair-royal do I wait in death' (V. ii. 136). In the same way the self-integrity expressed in the deliberate artifice with which these characters author their own ends is calculated to make death seem not merely a consequence of inner division, but also a way of reintegrating the sundered self. Calantha's death symbolically reunites these sundered opposites, as 'the Lifeless Trunk' is wedded to 'the Broken Heart' (V. iii. 100). In this way death, from being the agent of disintegration, is magically co-opted to become the restorative of essential integrity—a transformation, the play suggests, which only 'art' makes possible.

'*Art*' according to the play's final song 'Can find no comfort for a broken heart' (lines 93–4); yet the ending is full of reminders of artifice—that of the characters, and, by extension, that of the dramatist himself. In this there are significant parallels with the last scene of *Anthony and Cleopatra*: as the magnificent theatre of Cleopatra's death was conducted according to a decorum that made it '*fitting* for a princess | Descended of so many royal kings' (V. ii. 326–7; emphasis added), so Calantha orchestrates her going with a song which she has meticulously '*fitted* for mine end' (line 80; emphasis added), compelling Bassanes' admiration for the 'brave' performance of her 'part' (lines 96–7); and the inheritor of her kingdom, Nearchus, responds, like Octavius Caesar, by commanding her funeral triumph: 'wait in order | Upon these faithful lovers, as becomes us' (lines 103–4)—though, unlike the 'high order' of the 'solemnity' which Octavius offers his 'pair so famous', this is a ceremonial apparently untouched by political interest.

Calantha, as the setting of her death to music reminds us, is by no means the play's only exponent of the art of dying. Her song not only echoes the painfully preserved harmonies of the dance scene, but once again recalls Penthea, whose parting from life is described by Philema and Christalla:

PHILEMA. She called for music,
And begged some gentle voice to tune a farewell
To life and griefs. Christalla touched the lute;
I wept the funeral song.
CHRISTALLA. Which scarce was ended,
But her last breath sealed up these hollow sounds....
So down she drew her veil, so died.
(IV. iv. 4–10)

In each case the woman makes herself author of her own death by timing it to coincide with the close of the song she has fitted to her last moments, so that a dramatic end becomes a kind of enacted figure for mortal ending, the heart breaking as the art falls silent; in this way both women can lay claim to the stoical autonomy of suicide and yet remain untainted by its moral ambivalence. In each case too, the conscious artifice of the occasion is enhanced by deliberate ceremonial gesture—Calantha's ritual with the ring and Penthea's drawing of her veil—as though to signal the performers' awareness of completing a role prescribed by the old trope of life-as-theatre, of which Penthea offers Calantha a characteristically nostalgic version:

on the stage
Of my mortality my youth hath acted
Some scenes of vanity, drawn out at length
By varied pleasures, sweetened in the mixture,
But tragical in issue. (III. v. 15–19)

A similar concern with the artifice of making a good end is apparent in the death scenes of the rival male protagonists Ithocles and Orgilus. So impressed is Orgilus by Ithocles' 'goodly language' in the face of death (IV. iv. 52) that he is not only prepared to surrender the absolute aesthetic control that is always crucial to the satisfactions of revenge, but willing to grant his rival the desired 'monument [of] a happy name' (line 76) by himself becoming the chronicler of Ithocles' splendidly self-authored death: 'Bravery | Of an undaunted spirit,' he announces, 'conquering terror, | Proclaimed his last act triumph over ruin' (V. ii. 41–3). Calantha responds to the generosity of this 'honourable mention' (line 80) by according Orgilus the same privilege of orchestrating his own execution. Like Bussy D'Ambois, he chooses to meet his death standing, as though he were already metamorphosing into one of those 'senseless marble statue[s]' that Bassanes seeks to emulate (V. i. 46); and as he and Ithocles became collaborators in the theatre of the general's 'last act', so Orgilus now joins his 'skill' with his rival's 'art' (V. ii. 101–8) to produce the triumphant spectacle which Bassanes so admires:

> This pastime
> Appears majestical; some high-tuned poem
> Hereafter shall deliver to posterity
> The writer's glory and the subject's triumph. . . .
> 'A has shook hands with time. His funeral urn
> Shall be my charge. Remove the bloodless body.
>
> (V. ii. 131–4)

In that invocation of his own 'high-tuned poem' it is as though Ford were remembering his praise of Webster's *Duchess* and his celebration its power to create for its author 'A lasting fame, to raise his monument'. The effect is to give a new and strikingly self-referential twist to the gnomic tautology with which Orgilus announced his embarkation on the journey of revenge: 'Great arts best write themselves in their own stories' (I. ii. 182). *The Broken Heart* was written for the Blackfriars, a theatre which of all the new breed of exclusive 'private' playhouses became most closely associated with the court and its coterie drama; and, compared with *The Duchess of Malfi*, or even *Anthony and Cleopatra*, it can seem strikingly single-minded in its celebration of the values of courtly *maniera*—style produced as an absolute value. The Calantha who stakes everything upon preserving 'The custom of this ceremony' (V. ii. 27) identifiably belongs to the same courtly culture as Ford's patron Newcastle, who counselled Charles II that 'Ceremony though it is nothing in itself, yet it doth everything.'[16]

Ceremony indeed does everything in *The Broken Heart*: Calantha's rite of coronation-and-wedding-in-funeral is attended by none of those ironies that Cleopatra takes defiant pride in outfacing. Yet it would be wrong to think of the play's ending as wholly unambiguous. Significantly, perhaps, Ford's sources for *The Broken Heart* appear to have included Castiglione's *The Courtier*,[17] that Renaissance 'handbook of self-making'.[18] In *The Courtier* the key to virtuous action lies in the cultivation of 'an artificial following of nature',[19] a perfection of pure style; but when Castiglione talks about what lies behind this finely contrived mask, he seems to imagine a 'self' as chameleon and devious as Montaigne's: 'there are in our minds so many dens and corners, that it is unpossible for the wit of man to know the dissimulations that lie lurking in them'.[20] The play's ending is from one point of view a celebration of Calantha's 'artificial following of nature'—the moral equivalent of Bassanes' 'mastery | In art to fatten and keep smooth the outside ... Without the help of food' (IV. ii. 162–5). But desire will not abandon its cry for satisfaction, for the 'real, visible, material happiness' on which Ithocles insists (IV. i. 50). Penthea's starvation is a metaphor for the inner wasting which the marmoreal postures of art conceal even in Calantha: 'I but deceived your eyes with antic gesture. ... They are the silent griefs which cut the heart-strings' (V. iii. 68–75). The music of her last song represents art's answer to that terminal silence, even as its lyrics seem to repudiate such consolation. The wedding of Ithocles' Lifeless Trunk to Calantha's Broken Heart is a consummation, perhaps

[16] William Cavendish, Earl of Newcastle, 'Advice to Charles II' (1659), cited from Thomas P. Slaughter, *Ideology and Politics on the Eve of the Restoration: Newcastle's Advice to Charles II* (Philadelphia: American Philosophical Society, 1984), 44. The whole section 'For Seremoney, & Order' (pp. 44–9) repays attention. Ford dedicated *Perkin Warbeck* to Newcastle in 1634, a year after the publication of *The Broken Heart*.

[17] See Frederick M. Burelbach, '"The Truth" in John Ford's *The Broken Heart* Revisited', *Notes and Queries*, 212 (1967), 211–12.

[18] The phrase is Rosalie Colie's in *Paradoxia Epidemica*, 361; cf. also R. B. Hinman, 'The Apotheosis of Faust: Poetry and New Philosophy in the Seventeenth Century', in D. J. Palmer and Malcolm Bradbury (eds.), *Metaphysical Poetry*, Stratford-upon-Avon Studies, no. 11 (London: Edward Arnold, 1970), 169.

[19] Baldassare Castiglione, *The Book of the Courtier*, trans. Sir Thomas Hoby (London: Dent, 1928), 79.

[20] Ibid. 118.

the one kind truly available in a world where 'Love only reigns in death' (line 93); but Armostes' reminder that in it Tecnicus' gnomic couplet 'is here fulfilled' (line 101) speaks of a quite different kind of fulfilment, an ending that lies beyond the power of art to control.

If the performed self is an artefact set up to control the dangerous secrets of the heart, it must also contend with secrets of another sort, the 'mysteries locked up in Jove's own bosom' (v. i. 50) which are, after all, the primary referent of the enigmatic Delphic casket. *The Broken Heart* is full of reflections upon the omniscience of the gods and the omnipotence of their fatal designs:

Heaven
Does look into the secrets of all hearts.
(I. i. 113–14)

our mortal eyes
Pierce not the secrets of your hearts, the gods
Are only privy to them. (III. i. 10–12)

But let the gods be moderators still,
No human power can prevent their will.
(III. i. 57)

Leave to the powers
Above us the effects of their decrees.
(IV. i. 145–6)

For all its busyness in the characters' lives, however, the designs and purposes of Fate remain obscure, its decrees as far beyond human scrutiny as beyond prevention. Even when Orgilus sees himself as the chosen minister of destiny, his hubris is undercut by a humiliating sense of ignorance:

Ingenious Fate has leapt into mine arms,
Beyond the compass of my brain. Mortality
Creeps on the dung of earth, and cannot reach
The riddles which are purposed by the gods.
(I. iii. 178–81)

King Amyclas attempts to accommodate himself to fatal necessity by consulting the Delphic Oracle. But if it is the mouthpiece of divine will, the Oracle speaks with extraordinary obliquity, yielding him nothing beyond an elaborate riddle—'Dark sentences are for Apollo's priests,' as Orgilus contemptuously puts it (IV. i. 140).

The notorious obscurity of his riddles won for Pythian Apollo the name of Loxias ('Crooked', 'Ambiguous');[21] and Ford's god fully justifies the appellation—far from unveiling the 'mysteries lock'd up in Jove's own bosom' (v. i. 50), he keeps his meanings until the end 'clouded in hid sense' (IV. iii. 32). The prophecies of the Oracle are contained in the 'sealed box', whose opening results in an interpretation which bafflingly seems 'but itself a riddle' (IV. iii. 25), its rhetorical opacity compounded by a deliberate sequestration of knowledge:

> the thing
> Of most importance, not to be revealed,
> Is a near prince, the elm: the rest concealed.
>
> (IV. iii. 20–3)

The result is a kind of enigmatic tautology in which

> The pith of oracles
> Is then to be digested when th'events
> Expound their truth
>
> (lines 36–8)

With its Chinese box of riddles within riddles, the Oracle serves to signal the immanence of the end in the play's action, while simultaneously stressing its tantalizingly secret nature. Within the framework of puzzled expectation set up by this device even Calantha's supreme accomplishment of her 'part' can seem less like a self-authored consummation than the mechanical performance of a script she never really learned to scan. Paradox, after all, is never *quite* allowed to dissolve into mystery in this play. Nearchus' concluding speech, as though articulating the ambivalence of all tragic endings, looks in two directions: on the one hand, announcing a funeral rite whose artifice 'becomes' the human need to put a form of order upon the indistinction of death; on the other, acknowledging the subordination of that order to a larger scheme beyond human scrutiny. Looked at from this final perspective, the ending becomes the unpacking of a superhuman mystery, the resolution of the greatest and most oppressive of those 'secrets' with which

[21] Rabelais's Pantagruel remarks on 'the ambiguities, equivocations, and obscurities in the words [of the Oracle]. For which reason Apollo, the god of prophecy, was named Loxias—the Indirect'; *The Histories of Gargantua and Pantagruel*, trans. J. M. Cohen (Harmondsworth: Penguin, 1955), III. xix. 339.

the action of the play has been so preoccupied; and Nearchus' concluding couplet, significantly leaving his dutiful gestures to human 'order' behind it, places the consolations of art and the distinction of performance where they belong, within the realm of rhetoric, magnificent and frail: 'The counsels of the gods are never known. | Till men can *call* the effects of them their own.'

The barely concealed irony of this aphorism is that it celebrates a mode of anagnorisis which, the play suggests, is attainable only at the point of death; and if the final opening of Apollo's secrets is possible then, that is ironically because death itself is what waits to be discovered. Ford's sense of this reductive truth is most famously exhibited in the self-consciously staged 'riddle' that crowns the catastrophe of *'Tis Pity She's a Whore*, where Giovanni's display, at once frantic and boastful, of his sister's impaled heart gives hallucinatory life to the recurrent imagery of the human heart as the repository of tormenting secrets. That extraordinary scene mimics not merely the emblematic violence of seventeenth-century scaffolds, but the ambiguous triumphs of the anatomy theatre, whose patient unstitching of the body's fabric only produced a heightened sense of the maddening opacity of human flesh, even as it contrived to suggest that the true answers to Delphic Apollo's 'paradoxal commandment',[22] *nosce teipsum*, were to be found in the signs of death so intransigently engraved upon the body's innermost core.

There is, however, an important difference between these two catastrophes, which between them represent the logical end-point of that drive for the mastery of death from which early modern drama drew so much of its energy. In its unripping of Annabella's heart, the catastrophe of *'Tis Pity* carries to its frenzied extreme the anatomical will-to-knowledge that informs the bodily dismemberments of the Renaissance stage; but what it discovers is only an impenetrable enigma. As though acknowledging inevitability of that defeat, the catastrophe of *The Broken Heart* stakes everything on a refinement of monumental art that seeks (as in Penthea's self-starvation) to will the body out of existence, or to sublimate the flesh in postures of marmoreal calm. Its title speaks of a heart

[22] See Montaigne, *Essays*, III. ix. 252–3: 'It was a paradoxal commandment, which the God of Delphos laid heretofore upon us, saying: *View yourselves within; know your selves.* . . . Thou art the scrutator without knowledge.'

that is not merely crushed by emotion, but broken as a body might be 'broken' upon a torturer's wheel to extract its secrets. But the physical presence of this 'cabinet' of privacy is registered by a cracking of heart-strings that is audible only to the dying Calantha. With its transformed Dance of Death, its displays of surgical violence, its loving elaboration of funeral motifs, and its *précieux* celebration of the crowning end, *The Broken Heart* offers what now seems like a nostalgic retrospect of Renaissance drama's confrontation with death, even as it writes a *ne plus ultra* to the path of tragic discovery.

Appendix

The Plague and the Dance of Death

Although the connection has been challenged by some historians, there are good grounds for supposing that the overwhelming experience of the Black Death, that devastating pandemic which carried off up to one-third of the population of Europe,[1] was crucial to the conception of the *danse macabre*—just as the continuing ravages of the plague helped to sustain the popularity of the motif and its derivatives until the latter part of the seventeenth century.[2] The relationship between the plague and macabre art has been challenged by Clark, who points out that the Paris *Danse* 'was painted in one of the brighter intervals which occur in this most depressing of periods';[3] while Ariès argues that macabre art, rather than reflecting the mood of morbid despair described by Huizinga and others in their account of the crisis of the late Middle Ages, is the expression of a passionate attachment to life. But such an attitude can be read as a perfectly comprehensible reaction to the trauma of mass death, confirming the indictments of contemporary moralists against the careless hedonism produced by the plague. In the case of some *danses macabres*, moreover, there are historical traditions which link the paintings to particular outbreaks of pestilence. According to Merian, for example, the Basel *Tod* was commissioned

[1] Some estimates still run as high as 50%—a figure which may well hold good for particular localities. Although the statistics have been widely debated, especially since J. F. D. Shrewsbury's radically revisionist *History of the Bubonic Plague in the British Isles* (Cambridge: Cambridge University Press, 1970), which argued for an overall rate of only 5%, the weight of current opinion still favours a figure of about one-third. See J. M. W. Bean, 'The Black Death: The Crisis and its Social and Economic Consequences', in Daniel Williman (ed.), *The Black Death: The Impact of the Fourteenth Century Plague* (Binghamton, NY: Center for Medieval and Early Renaissance Studies, 1982), 22–38; Robert S. Gottfried, *The Black Death* (New York: Free Press, 1984), pp. xiii–xv; Christopher Morris, 'Plague in Britain', in Paul Slack *et al.*, *The Plague Reconsidered* (Matlock: Local Population Studies, 1977), 37–47; Ziegler, *Black Death*, 230–1.

[2] See e.g. Joseph Polzer, 'Aspects of Fourteenth-Century Iconogography of Death and the Plague', in Williman (ed.), *Black Death*, 107–30; and Douce, *Holbein's Dance of Death*, 31. Among recent historians of death, Clare Gittings (*Death, Burial and the Individual in Early Modern England*) accepts the relation between macabre art and the trauma of plague, observing only that 'it is perhaps surprising that there was not even greater anxiety and despair aroused by death' (p. 35).

[3] Ariès, *Hour of our Death*, 124–32; Clark, *Dance of Death*, 23.

in the immediate wake of the plague that swept through the city in 1439; its victims included several participants in the great Council of Basel (1431–49), and Merian identified a number of its figures as portraits of leading members of that Council.[4] Similarly the Lübeck *Totentanz* was painted in 1463 in anticipation of a major epidemic;[5] while the last of the great mural *Danses macabres*, painted at Lucerne in 1635, was commissioned by the city fathers as a response to a decade of war and devastating plague.[6] The *Danse macabre des femmes*, apparently written during the great Parisian plague of 1481–4,[7] is introduced by Death's Musicians, who call on their female victims to remember the mass burials of Paris with their

> heap
> Of bones from people who have died . . .
> And who now are piled
> One on another, fat and thin

—and the poem makes explicit reference to the plague in the Wetnurse's reply to Death:

> I feel a swelling under my clothing,
> Between my arms, when I breathe.
> The child is dying of plague.[8]

In any case the argument which sees the popularity of the *danse macabre* as a response to the trauma of mass death need not depend on exact chronological coincidence, since plague remained endemic in Europe—and hence a formative influence on the European consciousness—for more than 300 years after the outbreak of the Black Death in 1347.

[4] See Clark, *Dance of Death*, 64–5. According to Merian, the Pabst represented Felix V, the Kaiser Emperor Sigismund, and the Koenig Albrecht II, King of the Romans. Clark suggests the further identification of the pregnant Kaiserin with Sigismund's daughter, who bore a child to her husband, Albrecht II, after his death in 1440.

[5] Polzer, 'Iconography of Death', 117.

[6] Clark, *Dance of Death*, 76; the Lucerne *Tod* replaced their original project for a cheerful and decorative design. A good portion of the narrative in Samuel Rowlands's *Terribel Battell betweene . . . Time, and Death*, a late response to the plague which ravaged London at the beginning of James I's reign, is devoted to a Dance of Death sequence in which Death arrests a series of figures representing 'Each faculty, profession, and degree': 'About this time much work I had to do, | As woeful London did both feel and see, | A dreadful plague began six hundred two, | Which did continue out six hundred three'; sig. D1^{v}.

[7] See Harrison's edition, 8. Harrison is among those who see a strong connection between the *danse macabre* and 'the psychological trauma resulting from the great plagues'.

[8] Ibid. 90.

Bibliography

PRIMARY SOURCES

Archaeologia; or, Miscellaneous Tracts relating to antiquity, i (London: Society of Antiquaries, 1770).

BACON, FRANCIS, 'Of Love', in *Essays*, intro. Oliphant Smeaton (London: Dent, 1906).

BANISTER, JOHN, *The Historie of Man, sucked from the sappe of the most approued Anathomistes* (London, 1578).

BEDDOES, THOMAS LOVELL, *The Works of Thomas Lovell Beddoes*, ed. H. W. Donner (Oxford: Clarendon Press, 1935).

BOND, EDWARD, *Lear* (London: Methuen, 1972).

The Book of Beasts, trans. and ed. T. H. White (London: Jonathan Cape, 1954).

BRATHWAITE, RICHARD, *The English Gentleman*, 3rd edn. (London, 1641).

BROWNE, SIR THOMAS, *Religio Medici and Other Writings*, intro. M. R. Ridley (London: Dent, 1965).

CASTIGLIONE, BALDASSARE, *The Book of the Courtier*, trans. Sir Thomas Hoby (London: Dent, 1928).

CHARRON, PIERRE, *Of Wisdome Three Bookes*, trans. Samson Lennard, 2nd edn. (London, 1630).

CHETTLE, HENRY, *The Tragedy of Hoffman* (Oxford: Malone Society, 1950–1).

CONGREVE, WILLIAM, *The Comedies of William Congreve*, ed. Anthony G. Henderson (Cambridge: Cambridge University Press, 1982).

COTTA, JOHN, *The Triall of Witchcraft, shewing The Trew and Right Methode of the Discovery* (London, 1616).

CROOKE, HELKIAH, *Mikrocosmographia: A Description of the Body of Man* (London, 1618).

The Danse Macabre of Women, ed. Anne Tukey Harrison (Kent, Ohio: Kent State University Press, 1994).

[DAY, RICHARD], *A Booke of Christian Prayers* (London, 1569).

DEKKER, THOMAS, *The Plague Pamphlets of Thomas Dekker*, ed. F. P. Wilson (Oxford: Clarendon Press, 1925).

—— *Newes from Graues-end: Sent to Nobody* (London, 1604).

DONNE, JOHN, *Devotions upon Emergent Occasions Together with Death's Duel* (Ann Arbor: University of Michigan Press, 1959).

—— *The Poems of John Donne*, ed. H. J. C. Grierson (Oxford: Oxford University Press, 1912).

DONNE, JOHN, *The Sermons of John Donne*, ed. Evelyn M. Simpson and George R. Potter, 10 vols. (Berkeley and Los Angeles: University of California Press, 1954).

ELIOT, T. S., *Selected Essays* (London: Faber, 1961).

F[LETCHER], P[HINEAS], *The Purple Island; or, The Isle of Man* (Cambridge, 1633).

FORD, JOHN, *The Broken Heart*, ed. Brian Morris, The New Mermaids (London: Ernest Benn, 1965).

—— *John Fordes Dramatische Werke*, ed. W. Bang, Materialen zur Kunde des älteren Englischen Dramas, ser. 1, vol. 23 (Louvain: A. Uystpruyst, 1908).

FRASER, RUSSELL A., and RABKIN, NORMAN (eds.), *Drama of the English Renaissance*, 2 vols. (New York: Macmillan, 1976).

HAKLUYT, RICHARD, *The Principal Navigations, Voyages, Traffiques and Discoveries of the English Nation*, ed. Walter Raleigh (Glasgow: J. MacLehose, 1903–5).

HARVEY, WILLIAM, *The Anatomical Lectures of William Harvey*, trans. Gweneth Whitteridge (Edinburgh: E. and S. Livingston for the Royal College of Physicians, 1964).

HEANEY, SEAMUS, *Selected Poems, 1965–1975* (London: Faber, 1980).

HEYWOOD, THOMAS, *An Apology for Actors* (London, 1612).

[? HEYWOOD, THOMAS], *A Warning for Fair Women*, ed. Charles D. Cannon (The Hague: Mouton, 1975).

HOLBEIN, HANS, *The Dance of Death*, ed. James M. Clark (London: Phaidon, 1947).

—— *'The Dance of Death' by Hans Holbein the Younger: A Complete Facsimile of the Original 1538 Edition of 'Les simulachres et historiees faces de la Mort'*, intro. Werner L. Gundersheimer (New York: Dover, 1971).

I. H., *This Worlds Folly; or, A Warning-Peece discharged upon the Wickedness thereof* (London, 1615).

JAMES I, *The Political Works of James I*, ed. Charles Howard McIlwain (Cambridge, Mass.: Harvard University Press, 1918).

KYD, THOMAS, *The Works of Thomas Kyd*, ed. F. S. Boas (Oxford: Oxford University Press, 1941).

KNOWLAND, A. S. (ed.), *Six Caroline Plays* (London: Oxford University Press, 1962).

LYDGATE, JOHN, *The Dance of Death*, ed. Florence Warren (London: Early English Text Society, 1931).

MARCHANT, GUYOT, *La Grande Danse macabre des hommes et des femmes* (Paris: Baillieu, n.d.), and as *La Danse macabre de Guy Marchant*, ed. Pierre Champion (Paris: editions des Quatre Chemins, 1925).

MARSTON, JOHN, *Antonio's Revenge*, ed. G. K. Hunter (London: Edward Arnold, 1964).

—— *Antonio's Revenge*, ed. Reavley Gair (Manchester: Manchester University Press, 1978).

—— *The Plays of John Marston*, ed. W. Harvey Wood, 3 vols. (Edinburgh: Oliver & Boyd, 1934–9).

—— *The Selected Plays of John Marston*, ed. MacDonald P. Jackson and Michael Neill (Cambridge: Cambridge University Press, 1986).

MARVELL, ANDREW, *The Poems and Letters*, ed. H. M. Margoliouth (Oxford: Clarendon Press, 1927).

MONTAIGNE, MICHEL DE, *Montaigne's Essays*, trans. John Florio, ed. J. C. Harmer, 3 vols. (1910; London: J. M. Dent, 1965).

MORE, JOHN, *A Lively Anatomie of Death . . . Tending to teach men to lyue, and die well to the Lord* (London, 1596).

MORE, SIR THOMAS, *The English Works of Sir Thomas More*, ed. W. E. Campbell, 7 vols. (London: Eyre & Spottiswoode, 1931).

NICHOLS, JOHN, *The Progresses and Public Processions of Queen Elizabeth*, 3 vols. (London: John Nichols, 1823).

PEELE, GEORGE, *The Old Wives Tale*, ed. Patricia Binnie, The Revels Plays (Manchester and Baltimore: Manchester University Press and Johns Hopkins University Press, 1980).

PLUTARCH, *The Lives of the Noble Grecians and Romanes*, trans. Sir Thomas North (London, 1579).

PURCHAS, SAMUEL, *Haklvytvs Posthumus: Pvrchas his Pilgrimes: Microcosmvs; or, The Historie of Man. Relating the Wonders of his Generation, Vanities of his Degeneration, Necessity of his Regeneration. Meditated on the words of David. Ps. 39.5. Verily, every Man at his best state is altogether Vanitie* (London, 1619).

RABELAIS, FRANÇOIS, *The Histories of Gargantua and Pantagruel*, trans. J. M. Cohen (Harmondsworth: Penguin, 1955).

The Roxburghe Ballads, 9 vols. (Hertford: printed for the Ballad Society by S. Austin, 1871–99).

ROWLANDS, SAMUEL, *A Terrible Battell betweene the two consumers of the Whole world: Time, and Death* (London, [?1606]).

SEGAR, WILLIAM, *Honor Military, and Civill, Contained in Foure Bookes* (London, 1602).

SENECA, L. A., *The Works of Lucius Annaeus Seneca both Morall and Naturall*, trans. Thomas Lodge (London, 1620).

SHAKESPEARE, WILLIAM, *Anthony and Cleopatra*, ed. Michael Neill (Oxford: Oxford University Press, 1994).

—— *Hamlet*, ed. G. R. Hibbard (Oxford: Clarendon Press, 1987).

—— *The Riverside Shakespeare*, ed. G. Blakemore Evans (Boston, Mass.: Houghton Mifflin, 1974).

SIDNEY, SIR PHILIP, 'An Apology for Poetry', in Edmund D. Jones (ed.), *English Critical Essays (Sixteenth, Seventeenth and Eighteenth Centuries)*, 2nd edn. (London: Oxford University Press, 1947), 1–54.

STOCKWOOD, JOHN, *A Sermon Preached at Paules Crosse* (London, 1578).

Totentanz der Stadt Basel (Basel: G. S. Beck, n.d.).

TOURNEUR, CYRIL, *The Atheist's Tragedy*, ed. Irving Ribner, The Revels Plays (London: Methuen, 1964).

—— [Thomas Middleton], *The Revenger's Tragedy*, ed. Brian Gibbons, 2nd edn. (London: A. C. Black, 1990).

VAN LINSCHOTEN, JOHN HUIGHEN, *John Huighen Van Linschoten his Discours of Voyages into ye Easte and West Indies* (London, 1598).

VESALIUS, ANDREAS, *De Humani Corporis Fabrica* (Basel, 1543).

—— *The Illustrations from the Works of Andreas Vesalius of Brussels*, ed. J. B. deC. Saunders and C. B. O'Malley (Cleveland: World Publishing, 1950).

VICARY, THOMAS, *A Profitable Treatise of the Anatomie of mans body* (London, 1577).

WEBSTER, JOHN, *The Duchess of Malfi*, ed. John Russell Brown, The Revers Plays (London: Methuen, 1964).

—— *Works*, ed. F. L. Lucas, 4 vols. (London: Chatto & Windus, 1927).

WEEVER, JOHN, *Ancient Funerall Monuments Within the United Monarchie of Great Britaine, Ireland, and the Ilands adjacent* (London, 1631).

WENTWORTH, PETER, *A Pithie Exhortation to her Majestie for establishing her successor to the crowne* (Edinburgh, 1598).

WITHER, GEORGE, *Juvenilia* (London, 1622; Menston: Scolar Press facsimile, 1970).

SECONDARY SOURCES

Books

ADELMAN, JANET, *The Common Liar* (New Haven: Yale University Press, 1973).

ANDREWS, MICHAEL CAMERON, *The Action of our Death: The Performance of Death in English Drama* (Newark, NJ: University of Delaware Press, 1989).

ARIÈS, PHILIPPE, *The Hour of our Death*, trans. Helen Weaver (London: Allen Lane, 1981).

—— and DUBY, GEORGES (gen. eds.), *A History of Private Life*, trans. Arthur Goldhammer, 5 vols. (Cambridge, Mass.: Belknap Press, 1987–91).

ARTAUD, ANTONIN, *The Theatre and its Double* (London: Calder & Boyars, 1970).

BAKHTIN, MIKHAIL, *Rabelais and his World*, trans. Helene Iswolsky (Cambridge, Mass.: MIT Press, 1968).

BARBER, C. L., *Shakespeare's Festive Comedy: A Study of Dramatic Form and its Relation to Social Custom* (Princeton: Princeton University Press, 1959).

BARISH, JONAS, *The Anti-theatrical Prejudice* (Berkeley: University of California Press, 1981).

BARKAN, LEONARD, *The Gods Made Flesh: Metamorphosis and the Pursuit of Paganism* (New Haven: Yale University Press, 1985).

BARKER, FRANCIS, *The Tremulous Private Body: Essays on Subjection* (London: Methuen, 1984).

BARROLL, LEEDS, *Politics, Plague, and Shakespeare's Theatre: The Stuart Years* (Ithaca, NY: Cornell University Press, 1991).

BARTON, ANNE, *Ben Jonson, Dramatist* (Cambridge: Cambridge University Press, 1984).

BEIER, LUCINDA MCCRAY, *Sufferers and Healers: The Experience of Illness in Seventeenth-Century England* (London: Routledge & Kegan Paul, 1987).

BELSEY, CATHERINE, *The Subject of Tragedy: Identity and Difference in Renaissance Drama* (London: Methuen, 1985).

BENJAMIN, WALTER, *The Origin of German Tragic Drama* (London: Verso, 1985).

BERGERON, DAVID, *Pageantry in the Shakespearean Theatre* (Athens: University of Georgia Press, 1985).

BERRY, EDWARD, *Shakespeare's Comic Rites* (Cambridge: Cambridge University Press, 1984).

BEVINGTON, DAVID, *Action is Eloquence: Shakespeare's Language of Gesture* (Cambridge, Mass.: Harvard University Press, 1984).

BOASE, T. S. R., *Death in the Middle Ages: Mortality, Judgement and Remembrance* (London: Thames & Hudson, 1972).

BOOTH, STEPHEN, *'King Lear', 'Macbeth', Indefinition and Tragedy* (New Haven: Yale University Press, 1983).

BRADBROOK, M. C., *John Webster, Citizen and Dramatist* (London: Weidenfeld & Nicolson, 1980).

—— *Themes and Conventions of Elizabethan Tragedy*, 2nd edn. (Cambridge: Cambridge University Press, 1980).

BRISTOL, MICHAEL D., *Carnival and Theatre: Plebeian Culture and the Structure of Authority in Renaissance England* (London: Methuen, 1985).

BURKE, KENNETH, *Language as Symbolic Action* (Berkeley: University of California Press, 1966).

CALDERWOOD, JAMES L., *Shakespeare and the Denial of Death* (Amherst: University of Massachusetts Press, 1987).

CANETTI, ELIAS, *Crowds and Power*, trans. Carol Stewart (London: Penguin, 1981).

CARROLL, WILLIAM C., *The Metamorphoses of Shakespearean Comedy* (Princeton: Princeton University Press, 1985).

CHAMBERS, E. K., *The Elizabethan Stage*, 4 vols. (Oxford: Clarendon Press, 1951), iv.

CHAMBERLIN, E. R., *The Black Death* (London: Jonathan Cape, n.d.).

CERTEAU, MICHEL de, *The Writing of History*, trans. Tom Conley (New York: Columbia University Press, 1988).

CLARK, JAMES M., *The Dance of Death in the Middle Ages and the Renaissance* (Glasgow: Jackson, 1950).

COLIE, ROSALIE, *Paradoxia Epidemica* (Princeton: Princeton University Press, 1966).

COPE, JACKSON I., *The Theater and the Dream: From Metaphor to Form in Renaissance Drama* (Baltimore: Johns Hopkins University Press, 1973).

CRAWFURD, RAYMOND, *Plague and Pestilence in Literature and Art* (Oxford: Clarendon Press, 1914).

CUSHING, HARVEY, *A Bio-bibliography of Andreas Vesalius* (Hamden, Conn.: Archon Books, 1962).

DEAUX, GEORGE, *The Black Death 1347* (London: Hamish Hamilton, 1969).

DOLLIMORE, JONATHAN, *Radical Tragedy* (Brighton: Harvester, 1983).

DONALDSON, IAN (ed.), *Jonson and Shakespeare* (London and Canberra: Macmillan/HRC, 1983).

DOUCE, FRANCIS, *Holbein's Dance of Death* (London: G. Bell, 1902).

DOUGLAS, MARY, *Purity and Danger: An Analysis of Concepts of Pollution and Taboo* (New York: Praeger, 1966).

ELIAS, NORBERT, *The Civilizing Process: The History of Manners*, trans. Edmund Jephcott (London: Basil Blackwell, 1978).

ENGEL, WILLIAM E., *Mapping Mortality: The Persistence of Memory and Melancholy in Early Modern England* (Amherst: University of Massachusetts Press, 1995).

ENRIGHT, D. J. (ed.), *The Oxford Book of Death* (Oxford: Oxford University Press, 1983).

FARNHAM, WILLARD, *The Medieval Heritage of Elizabethan Tragedy* (Oxford: Basil Blackwell, 1956).

FARRELL, KIRBY, *Play, Death and Heroism in Shakespeare* (Chapel Hill: University of North Carolina Press, 1989).

FERRY, ANNE, *The 'Inward' Language: Sonnets of Wyatt, Sidney, Donne and Shakespeare* (Chicago: University of Chicago Press, 1983).

FOREMAN, WALTER C., Jr., *The Music of the Close: The Final Scenes of Shakespeare's Tragedies* (Lexington: University of Kentucky Press, 1978).

FRYE, ROLAND MUSHAT, *The Renaissance Hamlet: Issues and Responses in 1600* (Princeton: Princeton University Press, 1984).

GARBER, MARJORIE, *Coming of Age in Shakespeare* (London: Methuen, 1981).

—— *Shakespeare's Ghost Writers* (New York: Methuen, 1987).

GENT, LUCY, and LLEWELLYN, NIGEL (eds.), *Renaissance Bodies: The Human Figure in English Culture c.1550–1660* (London: Reaktion Books, 1990).

GILLIES, JOHN, *Shakespeare and the Geography of Difference* (Cambridge: Cambridge University Press, 1994).

GIRARD, RENÉ, *To Double Business Bound: Essays on Literature, Mimesis, and Anthropology* (Baltimore: Johns Hopkins University Press, 1978).

—— *Violence and the Sacred* (Baltimore: Johns Hopkins University Press, 1977).

GITTINGS, CLARE, *Death, Burial and the Individual in Early Modern England* (London: Croom Helm, 1984).

GOLDBERG, JONATHAN, *Writing Matter: From the Hands of the English Renaissance* (Stanford, Calif.: Stanford University Press, 1990).

GOTTFRIED, ROBERT S., *The Black Death* (New York: Free Press, 1984).

GURR, ANDREW, *The Shakespearean Stage 1574–1642* (Cambridge: Cambridge University Press, 1970).

HANKEY, JULIE (ed.), *Plays in Performance: Othello* (Bristol: Bristol Classical Press, 1987).

HATTAWAY, MICHAEL, *English Popular Theatre* (London: Routledge & Kegan Paul, 1982).

HECKSCHER, WILLIAM S., *Rembrandt's Anatomy of Dr Nicolaas Tulp* (New York: New York University Press, 1958).

HODGES, DEVON, *Renaissance Fictions of Anatomy* (Amherst: University of Massachusetts Press, 1985).

HOULBROOKE, RALPH (ed.), *Death, Ritual and Bereavement* (London: Routledge, 1989).

HOWARD, JEAN E., and O'CONNOR, MARION (eds.), *Shakespeare Reproduced: The Text in History and Ideology* (London: Methuen, 1987).

HUNTER, G. K. and S. K. (eds.), *John Webster*, Penguin Critical Anthologies (Harmondsworth: Penguin, 1969).

KERMODE, FRANK, *The Sense of an Ending: Studies in the Theory of Fiction* (New York: Oxford University Press, 1979).

KERNAN, ALVIN (ed.), *Two Renaissance Mythmakers* (Baltimore: Johns Hopkins University Press, 1977).

KERNODLE, GEORGE R., *From Art to Theatre: Form and Convention in the Renaissance* (Chicago: University of Chicago Press, 1944).

KOERNER, JOSEPH LEO, *The Moment of Self-Portraiture in German Renaissance Art* (Chicago: University of Chicago Press, 1993).

LANDOLT, ELISABETH, *The Basel Dance of Death*, Basel Historical Museum pamphlet (Basel, n.d.).

LAQUEUR, THOMAS, *Making Sex: Body and Gender from the Greeks to Freud* (Cambridge, Mass.: Harvard University Press, 1992).

LASSEK, A. M., *Human Dissection: Its Drama and Struggle* (Springfield, Ill.: C. C. Thomas, 1958).

LESTRINGANT, FRANK, *Mapping the Renaissance World*, trans. David Fausett (Berkeley: University of California Press, 1994).

LEVIN, HARRY, *The Question of Hamlet* (New York: Oxford University Press, 1959).

LITTEN, JULIAN, *The English Way of Death: The Common Funeral since 1450* (London: Robert Hale, 1991).

LLEWELLYN, NIGEL, *The Art of Death: Visual Culture in the English Death Ritual* (London: Reaktion Books in association with the Victoria and Albert Museum, 1991).

MACK, MAYNARD, JR., *Killing the King* (New Haven: Yale University Press, 1973).

MÂLE, ÉMILE, *L'Art réligieux de la fin du moyen âge en France* (Paris: A. Colin, 1908).

MAURER, FRANÇOIS, *Die Kunstdenkmäler des Kantons Basel-Stadt* (Basel: Birkhäuser Verlag, 1966).

MAUS, KATHARINE, *Inwardness and Theatre in the English Renaissance* (Chicago: University of Chicago Press, 1995).

MERCER, ERIC, *English Art 1553–1625* (Oxford: Oxford University Press, 1962).

MORETTI, FRANCO, *Signs Taken for Wonders: Essays in the Sociology of Literary Form*, trans. Susan Fischer, David Forgacs, and David Millar (London: Verso, 1983).

MORRIS, HARRY, *Last Things in Shakespeare* (Tallahassee: Florida State University Presses, 1985).

NEELY, CAROL THOMAS, *Broken Nuptials in Shakespeare* (New Haven: Yale University Press, 1985).

NEILL, MICHAEL (ed.), *John Ford: Critical Re-visions* (Cambridge: Cambridge University Press, 1989).

NOHL, JOHANNES, *The Black Death: A Chronicle of the Plague*, trans. C. H. Clarke (London: George Allen & Unwin, 1926).

O'MALLEY, C. D., *Andreas Vesalius of Brussels, 1514–1564* (Berkeley: University of California Press, 1964).

ONG, WALTER J., *Fighting for Life: Contest, Sexuality and Consciousness* (Ithaca, NY: Cornell University Press, 1981).

PAGDEN, ANTHONY, *European Encounters with the New World* (New Haven: Yale University Press, 1993).

PANOFSKY, DORA and ERWIN, *Pandora's Box: The Changing Aspects of a Mythical Symbol* (New York: Pantheon Books, 1956).

PANOFSKY, ERWIN, *Tomb Sculpture: Its Changing Aspects from Ancient Egypt to Bernini*, ed. H. W. Janson (London: Thames & Hudson, 1964).

PARKER, PATRICIA, *Literary Fat Ladies: Rhetoric, Gender, Property* (London: Methuen, 1987).

—— *Shakespeare from the Margins: Language, Culture, Context* (Chicago: University of Chicago Press, 1996).

—— and HARTMANN, GEOFFREY (eds.), *Shakespeare and the Question of Theory* (New York: Methuen, 1985).

PASTER, GAIL KERN, *The Body Embarrassed* (Ithaca, NY: Cornell University Press, 1992).

PERSAUD, T. V. N., *Early History of Human Anatomy* (Springfield, Ill.: C. C. Thomas, 1984).

PFISTER, A., *Tod und Totentanze* (Basel: Henning Oppermann, 1927).

PUCKLE, BERTRAM S., *Funeral Customs: Their Origin and Development* (London: T. Werner Laurie, 1926).

ROBERTS, K. B., and TOMLINSON, J. D. W., *The Fabric of the Body: European Traditions of Anatomical Illustration* (Oxford: Clarendon Press, 1992).

ROSENBERG, MARVIN, *The Masks of King Lear* (Berkeley: University of California Press, 1972).

SAWDAY, JONATHAN, *The Body Emblazoned: Dissection and the Human Body in Renaissance Culture* (London: Routledge, 1995).

SHREWSBURY, J. F. D., *History of the Bubonic Plague in the British Isles* (Cambridge: Cambridge University Press, 1970).

SLACK, PAUL, *et al.*, *The Plague Reconsidered* (Matlock: Local Population Studies, 1977).

SLAUGHTER, THOMAS P., *Ideology and Politics on the Eve of the Restoration: Newcastle's Advice to Charles II* (Philadelphia: American Philosophical Society, 1984).

SMITH, NIGEL, *Perfection Proclaimed: Language and Literature in English Radical Religion* (Oxford: Clarendon Press, 1989).

SNYDER, SUSAN, *The Comic Matrix of Shakespeare's Tragedies* (Princeton: Princeton University Press, 1979).

—— (ed.), *Othello: Critical Essays* (New York: Garland, 1988).

SPENCER, THEODORE, *Death and Elizabethan Tragedy* (Cambridge, Mass.: Harvard University Press, 1936; repr. New York: Pageant Books, 1960).

SPINRAD, PHOEBE S., *The Summons of Death on the Renaissance Stage* (Columbus: Ohio State University Press, 1987).

STALLYBRASS, PETER, and WHITE, ALLON, *The Politics and Poetics of Transgression* (London: Methuen, 1986).

STEIN, ARNOLD, *The House of Death: Messages from the English Renaissance* (Baltimore: Johns Hopkins University Press, 1986).

STONE, LAWRENCE, *The Crisis of the Aristocracy 1558–1641* (Oxford: Oxford University Press, 1965).

—— *The Family, Sex, and Marriage in England 1500–1800* (London: Weidenfeld & Nicolson, 1977).

STRONG, ROY, *The Cult of Elizabeth: Elizabethan Portraiture and Pageantry* (London: Thames & Hudson, 1977).

VALE, MALCOLM, *War and Chivalry* (London: Duckworth, 1981).

WAGNER, ANTHONY, *Heralds of England: A History of the Office and College of Arms* (London: HMSO, 1967).

WALLACE, M. W., *The Life of Sir Philip Sidney* (Cambridge: Cambridge University Press, 1915).

WARTHIN, ALDRED SCOTT, *The Physician of the Dance of Death: A Historical Study of the Evolution of the Dance of Death Mythus in Art* (New York: Paul B. Hoeber, 1931).

WATSON, ROBERT N., *The Rest is Silence: Death as Annihilation in the English Renaissance* (Berkeley: University of California Press, 1994).

WEIMANN, ROBERT, *Shakespeare and the Popular Tradition in the Theater: Studies in the Social Dimension of Dramatic Form*, ed. Robert Schwartz (Baltimore: Johns Hopkins University Press, 1979).

WHALLEY, JOACHIM (ed.), *Studies in the Social History of Death* (London: Europa, 1981).

WHITE, R. S., *Let Wonder Seem Familiar: Endings in Shakespeare's Romance Vision* (Atlantic Heights, NJ, and London: Humanities Press and Athlone Press, 1985).

WICKHAM, GLYNNE, *Early English Stages 1300–1600*, 3 vols. (London: Routledge & Kegan Paul, 1959–72).

WILDERS, JOHN, *The Lost Garden* (London: Methuen, 1978).

WILLIMAN, DANIEL (ed.), *The Black Death: The Impact of the Fourteenth-Century Plague* (Brighampton, NY: Center for Medieval and Early Renaissance Studies, 1982).

WILSON, F. P., *The Plague in Shakespeare's London* (Oxford: Oxford University Press, 1963).

WILSON, JEAN, *The Archaeology of Shakespeare: The Material Legacy of Shakespeare's Theatre* (Stroud: Alan Sutton, 1995).

ZIEGLER, PHILIP, *The Black Death* (London: Collins, 1969).

ZUCKER, DAVID HARD, *Stage and Image in the Plays of Christopher Marlowe*, Salzburg Studies in English Literature (Salzburg: University of Salzburg, 1972).

Articles and Essays

BARISH, JONAS A., '*The Spanish Tragedy*, or the Pleasures and Perils of Rhetoric', in John Russell Brown and Bernard Harris (eds.), *Elizabethan Theatre*, Stratford-upon-Avon Studies, no. 9 (London: Edward Arnold, 1966), 58–85.

BARNARD, JOHN, Introduction to George Etherege, *The Man of Mode* (London: Ernest Benn, 1979).

BARTELS, EMILY, 'Making More of the Moor: Aaron, Othello, and Renaissance Refashionings of Race', *Shakespeare Quarterly*, 41 (1990), 432–54.

BARTON, ANNE, '*As You Like It* and *Twelfth Night*: Shakespeare's Sense of an Ending', in Malcolm Bradbury and David Palmer (eds.), *Shakespearean Comedy*, Stratford-upon-Avon Studies, no. 14 (London: Arnold, 1972), 160–80.

—— Introduction to *Hamlet*, ed. T. J. B. Spencer (Harmondsworth: Penguin, 1980).

—— 'Nature's Piece 'Gainst Fancy: The Divided Catastrophe of *Antony and Cleopatra*', *Bedford College Inaugural Lecture* (London: Bedford College, University of London, 1973).

—— 'Oxymoron and the Structure of Ford's *The Broken Heart*', *Essays and Studies*, 33 (1980), 70–94.

BERGER, THOMAS L., 'The Petrarchan Fortress of *The Changeling*', *Renaissance Papers* (1969), 37–46.

BERGERON, DAVID M., 'The Restoration of Hermione in *The Winter's Tale*', in Carol McGinnis Kay and Henry M. Jacobs (eds.), *Shakespeare's Romances Reconsidered* (Lincoln: University of Nebraska Press, 1978), 125–33.

—— 'The Wax Figures in *The Duchess of Malfi*', *Studies in English Literature*, 18 (1978), 331–39.

BLISS, LEE, '"Plot mee no Plots": The Life of Drama and the Drama of Life in *The Knight of the Burning Pestle*', *Modern Language Quarterly*, 45 (1984), 3–21.

BOOSE, LYNDA, 'Othello's Handkerchief: "The Recognizance and Pledge of Love"', *English Literary Renaissance*, 5 (1975), 360–74.

BOWERS, JOHN M., '"I am marble-constant": Cleopatra's Monumental End', *Huntington Library Quarterly*, 46 (1983), 283–97.

BURELBACH, FREDERICK M., '"The Truth" in John Ford's *The Broken Heart* Revisited', *Notes and Queries*, 212 (1967), 211–12.

CODDON, KARIN S., '"Suche Strange Desygns": Madness, Subjectivity, and Treason in *Hamlet* and Elizabethan Culture', *Renaissance Drama*, 20 (1989), 51–75.

DAVIS, NATALIE ZEMON, 'Ghosts, Kin, and Progeny: Some Features of Family Life in Early Modern France', *Daedalus*, special issue on The Family (1977), 87–114.

FERRARI, GIOVANNA, 'Public Anatomy Lessons and the Carnival in Bologna', *Past and Present*, 117 (1987), 50–107;

FLACHMANN, MICHAEL, 'Fitted for Death: *Measure for Measure* and the *Contemplatio Mortis*', *ELR* 22 (1992), 222–41.

FLY, RICHARD, 'Accommodating Death: The Ending of *Hamlet*', *Studies in English Literature*, 24 (1984), 257–74.

GARBER, MARJORIE, 'Hamlet's Dull Revenge', in Patricia Parker and David Quint (eds.), *Literary Theory/Renaissance Texts* (Baltimore: Johns Hopkins University Press, 1986), 280–302.

—— '"Remember me": *Memento Mori* Figures in Shakespeare's Plays', *Renaissance Drama*, 12 (1981), 3–25.

GARBER, MARJORIE, '"Wild Laughter in the Throat of Death": Darker Purposes in Shakespearean Comedy', *New York Literary Forum*, 5–6 (1980), 121–6.

GORDON, D. J., 'Name and Fame: Shakespeare's *Coriolanus*', in Stephen Orgel (ed.), *The Renaissance Imagination* (Berkeley and Los Angeles: University of California Press, 1975), 203–19.

GRAZIANI, RENÉ, 'M. Marcadé and the Dance of Death: *Love's Labour's Lost*, v. ii. 705–11', *Review of English Studies*, 37 (1986), 392–5.

HAMILTON, DONNA B., '*The Spanish Tragedy*: A Speaking Picture', *ELR* 4 (1974), 203–17.

HAMMERSMITH, JAMES P., '*Hamlet* and the Myth of Memory', *ELH* 45 (1978), 597–605.

HARDY, BARBARA, 'Aspects of Narration in *King Lear*', *Deutsche Shakespeare-Gesellschaft West Jahrbuch* 1987, 100–8.

—— 'The Figure of Narration in *Hamlet*', in Robert Druce (ed.), *A Centre of Excellence: Essays Presented to Seymour Betsky* (Amsterdam: Costerus Rodopi, 1987), 1–14.

—— 'The Narrators in *Macbeth*', *Hilda Hume Memorial Lecture, 1986* (London: University of London, 1987).

HARRIS, DUNCAN, 'Tombs, Guidebooks, and Shakespearean Drama: Death in the Renaissance', *Mosaic*, 15, special issue on Death and Dying (1982), 13–28.

HELGERSON, RICHARD, 'What Hamlet Remembers', *Shakespeare Studies*, 10 (1977), 67–97.

HILLMAN, RICHARD, 'Hamlet and Death: A Recasting of the Play within the Play', *Essays in Literature*, 13 (1986), 201–18.

HINMAN, R. B., 'The Apotheosis of Faust: Poetry and New Philosophy in the Seventeenth Century', in D. J. Palmer and Malcolm Bradbury (eds.), *Metaphysical Poetry*, Stratford-upon-Avon Studies, no. 11 (London: Edward Arnold, 1970), 149–79.

HOLLERAN, JAMES V., 'Maimed Funeral Rites in *Hamlet*', *ELR* 19 (1989), 65–93.

HOSLEY, RICHARD, 'The Staging of Desdemona's Bed', *Shakespeare Quarterly*, 14 (1963), 57–65.

JOHNSON, S. F., '*The Spanish Tragedy*, or Babylon Revisited', in Richard Hosley (ed.), *Essays on Shakespeare and Elizabethan Drama in Honor of Hardin Craig* (Columbia: University of Missouri Press, 1963), 23–36.

KAUFMANN, R. J., 'Ford's "Waste Land": *The Broken Heart*', *Renaissance Drama*, NS 3 (1970), 167–87.

KAY, DENNIS, '"To hear the rest untold": Shakespeare's Postponed Endings', *Renaissance Quarterly*, 37 (1984), 207–27.

KERRIGAN, JOHN, '*Henry IV* and the Death of Old Double', *Essays in Criticism*, 40 (1990), 25–53.

—— 'Hieronimo, Hamlet, and Remembrance', *Essays in Criticism*, 31 (1981), 105–26.

KOWSAR, MOHAMMED, 'Middleton and Rowley's *The Changeling*: The Besieged Temple', *Criticism*, 28 (1986), 145–64.

LANCASHIRE, ANNE, 'The Emblematic Castle in Shakespeare and Middleton', in J. C. Gray (ed.), *Mirror up to Shakespeare: Essays in Honour of G. R. Hibbard* (Toronto: University of Toronto Press, 1984), 223–41.

LITTLE, ARTHUR L. Jr., '"An essence that's not seen": The Primal Scene of Racism in *Othello*', *Shakespeare Quarterly*, 44 (1993), 304–24.

LORD, JOAN M., '*The Duchess of Malfi*: "The Spirit of Greatness" and "of Woman"', *Studies in English Literature*, 16 (1976), 305–17.

MACDONALD, MICHAEL, 'Ophelia's Maimèd Rites', *Shakespeare Quarterly*, 37 (1986), 309–17.

MACK, MAYNARD, 'The World of *Hamlet*', *Yale Review*, 41 (1952), 502–23.

MCMILLIN, SCOTT, 'The Figure of Silence in *The Spanish Tragedy*', *ELH* 39 (1974), 203–17.

MARCHITELLO, HOWARD, 'Vesalius's *Fabrica* and Shakespeare's *Othello*: Anatomy, Gender, and the Narrative Production of Meaning', *Criticism*, 34 (1993), 529–58.

MAUS, KATHARINE EISAMAN, 'Proof and Consequences: Inwardness and its Exposure in the English Renaissance', *Representations*, 34 (1991), 29–52.

MORRIS, HARRY, 'The Dance of Death Motif in Shakespeare', *Studies in English Literature*, 14 (1984), 15–28.

NEILL, MICHAEL, 'Amphitheaters in the Body: Playing with Hands on the Shakespearian Stage', *Shakespeare Survey*, 48 (1995), 23–50.

—— 'Changing Places in *Othello*', *Shakespeare Survey*, 37 (1984), 115–31.

—— 'Exeunt with a Dead March: Funeral Pageantry on the Shakespearean Stage', in David Bergeron (ed.), *Pageantry in the Shakespearean Theatre* (Athens: University of Georgia Press, 1985), 154–93.

—— '"Feasts put down funerals": Death and Ritual in Renaissance Comedy', in Linda Woodbridge (ed.), *True Rites and Maimed Rites: Ritual and Anti-ritual in Shakespeare and his Age* (Urbana: University of Illinois Press, 1992), 47–74.

—— 'Ford's Unbroken Art: The Moral Design of *The Broken Heart*', *Modern Language Review*, 75 (1980), 249–68.

—— '*Hamlet*: A Modern Perspective', in Barbara A. Mowat and Paul Werstine (eds.), *Hamlet*, The Folger Shakespeare (New York: Washington Square Press, 1992), 307–26.

—— 'Remembrance and Revenge: *Hamlet*, *Macbeth*, and *The Tempest*', in Ian Donaldson (ed.), *Jonson and Shakespeare* (London and Canberra: Macmillan/HRC, 1983), 35–56.

NEILL, MICHAEL, '"Unproper Beds": Race, Adultery and the Hideous in *Othello*', *Shakespeare Quarterly*, 40 (1989), 383–412.

ORGEL, STEPHEN, 'Shakespeare and the Kinds of Drama', *Critical Inquiry*, 6 (1979), 107–123.

PARKER, PATRICIA, '"Dilation" and "Delation" in *Othello*', in Patricia Parker and Geoffrey Hartmann (eds.), *Shakespeare and the Question of Theory* (New York: Methuen, 1985).

—— 'Fantasies of "Race" and "Gender": Africa, Othello, and Bringing to Light', in Margo Hendricks and Patricia Parker (eds.), *Women, 'Race', and Writing in the Early Modern Period* (London: Routledge, 1994), 84–100.

PASTER, GAIL KERN, 'Leaky Vessels: The Incontinent Women of Jacobean City Comedy', *Renaissance Drama*, NS 18 (1987), 71–86.

RICHARDS, SUSAN, 'Marlowe's *Tamburlaine II* as a Drama of Death', *Modern Language Quarterly*, 26 (1965), 375–87.

ROSAND, DAVID, 'The Portrait, the Courtier, and Death', in Robert W. Hanning and David Rosand (eds.), *Castiglione: The Ideal and the Real in Renaissance Culture* (New Haven: Yale University Press, 1983), 91–129.

ROSS, CHERYL LYNN, 'The Plague of *The Alchemist*', *Renaissance Quarterly*, 41 (1988), 439–58.

SCHOENBAUM, SAMUEL, '*The Revenger's Tragedy*: Jacobean Dance of Death', *Modern Language Quarterly*, 15 (1954), 201–7.

SNYDER, SUSAN, '*Romeo and Juliet*: Comedy into Tragedy', *Essays in Criticism*, 20 (1970), 391–401.

STALLYBRASS, PETER, 'Patriarchal Territories: The Body Enclosed', in Susan Snyder (ed.), *Othello: Critical Essays* (New York: Garland, 1988), 251–74.

—— 'Reading the Body: *The Revenger's Tragedy* and the Jacobean Theater of Consumption', *Renaissance Drama*, NS 18 (1987), 121–48.

STANFORD, MICHAEL, 'The Terrible Thresholds: Sir Thomas Browne on Sex and Death', *English Literary Renaissance*, 18 (1988), 413–23.

STEWART, ALAN, 'The Early Modern Closet Discovered', *Representations*, 50 (1995), 76–100.

STRICKLAND, RONALD, 'Pageantry and Poetry as Discourse: The Production of Subjectivity in Sir Philip Sidney's Funeral', *ELH* 57 (1990), 19–36.

WATSON, ROBERT N., 'Giving up the Ghost in a World of Decay', *Renaissance Drama*, 21 (1990), 199–223.

WHIGHAM, FRANK, 'Reading Social Conflict in the Alimentary Tract: More on the Body in Renaissance Drama', *ELH* 55 (1988), 333–50.

WICKHAM, GLYNNE, 'Romance and Emblem: A Study in the Dramatic Structure of *The Winter's Tale*', in David Galloway (ed.), *The Elizabethan Theatre*, 3 (Toronto: Macmillan, 1972), 82–99.

WILSON, LUKE, 'William Harvey's *Prelectiones*: The Performance of the Body in the Renaissance Theatre of Anatomy', *Representations*, 17 (1987), 62–95.

WIND, EDGAR, 'Amor as a God of Death', in his *Pagan Mysteries in the Renaissance* (Harmondsworth: Penguin, 1967).

Index